Publisher's Letter

Safe Boating, Travel, and Adventure

As we embark on another exciting year of delivering the 2025 editions of Waterway Guide into your hands and on your boat, I am reminded of the responsibility and privilege we share as stewards of these incredible resources. To continue to do our part for as long as we have (78 years), our mission has always been clear: promote safe boating, travel, and adventure on our waterways.

Boating is about more than just getting from point A to point B—it's about discovering the unique destinations that lie along the way. From bustling marinas to quiet, untouched coves, each stop is an opportunity to connect with new communities, experience local cultures, and uncover hidden gems. Whether it's the charm of a historic coastal town or the serenity of a secluded anchorage, every journey is enriched by the destinations you encounter. At Waterway Guide, we're committed to helping you find those special places that turn a routine trip into an unforgettable adventure.

We understand that every boater has their own way of accessing information, which is why we offer our content across a variety of platforms to suit your needs. Whether you prefer planning with the online Waterway Explorer, using the Waterway Guide App, or relying on our popular and cockpit-enhancing printed guides, we have you covered. You can also access extensive details on marinas, anchorages and points of interest through our presence on third-party navigation apps and chart plotters, ensuring that you have the information you need, wherever and whenever you need it.

As we look to the future, our dedication to this mission only grows stronger. We are committed to expanding our resources, enhancing our coverage, and leveraging the latest technology to continuously improve and deliver the content we provide. Whether through digital platforms, navigation apps, or chart plotters, we aim to deliver the highest standards of quality and reliability. Your safety, enjoyment, and the preservation of our waterways will always be at the forefront of everything we do.

Thank you for being a part of the Waterway Guide community. I encourage you to visit us and join the community at waterwayguide.com and look at everything we have available for you to plan, contribute, and connect with others. Together, we can continue to explore, protect, and celebrate the incredible waterways that connect us all.

Safe travels and happy boating!

Sincerely,
Graham Jones

Publisher, Waterway Guide

WATERWAY GUIDE MEDIA, LLC

P.O. Box 419, Midlothian, VA 23113

Phone: 800-233-3359
Fax: 888-951-7890
www.waterwayguide.com

BOOK SALES
waterwayguide.com/ship-store
Phone: 800-233-3359
Support@waterwayguide.com

Waterway Guide is published in the following editions—Bahamas, Southern, Florida Keys, Gulf Coast, Mid-Atlantic, Chesapeake Bay, Northern, Great Lakes Vol. 1, Great Lakes Vol. 2 and Cuba—by Waterway Guide Media, LLC © 2024. All rights reserved. Reproduction in whole or part or use of any data compilation without written permission from the publisher is prohibited. The title Waterway Guide is a registered trademark. ISBN Number: 979-8-9903530-4-6 for the Mid-Atlantic 2025 Edition. Purchase and use of Waterway Guide constitutes acceptance of the restrictions set forth herein.

Waterway Guide Media, LLC, the publisher of Waterway Guide (Guide), makes reasonable efforts to ensure the accuracy of the information in this Guide. However, Waterway Guide must rely on others over which it has no control for certain information. In addition, no book or guide is a substitute for good judgment, experience and firsthand knowledge. Therefore, Waterway Guide hereby gives notice that the charts, descriptions, and illustrations in this Guide are not to be used for navigation. The use of any navigational reference or description contained in the Guide is at the user's own risk. Inclusion in the Waterway Guide of marine facilities, services, restaurants and other information is for informational purposes only; no guarantee is provided as to the accuracy or current status of this information, nor does Waterway Guide Media, LLC endorse any of the facilities or services described herein.

Because Waterway Guide Media, LLC cannot and does not guarantee or warrant that the information in the Guide is complete or current, Waterway Guide Media, LLC disclaims all warranties, express or implied, relating to the information in any manner, including, without limitation, implied warranties of merchantability and fitness for a particular purpose.

Waterway Guide Media, LLC shall not be liable to the purchaser or any third party for any loss or injury allegedly caused, in whole or in part, by Waterway Guide Media, LLC and/or Waterway Guide (or the information contained therein) or for consequential, exemplary, incidental or special damages. Furthermore, in any event, Waterway Guide Media, LLC's liability, if any, shall never exceed the amount paid by the original purchaser for the directory.

To provide the most complete and accurate information, all facilities have been contacted within the past year. Although facility operators supplied this data, we cannot guarantee accuracy or assume responsibility for errors. Entrance and dockside soundings tend to fluctuate. Always approach marinas carefully. Reference numbers on spotting charts indicate marina locations. Aerial photos are for general overview only and are not to be used for navigation.

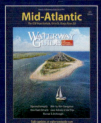

On the cover:
Sailing into Masonboro Inlet near Wrightsville Beach, NC

FOUNDED IN 1947

Publisher	**JEFF JONES**
	jjones@waterwayguide.com
President	**GRAHAM JONES**
	graham@waterwayguide.com
Editor-in-Chief	**ED TILLETT**
	etillett@waterwayguide.com
Operations Manager	**HEATHER SADEG**
	heather@waterwayguide.com
Managing Editor	**JANI PARKER**
	jparker@waterwayguide.com
Art Director/ Production Manager	**SCOTT MCCONNELL**
	scott@waterwayguide.com
Customer Success Manager	**KARLA LOCKE**
	karla@waterwayguide.com
Marketing/News Editor	**WHITNEY LAW**
	whitney@waterwayguide.com
Customer Support Specialists	**LINDA JERNIGAN**
	linda@waterwayguide.com
	ANNE EMERSON
	anne@waterwayguide.com
Data Support Specialist	**RILEY VAUGHN**
	riley@waterwayguide.com
Senior Advisor/ Skipper Bob Editor	**TED STEHLE**
	tstehle@waterwayguide.com
Software Engineer	**MIKE SCHWEFLER**
National Sales	**GRAHAM JONES**
	graham@waterwayguide.com
Sales & Marketing Manager	**KELLY CROCKETT**
	kelly@waterwayguide.com
Regional Account Executives	**KIM EATON**
	kim@waterwayguide.com
	MARLÈNE CROCKETT
	marlene@waterwayguide.com
	BOB BOWER
	bobby@waterwayguide.com

REGIONAL CRUISING EDITORS

SCOTT RICHARD BERG
MATT & LUCY CLAIBORNE
GINA L. CICOTELLO
EMILY KIZER
BOB SHERER (CONTRIBUTING EDITOR)
ONNE VAN DER WAL (CONTRIBUTING EDITOR)

CUBA CRUISING EDITORS

ADDISON CHAN
NIGEL CALDER (CONTRIBUTING EDITOR)

Printed In Canada

@Waterway Guide   @waterway_guide

Mid-Atlantic Chapter Guide

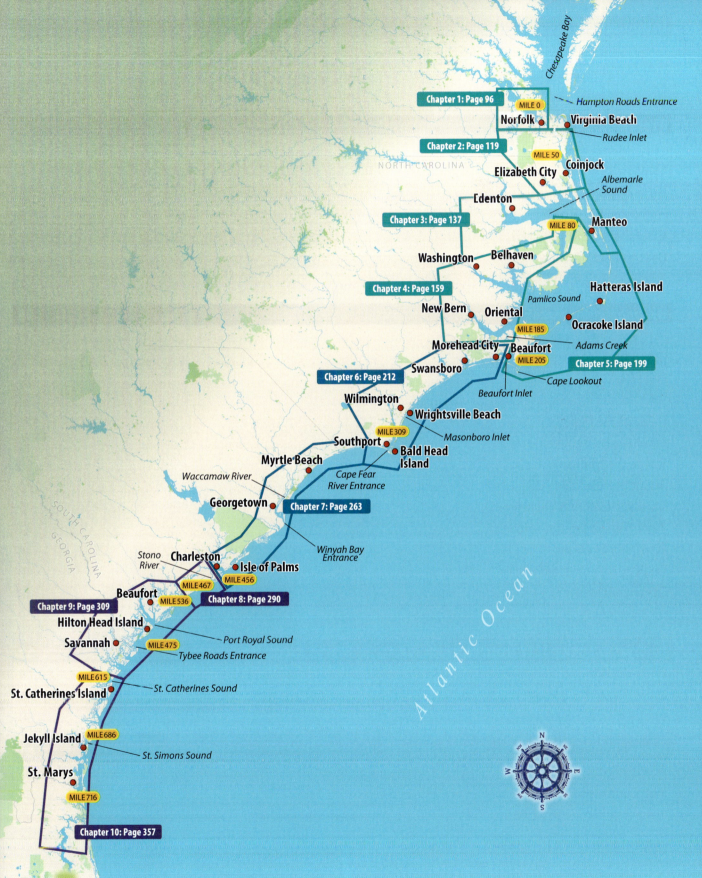

MID-ATLANTIC EDITION

Table of Contents — 2025 Mid-Atlantic Edition

Introduction
- Publisher's Letter 1
- Mid-Atlantic Chapter Guide 3
- Meet Our Cruising Editors 8

Preferred Destinations 13
- Westmoreland County, VA 14
- Onancock, VA 16
- Urbanna, VA 18
- Hampton, VA 20
- Washington, NC 22
- Beaufort & Port Royal, SC 24
- Florida's Forgotten Coast 26

Skipper's Handbook 29
- Port Security 30
- Customs Reporting Procedures 32
- Float Plan 33
- VHF Communications 34
- Rules of the Road 36
- Coast Guard Requirements 38
- Reference Materials 39
- About the Weather 40
- Tropical Weather & Hurricanes 42
- Picking an Anchorage (excerpt) 44
- Ditch Bag Checklist 45
- Dealing with Onboard Waste 46
- Distance Tables 48
- GPS Waypoints 50

Bridges & Locks: ICW from Norfolk, VA to St. Marys River, GA 53
- Bridge Basics 54
- Locks & Locking Through 56
- Bridge & Lock Schedules 58

Inlets: 61
- Introduction 61
- Inlet Distances 64
- Inlets: Norfolk, VA to St. Marys, GA 66

America's Waterway Guide Since 1947

Section 1: Hampton Roads, VA to the Neuse River, NC 95
Chapter 1 Hampton, Norfolk & Portsmouth, VA 96
Chapter 2 Virginia Cut & Dismal Swamp Routes, VA/NC 119
Chapter 3 Side Trip: The Albemarle & Roanoke Sounds, NC 137
Chapter 4 Albemarle Sound to the Neuse River, NC 159
Chapter 5 Side Trip: The Pamlico Sound & Outer Banks, NC 199

Before you can begin your journey down the ICW, you must traverse the 10-mile stretch through the Hampton Roads area. This is the home to the world's largest naval base and is one of the busiest harbors on the ICW. The "official" beginning of the ICW is at Mile Zero in Norfolk, VA. At Mile 7.3 you must choose one of two very different routes south: the Albemarle-Chesapeake Canal or the Dismal Swamp Canal. The two routes converge on the southern side of the Albemarle Sound. North Carolina's sounds (Inner Banks) and the Outer Banks are rewarding side trips and are unlike any other regions along the Mid-Atlantic coast. The barrier islands extend in a crescent from the Virginia state line, then swing back at Cape Hatteras.

Section 2: Beaufort, NC to Isle of Palms, SC 211
Chapter 6 Beaufort to Southport, NC 212
Chapter 7 Lockwoods Folly, NC to McClellanville, SC 263

After passing through the sister cities of Beaufort and Morehead City (Mile 205), the ICW follows the open Bogue Sound and New and Cape Fear Rivers to an area known as "The Ditch." The dredged channel cuts through low marshy islets, across several small rivers and finally through a long land cut that ends in Charleston Harbor. This is where the Cooper and Ashley Rivers meet and is a favorite destination for cruisers.

Section 3: Charleston, SC to St. Marys, GA 289
Chapter 8 Charleston Area 290
Chapter 9 Stono River, SC to Ossabaw Sound, GA 309
Chapter 10 St. Catherines Sound to St. Marys, GA 357

It's 244 miles along the ICW from Charleston to Florida's state line. During this stretch of the ICW, you will wend your way across wide river mouths, through a series of sounds and past numerous coastal inlets. The banks are lined with woods, moss-covered live oaks and marshland. You may even glimpse the ocean. When you leave Georgia, you will notice a change from open sounds and rivers to creeks connected by narrow land cuts.

INDEXES
Marina / Sponsor Index* 381
Subject Index 385
Inlets & Goin' Ashore Index 388

*Sponsors are listed in **BOLD** and are highlighted in yellow in marina tables.

The adventure of a lifetime
America's Great Loop

2+ Countries • 14+ States and Provinces • 100+ Locks • 5,250+ Miles...
... all aboard your own boat!

Are you ready for a journey that is both high-adventure and low-risk?

Join our group of likeminded boaters exploring the 6,000-mile waterway known as the Great Loop. There's no better way to travel extensively while remaining socially distant than aboard your own vessel! Whether you're brand new to the idea of the Great Loop, actively planning your trip, or ready to drop the dock lines and head out, we offer something for you!

**Visit us at
www.greatloop.org
or call 877-GR8-LOOP**

Membership in America's Great Loop Cruisers' Association includes:

- Access to hundreds of harbor hosts to assist you with local knowledge around the route
- Participation in our discussion forum that offers a deep-dive into Great Loop-related questions and topics
- Webinars exclusively for members
- Discounts on dockage, fuel, equipment, and more
- Monthly digital magazines and newsletters
- Access to our distinctive AGLCA burgee
- Members-only events

and so much more!

**Scan the QR code
to start your adventure**

Meet Our Cruising Editors

Waterway Guide's on-the-water Cruising Editors bring us firsthand information about the navigation, news and trends along the waterways we cover. In addition to contributing to the annual guide, they provide daily updates on the Waterway Explorer at www.waterwayguide.com. We are pleased to introduce you to our crew.

Scott Richard Berg has been sailing, racing and cruising for the past 50 years and has experience on a range of power and sailing vessels from an El Toro Pram to a 135' Baltic Trader. Scott is an experienced delivery and commercial captain and the owner of Chardonnay Boatworks, a full service marine repair and consulting company focusing on the repair and re-engineering of sail and motor yachts. He frequently lectures on marine electrical systems, communication, electronics, and yacht systems for off shore cruising. Scott holds multiple certifications from the ABYC and NMEA. He is the co-founder of the SSCA HF Radio Network (KPK), holds both commercial and amateur radio licenses, and represents recreational boaters as member of the USCG's Global Maritime Distress & Safety System(GMDSS) Task Force. Scott is a member of the Capital Yacht Club, the Ocean Cruising Club and the Seven Seas Cruising Association (Past President). He holds a USCG 100T Masters license and currently lives on his 60-foot Seaton Ketch, *CHARDONNAY*.

Addison Chan is an experienced software entrepreneur, a world traveler and a committed sailing cruiser. He is the founder of Land and Sea Software Corp., which has engineered a revolutionary platform to produce mobile friendly, piracy-resistant, interactive content for traditional publishers. Waterwayguide Media is using the platform to provide its users with an enhanced digital experience that always delivers the most currently available information to mobile devices. Addison and his wife, Pat, have traveled extensively through Cuba, Mexico and the Bahamas on their 42-foot Catalina sailboat, acquiring deep local knowledge over the years. The depth of his local knowledge and understanding of local culture is evident in his work as the coauthor of *Waterway Guide Cuba*, which is the gold standard of cruising guides for Cuba. His latest project has the working title of "A Handbook for Comfortable Cruising in The Bahamas" which will be representative of a new breed of interactive cruising guides. He is active within the cruising community and maintains the popular Cuba, Land and Sea and Bahamas Land and Sea groups on Facebook.

Capts. Matt & Lucy Claiborne are full-time cruising sailors and storytellers. After college, Matt and Lucy lived on a 32-foot sailboat in the Florida Keys. Even while working in the "real-world" as professors at a university, they continued cruising and camping with a trailerable 21-foot cuddy cabin. In 2014, they cast off on a full-time sailing adventure on a 38-foot Lagoon catamaran. Both Matt and Lucy have USCG Master and FAA pilot licenses. They are full-time digital nomads who work from their boat. Their favorite offices are quiet anchorages; their favorite coworkers are dolphins and pelicans. Matt and Lucy are passionate about education and helping new boaters fulfill their cruising dreams. In 2019, they purchased their "forever dream boat"–a Cabo Rico 38 named *Dulcinea*. After a year outfitting for off-the-grid living and long-distance cruising, you'll now find them cruising Chesapeake Bay, the ICW, Bahamas and beyond with their adventure dog, Chelsea.

Gina L. Cicotello and Peter Henry share an irrational love of old wooden boats. Together they became caretakers of a 1958 Laurent Giles Vertue. *Ariel* didn't need a full restoration, but her new owners find endless opportunities to practice their skills in woodworking, old school rigging, and proper techniques for varnishing. Once they had a boat, Gina's next challenge was learning to sail. She started with classes sailing Flying Scots around the Anacostia River, and they've been cruising around the Chesapeake Bay ever since. Someday *Ariel* and her crew will broaden their adventures beyond the estuary. Gina lives in Arlington, VA. She's had a long career working for various publishers, which culminated in a dream job with National Geographic that lasted 14 years. She managed technology systems while collaborating with the cartographers, explorers and storytellers. After easing out of the corporate world she started freelancing and became her own boss, which means spending more time on the boat.

Emily Kizer and her husband, Lucas, are currently cruising the US East Coast. Emily has spent the past 10 years building a career in communications with a focus on infrastructure communications. In 2018, a random Reddit post sparked a dream of cruising full-time on a sailboat. Over the next five years, Emily and Lucas saved money, learned how to sail and fixed up their 1986 Solum 43 sailboat, *Alaya*. They left their land life in 2023, moving on board *Alaya* full-time after quitting their jobs and selling their house. Originally from Southeast Michigan, the Kizers have sailed for the past four years on the Great Lakes, mostly in Lake Erie. They did a 700-mile shakedown sail traveling from Lake Erie to Lake Michigan before turning back around and traversing the Erie Canal and Hudson River on their way east. Future cruising dreams include exploring the Bahamas and Caribbean islands.

Bob & Ann Sherer started sailing in 1985 with charters in Maine, Florida and the Caribbean followed by their first sailboat in 1986, which then lead to a 38-foot Ericson, followed by their present boat, a 42-foot Beneteau 423 in 2004. They started their yearly cruises on the ICW from New York to Key West in 2010 and Bob became known as Bob423, the person to follow for advice navigating through the many shoals of the ICW. He published his first *ICW Cruising Guide* in 2015 and has published an updated edition every year. The guide not only includes charts to avoid groundings but also tips learned from years of boating and a review of basic and advanced topics covering the ICW. In 2018, Bob started the ICW Cruising Guide Facebook page, which has grown to 13,500 members. His most recent efforts include the publishing of Bob423 Tracks in GPX format for free downloading, which follow the deep-water path around the shoals of the ICW to enable a less stressful cruise in staying out of the mud. He is routinely consulted by NOAA, the USACE, and the Coast Guard on matters affecting the boating public. Bob and Ann reside 9 months of the year aboard their latest boat, a 42-foot Beneteau 423 sailboat, with their fearless dog, Hoolie, a Brittany.

Onne van der Wal is one of the most prolific and talented marine photographers in the world of sailing. Before he learned to walk, he learned to sail aboard his grandfather's boat, and after progressing through youth sailing training programs he discovered his passion for ocean racing. As the bowman and engineer aboard the Dutch maxi-boat *Flyer II*, Onne won all four legs of the 1981-82 Whitbread Round the World Race. Along the way, he took his camera everywhere to document the experience, even to the top of the mast and the end of the spinnaker pole. Many admirers of Onne's work believe that his background as a world-class sailor informed the artistic choices he made as a world-class artist. In addition to editorial work, Onne has shot for blue chip commercial clients, including the likes of Hinckley Yachts, J Boats, Sperry, Patagonia, North Sails, and Harken. Despite all of the accolades and accomplishments over a career that has covered more than three decades and all seven seas, Onne is always looking forward to the next assignment.

Other Contributors: Waterway Guide gathers information and photos from a variety of sources, including boaters, marinas, communities and tourism divisions. We thank everyone who has contributed to our updates through their comments, reviews, and email. Your efforts are most appreciated.

NOAA Chart Numbers No Longer Needed

The end of the National Oceanic and Atmospheric Administration's (NOAA) updates to paper charts has arrived. When sunsetting of the paper charts was first announced in 2019, concern for how the transition would come about was palpable among many veteran skippers who had grown up using all manner of NOAA printed charts in various formats and from a multitude of vendors. Common denominators across all charts were nomenclature, design and a unique reference number that identified geographical coverage areas.

NAVIGATION: Use NOAA Charts 12358 and 13209. Just north of Long Beach Point, Orient Harbor is open to the southwest. The village of Orient is located on its northeastern shore. Do not cut between flashing...

Waterway Guide used the chart numbers to provide cross-references for locating specific areas we covered. Now that the charts and numbers have been replaced with a new digital methodology Waterway Guide is removing chart numbers from our publications, including legacy numbers used by the Canadian Hydrographic Service (CHS).

For those who have printed charts in their collections and want to maintain knowledge and access to the traditional library, NOAA has created a repository of every printed (raster) chart produced by the agency. *The Historical Chart & Map Collection* is located online at www.historicalcharts.noaa.gov from the Office of Coast Survey. The portal offers search options and displays original printed charts from different eras and sources.

You may feel a little overwhelmed initially attempting to get to specific charts but remain vigilant. There is a wealth of information alongside valuable historical charts and maps in the portal, including guidance from NOAA on how to locate what you want.

As this transition to digital vector-based or Electronic Nautical Charts (ENCs) continues, the ways in which we use various media and sources to access them are also evolving. Chart plotters, mobile navigation applications, chart viewers via the internet and data distribution across different delivery platforms provide choices for improving safe navigation as never before. The transition, though, is not without complications.

Information from years of drawings on paper charts has not all been converted and stored in the databases. And errors and omissions are sometimes obvious when cross-referencing legacy paper charts against digital versions of the same region, whether using NOAA's online ENC chart viewer or other sources such as Navionics, Raymarine, Garmin or other ENC offerings. But the work continues, and NOAA and other members of the International Hydrographic Organization (IHO) are committed to accuracy and coverage.

As Waterway Guide develops solutions to the changing landscape of charts and charting, our most recent response has been to publish chart extracts from the cartographers at Aqua Map who use NOAA data in their nautical charts for the U.S. The Aqua Map mobile app is a respected source and effective tool for navigation when employed as part of an overall plan of course-plotting and routing. The chart extract images we provide from Aqua Map in our guidebooks are designed for situational awareness and to show the locations of marinas and harbors at appropriate scale and detail.

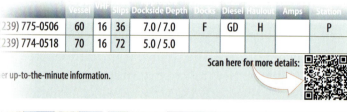

Legacy NOAA chart numbers are no longer relevant to a subjective view of a geographical area, which is how NOAA's data is now provided in their online ENC viewers and custom chart portal, where you can now design your own charts, save, and print them. Borders and scale are not necessary when employing a screen that allows you to zoom and slide to reveal what you want.

Removing chart numbers from Waterway Guide's publications is our response to a changing environment. NOAA's chart numbers, an integral reference tool for navigators for many years, no longer serve the purpose for which they were intended originally. The sun has set.

America's Waterway Guide Since 1947

ANNAPOLIS BOAT SHOWS

ANNAPOLIS POWERBOAT SHOW
OCTOBER 2-5, 2025
CITY DOCK | ANNAPOLIS, MD

ANNAPOLIS SAILBOAT SHOW
OCTOBER 9-13, 2025
CITY DOCK | ANNAPOLIS, MD

For tickets and more info, visit AnnapolisBoatShows.com

Waterway Guide is proud to be an AuxA Affiliate. We support the missions of the Coast Guard Auxiliary in its support of the United States Coast Guard.

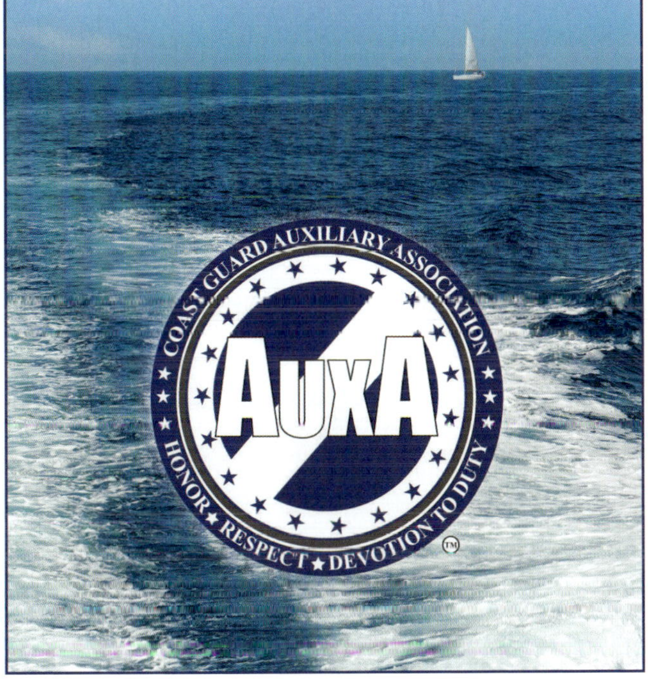

LIVE THE DREAM

Join Seven Seas Cruising Association and turn your cruising dreams into reality.

Benefits include:
- Connection, Advocacy and Much More
- Seven Seas U Webinars & Member Discounts
- Cruisers' Bulletin & Destination Information
- Cruising Stations Worldwide —instant help and local knowledge around the globe
- Member Locator
- Online Discussion Forum

Check out our website www.ssca.org

SEVEN SEAS CRUISING ASSOCIATION
Est. 1952
www.SSCA.org
(754) 702-5068

MID-ATLANTIC EDITION

America's Waterway Guide Since 1947

Preferred Destinations from Waterway Guide Media

Preferred Destinations

MID-ATLANTIC EDITION

Rich in History & Natural Beauty
Westmoreland County, Virginia

Formed in 1653 from Northumberland County, Westmoreland County is the birthplace to George Washington, and James Monroe, and home to Declaration of Independence signers Richard Henry Lee and Francis Lightfoot Lee. George Washington Birthplace National Monument, James Monroe Birthplace, and Stratford Hall are all welcome the public and provide the context and stories of those who lived and worked in Westmoreland County centuries ago.

The county seat of Montross recently was designated an historic district, and hosts a Courthouse Green, town park and playground, restaurant, coffee shop, local fine art and jewelry, a brewery, and the Westmoreland County Museum. Outside of Montross is Westmoreland State Park, an historic district due to its history as one of the original Civilian Conservation Corps-constructed state parks. If you want to stretch your legs on another beautiful trail, the Voorhees Nature Preserve has overlooks onto the Rappahannock River.

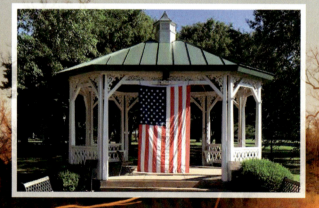

America's Waterway Guide Since 1947

Colonial Beach

Colonial Beach has several marinas and is a haven for mariners of the mid-Potomac. The town is walkable, and a golf cart community, with a summer trolley to the town beach, seafood restaurants, and charming boutique retail shops.

Kinsale

In a protected tributary off the Potomac River, the port village of Kinsale welcomes visitors to its marinas, and historic district. A site on the Star-Spangled Banner National Historic Trail, this waterfront village saw action during the War of 1812, during one of the many British raids of the Northern Neck from 1813-1814. Due to the expanse of shoreline on the Potomac River, Westmoreland County has two other sites on the Star-Spangled Banner National Historic Trail further up the Potomac: George Washington Birthplace National Monument and Westmoreland State Park: nps.gov/stsp

Locally, kayak and canoe rentals are available at The Slips to explore the Yeocomico River, lined with historic homes, and pristine waterfront. The Kinsale Museum and Gift Shop is open year-round and offers visitors stories of the Northern Neck waterfront and historic sites along the Westmoreland shoreline. Animated by the activities of the centrally located Kinsale Museum, the village is walkable, and quiet, with amenities at The Slips Marina, walkable to the Kinsale Museum. Through the activities of the Museum, the village celebrates the Fourth of July, Kinsale Day in September, and Christmas in Kinsale in early December. kinsalefoundation.org

Virginia Wineries

Westmoreland County is home to four wineries: General's Ridge Vineyard, The Hague Winery, Ingleside Winery, and Monroe Bay Winery. Two breweries operate in Colonial Beach and Montross. Look for food truck and live music events at the wineries.

MID-ATLANTIC EDITION

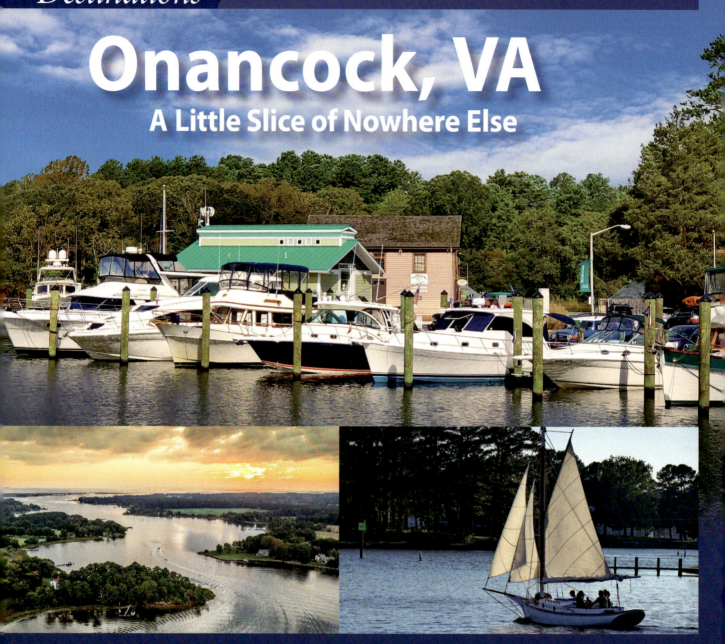

Onancock, VA
A Little Slice of Nowhere Else

Onancock, located between the bay and the sea, has a fascinating history that connects the past and present through its people, places, food, and art. This hidden treasure on Virginia's Eastern Shore impressed Captain John Smith over four centuries ago, and it's likely to leave a lasting impression on you too.

Chartered in 1680, Onancock has a history spanning over 300 years as a deep-water port with a safe harbor, catering to pleasure boats cruising the Chesapeake and offering convenient access for kayakers and day sailors.

It takes a full day's sail at an average speed of 6 knots to reach Onancock from most bayfront points on Virginia's western shores. However, keep in mind that the weather on Chesapeake Bay can be unpredictable, so it's crucial to consider this when planning a boat trip. Once you arrive, the six-mile journey up Onancock Creek by boat provides a pleasant respite from the open waters of the Chesapeake, giving you ample time to contemplate the area's rich history. The town offers a charming marina with floating docks, and you can make reservations online at Onancock.com/Wharf.

Where To Dine

Onancock, Virginia, boasts a diverse dining scene that captures the coastal charm of the town. From fresh seafood to farm-to-table options, there are various restaurants catering to different tastes. Whether it's cozy cafes or family-owned eateries, locals and visitors have plenty of choices. The town's proximity to the Chesapeake Bay ensures that you can savor the freshest seafood, making dining in Onancock a truly enjoyable experience that reflects the region's heritage.

If you're looking for a great waterfront dining experience in Onancock, we highly recommend Mallards at the Wharf. Located in the historic Hopkins and Brothers Store dating back to 1842 and positioned at the head of Onancock Creek, this restaurant offers a friendly and relaxed atmosphere. Johnny Mo and his team provide excellent service, ensuring you have a memorable time.

Things To Do Ashore

The town's wharf serves as a central hub for marine activities, offering kayak tours and boat excursions.

Taking a stroll east on Market Street, you'll encounter a cluster of well-preserved 19th-century homes and churches. On College Avenue lies the Historic Onancock School, a 13-acre oasis within the town, offering recreational activities and a Nature Trail alongside Onancock Creek. Inside, you'll encounter many artisans working in their studios (often by appointment), and the Eastern Shore Watermen's Museum & Research Center, which delves into the rich history and culture of those making their livelihood from the surrounding waters.

When the sun sets, Onancock comes alive with a surprisingly sophisticated selection of evening entertainment. Catch first-run films at the Roseland Theater, which also hosts monthly international films. For live performances, head to the North Street Playhouse, featuring a range of plays and other productions throughout the year. Several eateries in town offer live music, spanning from soothing jazz to soulful Celtic ballads.

This hidden gem on Virginia's Eastern Shore has a charm that has withstood the test of time, leaving a lasting impression on all who visit. Onancock offers a fulfilling experience for every traveler. Whether you're drawn to its coastal allure, its welcoming community, or its deep-rooted heritage, Onancock is a place that will captivate your heart and beckon you to return for more unforgettable memories.

Preferred Destinations from WATERWAY GUIDE MEDIA®

Unveiling the Charms of
Washington, NC

Nestled on the picturesque banks of the Pamlico River, Washington, North Carolina, holds a special allure for boating enthusiasts in search of a coastal adventure. With its rich historical significance, scenic waterfront, and abundant natural beauty, Washington, NC presents an enticing destination for boaters of all levels of expertise.

First called Forks of the Tar, the city name was changed in 1776 in honor of Gen. George Washington. Because it was America's first city to be named for Gen. Washington, it is sometimes referred to as "The Original Washington" or "Little Washington" to avoid confusion. "Little" does not, however, describe the amenities here.

Whether you're an experienced captain or a novice sailor eager to dip your toes into new waters, Washington, NC promises tranquility, scenic beauty, and a warm hospitality that will make your boating experience truly memorable.

Curious Foodies Welcome

Washington, NC, beckons curious foodies to embark on a culinary adventure, where they can indulge in a wide array of flavors and delights. The town boasts several noteworthy eateries that showcase the region's culinary treasures. Among the must-visit establishments, Bill's Hot Dogs stands as a true local institution since 1928. Renowned for their mouthwatering classic hot dogs topped with their signature, original-recipe chili and an array of fixings, Bill's Hot Dogs guarantees a taste of tradition.

To help wash things down, a visit to Pitt Street Brewing on the Pamlico is in order. Housed in a converted waterfront craft brewery that was once a rowing club, Pitt Street Brewing invites patrons to enjoy the gentle breezes of the Pamlico while sipping on a refreshing selection of lagers, ales, and stouts. The brewery offers a perfect setting to relax and savor the craft beer experience.

Things To Do Ashore

For boaters venturing ashore in Washington, NC, an array of enjoyable activities awaits, showcasing the town's natural beauty, cultural exploration, and historical charm. Goose Creek State Park, a hidden gem, provides an idyllic escape into nature. With its tranquil waterways, lush forests, and scenic trails, the park beckons outdoor enthusiasts for hiking, boating, fishing, and wildlife spotting.

Continue your journey of discovery at the North Carolina Estuarium, where the fascinating world of estuaries comes to life. Explore interactive exhibits, aquariums, and educational displays that highlight the unique ecosystems of the Pamlico River and its surrounding estuarine environments. Dive into the diverse marine life, ecological importance, and conservation efforts of this captivating coastal region.

To further immerse yourself in the town's history and architecture, embark on self-guided audio tours of Washington's Historic Districts. Wander through the charming streets and listen to informative narratives that bring the town's rich heritage to life. From well-preserved homes to significant landmarks, these tours offer a glimpse into Washington's storied past and its contributions to North Carolina's history.

Discover the allure of Washington, NC—an enchanting blend of natural beauty, rich history, and warm hospitality. From serene waters to captivating museums, this coastal gem offers a truly unforgettable experience.

Urbanna, Virginia

Where History Meets Harbor

Whether you're docking for a weekend or seeking a picturesque escape, Urbanna, Virginia, invites you to experience its colonial charm, vibrant community events, and rich maritime heritage. It's a place where history can be learned and lived, making every visit a memorable journey into the heart of Virginia's colonial past.

Founded in 1680 and named for Queen Anne of England, it was originally intended as a trade hub and was one of America's original colonial ports, with deep draft ships loading tobacco from area plantations. Urbanna retains its historical allure with architecture dating back to the 18th century, including one of Virginia's surviving colonial courthouse; a delightful, hospitable, and walkable town.

Enhance Your Urbanna Experience with the Explore Middlesex App!

EXPLORE Middlesex Co. Virginia
VIRGINIA IS FOR LOVERS

20   WATERWAY GUIDE 2025   www.waterwayguide.com

Watermen Heritage

In the 1930s, Urbanna experienced significant growth when it became a refuge for 14 families from Tangier Island following the catastrophic "August Storm" that inundated their homes. The Tangier families were already familiar with Urbanna, or "Banna" as they called it, due to their seasonal work in the oyster beds when the State of Virginia's Public Oyster Hand Tong season opened each October. By the 21st century, the town became known for its oyster packing plants and as a charming, waterside destination.

Dock the Boat and Explore

Urbanna has two main marinas. Urbanna Boat Yard and Marina (URBBY) offers 160 slips with facilities for vessels up to 100ft. The Urbanna Town Marina anchors the northern section of the waterfront offering 15 transient slips for vessels up to 65 ft. Both are a short jaunt up the hill into town.

Just steps from the Urbanna Town Marina, visitors can immerse themselves in history at the Friends of Urbanna Museum and James Mills Scottish Factor Store, home to the John Mitchell Map. You can also take to the streets with Urbanna's Museum in the Streets—a self-guided walking tour with QR-coded markers narrated by historian Larry Chowning. For paddling enthusiasts, the Urbanna Creek Kayak Trail offers a trip through history, accessible from the town marina.

Home to the Urbanna Oyster Festival

The Urbanna Oyster Festival, established in 1958 as "Urbanna Days," has grown into a major annual event that draws over 50,000 visitors from Virginia and beyond. As the official oyster festival of the Commonwealth, it honors the rich oyster culture of the region. The festival features numerous highlight events, including an almost deafening display of sirens and lights during the Fireman's Parade and the Virginia State Oyster Shucking Competition, where winners advance to compete in the National Shucking Competition in Maryland.

Urbanna for All Seasons

Throughout the year, the town offers abundant dining options. The Town of Urbanna is more notably a seafood lover's delight with local aquaculture ensuring fresh oysters are available year round and local watermen's daily catch of Chesapeake Bay blue crabs throughout the summer.

The monthly Urbanna Farmers Market and Second Saturdays feature local produce, handmade goods, live music, and wine tasting with a festive atmosphere that celebrates the best of local culture.

Preferred *Destinations* from WATERWAY GUIDE MEDIA

Visit a Place Where Adventures are as Vast as the Sea

Hampton, VA.

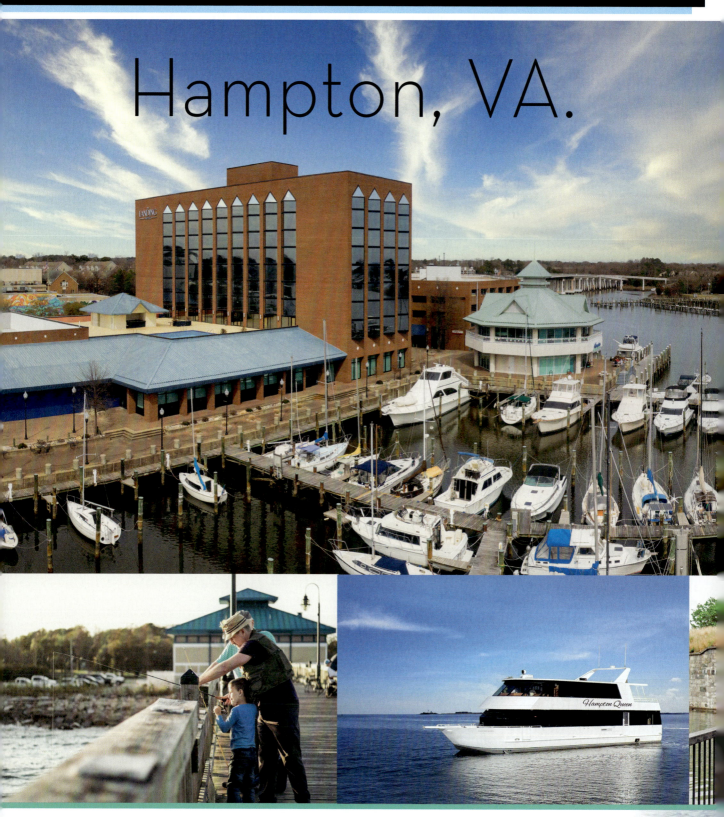

We're home to a vibrant boating, fishing and ocean-faring culture that dates back centuries. Tour the Chesapeake Bay and cast your line for an incredible time on the James T. Wilson Fishing Pier. Soak up the sun and the fun at Buckroe beach where you can fulfill your thrill with watersports, jet skiing, kayaking and paddle-boarding. Savor the moment, and the flavors, with waterfront dining and fresh, delicious seafood.

Looking for something more personal? Charter a boat for a private tour, and savor fresh seafood straight from the Atlantic, with the world's greatest natural harbor as your backdrop. Starting this Spring, climb aboard the all-new Hampton Queen and see the sea!

Need an adventure outside the water? Experience our attractions, history and culture. Hampton's numerous world-class attractions, including Fort Monroe National Monument, the Virginia Air & Space Science Center, and the Hampton University Museum, have been inspiring visitors for decades. See history and adventure come alive in Hampton.

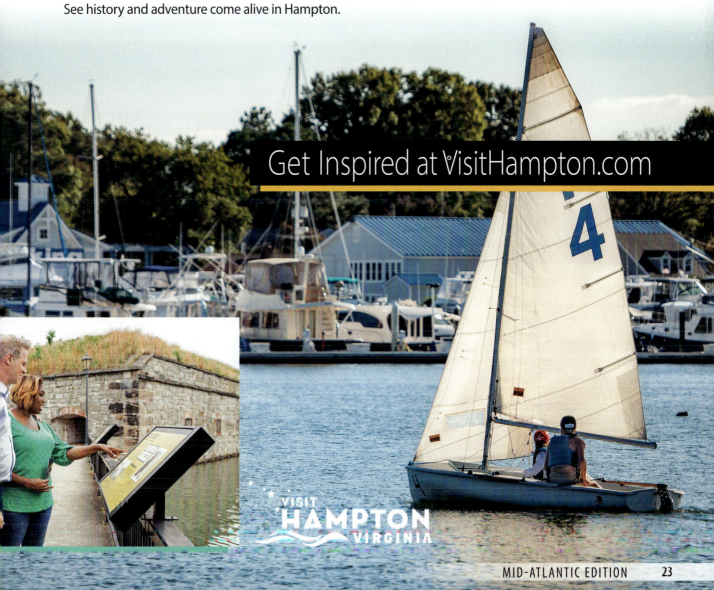

Get Inspired at VisitHampton.com

VISIT HAMPTON VIRGINIA

Preferred Destinations from WATERWAY GUIDE MEDIA

Discovering Timeless Treasures In
Beaufort & Port Royal
South Carolina

Welcome to the picturesque haven of Beaufort and Port Royal, South Carolina, where a delightful blend of southern hospitality, rich culture, and tantalizing cuisine awaits your discovery. Nestled between the Beaufort River and Battery Creek, these enchanting twin cities are loved by history enthusiasts, nature lovers, and those yearning for a peaceful escape.

Founded in 1562, Port Royal Island has been a beacon of attraction for explorers throughout its rich history. Upon your arrival, you'll be transported to a bygone era, where exquisitely preserved pre-Civil War architecture graces every corner. Wander through the historic downtown, a designated district that offers a glimpse into the past, and lose yourself in the splendor of the south's most extraordinary bed and breakfasts, restaurants, and hotels.

America's Waterway Guide Since 1947

Where To Dine

This area boasts a wide array of restaurants, catering to every preference, from laid-back coastal cuisine to elegant fine dining.

When it comes to seafood, the Beaufort & Port Royal area is a reigning champion, and your visit here would be incomplete without savoring the culinary delights offered by its many local eateries, where seafood dishes take center stage on the menus. Witness the docks of Battery Creek bustling with activity as a vibrant fleet of trawlers sets sail daily, ensuring a continuous supply of the freshest catches. Prepare to revel in a delightful assortment of oysters, shrimp, crab, and freshly caught fish, all sourced from the local waters.

For an authentic taste of Lowcountry living, head over to Fishcamp on 11th Street – a beloved spot cherished by locals and visitors alike. The menu here is a true treasure trove, featuring mouthwatering seafood delicacies alongside succulent steaks, catering to the diverse preferences of every palate.

If you're looking for a fine dining experience, head to the Ribaut Social Club, a fine dining and social space for Beaufort locals and visitors to mingle over cocktails and impeccable regional cuisine. The concise menu presents imaginative interpretations of meats, seafood, and fresh vegetables. Be sure to secure reservations ahead of time, as this culinary haven is in high demand and promises an unforgettable dining experience.

Local Events & Festivals

Throughout the year, Beaufort, South Carolina, is a bustling hub of annual festivals and events, ensuring there is never a dull moment for both locals and visitors. Mark your calendars and embrace the opportunity to partake in these local events.

Take a Journey into Gullah Culture

Delve into the rich heritage of the Gullah people, African Americans who have made their home in the Lowcountry region of South Carolina and Georgia, including the coastal plains and Beaufort Sea Islands. Immerse yourself in the culture and history of the Gullah community with a guided tour by native experts from St. Helena, courtesy of Gullah-N-Geechie Mahn Tours. The Gullah culture is a source of immense pride and has inspired documentary films, children's books, and popular novels that celebrate its unique traditions and contributions.

Travel Back in Time

Exploring the local history of Beaufort and Port Royal is like stepping into a living time capsule, where every street corner and historic landmark reveals fascinating stories from the past. Beaufort and Port Royal, both deeply intertwined with the nation's history, boast an exquisitely preserved charm that takes visitors on a captivating journey through time.

Founded in 1711, Beaufort holds a significant place in history as the second oldest city in South Carolina, only trailing behind Charleston. With its roots intertwined with early European explorations, this charming city thrived as one of the economic hubs of the Lowcountry throughout the 1800s.

To truly immerse oneself in the past, a visit to the numerous cultural sites scattered across historic Beaufort is a must. Step back in time and witness the echoes of bygone eras as you explore the rich heritage that has shaped this captivating city.

Discover a haven that effortlessly transforms overnight anchorages into week-long retreats, and visitors into locals captivated by the enchanting allure of this coastal gem. Learn more about the Beaufort and Port Royal area at https://www.beaufortsc.org/

Preferred Destinations from **WATERWAY GUIDE MEDIA**

Florida's Forgotten Coast
is a Boater's Paradise

Florida's Forgotten Coast, along the North Florida Gulf Coast, is a boater's paradise with hundreds of miles of freshwater creeks, sloughs and rivers that empty into nutrient-rich bays and out to the Gulf of Mexico.

Getting out on the water is easy here. The area features more than 40 boat ramps stretching from Alligator Point to Apalachicola. Bring your boat and tie up at one of the area's 10 commercial marinas.

America's Waterway Guide Since 1947

APALACHICOLA
The downtown historic district of Apalachicola stretches three blocks deep from where the historic Apalachicola River meets the oyster-famous Apalachicola Bay. Everything is walkable here - stroll along the wide tree-lined streets with historic homes or hole up along the waterfront and enjoy the music scene in pubs and local eateries just blocks from the waterfront. Apalachicola's commercial marina facilities include the Scipio Creek, Water Street and Apalachicola Marina with services and available at Scipio Creek.

EASTPOINT
Across the bay from Apalachicola, Eastpoint features rustic seafood houses, weather-worn docks and fresh seafood markets run by families four generations deep. There are RV parks here, two boat ramps, a full-service bait and tackle shop, fresh seafood restaurants, causal fare and even a waterfront brewery!

ST. GEORGE ISLAND
Just offshore, St. George Island is a 22- mile barrier island that hosts some of Florida's most beautiful and serene beaches. There is a protected anchorage spot on the bayside of St. George Island. Don't expect to walk to amenities from this anchorage but it's not far from the Julian G. Bruce St. George Island State Park which boasts some of the best camping facilities in the region. Elsewhere on the island, accommodations range from quaint beach cottages to luxurious beach homes and can be reserved with any of the island's vacation rental companies. The historic St. George Island Lighthouse is located at the St. George Island public beach park.

CARRABELLE
Carrabelle is about 30 nautical miles from Apalachicola and it's a must stop spot for boaters and fishermen. Carrabelle features three public commercial marinas along the Carrabelle River and all are located within walking distance of restaurants, a grocery and all three offers either fuel or service facilities. There is public dockage along the river and a private boat club nearby on Timber Island.

Carrabelle is considered ground zero for fishing enthusiasts because of its easy access to offshore fishing and boating. The town features a natural deep-water harbor plus a nearby renowned golf resort. The nearby Crooked River Lighthouse reminds you of the town's maritime importance and features monthly full moon climbs.

To learn more about Franklin County boating, fishing charters, restaurants, and accomodations, visit Floridasforgottencoast.com/waterways

MID-ATLANTIC EDITION

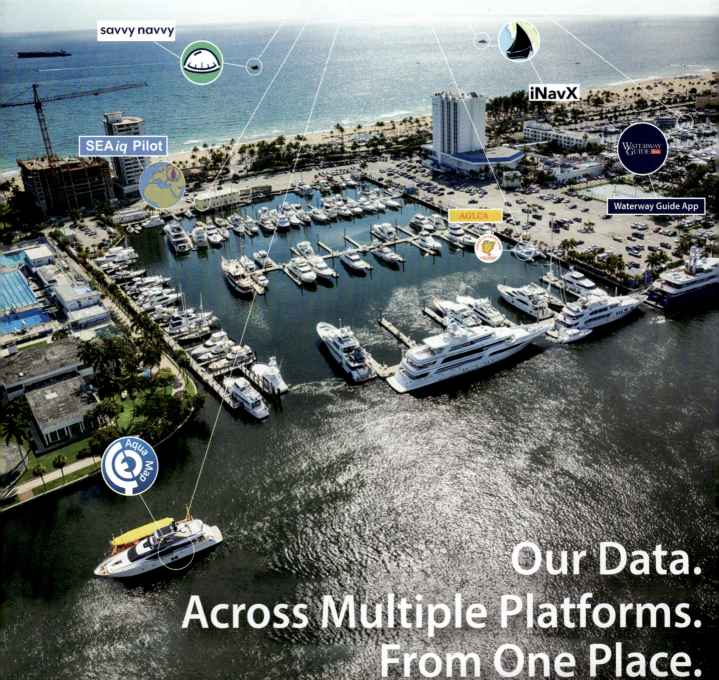

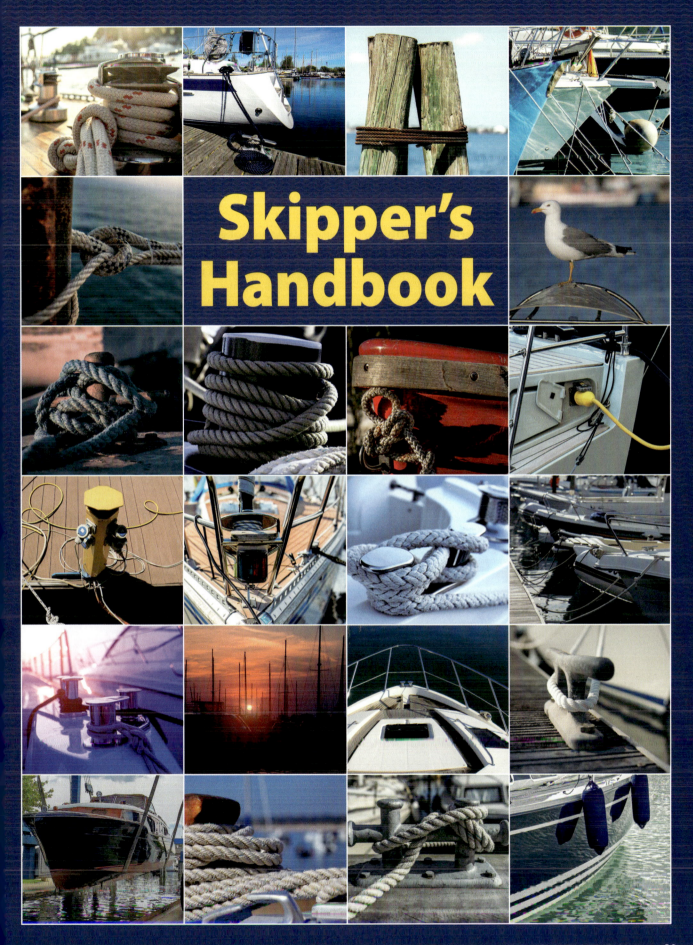

Skipper's Handbook

MID-ATLANTIC EDITION

Skipper's Handbook

Port Security

The U.S. Coast Guard and Customs and Border Patrol–both components of the Department of Homeland Security–handle port security in the United States. Local law enforcement agencies and the FBI also have a role in port security at the local and regional level. Each year more than 11 million maritime containers arrive at our seaports. At land borders, another 11 million arrive by truck and 2.7 million by rail. Homeland Security is responsible for knowing what is inside those containers, whether it poses a risk to the American people and ensuring that all proper revenues are collected.

As an example, one in five food items is now imported. American consumers demand fresh limes and blueberries all year round and, as a result, during the winter months in the U.S. nearly 80 percent of the fresh fruits and vegetables on our tables come from other countries. With the ever-increasing amount of trade, the agricultural risks to the United States grow. The threat to crops and livestock is real.

In response to this threat and others, the U.S. Coast Guard has established "protection zones" around all U.S. Navy vessels, tank vessels and large-capacity cruise vessels, even when underway. U.S. Navy bases, U.S. Coast Guard bases and some shoreside facilities such as nuclear power plants are also in protection zones. Non-military vessels (this means YOU) are not allowed within 100 yards of these protection zones. To do so can rack up serious civil penalties and even imprisonment. These protection zones vary from port to port and from facility to facility but ignorance of the protection zones is not a viable excuse. Having said that, law-abiding boaters sometimes find themselves unable to comply with the letter of the law without hitting a jetty, for example. In such cases, common sense and good communication should prevail.

America's Waterway Watch Program

Government officials view the recreational boating community as an ally. We can do our part (and perhaps stave off more stringent regulations and surveillance measures) by becoming familiar with the Coast Guard's America's Waterway Watch program. Think of it as a neighborhood watch program for the waterways.

It is not the intent of America's Waterway Watch to spread paranoia or to encourage spying on one another and it is not a surveillance program; it is instead a simple deterrent to potential terrorist activity. The purpose of the program is to allow boaters and others who spend time along the water to help the authorities counter crime and terrorism. To report suspicious behavior, call the National Response Center at 877-249-2824 (877-24WATCH). For immediate danger to life or property, call 911 or contact the U.S. Coast Guard on Marine VHF Channel 16.

Staying safe and responsible requires a little forethought and vigilance on your part. Following the steps outlined below will help ensure a trouble-free journey and keep you and your crew out of the headlines.

Be Prepared

- Before you leave, check the current charts for the area in which you will be traveling and identify any security areas. Security zones are highlighted and outlined in magenta with special notes regarding the specific regulations pertaining to that area.

- Check the latest *Local Notice to Mariners* (available online at www.navcen.uscg and posted at some marinas) and identify any potential security areas that may not be shown on the chart.

- Prior to your departure, listen to VHF Channel 16 for any Sécurité alerts from the Coast Guard (departing cruise ships, U.S. Navy vessels, fuel tankers, etc.) for the area you will be cruising.

- Talk to other boaters in your anchorage or marina about the areas where you will be traveling. They may have tips and suggestions on potential security zones or special areas they may have encountered along the way.

Stay Alert While Underway

- Mind the outlined magenta security areas noted on your charts.

- Look for vessels with blue or red warning lights in port areas and, if approached, listen carefully and strictly obey all instructions given to you.

- Keep your VHF radio switched to VHF Channel 16 and keep your ears tuned for bulletins, updates and possible requests for communication.

- Avoid commercial port operation areas, especially those that involve military, cruise line or petroleum facilities. Observe and avoid other restricted areas near power plants, national monuments, etc.

- If you need to pass within 100 yards of a U.S. Navy vessel for safe passage, you must contact the U.S. Navy vessel or the Coast Guard escort vessel on VHF Channel 16 to let them know your intentions.

- We advise that if government security or the U.S. Coast Guard hails you, do exactly what they say, regardless of whether or not you feel their instructions have merit.

Additional Resources

Atlantic Intracoastal Waterway Association:
www.atlanticintracoastal.org.

America's Waterway Watch:
www.americaswaterwaywatch.org

Department of Homeland Security:
www.dhs.gov

U.S. Customs and Border Protection:
www.cbp.gov

Skipper's Handbook

Customs Reporting Procedures

Operators of small pleasure vessels, arriving in the U.S. from a foreign port are required to report their arrival to Customs and Border Patrol (CBP) immediately. The master of the vessel reports their arrival at the nearest Customs facility or other designated location. These reports are tracked in the Pleasure Boat Reporting System. An application to lawfully enter the U.S. must be made in person to a CBP officer at a U.S. port-of-entry when the port is open for inspection.

CBP has designated specific reporting locations within the Field Offices that are staffed during boating season for pleasure boats to report their arrival and be inspected by CBP. The master of the boat must report to CBP telephonically and be directed to the nearest Port of Entry to satisfy the face-to-face requirement, or report to the nearest designated reporting location, along with the boat's passengers for inspection.

You may be required to rent a car or take a cab to the nearest airport or federal office several miles away for the inspection. These offices are often closed on weekends. If your arrival is after working hours, you are required to stay on board and clear in the next morning. You must, however, clear in within 24 hours of your arrival. Everyone on board, regardless of nationality, has to report in person. U.S. nationals must take their passports or passport cards. All non-U.S. Nationals should take their passports with valid visas and a Green Card, if held. Take your boat papers, either U.S. documentation or state registration with state decal number. You should also present a list of firearms and ammunition on board.

Clearing In with the ROAM App

Travelers arriving by boat into many popular U.S. ports can check into the country on their phones or tablets. The Reporting Offsite Arrival–Mobile (ROAM) app is the official replacement for the Local Boater Option (LBO) and Small Vessel Reporting System (SVRS) programs that have been used over the years. These programs required an initial interview to get in but usually resulted in a quick phone call instead of a face-to-face meeting to re-enter the U.S.

If you have a www.Login.gov account, you can log into the app immediately. If you need a password, the app directs you to the website. Then it walks you through the steps, including entering the specifics for each person on board and for your vessel. Once you've entered all of the details and submitted it for a review, an officer may initiate a video call to discuss the trip or to ask any necessary questions. All of this happens directly inside the app. Of course, there are still instances where in-person reporting is required. If you require an I-94, need to pay customs fees or duties, or need to obtain a cruising permit, you will still need to check in in-person. Boaters are still required to have a current fee decal onboard.

Now that the app has been implemented on a larger scale, travelers entering by boat in the Great Lakes; most of the East Coast (Delaware to Florida); Texas and San Diego, CA; and the U.S. territories in the Caribbean can use the app. New locations are continually being added, and because the program is new, it's probably a good idea to call your port of arrival to ensure they are using the ROAM app.

To download the ROAM app, just search the Apple App Store or the Google Play Store on your device. For more information, visit the CBP website or contact the CBP office at your port of arrival.

Additional Resources

U.S. Customs and Border Control:
www.cbp.gov/travel/pleasure-boats-private-flyers

Designated Port of Entry (Key West):
301 Simonton St., Ste. 20, 305-296-5411

America's Waterway Guide Since 1947

 # Float Plan   BoatU.S.

1. Phone Numbers

Coast Guard: _____

Marine Police: _____

Local TowBoatU.S. Company: _____

2. Description of the Boat

Boat Name: _____ Hailing Port: _____

Type: _____ Model Year: _____

Make: _____ Length: _____ Beam: _____ Draft: _____

Color, Hull: _____ Cabin: _____ Deck: _____ Trim: _____ Dodger: _____

Other Colors: _____ # of Masts: _____

Distinguishing Features: _____

Registration No: _____ Sail No: _____

Engine(s) Type: _____ Horsepower: _____ Cruising Speed: _____

Fuel Capacity, Gallons: _____ Cruising Range: _____

Electronics/Safety Equipment Aboard

VHF Radio: _____ Cell Phone: _____ CB: _____ SSB: _____

Frequency Monitored: _____ Loran: _____ SatNav: _____

Depth Sounder: _____ Radar: _____ GPS: _____

Raft: _____ Dinghy: _____ EPIRB: _____ A/B/C/406M
(Indicate Type)

3. Trip Details

Owner/Skipper (Filing Report): _____

Phone: _____ Age: _____

Address: _____

Additional Persons Aboard, Total: _____

Name: _____ Age: _____
Address: _____ Phone: _____
Boating Experience: _____

Name: _____ Age: _____
Address: _____ Phone: _____
Boating Experience: _____

Name: _____ Age: _____
Address: _____ Phone: _____
Boating Experience: _____

Name: _____ Age: _____
Address: _____ Phone: _____
Boating Experience: _____

Name: _____ Age: _____
Address: _____ Phone: _____
Boating Experience: _____

Departure Date/Time: _____ Return No Later Than: _____
Depart From: _____

Marina (Home Port): _____ Phone: _____

Auto Parked At: _____

Model/color: _____ Lic. # _____

Destination Port: _____

_____ ETA: _____ No Later Than: _____
Phone: _____

Anticipated Stopover Ports: _____

_____ ETA: _____ No Later Than: _____
Phone: _____

_____ ETA: _____ No Later Than: _____
Phone: _____

_____ ETA: _____ No Later Than: _____
Phone: _____

_____ ETA: _____ No Later Than: _____
Phone: _____

_____ ETA: _____ No Later Than: _____
Phone: _____

Plan Filed With: _____

Name: _____ Phone: _____

Get in the habit of filing a Float Plan. It can assure quicker rescue in the event of a breakdown, stranding or weather delay. Fill out the permanent data in Sections 1 and 2. Then, make enough copies to last for the season. If you file a Float Plan with someone not at your home, such as a harbormaster or boating friend, be sure to notify them as soon as you return. Don't burden friends or authorities with unnecessary worry and responsibility if you are safe.

Check your *BoatU.S. Towing Guide*. Some listed companies will accept a verbal Float Plan via telephone or VHF.

MID ATLANTIC EDITION

Skipper's Handbook

VHF Communications

Skippers traveling the U.S. inland waterways use their VHF radios almost every day to contact other vessels and bridgetenders, make reservations at marinas, arrange to pass other vessels safely and conduct other business. Waterway Guide has put together the following information to help remove any confusion as to what frequency should be dialed in to call bridges, marinas, commercial ships or your friend anchored down the creek.

Remember to use low power (1 watt) for your radio transmission whenever possible. If you are within a couple of miles of the responding station (bridge, marina or other craft), there is no need to broadcast at 25 watts and disturb the transmissions of others 25 miles away.

Channel Usage Tips

- VHF Channel 16 (156.8 MHz) is by far the most important frequency on the VHF-FM band. VHF Channel 16 is the international distress, safety and calling frequency.

- If you have a VHF radio on your boat, Federal Communications Commission (FCC) regulations require that you maintain a watch on either VHF Channel 09 or 16 whenever you are underway and the radio is not being used to communicate on another channel. Since the Coast Guard does not have the capability of announcing an urgent marine information broadcast or weather warning on VHF Channel 09, it recommends that boaters remain tuned to and use VHF Channel 16.

- Recreational craft typically communicate on VHF Channels 68, 69, 71, 72 or 78A. Whenever possible, avoid calling on VHF Channel 16 altogether by prearranging initial contact directly on one of these channels. No transmissions should last longer than 3 minutes.

- The Coast Guard's main working VHF Channel is 22A and both emergency and non-emergency calls generally are switched there to keep VHF Channel 16 clear. Calling the Coast Guard for a radio check on VHF Channel 16 is prohibited.

- Radio-equipped bridges on the Atlantic ICW use VHF Channel 09 with a few exceptions.

- The Bridge-to-Bridge Radio Telephone Act requires many commercial vessels, including dredges and tugboats, to monitor VHF Channel 13. VHF Channel 13 is also the frequency used by bridges in several states.

Distress Calls

MAYDAY: The distress signal "MAYDAY" is used to indicate that a vessel is threatened by grave and imminent danger and requests immediate assistance.

PAN PAN: The urgency signal "PAN PAN" is used when the safety of the ship or person is in jeopardy.

SÉCURITÉ: The safety signal "SÉCURITÉ" is used for messages about the safety of navigation or important weather warnings.

VHF Channel 16 is the distress call frequency. The codeword "MAYDAY" is the international alert signal of a life-threatening situation at sea. After a MAYDAY message is broadcast, VHF Channel 16 must be kept free of all traffic, other than those directly involved in the rescue situation, until the rescue has been completed.

If you hear a MAYDAY message and no one else is responding, it is your duty to step in to answer the call, relay it to the nearest rescue organization and get to the scene to help. Remember, a MAYDAY distress call can only be used when life is threatened. For example, if you have run on the rocks but no one is going to lose their life, that is NOT a MAYDAY situation.

> Note: The Coast Guard has asked the FCC to eliminate provisions for using VHF Channel 09 as an alternative calling frequency to VHF Channel 16 when it eliminates watch-keeping on VHF Channel 16 by compulsory-equipped vessels. Stay tuned for updates.

America's Waterway Guide Since 1947

How to Make a Distress Call

MAYDAY! MAYDAY! MAYDAY!

This is: Give your vessel name and call sign.

Our position is: Read it off the GPS or give it as something like "2 miles southwest of Royal Island." (Your rescuers must be able to find you!)

We are: Describe what's happening (e.g., on fire/hit a reef/sinking).

We have: Report how many people are on board.

At this time we are: Say what you're doing about the crisis (e.g., standing by/abandoning ship).

For identification we are: Describe your boat type, length, color, etc. (so your rescuers can more readily identify you).

We have: List safety equipment you have (e.g., flares/smoke/ocean dye markers/EPIRB).

We will keep watch on Channel 16 as long as we can.

VHF Channels	
09	Used for radio checks and hailing other stations (boats, shoreside operations). Also used to communicate with drawbridges in Florida.
13	Used to contact and communicate with commercial vessels, military ships and drawbridges. Bridges in several states monitor VHF Channel 13.
16	*Emergency use only.* May be used to hail other vessels, but once contact is made, conversation should be immediately switched to a working (68, 69, 71, 72, 78A) VHF channel.
22	Used for U.S. Coast Guard safety, navigation and Sécurité communications.
68 69 71 72 78A	Used primarily for recreational ship-to-ship and ship-to-shore communications.

MID-ATLANTIC EDITION

Skipper's Handbook

Rules of the Road

Anyone planning to cruise U.S. waterways should be familiar with the rules of the road. *Chapman Piloting: Seamanship and Small Boat Handling* and *The Annapolis Book of Seamanship* are both excellent on-the-water references with plentiful information on navigation rules. For those with a penchant for the exact regulatory language, the U.S. Coast Guard publication *Navigation Rules: International–Inland* covers both international and U.S. inland rules. (Boats over 39.4 feet are required to carry a copy of the U.S. Inland Rules at all times.)

Following is a list of common situations you may likely encounter on the waterways. Make yourself familiar with them, and if there is ever a question as to which of you has the right-of-way, let the other vessel go first.

Sailors need to remember that a boat under sail with its engine running is considered a motorboat.

Passing or Being Passed:

- If you intend to pass a slower vessel, try to hail them on your VHF radio to let them know you are coming.

- In close quarters, BOTH vessels should slow down, which normally allows the faster vessel to pass quickly without throwing a large wake onto the slower boat.

- A boat passing another is the "give-way" vessel and is required to keep clear of the slower "stand-on" vessel until past and well clear of it.

- Sound signals when overtaking (both vessels heading the same way):
"See you on the one (whistle)" = overtake on his starboard (your port)
"See you on the two (whistle)" = overtake on his port (your starboard)

- Sound signals when passing (vessels going in opposite directions):
"See you on the one (whistle)" = pass port to port
"See you on the two (whistle)" = pass starboard to starboard

- As you pass a slower boat, take a look back to see how they were affected by your wake. Remember: YOU are responsible for your wake. It is the law to slow down and it is common courtesy.

At Opening Bridges:

- During an opening, boats traveling with the current go first and generally have the right-of-way.

- Boats constrained by their draft, size or maneuverability (e.g., dredges, tugs and barges) take priority.

- Standard rules of the road apply while circling or waiting for a bridge opening.

Tugs, Freighters, Dredges & Naval Vessels:

- These vessels are usually constrained by draft or their inability to easily maneuver. For this reason, you will almost always need to give them the right-of-way and keep out of their path.

- You must keep at least 100 yards away from any Navy vessel. If you cannot safely navigate without coming closer than this, you must notify the ship of your intentions over VHF Channel 16.

- Keep a close watch for freighters, tugs with tows and other large vessels while offshore or in crowded ports. They often come up very quickly, despite their large size.

- It is always a good practice to radio larger vessels (VHF Channel 13 or 16) to notify them of your location and your intentions. The skippers of these boats are generally appreciative of efforts to communicate with them. This is especially true with dredge boats on all the waterways.

Additional Resources

U.S. Coast Guard Boating Safety Division:
www.uscgboating.org

U.S. Coast Guard Navigation Center:
www.navcen.uscg.gov

In a Crossing Situation:

- When two vessels under power are crossing and a risk of collision exists, the vessel that has the other on her starboard side must keep clear and avoid crossing ahead of the other vessel.

- When a vessel under sail and a vessel under power are crossing, the boat under power is usually burdened and must keep clear. The same exceptions apply as per head-on meetings.

- On the Great Lakes and western rivers (e.g., the Mississippi River system), a power-driven vessel crossing a river shall keep clear of a power-driven vessel ascending or descending the river.

Power Vessels Meeting Any Other Vessel:

- When two vessels under power (either sailboats or powerboats) meet "head-to-head," both are obliged to alter course to starboard.

- Generally, when a vessel under power meets a vessel under sail (i.e., not using any mechanical power), the powered vessel must alter course accordingly.

- Exceptions are vessels not under command, vessels restricted in ability to maneuver, vessels engaged in commercial fishing or those under International Rules such as a vessel constrained by draft.

Two sailboats meeting under sail:

- When each has the wind on a different side, the boat with the wind on the port side must keep clear of the boat with the wind on the starboard side.

- When both have the wind on the same side, the vessel closest to the wind (windward) will keep clear of the leeward boat.

- A vessel with wind to port that sees a vessel to windward but cannot determine whether the windward vessel has wind to port or starboard will assume that windward vessel is on starboard tack and keep clear.

Keep Watch for Crab Pots!

While crab pots with marker buoys are not intentionally placed inside navigational channels, they sometimes break loose and find their way there. The terms "pot" refers to the enclosed traps (usually a framework of wire) used to catch crabs in shallow waters. The attached retrieval markers can range from colorful buoys to empty milk jugs (or anything else that floats). Most buoys are painted in a color that contrasts the water surface but some are black or even dark blue, which are especially difficult to see in the best of conditions. You do NOT want to get a line wrapped around your prop so it is advisable to have a spotter on the foredeck when traversing fields of pots.

Skipper's Handbook

Coast Guard Requirements

The U.S. Coast Guard stands watch at all times to aid vessels of all sizes and the persons on board. In some areas, you can quickly reach the Coast Guard by dialing *CG on a cellular phone. If you have a question of a non-emergency nature, the Coast Guard prefers that you telephone the nearest station. As always, if there is an emergency, initiate a "MAYDAY" call on VHF Channel 16.

In addition to aiding boaters in distress, the Coast Guard also enforces maritime law and conducts safety inspections. While a Coast Guard boarding can be unnerving, if you are responsible and prepared, it will only take 15 to 30 minutes and will be a non-event. First, have your boat in order. This includes having your vessel documentation, registration and insurance documents on hand, as well as your passport. Organize this in a binder and keep it in the nav station so you don't have to fumble around looking for documents and paperwork. You will need to acknowledge the location of any weapons on board and show a permit (when required by state law). The officers will likely focus on areas with the largest safety concerns including the following.

Note that state and local requirements are also considered. If there is a minor violation, they may give you a written warning explaining what needs to be fixed to be in compliance. If you are found with a small violation and correct it quickly, then this will merely be a chance to interact with those whose goal is to keep you as safe as possible on the water.

Life Jackets: One Type I, II, II or V per person plus one Type IV throwable device is required. PFDs must be U.S. Coast Guard-approved, wearable by the intended user and readily accessible. The Type IV throwable device must be located so that it is immediately available.

Visual Distress Signals: All vessels 16 feet and over must be equipped with minimum of 3 day-use and 3 night-use or 3 day/night combination pyrotechnic devices. Non-pyrotechnic substitutes are orange flag (for day use) and electric S-O-S signal light (for night use). Flares must be up to date (e.g., not expired).

Sound Producing Devices: A whistle, horn, siren, etc. capable of a 4-second blast audible for 0.5 mile must be on board for use during periods of reduced visibility. Boats 65 feet and over must have a bell and one whistle or horn required to signal intentions.

Navigation Lights: All powered vessels under 12 meters (39.4 feet) must have working navigational lights and an independent all-around anchor light. Sailboats under power are considered powerboats and must follow "power" rules.

Fire Extinguisher: U.S. Coast Guard-approved, marine-type fire extinguishers are required on any boat with enclosed fuel or engine spaces, enclosed living spaces or permanent (not movable by one person) fuel tanks. They must be in good working condition and readily accessible. (Number of units required depends on vessel length.)

Ventilation: Boats built after August 1, 1980, with enclosed gasoline engines must have a powered ventilation system with one or more exhaust blowers.

Backfire Flame Arrester: All gasoline-powered inboard/outboard or inboard motor boats must be equipped with an approved backfire flame arrester.

Pollution Placard: It is illegal to discharge oil or oily waste into any navigable waters of the U.S. Boats over 26 feet must display a durable oily waste pollution placard of at least 5 by 8 inches in a prominent location.

MARPOL Trash Placard: It is illegal to dump plastic trash anywhere in the ocean or navigable waters of the U.S. Boats over 26 feet must display a durable trash placard at least 4 by 9 inches in a prominent location.

Navigation Rules: Boats 39.4 feet and over must have a copy of current Navigation Rules on board. You can download a copy at www.uscgboating.org.

Marine Sanitation Devices: The discharge of treated sewage is allowed within 3 nm of shore except in designated "No Discharge Zone" areas. The Coast Guard will check that overboard discharge outlets can be sealed (and remain sealed if within 3 nm of shore).

Reference Materials

U.S. Coast Guard Local Notice to Mariners

The U.S. Coast Guard provides timely marine safety information for the correction of all U.S. Government navigation charts and publications from a wide variety of sources, both foreign and domestic via the *Local Notice to Mariners*. These are divided by district, updated weekly and available as a PDF at www.navcen.uscg.gov. (Select LNMs tab at top of page.)

Cruising Guides

- *ICW Cruising Guide (by Bob423)*, Robert A. Sherer
- *Skipper Bob Cruising Guides*, Ted Stehle (editor)

Navigation

- *A Boater's Guide to Federal Requirements for Recreational Boaters*. Covers equipment requirements, navigation rules and aids to navigation, a sample float plan and safety and survival tips. Can be downloaded as a PDF at www.uscgboating.org/images/420.PDF.
- *NAVIGATION RULES, INTERNATIONAL—INLAND*, U.S. Dept. of Homeland Security. The U.S. Coast Guard requires all vessels over 39 feet carry this book of the national and international rules of the road. Can be downloaded as a PDF at www.navcen.uscg.gov.
- *U.S. Coast Pilot (1-5)*, NOAA. Includes piloting information for coasts, bays, creeks and harbors. Also includes tide tables and highlights restricted areas. Updated weekly and can be downloaded as a PDF at www.nauticalcharts.noaa.gov/publications/coast-pilot/index.html.
- *U.S. Chart No 1. (Chart Symbols)*. Describes the symbols, abbreviations and terms used on NOAA nautical charts. Available online at www.nauticalcharts.noaa.gov/publications/us-chart-1.html.
- *U.S. Aids to Navigation System* is a downloadable guide from the U.S. Coast Guard with basic information on the recognition of U.S. Aids to Navigation System (ATONS). Find it at www.uscgboating.org/images/486.PDF.

Maintenance

- *Boatowner's Mechanical & Electrical Manual* (4th Edition), Nigel Calder
- *Boatowner's Illustrated Electrical Handbook*, Charlie Wing
- *Boat Mechanical Systems Handbook*, David Gerr

Seamanship

- *Anchoring: A Ground Tackler's Apprentice*, Rudy and Jill Sechez
- *Boater's Pocket Reference*, Thomas McEwen
- *Chapman Piloting & Seamanship* (68th Edition), Charles B. Husick
- *Eldridge Tide and Pilot Book* (Annual), Robert E. and Linda White
- *Heavy Weather Sailing* (7th Edition), Peter Bruce
- *Nigel Calder's Cruising Handbook*, Nigel Calder
- *Offshore Cruising Encyclopedia*, Steve & Linda Dashew
- *The Annapolis Book of Seamanship* (4th Edition), John Rousmaniere
- *The Art of Seamanship*, Ralph Naranjo
- *World Cruising Essentials*, Jimmy Cornell

First Aid & Medical

- *Advanced First Aid Afloat* (5th Edition), Dr. Peter F. Eastman
- *DAN Pocket Guide to First Aid for Scuba Diving*, Dan Orr & Bill Clendenden
- *First Aid at Sea*, Douglas Justin and Colin Berry
- *Marine Medicine: A Comprehensive Guide* (2nd Edition), Eric Weiss and Michael Jacobs
- *On-Board Medical Emergency Handbook: First Aid at Sea*, Spike Briggs and Campbell Mackenzie

Skipper's Handbook

About the Weather

Every day on the water can't have balmy breezes, abundant sunshine and consistently warm weather; however, staying out of bad weather is relatively easy if you plan ahead. The National Weather Service (NWS) provides mariners with continuous broadcasts of weather warnings, forecasts, radar reports and buoy reports over VHF-FM and Single Side Band (SSB) radio. There are almost no areas on the Atlantic ICW where a good quality, fixed-mount VHF cannot pick up one or more coastal VHF broadcasts. Also, there is no substitute for simply looking at the sky, and either stay put or seek shelter if you don't like what you see.

Reading the Skies

Water and metal are excellent conductors of electricity, making boating in a thunderstorm a risky prospect. While the odds of a given boat being hit are small, the consequences are severe and deadly. Do not try and play the odds! The best advice if you are out on the water and skies are threatening is get back to land and seek safe shelter, but that's not always practical for cruisers who live aboard or are not near land.

Thunderstorms occur when air masses of different temperatures meet over inland or coastal waters. An example of this would be when air with a high humidity that is warm near the ground rises and meets cooler air, which condenses and creates water droplets. This releases energy, which charges the atmosphere and creates lightning. This is why thunderstorms are a daily occurrence between March and October near southern waterways.

A tell-tale sign of a thunderstorm is cumulonimbus clouds: those tall clouds with an anvil-shaped (flat) top. Thunderstorms can also precede even a minor cold front. Keep in mind that thunderstorms generally move in an easterly direction so if you see a storm to the south or southwest of you, start preparing.

Don't Wait Until It's Too Late!

Almost all lightning will occur within 10 miles of its parent thunderstorm, but it can strike much farther than that. Also, the current from a single flash will easily travel for long distances. Because of this, if you see lightning or hear thunder, you CAN get struck!

Weather Apps (Free)
Boat Weather
Buoycast: NOAA Marine Forecast
National Hurricane Center Tracker
NOAA Marine Weather Radar
NOAA Weather
PredictWind
Wind Alert
Windfinder
Windy
Weather Online
Accuweather (www.accuweather.com)
BoatUS Hurricane Tracking & Resource Center (www.boatus.com/hurricanes/tracking)
Buoy Weather (www.buoyweather.com)
Coastal Marine Forecast (www.weather.gov/marine)
National Hurricane Center (www.nhc.noaa.gov)
National Weather Service (www.weather.gov)
Passage Weather (www.passageweather.com)
Predict Wind (www.predictwind.com)
Sailflow (www.sailflow.com)
The Weather Channel (www.weather.com)
Windfinder (www.windfinder.com)

The ability to see lightning will depend on the time of day, weather conditions and obstructions, but on a clear night it is possible to see a strike more than 10 miles away. Thunder can also be heard for about 10 miles, provided there is no background noise such as traffic, wind or rain.

If you see lightning, you can determine the distance by timing how long it takes before you hear thunder. The old rule that every 5 seconds of time equals 1 mile of distance works well. So if it takes 20 seconds to hear thunder after you see lighting, then the storm is 4 miles away. Time to drop anchor and "hunker down"!

Lightning Safety Tips

Lightning tends to strike the tallest object and boats on the open water fit this profile. The lightning will try to take the most direct path to the water, which is usually down the mast on a sailboat or the VHF antenna on a powerboat. However, both sailboats and powerboats with cabins–especially those with lightning protection systems properly installed–are relatively safe, provided you keep a few things in mind:

- Before the storm strikes, lower, remove or tie down all antennas, fishing rods and flag poles.

- Stay down below and in the center of the cabin. Avoid keel-stepped masts and chain plates (on sailboats) and large metal appliances such as microwaves or TVs. Remove any metal jewelry.

- Disconnect the power and antenna leads to all electronics including radios. Do not use the VHF radio unless absolutely necessary.

- If you are stuck on deck, stay away from metal railings, the wheel, the mast and stays (on sailboats) or other metal fittings. Do not stand between the mast and stays as lightning can "side-flash" from one to the other.

- Stay out of the water and don't fish or dangle your feet overboard. Salt water conducts electricity, which means that it can easily travel through the water toward you.

- Don't think rubber-soled deck shoes will save you; while rubber is an electric insulator, it's only effective to a certain point. The average lightning bolt carries about 30,000 amps of charge, has 100 million volts of electric potential and is about 50,000°F.

If You Are Struck:

1. **Check people first.** Many individuals struck by lightning or exposed to excessive electrical current can be saved with prompt and proper cardiopulmonary resuscitation (CPR). Contrary to popular belief, there is no danger in touching persons after they have been struck by lightning.

2. **Check the bilge** as strikes can rupture through-hull fittings and punch holes in hulls. Props and rudders are natural exit points on boats.

3. **Check electronics and the compasses.** Typically everything in the path of the lightning is destroyed on the way down to the water including instruments, computers and stereos.

4. **Consider a short haul** to check the bottom thoroughly. Lightning strikes sometimes leave traces of damage that may only be seen when the boat is out of the water.

Don't Rush Back Out

Because electrical charges can linger in clouds after a thunderstorm has passed, experts agree that you should wait at least 30 minutes after a storm before resuming activities. And remember: If you can hear thunder, you can still be struck by lightning!

Natural Seasickness Remedies

- *Take slow, deep breaths.* This helps soothe upset stomach and dizziness.

- *Focus on the horizon.* Keep your body still and head facing forward and watch a stationary object. Taking the helm always helps.

- *Ginger can help.* Eat ginger snaps, drink ginger tea or ginger ale or digest in capsule form ahead of time.

- *Peppermint works too.* Sucking on a peppermint candy, drinking peppermint tea or breathing in peppermint oil dabbed on a cloth can help with stomach issues.

- *Try acupuncture wristbands.* Apply pressure to specific points on your wrist to reduce nausea.

Skipper's Handbook

Tropical Weather & Hurricanes

While all coastal areas of the country are vulnerable to the effects of a hurricane (especially from June through November), the Gulf Coast, Southern and Mid-Atlantic states typically have been the hardest hit. But northern locales aren't immune; several destructive hurricanes have dealt a blow to areas in New England over the last 100 years including Hurricane Sandy in 2012 and Matthew in 2016. While hurricanes can create vast swaths of devastation, ample preparation can help increase your boat's chances of surviving the storm.

According to the National Weather Service, a mature hurricane may be 10 miles high with a great spiral several hundred miles in diameter. Winds are often well above the 74 mph required to classify as hurricane strength, especially during gusts. Hurricane damage is produced by four elements: tidal surge, wind, wave action and rain.

Distance from Eye	Force Level	Wind Speed
150 miles	Force 8	34–40 knots
100 miles	Force 11	56–63 knots
75 miles	Force 12	over 64 knots

■ Tidal surge is an increase in ocean depth prior to the storm. This effect, amplified in coastal areas, may cause tidal heights in excess of 15 to 20 feet above normal. Additionally, hurricanes can produce a significant negative tidal effect as water rushes out of the waterways after a storm.

■ Wind gusts can exceed reported sustained winds by 25 to 50 percent. For example, a storm with winds of 150 mph might have gusts of more than 200 mph, according to the National Weather Service.

■ Wave action is usually the most damaging element of a hurricane for boaters. The wind speed, water depth and the amount of open water determine the amount of wave action created. Storm surges can transform narrow bodies of water into larger, deeper waters capable of generating extreme wave action.

■ Rainfall varies but hurricanes can generate anywhere from 5 to 20 inches or more of rain.

Hurricane Categorization

CATEGORY	PRESSURE	WIND SPEED	SURGE
1	Above 980 mb (Above 28.91 in.)	64–82 knots (74–95 mph)	4–5 ft. (1–1.5 m)
	\multicolumn{3}{l}{Visibility much reduced. Maneuvering under engines just possible. Open anchorages untenable. Danger of poorly secured boats torn loose in protected anchorages.}		
2	965-979 mb (28.50-28.91 in.)	83-95 knots (96-110 mph)	6-8 ft. (1.5-2.5 m)
	Visibility close to zero. Boats in protected anchorages at risk, particularly from boats torn loose. Severe damage to unprotected boats and boats poorly secured and prepared.		
3	945-964 mb (27.91-28.50 in.)	96-113 knots (111-130 mph)	9-12 ft. (2.5-3.5 m)
	Deck fittings at risk and may tear loose, anchor links can fail and unprotected lines will chafe through. Extensive severe damage.		
4	920-944 mb (27.17-27.91 in.)	114-135 knots (131-155 mph)	13-18 ft. (3.5-5.4 m)
	Very severe damage and loss of life.		
5	Below 920 mb (Below 27.17 in.)	Above 135 knots (131-155 mph)	Above 18 ft. (Above 5.4 m)
	Catastrophic conditions with catastrophic damage.		

If your boat is in a slip, you have three options: Leave it where it is (if it is in a safe place); move it to a refuge area; or haul it and put it on a trailer or cradle. Some marinas require mandatory evacuations during hurricane alerts. Check your lease agreement and talk to your dockmaster before a hurricane if you are uncertain. Keep in mind that many municipalities close public mooring fields in advance of the storm. In some localities, boaters may be held liable for any damage that their boat inflicts to marina piers or property; check locally for details. Because of this, rivers, canals, coves and other areas away from large stretches of open water are best selected as refuges.

Consult your insurance agent if you have questions about coverage. Many insurance agencies have restricted or canceled policies for boats that travel or are berthed in certain hurricane-prone areas. Review your policy and check your coverage as many insurance companies will not cover boats in hurricane-prone areas during the June through November hurricane season. Riders for this type of coverage are notoriously expensive.

America's Waterway Guide Since 1947

Preparing Your Boat

- Have a hurricane plan made up ahead of time to maximize what you can get done in the amount of time you will have to prepare (no more than 12 hours in some cases). Plan how to tie up the boat or where to anchor before a hurricane is barreling down on you. Make these decisions in advance!

- Buy hurricane gear well in advance. When word of a hurricane spreads, local ship stores run out of storm supplies (anchors and line, especially) very quickly.

- Strip everything that isn't bolted down off the deck of the boat (e.g., canvas, sails, antennas, bimini tops, dodgers, dinghies, dinghy motors, cushions, unneeded control lines on sailboats) as this will help reduce windage and damage to your boat. Remove electronics and valuables and move them ashore.

- Any potentially leaky ports or hatches should be taped up. Dorades (cowls) should be removed and sealed with deck caps.

- Make sure all systems on board are in tip-top shape in case you have to move quickly. Fuel and water tanks should be filled, bilge pumps should be in top operating condition and batteries should be fully charged.

- You will need many lengths of line to secure the boat; make certain it is good stretchy nylon (not Dacron). It is not unusual to string 600 to 800 feet of dock line on a 40-foot-long boat in preparation for a hurricane. If you can, double up your lines (two for each cleat) as lines can break during a strong storm. Have fenders and fender boards out and make sure all of your lines are protected from chafing.

- If you are anchored out, use multiple large anchors; there is no such thing as an anchor that is too large. If you can, tie to trees with a good root system such as mangroves or live oaks. Mangroves are particularly good because their canopy can have a cushioning effect. Be sure mooring lines include ample scope to compensate for tides 10 to 20 feet above normal.

- Lastly, do not stay aboard to weather out the storm. Many people have been seriously injured (or worse) trying to save their boats during a hurricane. Take photos of the condition in which you left your boat and take your insurance papers with you.

Returning Safely After the Storm

- Before hitting the road, make sure the roads back to your boat are open and safe for travel. Beware of dangling wires, weakened docks, bulkheads, bridges and other structures.

- Check your boat thoroughly before attempting to move it. If returning to your home slip, watch the waters for debris and obstructions. Navigate carefully as markers may be misplaced or missing.

- If your boat should sink, arrange for engine repairs before floating it but only if it is not impeding traffic. Otherwise, you will need to remove it immediately. Contact your insurance company right away to make a claim.

Additional Resources

National Hurricane Center: www.nhc.noaa.gov

BoatUS Hurricane Tracking & Resource Center: www.boatus.com/hurricanes

Skipper's Handbook

Picking an Anchorage (excerpt)

We all know that unless it is an emergency, in addition to being verboten, it's just plain common sense and courteous to avoid encroaching on or anchoring in a marked channel, or in a location that inhibits a boat's access to or from a slip, mooring, boatyard, or marina, or that interferes with another anchored vessel. Otherwise, just about any other location is fair game, but there are a few prerequisites that should be met in order to qualify it as an acceptable anchorage.

First, there's a minimum acceptable depth of water, which is determined by your boat's draft, plus any additional distance the tide will drop, plus another foot or two–just in case. In dam controlled waterways, the height of the water level above normal pool should also be considered, as the elevated pool level can be lowered back to normal pool without notice, often quickly–think hours.

Also, the wind, depending on its direction can blow water out, anywhere from a few feet in gale force conditions, to ten feet or more in storms or hurricane force winds. Water levels can also become lower than normal when: the moon is in perigee, or during seiches, spring tides, and winter solstice. Neglecting these influences could leave the boat bottoming out, aground, or with too little water to get over a bar.

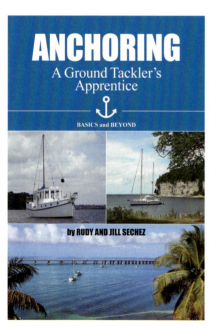

The amount of rode that you can deploy establishes the maximum depth in which you can anchor. If you're anchoring to 5:1 scope, then one fifth the length of your rode is the maximum depth where you can set your anchor; however, in demanding conditions you may need to use 10:1 scope; if so, one tenth the length of your rode would be the maximum depth where you'd want to set your anchor.

Fetch–the distance that the wind can blow over the water without obstruction–can also be a factor when choosing an anchorage, as it can affect comfort. The greater the fetch, the bigger the seas or waves, the more uncomfortable the boat's motion. Our goal is to try to anchor where the fetch is less than a few hundred yards, as beyond this, wave action becomes livelier.

It's prudent to enter unfamiliar anchorages slowly, remaining alert to potential hazards, not just below the surface, but overhead, too–you want enough clearance to prevent snagging bridges, tree limbs, or other dangers, and with power lines, to prevent arcing.

If obstructions are a concern or soundings reveal questionable depths, not only where the boat will initially be anchored, but later where the boat might swing if wind or current shifts direction or strength, then relocate the anchor, or set out an additional anchor or two in a manner that would keep the boat away from any danger.

And keep in mind that your anchor must be compatible with the type of seabed in which you will be anchoring, as well as sized for the wind speed and seas that you will encounter.

Cruising guides are a great resource for identifying anchorages, but if you keep the above guidelines in mind, you just might discover many others, perhaps some that are picturesque, others offering solitude… maybe both.

Rudy and Jill Sechez are the authors of "ANCHORING–A Ground Tackler's Apprentice." To read more, order a copy at www.waterwayguide.com or call 800-233-3359. Rudy and Jill are Trawler Training and Anchoring Consultants, providing one-on-one onboard sessions, consultations, and group seminars. They are also available to talk to groups and clubs. To arrange to have them speak to your organization, contact them at rudyandjill@yahoo.com.

America's Waterway Guide Since 1947

Ditch Bag Checklist

Rescue Items

- [ ] Functioning, registered EPIRB
- [ ] Handheld VHF radio (waterproof or in sealed pouch with extra batteries)
- [ ] Sea anchor, drogue and line
- [ ] Manual inflation pump
- [ ] Selection of flares (parachute and handheld) and smoke signals
- [ ] Strobe light (may be present in inflatable PFD)
- [ ] Flashlight & batteries (headlamp is ideal)
- [ ] Whistle (may be present in inflatable PFD)
- [ ] Signal mirror
- [ ] Handheld GPS or compass (for position)
- [ ] Small pair of binoculars (to confirm a boat or plane spotting before using flares)

Survival Items

- [ ] Sponges and bailer (with handle)
- [ ] Patch kit for inflatable dinghy or life raft (or emergency clamps)
- [ ] Water (individually sealed or in collapsible containers)–at least 2 gallons per person
- [ ] Emergency food rations and can opener (if needed)
- [ ] Power Bars
- [ ] Prescription medications
- [ ] Seasickness medications/remedies
- [ ] First aid kit
- [ ] Multipurpose tool or sailor's knife
- [ ] Waterproof matches

Other Items

- [ ] Solar blanket
- [ ] Heavy-duty coated gloves
- [ ] Duct tape
- [ ] Sewing kit
- [ ] Simple fishing gear (line, jigs, hooks, etc.)
- [ ] Polypropylene line
- [ ] Waterproof sunscreen and zinc oxide
- [ ] Bug repellent
- [ ] Ziploc bags (gallon size)
- [ ] Paper and pen in Ziploc bag
- [ ] Spare prescription glasses and sunglasses (polarized to reduce glare)
- [ ] Laminated copies of passports or license
- [ ] Cash ($50 in small bills)
- [ ] Copy of the yacht's papers (including insurance)

MID-ATLANTIC EDITION

Skipper's Handbook

Dealing With Onboard Waste

Up until the late 1980s, many boaters simply discharged their untreated sewage overboard into the water. After a revision to the Clean Water Act was passed in 1987, the discharge of untreated sewage into U.S. waters within the 3-mile limit was prohibited. Shortly thereafter, pump-out stations became a regular feature at marinas and fuel docks throughout the U.S. waterways.

Simply stated, if you have a marine head installed on your vessel and are operating in coastal waters within the U.S. 3-mile limit (basically all of the waters covered in the guide you are now holding), you need to have a holding tank and you will obviously need to arrange to have that tank pumped out from time to time.

Government regulation aside, properly disposing of your waste is good environmental stewardship. While your overboard contribution to the waterways may seem small in the grand scheme of things, similar attitudes among fellow boaters can quickly produce unsavory conditions in anchorages and small creeks. The widespread availability of holding tank gear and shoreside pump-out facilities leaves few excuses for not doing the right thing.

No-Discharge Zones

■ No-Discharge means exactly what the name suggests: No waste, even waste treated by an onboard Type I marine sanitation device (MSD), may be discharged overboard. All waste must be collected in a holding tank and pumped out at an appropriate facility.

■ Keep in mind that there are some areas that forbid overboard discharge of any waste including gray water from showers or sinks. Familiarize yourself with local regulations before entering new areas to ensure you don't get hit with a fine.

The Law

■ If you have a marine head onboard and are operating on coastal waters within the U.S. 3-mile limit (basically all of the waters covered in this guide), you need to have an approved holding tank or Type I MSD. In a No-Discharge area even a Type I MSD system must have a holding tank.

■ All valves connected to your holding tank or marine head that lead to the outside (both Y-valves AND seacocks) must be wire-tied, padlocked or absent of the valve handle and in the closed position. Simply having them closed without the (non-releasable) wire ties will not save you from a fine if you are boarded.

■ You may discharge waste overboard from a Type I MSD in all areas except those designated as No-Discharge Zones. A Type I MSD treats waste by reducing bacteria and visible solids to an acceptable level before discharge overboard.

■ While small and inconvenient for most cruisers, "Port-A-Potties" meet all the requirements for a Type III MSD as the holding tank is incorporated into the toilet itself.

Pump-Out and Holding Tank Basics

■ Some marinas are equipped with pump-out facilities, normally located at the marina's fuel dock. Note that some marinas charge a fee for the service.

■ Several municipalities and local governments have purchased and staffed pump-out boats that are equipped to visit boats on request, especially those at anchor. Radio the local harbormaster to see if this service is available in the area you are visiting. There is normally a small fee involved.

■ You will want to keep an eye out on your holding tank level while you are cruising, especially if you are getting ready to enter an area where you many not have access to proper pump-out services for a few days. Plan a fuel stop or marina stay to top off the fuel and water tanks and empty the other tank before you set out into the wild.

America's Waterway Guide Since 1947

NEW: Pump-Out App

Pumpout Nav, a free iOS and Android app, uses a boater's location information to suggest the nearest public pump-out station on a map or list. The app helps boaters find the amenities they need and helps marinas promote their services. The app catalogs more than 250 pump-out stations along the coast and in some inland waterways and provides the cost, hours and detailed location for each facility.

Marine Sanitation Devices

- Type I MSD: Treats sewage before discharging it into the water using maceration. The treated discharge must not show any visible floating solids and must meet specified standards for bacteria content. Raritan's Electro Scan and Groco's Thermopure systems are examples of Type I MSDs. Not permitted in No-Discharge Zones.

- Type II MSD: Type II MSDs provide a higher level of waste treatment than Type I units and are larger as a result. They employ biological treatment and disinfection. These units are usually found on larger vessels due to their higher power requirements. These may not be discharged in No-Discharge Zones.

- Type III MSD: Regular holding tanks store sewage until the holding tank can either be pumped out to an onshore facility or at sea beyond the U.S. boundary waters (i.e., 3 miles offshore).

Composting Heads

Composting heads are essentially Type III MSDs but rather than simply storing sewage, composters separate liquid and solid waste, which speeds up decomposition and reduces odors. This "dry" system promotes decomposition through controlled composting in which the solid portion is converted into an easy-to-handle, safe, non-odorous humus. There is no need for plumbing, valves, pump or thru-hull and no components to break down, clog up or leak. Other advantages include no pump-outs, uses no water, reduces onboard weight and opens up storage space.

Penalties and Fines

- Misuse or failure to equip a vessel with a Marine Sanitation Device may result in a non-criminal infraction with a $56 penalty.

- Illegal dumping/discharge of a Marine Sanitation Device may result in a non-criminal infraction with a $250 penalty.

Additional Resources

BoatU.S. Guide to Overboard Discharge:
www.boatus.com/foundation/guide/environment_7.html

EPA Listing of No-Discharge Zones:
www.epa.gov/vessels-marinas-and-ports/no-discharge-zones-ndzs-state

Skipper's Handbook

Distances: Inside (ICW) Route–Norfolk, VA to Fernandina Beach, FL

Inside Route Distances - Norfolk, Virgina to Fernandina Beach, Florida
(nautical and statute miles)

	Fernandina Beach, FL	Brunswick, GA	Thunderbolt, GA	Savannah, GA	Beaufort, SC	Charleston, SC	McClellanville, SC	Georgetown, SC	Bucksport, SC	Little River, SC	Southport, NC	Wilmington, NC	Wrightsville, NC	Jacksonville, NC	Swansboro, NC	Morehead City, NC	Beaufort, NC	New Bern, NC	Oriental, NC	Ocracoke, NC	Washington, NC	Belhaven, NC	Manteo, NC	Plymouth, NC	Edenton, NC	Columbia, NC	Hertford, NC	Elizabeth City, NC	Norfolk, VA
Norfolk, VA	623	595	507	508	466	406	374	352	328	299	268	273	248	231	20	178	177	180	160	131	156	120	80	105	98	89	89	77*	•
Elizabeth City, NC	581	553	465	466	424	364	332	311	286	257	226	231	204	189	158	136	134	139	118	91	114	79	39	56	48	39	39	•	89
Hertford, NC	582	554	466	467	425	366	333	311	287	259	227	232	205	190	160	137	137	139	119	97	115	79	46	42	35	26	•	45	102
Columbia, NC	581	553	465	466	424	364	332	310	286	257	226	231	204	189	158	136	136	138	118	96	114	78	45	33	25	•	30	45	102
Edenton, NC	589	562	474	475	432	373	340	318	294	266	235	240	213	197	166	145	144	146	126	104	123	87	54	14	•	29	40	55	113
Plymouth, NC	596	570	482	483	441	381	349	327	303	274	243	248	221	206	175	152	152	155	134	113	130	95	61	•	16	38	48	64	121
Manteo, NC	555	527	439	440	397	337	306	283	260	232	201	205	178	162	132	110	110	110	91	61	105	70	•	70	62	52	53	45	92
Belhaven, NC	506	479	391	392	349	290	257	235	211	183	152	157	130	114	83	61	61	63	43	43	39	•	81	109	100	90	91	91	138
Washington, NC	519	491	403	404	362	302	270	248	224	195	164	169	142	127	96	74	74	76	56	60	•	45	121	150	142	131	132	131	180
Ocracoke, NC	504	477	389	390	347	288	255	233	209	181	150	155	128	112	81	59	59	62	41	•	69	49	70	130	120	110	112	105	151
Oriental, NC	467	440	352	353	310	251	218	196	172	144	113	118	91	75	44	22	22	23	•	47	64	49	105	154	145	136	137	136	184
New Bern, NC	484	456	368	369	327	267	235	213	188	160	129	134	107	91	60	38	38	•	26	71	87	72	127	178	168	159	160	160	207
Beaufort, NC	447	420	332	333	290	231	199	177	152	124	93	97	70	55	24	3	•	44	25	68	85	70	127	175	166	157	158	154	204
Morehead City, NC	445	418	330	331	288	229	196	174	150	122	91	96	69	53	22	•	3	44	25	68	85	70	127	175	167	157	158	157	205
Swansboro, NC	423	396	307	309	266	207	174	152	128	100	69	73	46	31	•	25	28	69	51	93	110	96	152	201	191	182	184	182	230
Jacksonville, NC	425	397	309	310	268	208	176	154	129	101	70	75	48	•	36	61	63	105	86	129	146	131	186	237	227	217	219	217	266
Wrightsville, NC	377	349	261	262	220	160	128	106	82	53	22	27	•	55	53	79	81	123	105	147	163	150	205	254	245	235	236	235	283
Wilmington, NC	376	349	260	261	219	159	127	105	81	52	21	•	31	86	84	110	112	154	136	178	194	181	236	285	276	266	267	266	314
Southport, NC	355	327	239	240	198	138	106	84	60	31	•	24	25	81	79	105	107	148	130	173	189	175	231	280	270	260	261	260	308
Little River, SC	324	296	208	209	167	107	75	53	28	•	36	60	61	116	115	140	143	184	166	208	224	211	267	315	306	296	298	296	344
Bucksport, SC	295	268	179	181	138	79	46	24	•	32	69	93	94	148	147	173	175	216	198	241	258	243	299	349	338	329	330	329	377
Georgetown, SC	273	246	157	159	116	56	24	•	28	61	97	121	122	177	175	200	203	245	226	268	285	270	326	376	366	357	358	358	405
McClellanville, SC	249	222	133	135	92	32	•	28	53	86	122	146	147	203	200	226	229	270	251	293	311	296	352	402	391	382	383	382	430
Charleston, SC	218	191	103	104	60	•	37	64	91	123	159	183	184	239	238	264	266	307	289	331	348	334	388	438	429	419	421	419	467
Beaufort, SC	157	130	41	43	•	69	106	133	159	192	228	252	253	308	306	331	334	376	357	399	417	402	457	508	497	488	489	488	536
Savannah, GA	130	102	14	•	49	120	155	183	208	241	276	300	302	357	356	381	383	425	406	449	465	451	506	556	547	536	537	536	585
Thunderbolt, GA	116	88	•	16	47	119	153	181	206	239	275	299	300	356	353	380	382	423	405	448	464	450	505	555	545	535	536	535	583
Brunswick, GA	35	•	101	117	150	220	255	283	308	341	376	402	402	457	456	481	483	525	506	549	565	551	606	656	647	636	638	636	685
Fernandina Beach, FL	•	40	133	150	181	251	287	314	339	373	409	433	434	489	487	512	514	557	537	580	597	582	639	688	678	669	670	669	717

Distances: Outside (Coastwise) Route–Norfolk, VA to Key West, FL

Coastwise Distances – Norfolk, Virginia to Key West, Florida (nautical miles)																			
	Straits of Florida	Key West, FL	Miami, FL	Port Everglades, FL	Port of Palm Beach, FL	Stuart, FL	Fort Pierce, FL	Cape Canaveral, FL	St. Augustine, FL	Jacksonville, FL	Fernandina Beach, FL	Brunswick, GA	Savannah, GA	Port Royal, SC	Charleston, SC	Georgetown, SC	Wilmington, NC	Southport, NC	Morehead City, NC	Diamond Shoals, NC	Norfolk, VA	Chesapeake Bay Entrance
Chesapeake Bay Entrance 36°56.3'N., 75°58.6'W.	942	881	743	720	678	666	647	612	557	560	533	527	476	465	402	365	336	315	222	117	27	–
Norfolk, VA 46°50.9'N., 76°17.9'W.	969	908	770	747	705	693	674	639	584	587	560	554	503	492	429	392	363	342	249	144	–	
Diamond Shoals, NC 35°08.0'N., 75°15.0'W.	825	764	626	603	561	549	530	495	440	443	416	410	359	348	285	248	219	198	105	–		
Morehead City, NC 34°42.8'N., 76°41.8'W.	772	711	573	550	509	497	476	438	377	379	352	346	295	284	220	184	154	133	–			
Southport, NC 33°54.8'N., 78°01.0'W.	707	646	508	485	443	423	407	367	296	294	265	260	206	191	130	87	21	–				
Wilmington, NC 34°14.0'N., 77°57.0'W.	728	667	529	506	464	444	428	388	317	315	286	281	227	212	151	108	–					
Georgetown, SC 33°21.4'N., 79°16.9'W.	671	610	472	449	407	391	368	324	246	247	216	210	154	141	79	–						
Charleston, SC 32°47.2'N., 79°55.2'W.	633	572	434	411	369	353	329	283	199	197	166	156	102	90	–							
Port Royal, SC 32°22.3'N., 80°41.6'W.	605	544	406	383	341	324	298	251	157	152	120	110	51	–								
Savannah, GA 32°05.0'N., 81°05.7'W.	604	543	405	382	340	324	298	251	152	145	115	104	–									
Brunswick, GA 31°08.0'N., 81°29.7'W.	549	488	350	327	285	268	242	195	90	82	50	–										
Fernandina Beach, FL 30°40.3'N., 81°28.0'W.	526	465	327	304	262	242	216	169	61	53	–											
Jacksonville, FL 30°19.2'N., 81°39.0'W.	523	462	324	301	256	240	214	167	56	–												
St. Augustine, FL 29°53.6'N., 81°18.5'W.	475	414	276	253	211	192	167	120	–													
Cape Canaveral, FL 28°24.6'N., 80°36.5'W.	374	313	175	152	110	91	69	–														
Fort Pierce, FL 27°27.5'N., 80°19.3'W.	316	255	117	94	52	32	–															
Stuart, FL 27°12.2'N., 80°15.6'W.	300	239	101	78	36	–																
Port of Palm Beach, FL 26°46.1'N., 80°03.0'W.	267	207	68	46	–																	
Port Everglades, FL 26°05.6'N., 80°07.0'W.	226	165	27	–																		
Miami, FL 25°47.0'N., 80°11.0'W.	211	151	–																			
Key West, FL 24°33.7'N., 81°48.5'W.	73	–																				
Straits of Florida 24°25.0'N., 83°00.0'W.	–																					

Skipper's Handbook

GPS Waypoints

The following list provides selected waypoints for the waters covered in this book. The latitude/longitude readings are taken from government light lists and must be checked against the appropriate chart and light list for accuracy. Some waypoints listed here are lighthouses and should not be approached too closely as they may be on land, in shallow water or on top of a reef. Many buoys must be approached with caution, as they are often located near shallows or obstructions. The positions of every aid to navigation should be updated using the Coast Guard's *Local Notice to Mariners* (www.navcen.uscg.gov/lnm).

The U.S. Coast Guard will continue to provide Differential GPS (DGPS) correction signals for those who need accuracy of 10 meters or less, even though most GPS receivers now come with an internal capability for receiving differential signals.

Prudent mariners will not rely solely on these waypoints to navigate. Every available navigational tool should be used at all times to determine your vessel's position.

Hampton Roads to Rudee Inlet

LOCATION	LATITUDE	LONGITUDE
Little Creek Entrance Lighted Buoy 1LC	N 36° 58.083'	W 076° 10.067'
Lynnhaven Roads Fishing Pier Light	N 36° 55.000'	W 076° 04.717'
Cape Henry Light	N 36° 55.583'	W 076° 00.433'
Rudee Inlet Lighted Whistle Buoy RI	N 36° 49.783'	W 075° 56.950'

Albemarle Sound to Neuse River

LOCATION	LATITUDE	LONGITUDE
Albemarle Sound Entrance Light AS	N 36° 03.733'	W 075° 56.133'
Albemarle Sound North Light N	N 36° 06.100'	W 075° 54.750'
Albemarle Sound South Light S	N 36° 01.083'	W 075° 57.617'
Pasquotank River Entrance Light PR	N 36° 09.367'	W 075° 58.650'
Pungo River Junction Light PR	N 35° 22.667'	W 076° 33.583'
Goose Creek Light 1	N 35° 20.400'	W 076° 35.750'
Bay Point Light	N 35° 10.350'	W 076° 30.317'
Bay River Light 1	N 35° 09.800'	W 076° 32.017'
Neuse River Junction Light	N 35° 08.783'	W 076° 30.183'
Whittaker Creek Light 2	N 35° 01.383'	W 076° 41.150'
Smith Creek (Oriental) Channel Light 1	N 35° 00.900'	W 076° 41.467'
Adams Creek Light 1AC	N 34° 58.500'	W 076° 41.767'

America's Waterway Guide Since 1947

Oregon Inlet to Cape Lookout

LOCATION	LATITUDE	LONGITUDE
Oregon Inlet Jetty Light	N 35° 46.433'	W 075° 31.500'
Hatteras Inlet Light	N 35° 11.867'	W 075° 43.933'
Diamond Shoal Lighted Buoy 12	N 35° 09.083'	W 075° 17.550'
Ocracoke Light	N 35° 06.533'	W 075° 59.167'

Beaufort Inlet to Florida Border

LOCATION	LATITUDE	LONGITUDE
Beaufort Inlet *(NOTE: This is not the location of a particular buoy.)*	N 34° 38.000'	W 077° 41.000'
Masonboro Inlet *(NOTE: This is not the location of a particular buoy.)*	N 34° 10.000'	W 077° 47.000'
Frying Pan Shoals Lighted Buoy 16	N 33° 28.783'	W 077° 35.083'
Cape Fear R. Ent. Lighted Whistle Buoy CF	N 33° 46.283'	W 078° 03.033'
Oak Island Light	N 33° 53.567'	W 078° 02.100'
Little River Inlet Lighted Whistle Buoy LR	N 33° 49.817'	W 078° 32.450'
Winyah Bay Lighted Whistle Buoy WB	N 33° 11.617'	W 079° 05.183'
Charleston Ent. Lighted Buoy C	N 32° 37.083'	W 079° 35.500'
North Edisto Rvr. Ent. Lig. Whistle Buoy 2NE	N 32° 31.350'	W 080° 06.850'

Beaufort Inlet to Florida Border (cont.)

LOCATION	LATITUDE	LONGITUDE
South Edisto Rvr. Approach Lig. Buoy A	N 32° 24.717'	W 080° 17.700'
St. Helena Sound Entrance Buoy 1	N 32° 21.667'	W 080° 18.450'
Port Royal Sound Lighted Whistle Buoy P	N 32° 05.133'	W 080° 35.033'
Calibogue Sound Entrance Daybeacon 1	N 32° 02.850'	W 080° 50.533'
Tybee Lighted Buoy T	N 31° 57.883'	W 080° 43.167'
Wassaw Sound Lighted Buoy 2W	N 31° 51.550'	W 080° 53.017'
Ossabaw Sound Ent. Lighted Buoy OS	N 31° 47.800'	W 080° 56.200'
St. Catherines Sound Lighted Buoy STC	N 31° 40.217'	W 081° 00.200'
Sapelo Sound Buoy S	N 31° 31.200'	W 081° 03.900'
Doboy Sound Lighted Buoy D	N 31° 21.233'	W 081° 11.400'
Altamaha Sound Shoal Light	N 31° 18.867'	W 081° 15.333'
St. Simons Sound Lig. Buoy STS	N 31° 02.817'	W 081° 14.417'
St. Andrew Sound Outer Ent. Buoy STA	N 30° 55.550'	W 081° 18.967'
St. Marys Rvr. Approach Lighted Buoy STM	N 30° 42.900'	W 081° 14.650'

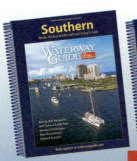    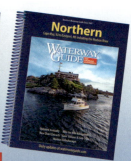

Plan with the experts

    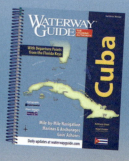

Scan to subscribe now at www.waterwayguide.com

Bridges & Locks: ICW from Norfolk, VA to St. Marys River, GA

Bridges & Locks: ICW from Norfolk, VA to St. Marys River, GA

Bridge Basics

Bridges have to be factored in when planning a trip. Depending on where you cruise, you may be dependent on bridge openings; a particular bridge's schedule can often decide where you tie up for the evening or when you wake up and get underway the next day. While many are high (over 65 feet) and some usually remain open (such as railroad bridges), others are restricted for different hours in specific months, closed during rush hours and/or open on the quarter-hour, half-hour or even at 20 minutes and 40 minutes past the hour.

To add to the confusion, the restrictions are constantly changing. Just because a bridge opened on a certain schedule last season does not mean it is still on that same schedule. Changes are posted in the Coast Guard's *Local Notice to Mariners* reports, which can be found online at www.navcen.uscg.gov/lnm. It is also a good idea to check locally to verify bridge schedules before your transit.

Measuring Vertical Clearance

Most bridges carry a tide board to register vertical clearance at "low steel" or the lowest point on the bridge. (Note that in the State of Florida waters the tide board figure–and the one noted on the chart–is generally for a point that is 5 feet toward the channel from the bridge fender.) In the case of arched bridges, center channel clearance is frequently higher than the tide gauge registers. Some bridges bear signs noting extra height at center in feet.

Calling a Bridge

Most bridges monitor VHF Channel 13, designated by the Federal Communications Commission as the "bridgetender channel" until you get to South Carolina (southbound), where it changes to VHF Channel 09. (The exception is the locks on the Okeechobee Waterway, which respond to VHF Channel 13).

In any waters, it is a good idea to monitor both the bridge channel and VHF Channel 16–one on your ship's radio and one on a handheld radio, if your main set doesn't have a dual-watch capability–to monitor oncoming commercial traffic and communications with the bridgetender.

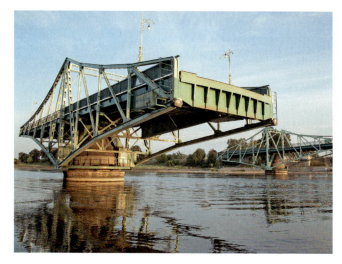

Swing bridges have an opening section that pivots horizontally on a central hub, allowing boats to pass on one side or the other when it is open.

Lift bridges normally have two towers on each end of the opening section that are equipped with cables that lift the road or railway vertically into the air.

When using VHF, always call bridges by name and identify your vessel by name and type (such as sailing vessel or trawler) and whether you are traveling north or south. If you are unable to raise the bridge using VHF radio, use a horn signal.

Note that some bridges are not required to open in high winds. If you encounter a bridge that won't open (for whatever reason), it is prudent to drop the hook in a safe spot until the situation is resolved.

America's Waterway Guide Since 1947

Pontoon bridges consists of an opening section that must be floated out of the way with a cable to allow boats to pass. Do not proceed until the cables have had time to sink to the bottom.

Bascule bridges are the most common type of opening bridge you will encounter. The opening section has one or two leaves that tilt vertically on a hinge like doors being opened skyward.

Bridge Procedures:

- First, decide if it is necessary to have the drawbridge opened. You will need to know your boat's clearance height above the waterline before you start. Drawbridges have "clearance gauges" that show the closed vertical clearance with changing water level but a bascule bridge typically has 3 to 5 feet more clearance than what is indicated on the gauge at the center of its arch at mean low tide. Bridge clearances are also shown on NOAA charts.

- Contact the bridgetender well in advance (even if you can't see the bridge around the bend) by VHF radio or phone. Alternatively, the proper horn signal for a bridge opening is one prolonged blast (four to six seconds) and one short blast (approximately one second). Bridge operators sound this signal when ready to open the bridge, and then usually the danger signal—five short blasts—when they are closing the bridge. The operator of each vessel is required by law to signal the bridgetender for an opening, even if another vessel has already signaled. Tugs with tows and U.S. government vessels may go through bridges at any time, usually signaling with five short blasts. A restricted bridge may open in an emergency with the same signal. Keep in mind bridgetenders will not know your intentions unless you tell them.

- If two or more vessels are in sight of one another, the bridgetender may elect to delay opening the bridge until all boats can go through together.

- Approach at slow speed and be prepared to wait as the bridge cannot open until the traffic gates are closed. Many ICW bridges, for example, are more than 40 years old and the aged machinery functions slowly.

- Once the bridge is open, proceed at no-wake speed. Keep a safe distance between you and other craft as currents and turbulence around bridge supports can be tricky.

- There is technically no legal right-of-way (except on the Mississippi and some other inland rivers) but boats running with the current should always be given the right-of-way out of courtesy. As always, if you are not sure, let the other boat go first.

- When making the same opening as a commercial craft, it is a good idea to contact the vessel's captain (usually on VHF Channel 13), ascertain his intentions and state yours to avoid any misunderstanding in tight quarters.

- After passing through the bridge, maintain a no-wake speed until you are well clear and then resume normal speed.

MID ATLANTIC EDITION

Bridges & Locks: ICW from Norfolk, VA to St. Marys River, GA

Locks & Locking Through

Many rivers in North America are a series of pools created by dams. When the dams also include locks, navigation is possible beyond the dam. Locks are watertight chambers with gates at each end. They raise and lower boats from one water level to the next. Many cruisers find locking through a pleasant experience and part of the adventure of boating.

Lock Types

- Conventional lift locks are single chambers that raise and lower boats.

- Flight locks are a series of conventional lift locks.

- Hydraulic lift locks have water-filled chambers supported by rams or pistons that move in opposite directions. The movement of one chamber forces the movement of the other via a connected valve. The chamber in the upper position adds sufficient water to cause it to drop, forcing the lower chamber to rise. The chambers have hinged gates fore and aft that contain the water and allow boats to enter or leave.

- Marine railways convey boats over obstacles, usually a landmass, by containing boats in a gantry crane that moves over the land and deposits the boat on the other side of the obstruction.

River locks are usually conventional lift locks. The dam deepens water around shoals and the lock allows vessels to bypass the dam. Conventional lift locks work by gravity alone. Water passively flows into or out of the lock. When the lock is filling, the valve at the upper end of the lock is opened and water flows in. The downstream lock gate is closed, preventing the escape of the water. This is the time of greatest turbulence in the locks and the time of greatest vigilance for boaters. When the upper water level is reached, the upper lock gate opens to allow boats to exit or enter.

When the lock empties, both lock doors are closed, a valve on the lower end of the lock is opened and water exits. This creates a surge of water outside the lock but inside the lock, the water recedes like water in a tub. When the water level in the lock is the same as the lower river level, the lower lock gate opens and vessels leave.

Locking Protocol

Call ahead on VHF Channel 13 (or sound three blasts) for permission to lock through. Indicate whether you are northbound (upbound) or southbound (downbound). Your presence and communication indicate to the locktender your desire to lock through.

Wait a safe distance from the lock or find an anchorage nearby and within sight of the lock.

Prepare for locking by placing large fenders fore and aft and having lines ready. Fender boards are useful because they protect your fenders and provide a skid plate against the dirt and algae on the lock wall.

When approaching the lock, stay back to allow outbound vessels to clear the lock. Do not enter until signaled to do so. Signals vary. Look for a telephone/pull rope at the lock wall; listen for a whistle blast–one long and one short blast or three blasts; look for a "traffic" light–green, yellow or red. Follow directions given by the locktender. The order of priority is:

1. U.S. Military
2. Mail boats
3. Commercial passenger boats
4. Commercial tows
5. Commercial fishermen
6. Pleasure Craft

When the locktender turns on the green light or calls for you to enter, enter in the order that boats arrived at the lock. The longest waiting boat goes first, unless directed by the locktender, who may call boats in according to size and the configuration of the lock. Do not jump the line, do not scoot in front of others and defer to faster boats so you do not have them behind you after you leave the lock.

When entering the lock, leave no wake, heed instruction and respect other boaters. If they are having trouble and appear unsettled, stand by until they are secure. Listen to the directives of

America's Waterway Guide Since 1947

the locktenders. Some lock systems require all line handlers to wear personal flotation devices (PFDs). Crew members on the bow should wear PFDs.

You will be directed by the locktender to a place along the lock wall. You will find an inset mooring pin (floating bollard), vertical cable or a rope.

If there is a floating bollard, secure the boat to the pin via a center cleat by wrapping the line around the pin then back to the boat cleat.

If there is a vertical cable, wrap the line around the cable and bring it back to the boat; the loop will ride up or down the cable.

If there is a drop-down line, bring the line around a cleat and hold it. DO NOT TIE THE LINES!

If you are asked to provide a line, throw it to the locktender. After the locktender has secured it, take the bitter end and wrap–but do not tie–around a cleat. Attend the bow and the stern, and adjust the line(s) as the boat rises or falls in the lock chamber.

In crowded locks, move forward as far as you can to make room for others coming in behind you. Small boats may raft to bigger boats. Set adequate fenders for fending off another vessel.

Inside the lock chamber, turn off engines when secure. Exhaust fumes contained in the lock chamber are an irritant to people in small, open boats. Attend the lines at all times. Be prepared for turbulence when the lock fills. Never use hands or feet to fend a boat off a lock wall. Stay alert to other boats. Be prepared to quickly cut a line if needed.

When the lock reaches its determined depth/height, the locktender will loosen the line and drop it to you if you are using a line attached at the top of the lock. After receiving a whistle blast by the locktender, recover any lines used, and prepare to exit. Leave the lock in the same order as entering. Do not rush ahead of those in front of you.

Great Bridge Lock at Mile 11.3

MID-ATLANTIC EDITION

Bridges & Locks: ICW from Norfolk, VA to St. Marys River, GA

Bridge & Lock Schedules

KEY: Statute Miles from ICW Mile 0 / Vertical Clearance

Drawbridge clearances are vertical, in feet, when closed and at Mean High Water in tidal areas. Bridge schedules are subject to schedule changes due to repairs, maintenance, events, etc. Check Waterway Explorer at www.waterwayguide.com for the latest schedules or call ahead.

East Coast ICW

VA BRIDGES MONITOR CHANNEL 13

2.6 / 6' — **Belt Line Railroad Bridge:** Usually open. Remote operation. When the bridge closes for any reason, the controller will announce 30 min. in advance, 15 min. in advance, and immediately proceeding the actual lowering over VHF Channel 13. 757-271-1741

2.8 / 145' — **Jordan Bridge:** Fixed

3.6 / 10' — **Norfolk & Western Railroad Bridge:** Usually open. Clearance of 9 feet or less has been reported. 757-494-7371

5.8 / 35' — **Gilmerton Bridge:** Opens on signal, except from 6:30 a.m. to 8:30 a.m. and 3:30 p.m. to 5:30 p.m., Mon. through Fri. (except federal holidays), when the draw need not open. Draw will not open if adjacent railroad bridge is closed. 757-485-5488

5.8 / 7' — **Norfolk Southern #7 Railroad Bridge:** Usually open. Remote operation. 757-924-5320

7.1 / 65' — **I-64 Bridge:** The draw will open on signal if at least 24-hour notice is given.

8.9 / 95' — **Veterans Bridge:** Fixed

11.3 — **Great Bridge Lock:** Opens on signal but coordinates with Battlefield Blvd. Bridge. 757-547-3311

12.0 / 8' — **SR 168 (Battlefield Blvd.) Bridge:** Opens on signal, except 6:00 a.m. to 7:00 p.m. daily, when the draw need only open on the hour. The drawtender may delay the hourly opening up to 10 min. past the hour for approaching vessels. Timed to open with Great Bridge Lock. 757-482-8250

13.0 / 65' — **Chesapeake Expressway (VA 168 Bypass) Bridge:** Fixed

13.9 / 7' — **Albemarle & Chesapeake Railroad Bridge:** Usually open.

15.2 / 4' — **Centerville Turnpike (SR 170) Bridge:** Opens on hour and half-hour, except Mon. through Fri. from 6:30 a.m. to 8:30 a.m. and 4:00 p.m. to 6:00 p.m. (except federal holidays), when the draw need not open. The drawtender may delay the hourly opening up to 10 min. past the hour or half hour for approaching vessels. 757-547-3631/-3632

20.2 / 6' — **SR 165 (North Landing) Bridge:** Opens on signal, except from 6:00 a.m. to 7:00 p.m., when the draw need only open on the hour and half-hour. 757-482-3081

28.3 / 65' — **Pungo Ferry (SR 726) Bridge:** Fixed

49.9 / 65' — **Coinjock (US 158) Bridge:** Fixed

Dismal Swamp Canal

VA & NC BRIDGES MONITOR CHANNEL 13

10.5 — **Deep Creek Lock:** Opens at 8:30 a.m., 11:00 a.m., 1:30 p.m. and 3:30 p.m. 757-487-0831

11.1 / 4' — **Deep Creek Bridge:** Openings coordinated with lock operation. 757-487-0831

28.0 / 0' — **Great Dismal Swamp Canal Visitor Center Foot Bridge:** Usually open. This is a floating pontoon bridge. 252-771-6593

31.5 / 65' — **US 17 Hwy. Bridge:** Fixed

32.6 / 4' — **South Mills Bridge:** Openings coordinated with lock operation. 252-771-5906

32.7 — **South Mills Lock:** Opens at 8:30 a.m., 11:00 a.m., 1:30 p.m. and 3:30 p.m. 252-771-5906

47.7 / 3' — **Norfolk Southern Railroad Bridge:** Usually open. (Note: Bridge is hand operated.) 866-527-3499 (emergencies only)

50.7 / 2' — **US 158 Hwy. Bridge:** Opens on signal, except from 7:00 a.m. to 9:00 a.m. and 4:00 p.m. to 6:00 p.m., Mon. through Fri., when the draw need only open at 7:30 a.m., 8:30 a.m., 4:30 p.m. and 5:30 p.m. if vessels are waiting to pass. 252-331-4772

East Coast ICW (cont.)

NC BRIDGES MONITOR CHANNEL 13

Mile	Clearance	Bridge
84.2	14'	**Alligator River (US 64) Bridge:** Opens on signal. (Note: Bridge may not open if wind speed exceeds 34 knots.) 252-796-7261
113.9	65'	**Fairfield (NC 94) Bridge:** Fixed
125.9	64'	**Wilkerson (US 264) Bridge:** (Also known as the Walter B. Jones Bridge.) Fixed. (Note: This bridge is lower than the authorized 65-foot fixed vertical clearance.)
157.2	65'	**Hobucken (NC 33/304) Bridge:** Fixed
195.8	65'	**Core Creek (NC 101) Bridge:** Fixed
203.8	65'	**Beaufort Channel (US 70) Bridge:** Fixed
203.8	4'	**Beaufort Channel Railroad Bridge:** Opens on signal.
206.7	65'	**Atlantic Beach Bridge:** Fixed
226.0	65'	**B. Cameron Langston Bridge:** (Also known as the Emerald Isle Bridge.) Fixed.
240.7	12'	**Onslow Beach Swing Bridge:** (Use northwest draw.) Opens on signal, except from 7:00 a.m. to 7:00 p.m., when the draw need only open on the hour and half hour. You MUST signal for an opening, even though the operator may see you waiting. 910-440-7376
252.3	64'	**NC 210 Hwy. Bridge:** Fixed. (Note: This bridge is lower than the authorized 65-foot fixed vertical clearance.)
260.7	65'	**Surf City (NC 50) Bridge:** Fixed
278.1	20'	**Figure Eight Island Swing Bridge:** Opens on the hour and half-hour. (Note: Bridge may not open if wind speed exceeds 30 mph.) 910-686-2018
283.1	20'	**SR 74 Bridge:** (Also known as Wrightsville Beach Bridge.) Opens on the hour 7:00 a.m. to 7:00 p.m. Schedule may change during special events. (Note: Actual clearance may be lower than charted.) 910-256-2886
295.7	65'	**Snows Cut (US 421) Bridge:** Fixed
311.8	65'	**Oak Island (NC 133) Bridge:** Fixed
316.8	67'	**Middleton Street Bridge:** Fixed
323.6	65'	**Holden Beach (NC 130) Bridge:** Fixed
333.7	65'	**Ocean Isle (NC 904) Bridge:** Fixed
337.9	65'	**Mannon C. Gore (Sunset Beach) Bridge:** Fixed

SC BRIDGES MONITOR CHANNEL 09

Mile	Clearance	Bridge
347.2	65'	**Nixon Crossroads Bridge:** Fixed
347.3	7'	**Captain Archie Neil "Poo" McLauchlin (Little River) Swing Bridge:** Opens on signal. 843-280-5919
349.1	65'	**Robert Edge Parkway Bridge:** (Also called the North Myrtle Beach Connector Bridge.) Fixed.
353.3	31'	**Barefoot Landing Swing Bridge:** Opens on signal. 843-361-3291
355.5	65'	**Conway Bypass (SC 22) Twin Bridges:** Fixed
357.5	65'	**Grande Dunes Bridge:** Fixed
360.5	65'	**Grissom Parkway Bridge:** Fixed
365.4	16'	**SCL Railroad Bridge:** (Referred to with adjacent railroad bridge as Combination Bridges.) Usually open.
365.4	65'	**US 501 Bridge:** Fixed
366.4	65'	**Fantasy Harbor Bridge:** Fixed
371.0	11'	**Socastee Swing Bridge:** (Use southeast draw.) Opens on signal. 843-347-3525

Bridges & Locks: ICW from Norfolk, VA to St. Marys River, GA

371.3 / 65' — **Socastee (SC 544) Hwy. Bridge:** (Note: Actual clearance may be less than charted.) Fixed.

372.3 / 65' — **Carolina Bays Parkway (SC 31) Bridge:** Fixed

402.1 / 65' — **Ocean Hwy. (US 17) Bridge:** Fixed

411.5 / 0' — **Estherville-Minim Canal Bridge:** Usually open, except when a vehicle needs to cross (infrequent). Watch for flashing yellow lights on sign. This is a floating swing bridge. The bridge rests against the east bank of the river when in the open position.

458.9 / 65' — **Isle of Palms Connector Bridge:** Fixed

462.2 / 31' — **Ben Sawyer Memorial (SC 703) Bridge:** Opens on signal, except from 7:00 a.m. to 9:00 a.m. and from 4:00 p.m. to 6:00 p.m., Mon. through Fri. (except federal holidays), when the draw need not open. On Sat., Sun. and federal holidays, the draw need open only on the hour. from 9:00 a.m. to 7:00 p.m. Use the west span. 843-883-3581

469.9 / 67' — **James Island Expressway Bridge:** Fixed

470.8 / 33' — **Wappoo Creek (SC 171) Bridge:** Opens on signal, except from 6:00 a.m. to 9:29 a.m. and 3:31 p.m. to 7:00 p.m., Monday through Friday, (except federal holidays), when the draw need not open. Between 9:30 a.m. and 3:30 p.m., Monday through Friday (except federal holidays), when the draw need only once an hour on the half hour. 843-852-4157

479.3 / 65' — **John F. Limehouse Hwy. Bridge:** Fixed

501.3 / 65' — **McKinley Washington Jr. (SR 174) Bridge:** Fixed

536.0 / 30' — **Lady's Island (Woods Memorial) Bridge:** Opens on signal, except from 6:30 a.m. to 9:00 a.m. and 3:00 p.m. to 6:00 p.m., Mon. through Fri. (except federal holidays), when the draw need not open to navigation; and from 9:00 a.m. to 3:00 p.m., when the draw need open only on the hour. During the months of Apr., May, Oct. and Nov., Mon. through Fri. (except federal holidays), the draw will open on signal except from 7:00 a.m. to 9:00 a.m. and from 4:00 p.m. to 6:00 p.m., when the draw need not open and from 9:00 a.m. to 4:00 p.m., when the draw need open only on the hour and half-hour. 843-521-2111

539.7 / 65' — **McTeer Memorial Twin Bridges:** Fixed

557.5 / 65' — **Wilton J. Graves (US 278) Hwy. Bridge:** Fixed

GA BRIDGES MONITOR — CHANNEL 09

579.8 / 65' — **Island Expressway Bridge:** Fixed. (Note: Adjacent Causton Bluff Bridge is no longer operational and permanently open.)

582.8 / 65' — **State of Georgia Memorial (U.S. 80) Bridge:** (Also called Thunderbolt Bridge.) Fixed

592.9 / 65' — **Diamond Causeway (Skidaway) Bridge:** Fixed

674.5 / 65' — **F.J. Torras Causeway Bridge:** Fixed

684.4 / 65' — **Jekyll Island (SR 520) Bridge:** Fixed

Ben Sawyer Memorial Bridge

Inlets: Norfolk, VA to St. Marys, GA

Introduction

Intracoastal Waterway (ICW): Cruising the "inside waterway" (the ICW) is a bit like driving down I-95. There are areas where every amenity and convenience you need is but an exit away (especially in FL), and then there are stretches with only marsh and woods as far as the eye can see (mostly in SC and GA). And like I-95 there is constant construction, varying speed-restricted areas, and many bridges to pass under or through. The main difference between the highway and the waterway is the "road maintenance." With federal funding for dredging being scarce, shoaling has been more commonplace on the ICW and the "projected depths" on the NOAA charts can no longer be considered valid. This, alone, will drive (pun intended) some vessels to take the offshore (Atlantic Ocean) route.

Offshore Runs: Some boaters choose the offshore run to save time or to get a break from the bridge openings and speed restrictions. Many sailboats will take this option to turn off the engine and unfurl the sails. You may be forced to take the offshore route due to vessel draft or vertical clearance. Regardless of your reasons for exiting the inland waterways, there are numerous inlets along both Atlantic Ocean that will allow you to duck in or back out should the weather turn.

Cautions & Warnings: Keep in mind that not all inlets are navigable and some are treacherous under certain conditions. This section will assist you in recognizing those but it is still important to study the charts, pay attention to the weather and seek current local knowledge before proceeding on an offshore run. Be sure to check for a suitable weather window and plan your passage based on inlets with sufficient depth.

Before you begin an offshore passage, take an honest accounting of your vessel, your crew and yourself. Is each of you up to the task? Is the vessel properly outfitted? Do you have the necessary safety equipment, charts, long distance communications gear such as single sideband radio (SSB), an Emergency Position Indicating Radio Beacon (EPIRB) and life raft? Do you and your crew have adequate experience in boating and navigation to attempt an offshore coastal passage?

Check the weather using as many sources as possible. If you have access to weather routing services, they are a good option, particularly for longer offshore passages. You are seeking a weather window with enough space on each side to get you safely out and back in, with room for unexpected contingencies.

Inlets: Norfolk, VA to St. Marys, GA

Of course, always file a float plan with a reliable person. A sample float plan is provided in the *Skippers Handbook* of this guide. You might also look into the free app BoatSafe Free, which allows you to create a float plan and email it to participants or emergency contacts.

Entering & Exiting: Plan your trip so that you enter in daylight, with the tide, particularly if your boat is slow or underpowered. Remember that wind against tide can create short, steep waves in an inlet that can quickly make even a ship channel impassable for slower boats. If conditions are bad when you reach the sea buoy for an inlet, you may find yourself being driven ashore by wind or waves and unable to find the inlet buoys. It may be better to remain well offshore in rough conditions, possibly continuing to a better inlet.

Be advised that the markers at some inlets are moved on a regular basis and the buoys should be honored. Should you find yourself at an inlet and needing direction, a call on VHF Channel 16 for local knowledge is likely to bring you a response. Sea Tow and TowBoatU.S. are two other knowledgeable sources. The Coast Guard may also be able to assist you, but only if it is indeed an emergency.

Overall Mileage: Heading north or south, many skippers mistakenly assume that they will shorten their trips by going out to sea and running down the coast. The distances shown here–both inside and outside (from inlet to inlet)–demonstrate that this is not necessarily true. Keep in mind that even if outside distances from sea buoy to sea buoy are virtually the same as the inside distances, the mileage in and out to the buoys adds to the total coastwise figure.

Resources: Prior to your voyage, there are a number of online sources that can familiarize you with the inlets, including the following:

- **Waterway Explorer** (www.waterwayguide.com): Provides chart and satellite views of the inlets plus cruising details from local boaters.
- **United States Coast Pilot** (www.nauticalcharts.noaa.gov): Nine-volume annual publication distributed by the Office of Coast Survey (NOAA) to supplement nautical charts.
- **Local Notice to Mariners** (www.navcen.uscg.gov, then select the LNMs tab): Weekly updates provided by the U.S. Coast Guard to provide corrections to navigational publications and nautical charts.
- **Tide Tables** (www.tidesandcurrents.noaa.gov): Provided by NOAA to provide tidal predictions (highs and lows) for specific areas.

Mid-Atlantic Inlets

Inlet	Page
Hampton Roads (Norfolk), VA	66
Beaufort Inlet, NC	68
Masonboro Inlet, NC	70
Cape Fear River Entrance, NC	72
Little River Inlet, SC	74
Winyah Bay Entrance, SC	76
Charleston Harbor Entrance, SC	78
North Edisto River Inlet, SC	80
Port Royal Sound Entrance, SC	82
Tybee Roads (Savannah River) Entrance, GA	84
Wassaw Sound Entrance, GA	86
St. Catherines Sound Entrance, GA	87
Sapelo Sound Entrance, GA	88
Doboy Sound Entrance, GA	89
St. Simons Sound Entrance, GA	90
St. Marys River Entrance, GA	92

America's Waterway Guide Since 1947

The decommissioned *Morris Island Lighthouse* at the entrance to Charleston Harbor, South Carolina

Inlet Distances

Hampton Roads to Beaufort Inlet:
222 nm (outside)/204 sm (ICW)

Beaufort Inlet to Cape Fear River Entrance:
115 nm (outside)/105 sm (ICW)

Cape Fear River Entrance to Winyah Bay Entrance:
65 nm (outside)/97 sm (ICW)

Winyah Bay Entrance to Charleston Harbor Entrance:
46 nm (outside)/58 sm (ICW)

Charleston Harbor Entrance to Port Royal Sound Entrance:
57 nm (outside)/85 sm (ICW)

Port Royal Sound Entrance to Tybee Roads (Savannah River) Entrance:
10 nm (outside)/27 sm (ICW)

Tybee Roads (Savannah River) Entrance to St. Simons Sound Entrance:
62 nm (outside)/102 sm (ICW)

St. Simons Sound Entrance to St. Marys River Entrance:
21 nm (outside)/36 sm (ICW)

Note: In keeping with standard NOAA conventions, outside (ocean and Gulf) distances are measured in nautical miles (nm), while ICW and GIWW distances are measured in statute miles (sm):

1 nm = 1.15 sm

Hampton Roads (Norfolk), VA

Overview: Strategically situated at Mile 0, the "official" beginning of the ICW, Norfolk offers nearly every type of marine service and equipment. Even with all its commercial and military activity, navigating through Norfolk Harbor is relatively easy during daylight hours.

Approach: Chesapeake Channel Lighted Buoy "2C" is at N 36° 57.303'/W 075° 58.378'.

Navigation: Pick up Thimble Shoal Channel Lighted Buoy "2" to the southwest at N 36° 57.168'/W 076° 01.361'. Follow the well-marked channel to the Elizabeth River Lighted Buoy "1ER" located just south of the Chesapeake Bay Bridge-Tunnel at N 36° 59.249'/W 076° 18.669'.

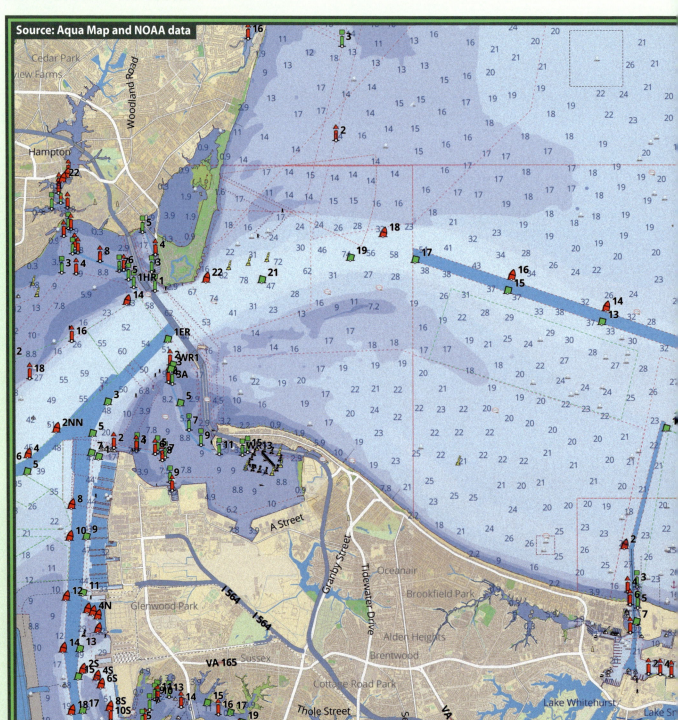

America's Waterway Guide Since 1947

Cautions & Hazards: This is a busy port. Naval Station Norfolk, the largest naval installation in the world, is homeport for the U.S. Navy's Atlantic Fleet, encompassing aircraft carriers, cruisers, destroyers, frigates, support ships, nuclear submarines and admiral's barges. The world's merchant fleet loads and unloads cargo at the Hampton Roads as well.

ICW Connection: Elizabeth River quick flashing red "32" just east of Hospital Point marks Mile 0, the beginning of the ICW.

MID-ATLANTIC EDITION 67

Beaufort Inlet, NC

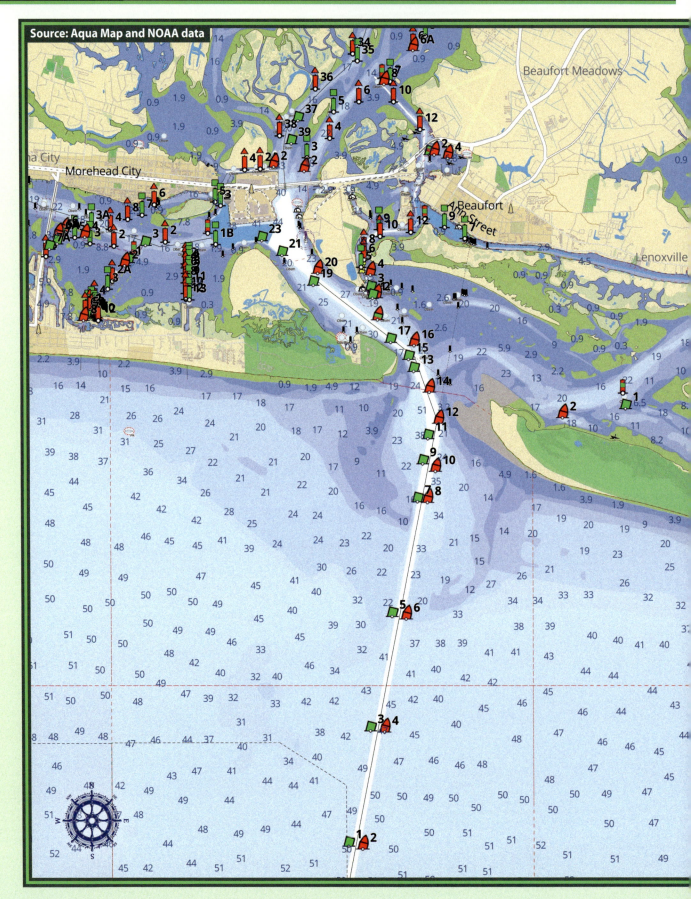

Source: Aqua Map and NOAA data

America's Waterway Guide Since 1947

Overview: Wide, deep and very well marked. Farthest "northerly" inlet recommended for transient recreational boaters. To the north lie the Outer Banks; rounding them entails a long passage in Atlantic Ocean waters.

Approach: Lighted red and white whistle buoy "BM" located at N 34° 34.830'/W 76° 41.550' (5 nm out).

Navigation: Use NOAA Chart 11544. You can forgo the sea buoy, which is more than 5 nm out, and start your approach from flashing green buoy "9" and flashing red bell buoy "10," which are just southwest of N 34° 40.000'/W 76° 40.000'. From here, follow the markers and stay in the center on a course slightly east of north to quick flashing red buoy "16" on Shackleford Point then bear west of north. (Shoaling has been reported at quick flashing red buoy "16.")

If you are headed for Beaufort itself, take the channel leading to the east side of Radio Island, taking care to round quick flashing red buoy "2." Don't cut flashing red buoy "20" short; it is very shallow out of the channel. If your destination is Morehead City, bear to port at flashing green buoy "21," and then continue to follow the channel markers under the bridge.

Cautions & Hazards: Areas of constant shoaling have been identified throughout the Beaufort Inlet and Harbor. Current runs 2 knots on the flood. Mariners are urged to use extreme caution when transiting the area.

ICW Connection: Proceed to the turning basin (ICW Mile 204) and bear to port if you are heading south on the ICW. If heading north, continue through the Beaufort Channel Railroad Bridge (4-foot closed vertical clearance, usually open), followed by the fixed Beaufort Channel (US 70) Bridge (65-foot vertical clearance) immediately ahead.

MID-ATLANTIC EDITION

Masonboro Inlet, NC

Overview: Uncomplicated entrance protected by jetties on both sides and with good depths within. Depths are maintained at 12 feet in the 400-foot-wide channel running midway between the jetties. Popular with sportfishers. Coast Guard Station Wrightsville Beach is just past red daybeacon "10."

Approach: Masonboro Inlet Lighted Whistle Buoy "A" is at N 34° 10.387'/W 077° 47.846'.

Navigation: The uncharted buoys are frequently relocated. Once inside, if you are heading to Wrightsville Beach, bear to starboard at green and red daybeacon "WC" into Banks channel and then turn to port at Motts Channel.

Cautions & Hazards: There are no particular difficulties with this inlet, although a southeasterly wind can cause difficult conditions for smaller boats.

ICW Connection: ICW Mile 285 lies straight ahead past Shinn Creek.

Looking south over Masonboro Inlet

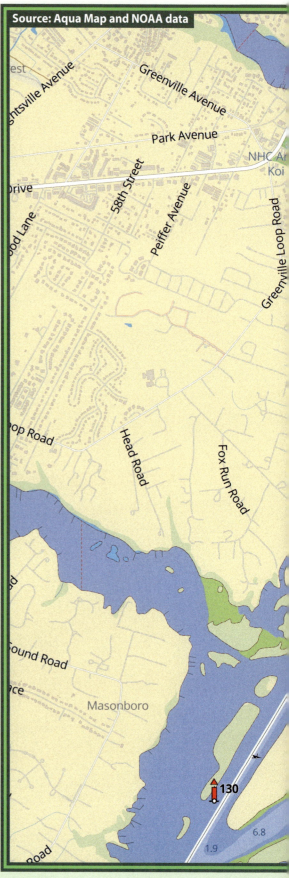

Source: Aqua Map and NOAA data

America's Waterway Guide Since 1947

MID-ATLANTIC EDITION

Cape Fear River Entrance, NC

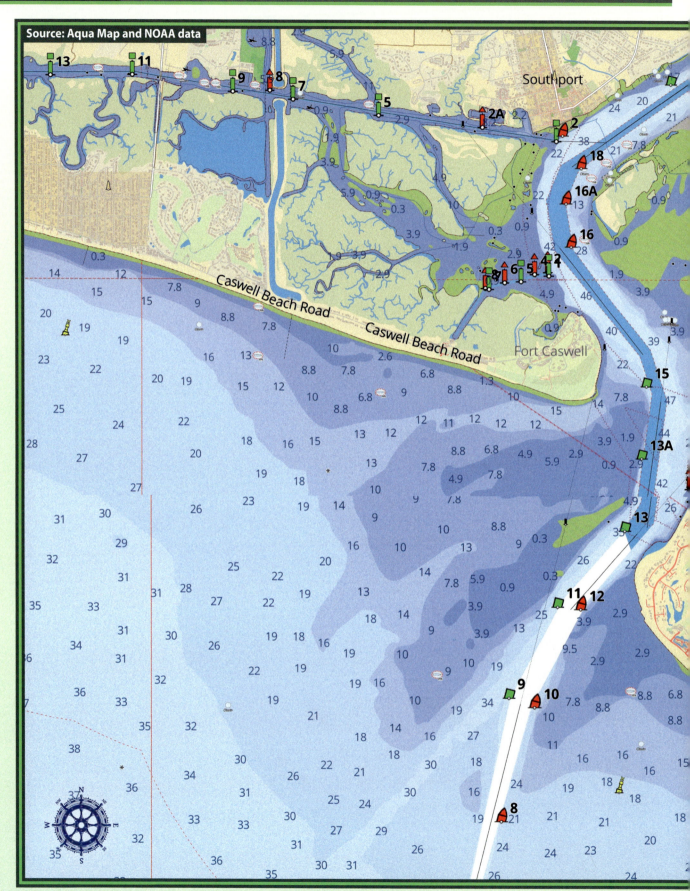

America's Waterway Guide Since 1947

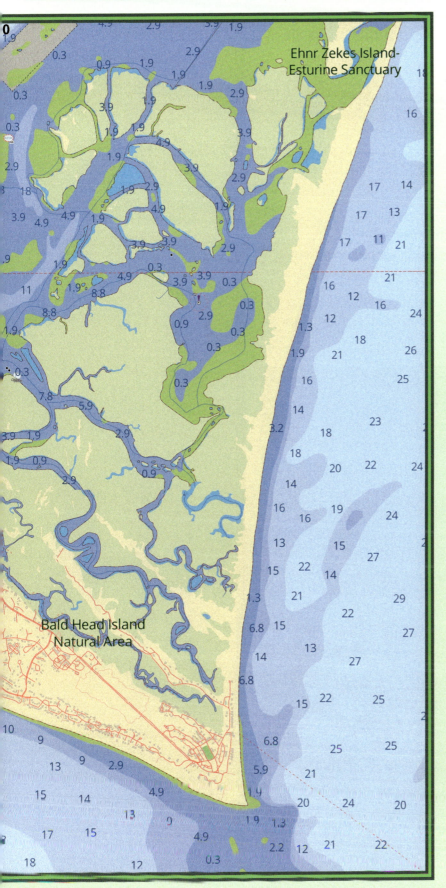

Overview: First port south of Morehead City suitable for all sizes of oceangoing vessels via a major deepwater channel. Well-marked channel protected from the north and an easy entrance day or night.

Approach: Cape Fear River Entrance Lighted whistle buoy "CF" is 5 nm out at N 33° 46.275'/W 078° 03.026'.

Navigation: Cruisers can approach using the waypoint N 33° 50.370'/W 78° 01.780', which is close to red buoy "8" where the surrounding waters begin to shallow. From flashing red buoy "8," proceed slightly east of north to quick flashing red buoy "10" and then to quick flashing red buoy "12" (flashing green "11" may be missing), where you can pick up the Bald Head Shoal Range. For those headed north, we advise you stay on the ICW here to avoid a significant detour around Frying Pan Shoals, which extend 30 nm out into the Atlantic.

Cautions & Hazards: As this is a busy inlet, keep a constant watch posted for big ships. The current is very strong; time your entrance to take advantage of the tides. Northbound slower boats would be well-advised to check the tides before attempting the Cape Fear River's strong currents.

ICW Connection: Connects with the ICW at Mile 308.5. Heading north, the ICW follows the big ship channel toward Wilmington. To head south on the ICW, bear to port at Southport.

MID-ATLANTIC EDITION

Little River Inlet, SC

Overview: Inlet has jetties and is relatively stable. Regularly used by casino boats and head boats docked at Little River. Casino boats are not required to have AIS transponders and many do not.

Approach: Little River Inlet Lighted Buoy "LR" is at N 33° 49.820'/W 078° 32.456'.

Navigation: Use NOAA Chart 11535. Proceed to the entrance markers on the ends of the twin breakwaters (green daybeacon "1" and red daybeacon "2," keeping clear of the shoal to your northeast. The inlet then sweeps west. The channel is well marked with a controlling depth of 10 feet MLW.

Cautions & Hazards: There is a 5-foot shoal just off the east jetty that is awash at low tide. Note that the aids to navigation are frequently moved here to mark shifting shoals. Seek local knowledge before traversing the inlet.

ICW Connection: Connects to the ICW a little more than 1 nm to the north at Mile 343.

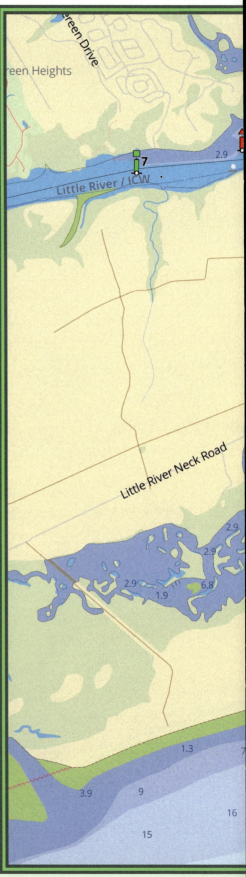

Looking southwest over the ICW, Little River, SC

America's Waterway Guide Since 1947

Source: Aqua Map and NOAA data

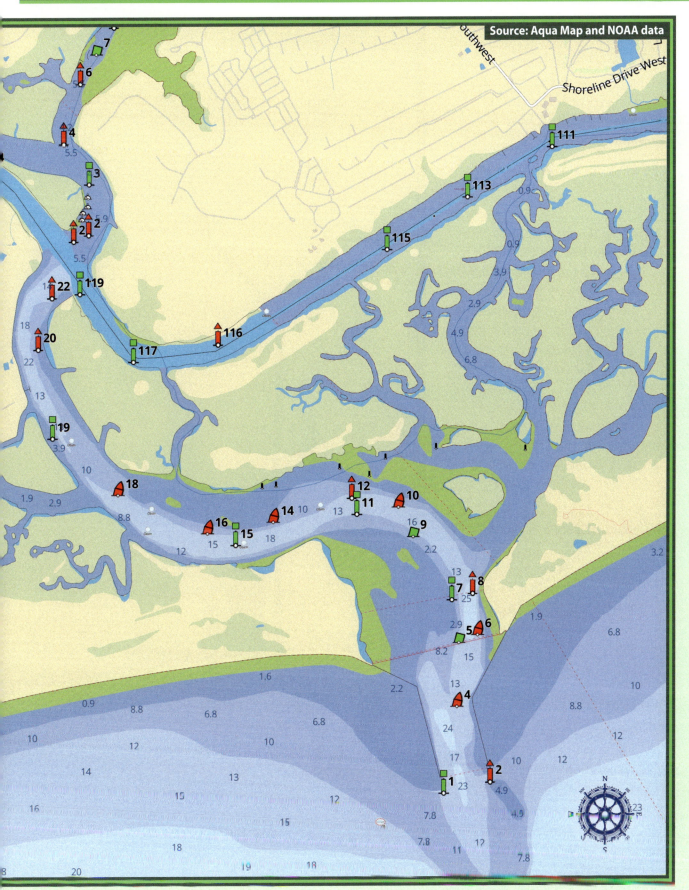

MID-ATLANTIC EDITION

Winyah Bay Entrance, SC

Overview: Well marked and deep. Presents a challenge for underpowered vessels with its strong currents. It pays to watch the tide here and enter or leave with the current. Night entry is feasible due to well-marked ranges.

Approach: Winyah Bay Lighted buoy "WB" is at N 33° 11.617'/W 079° 05.172'.

Navigation: Georgetown Light, 85 feet above the water, shines from a white cylindrical tower on the north side of Winyah Bay entrance. Smoke from one or another of the stacks in Georgetown can often be seen from well offshore. The sea buoy is well out; recreational vessels can safely approach waypoint N 33° 11.570'/W 79° 07.040', which is just east of red buoy "4." From the waypoint, entry is straightforward on a heading of due west, turning to northwest at red buoy "8" and north-northwest after that.

Cautions & Hazards: Conditions can be particularly bad at the ends of the jetties when tide opposes wind. Also, much of the south jetty is visible only at low water. Northbound vessels need to be aware of the shoals to the south and west of the channel and not stray west of the waypoint. Anything under 20 feet MLW indicates you are too far west on your approach.

ICW Connection: Connects to the ICW at Mile 406 (9 nm). Southbound traffic coming from offshore will want to leave the main shipping channel sooner, veering to port at flashing green buoy "17" to enter the ICW via the Western Channel.

Source: Aqua Map and NOAA data

America's Waterway Guide Since 1947

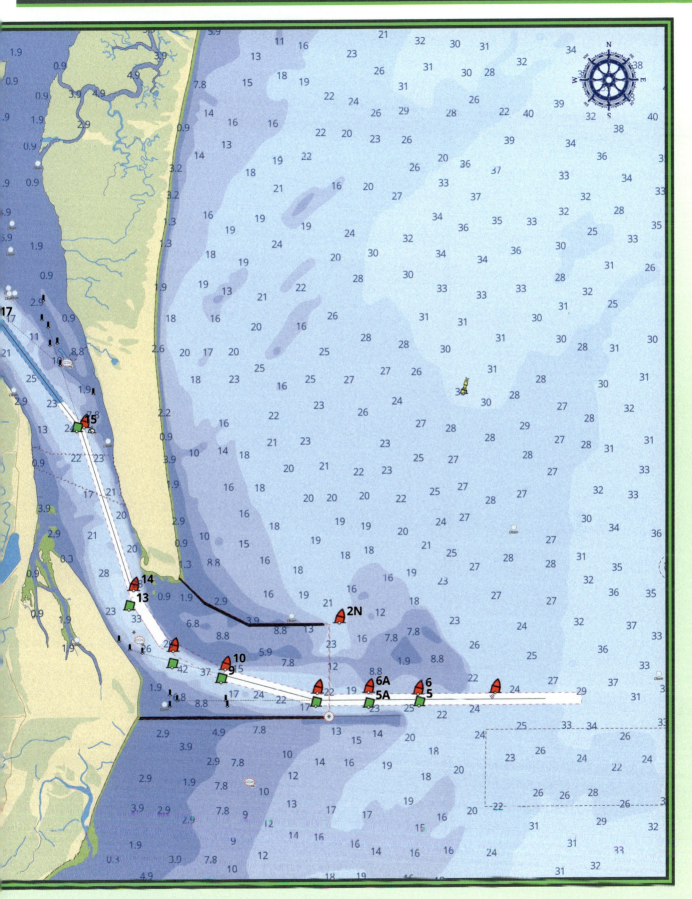

MID-ATLANTIC EDITION

Charleston Harbor Entrance, SC

Overview: This is a heavily used ship channel and there is a great deal of commercial traffic here day and night. The entrance markers and the forest of harbor buoys leading to Charleston Harbor are easy to sort out in daylight hours. Smaller vessels are advised to stay to the edge of the channel until reaching the inlet jetties.

Approach: Charleston Entrance Lighted Buoy "C" is located at N 32° 35.654'/W 079° 32.269'.

Navigation: The sea buoy is 10 nm farther out than necessary for recreational craft. A waypoint at N 32° 42.860'/W 79° 47.550' between green buoy "15" and red buoy "16" saves considerable time, although southbound vessels need to be aware of the shoaling to the north and guide their course appropriately, coming in on a southwesterly heading.

When entering Charleston Harbor from the ICW–anytime after low-water slack tide to about 2 hours before high-water slack for Charleston Harbor–the current will give slower boats a healthy boost up to the marinas on the Ashley River. When leaving Charleston to head north, slow boats should leave a couple of hours before low-water slack tide for an easier run.

Cautions & Hazards: Be aware of the partially submerged jetties north and south of the channel at quick flashing green buoy "17" and quick flashing red buoy "18." After clearing the jetties, do not proceed onto the charted Middle Ground without a harbor chart (NOAA Chart 11524) that provides expanded coverage. This inlet can be very confusing for nighttime entries due to the many lights both on the water and land, and the considerable traffic you'll encounter at all hours.

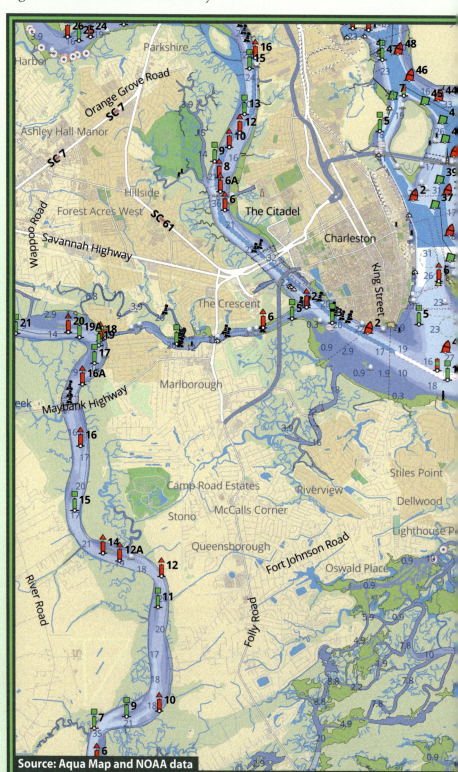

Source: Aqua Map and NOAA data

America's Waterway Guide Since 1947

ICW Connection: If continuing south on the ICW (Mile 464.1), bear to the west on the South Channel Range. Those northbound or heading for the Cooper River continue using the Mount Pleasant Range and follow it out of the channel, watching for flashing green "127" about 0.25 mile to the east, marking the entrance to the northbound ICW.

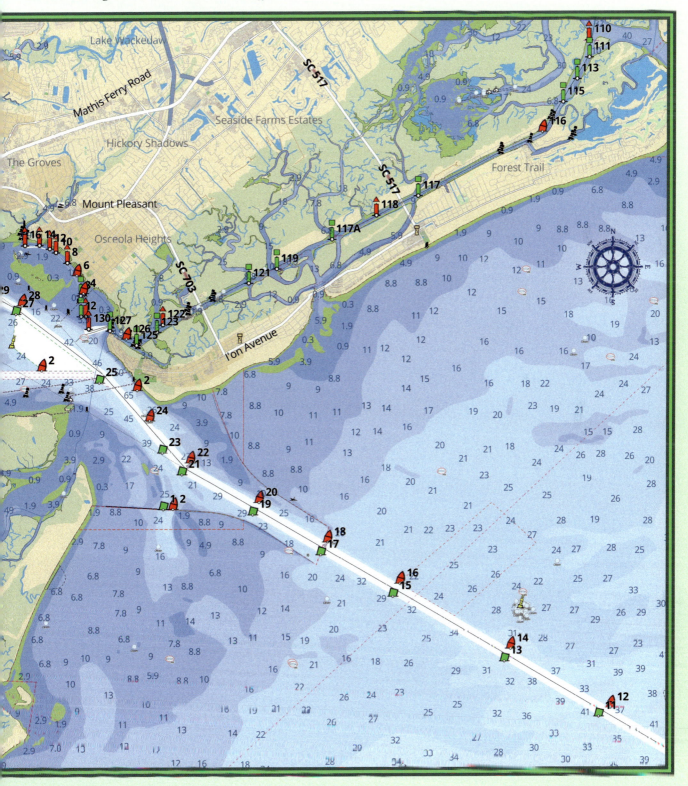

MID-ATLANTIC EDITION

North Edisto River Inlet, SC

Overview: Inlet provides a straight shot. Be aware of shoals to the west and breakers to the northeast.

Approach: North Edisto River Entrance Lighted Whistle Buoy "2NE" is at N 32° 31.348' / W 080° 06.844'.

Navigation: Proceed on a course of 286° M, leaving flashing red buoy "6" to starboard (red nun buoy "4" is close by). Then turn to 325° M, picking up green can buoy "7" before lining up with the charted range that leads you close alongside flashing green buoy "9."

Cautions & Hazards: The chart shows a 5-foot-deep section near flashing red buoy "6," which will not be a problem provided you keep the marker to starboard on entering.

ICW Connection: Connects to the ICW approximately 7.5 nm from the inlet at White Point (Mile 496.7).

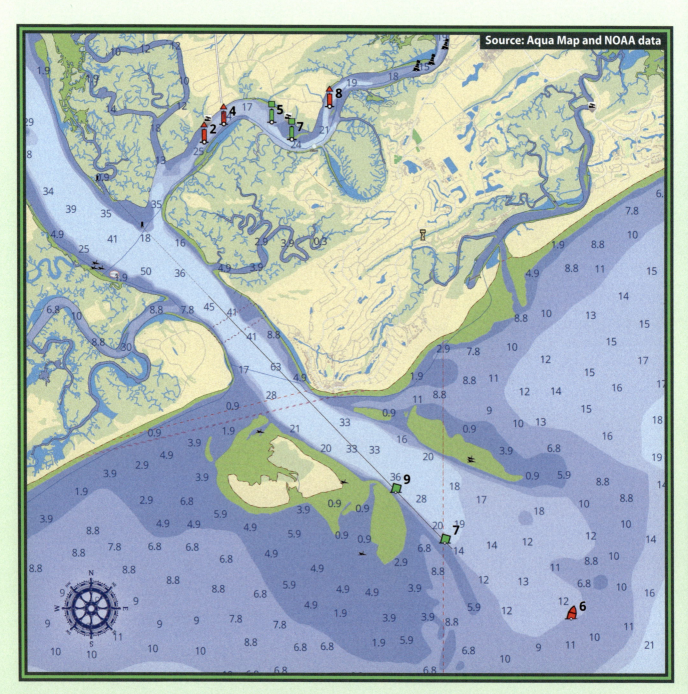

Scan to subscribe now at
www.waterwayguide.com

Navigate with the Cruising Authority

Port Royal Sound Entrance, SC

Overview: Wide, deep and very long. If headed south offshore, this is not the best option as a point of entry, as you will backtrack some distance to re-enter the ocean.

Approach: Port Royal Sound Lighted Buoy "P" is at N 32° 05.111'/W 080° 35.052'.

Navigation: From the sea buoy, head north and follow the range to flashing red buoy "14," then veer to the west to quick flashing green buoy "25," where you can head west as noted to the southbound ICW and Hilton Head Island, or north to Beaufort, SC. There are ranges northbound to quick flashing green buoy "37" on the Beaufort River.

Cautions & Hazards: When a cold front passes through the area, expect breaking ocean swells throughout the channel until rounding Bay Point. Under these conditions the going will be tedious but still negotiable for well-found vessels. More difficult is the combination of a stiff onshore breeze against an ebb tide (driven here by local tides of 9 feet); this is a situation best avoided.

ICW Connection: Connects to the ICW after quick flashing green buoy "25" at approximately Mile 548.6.

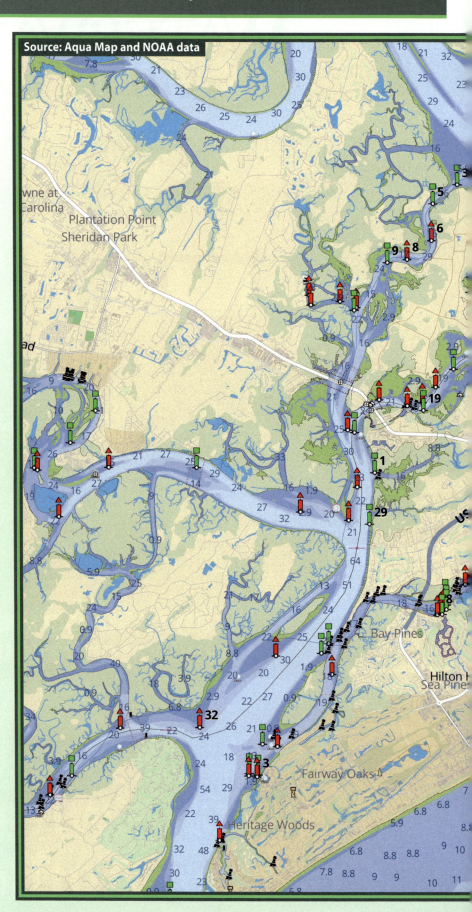

Source: Aqua Map and NOAA data

America's Waterway Guide Since 1947

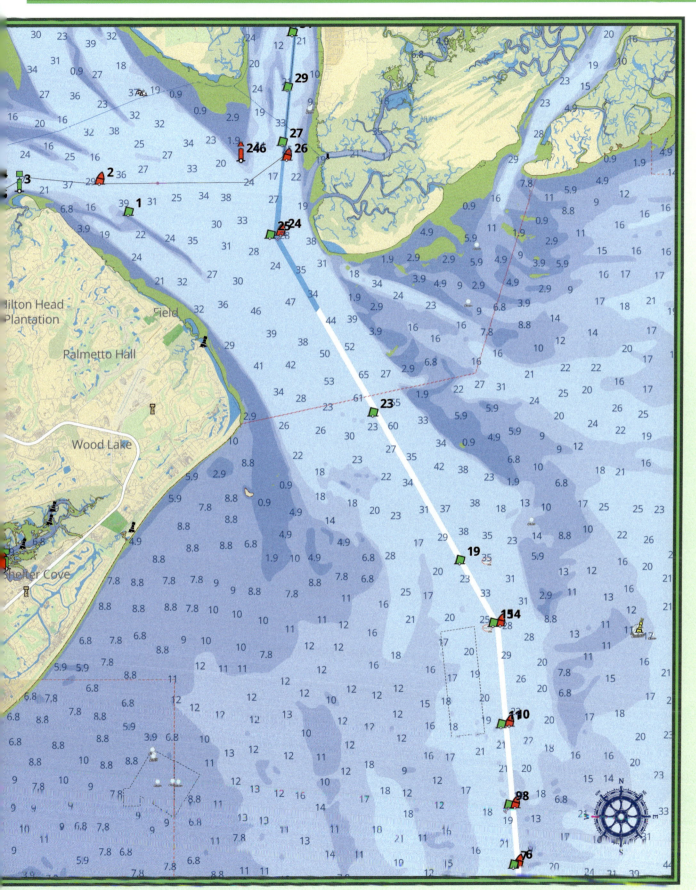

MID-ATLANTIC EDITION

Tybee Roads (Savannah River) Entrance, GA

Overview: This is an active inlet offering entry to Savannah via the ICW and Savannah River. Slower boats bound for the Savannah River on this route should enter Tybee Roads with a favorable current, if possible, as the effects of the current start many miles offshore in the Atlantic.

Approach: Savannah River Entrance Channel Lighted "T" is at N 31° 57.700'/W 80° 43.100'.

Navigation: Entering the channel from the sea buoy, follow the Tybee range to quick flashing red bell buoy "8," turning north to follow the Bloody Point Range to flashing red "14." Turning to port here, follow the Jones Island Range to flashing red buoy "18," and then turn slightly southwest and continue in on Tybee Knoll Cut Range to flashing red buoy "24." Here, you will have Oyster Bed Island to your north and Cockspur Island to the south. Pick up New Channel Range

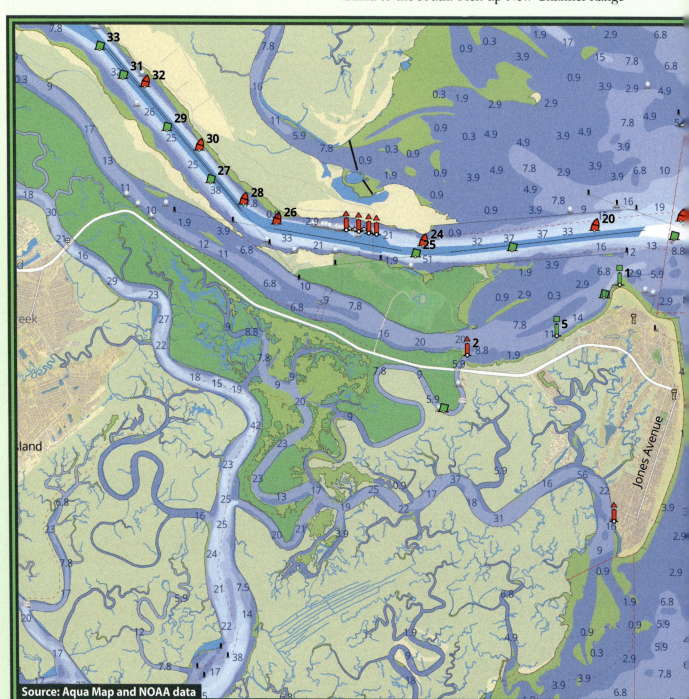

Source: Aqua Map and NOAA data

America's Waterway Guide Since 1947

and follow the channel markers. Note the partially submerged breakwater that begins just past flashing red buoy "18," which is marked by a flashing white light, noted as "Fl 4s 16ft 5M" on your chart.

Cautions & Hazards: Coming from the north, mariners need to be aware of Gaskin Banks, an extensive shoal area extending nearly 8 nm out from Hilton Head. Also to be avoided is a submerged breakwater north of and roughly parallel to flashing red buoy "12" and flashing red buoy "14."

ICW Connection: Savannah River crosses ICW at Fields Cut (Mile 575.7), directly opposite flashing green buoy "35."

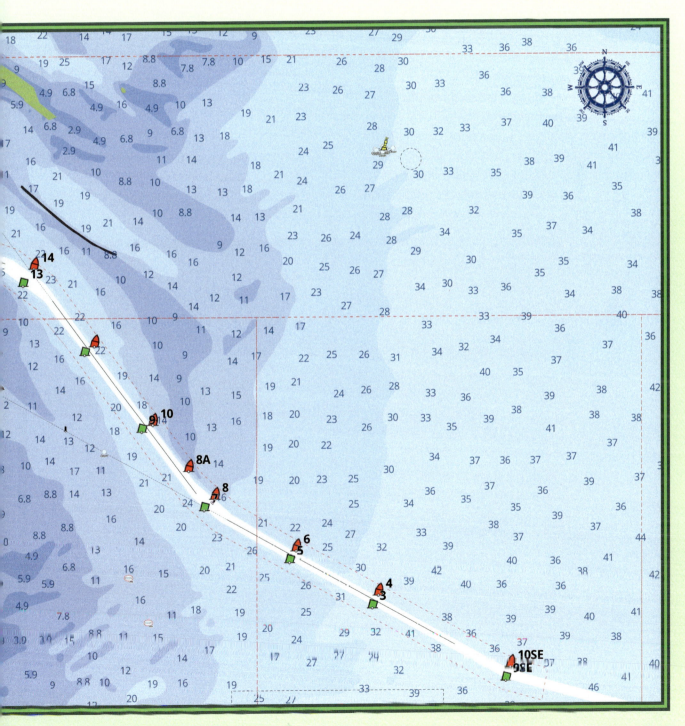

MID-ATLANTIC EDITION

Wassaw Sound Entrance, GA

Overview: A fair amount of local traffic regularly uses this inlet but we do not recommend it except with up-to-date local knowledge, excellent visibility, calm seas and at mid-tide. This inlet is sometimes used by vessels bound for Thunderbolt Marine and unable to clear the 65-foot State Of Georgia Memorial (U.S. 80) Bridge over the Wilmington River at Mile 582.8.

Approach: Wassaw Sound Lighted Buoy "2W" is at N 31° 51.555'/W 080° 53.030'.

Navigation: The entrance to Wassaw Sound changes continually, so red buoys "4," "6" and "8" are not charted. Before beginning this inlet, mark a boundary line on your chart running due south from flashing red buoy "10." From flashing red buoy "2W," head west-northwest and curve to the north around the shoal to starboard until you reach the above noted line from flashing red buoy "10." Head due north to green can buoy "9" and turn northwest to follow the markers; depths will be 20 feet MLW or better. Stay to the center of Wilmington River until you turn to the north after flashing red "22" and then stay to the east side of the river for deep water. Wassaw Sound and the Wilmington River carry about 25-foot MLW depths between flashing red buoy "10" in the Atlantic Ocean to flashing green daybeacon "29" at Skidaway River (Mile 585.5).

Cautions & Hazards: The 2 nm from the sea buoy to the first markers are tricky, with shoals on both sides, breakers and no markers. Just east of green can "9" and flashing red can "10" there is extensive shoaling. If you draw more than 5 feet, think twice before entering this inlet. This is not an inlet for dark and stormy arrivals, as it is poorly marked and surrounded by shoals nearly 5 nm out from the entrance.

ICW Connection: Wilmington River meets the ICW at Skidaway Narrows (Mile 585.5), about 3.5 nm north of flashing red buoy "20" at the river's entrance.

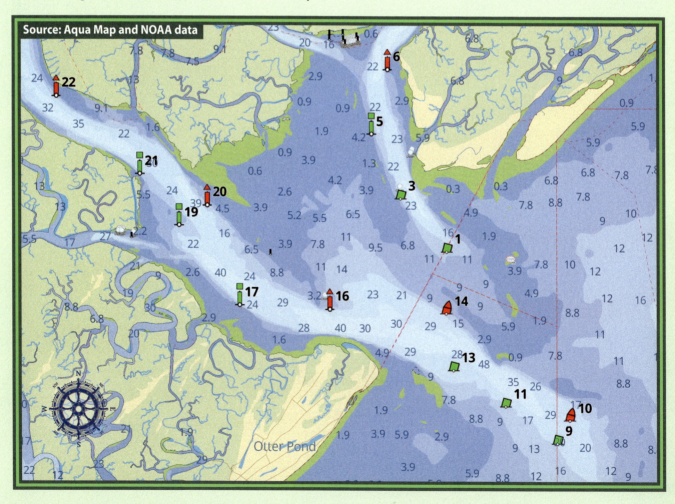

St. Catherines Sound Entrance, GA

Overview: This wide, uncomplicated entrance offers good depths within.

Approach: St. Catherines Sound Lighted Buoy "STC" is at N 31° 40.197'/W 081° 00.193'.

Navigation: Heading west from the sea buoy, turn in between green can "1" and flashing red "2" and head north to flashing green "5" in no less than 12 feet at MLW. (Or head straight from RW "STC" to flashing green "5" where you may see 9-foot MLW depths.) The channel turns west toward green can "7."

Cautions & Hazards: As with other smaller inlets in Georgia, channel markers are widely placed and it can be difficult to visually pick them out, even though the offshore sea buoys are in their charted position and easy to locate with GPS. Some of the smaller markers are frequently moved to locate better water. For slow-moving northbound or southbound boats, the best time to arrive at St. Catherines Sound Entrance (Mile 618) is at low slack water, which occurs within 20 minutes of low tide at the Bear River Entrance NOAA station (#8673171). Tidal range is 7 to 8 feet.

ICW Connection: St. Catherines Sound Entrance intersects the ICW at Mile 618, about 3nm from flashing green "5" at the entrance.

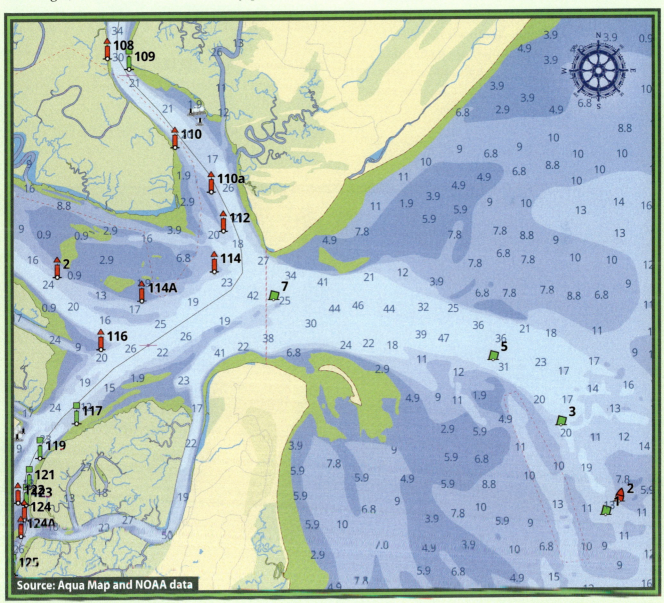

Source: Aqua Map and NOAA data

Sapelo Sound Entrance, GA

Overview: Used by fishermen and shrimpers, not to mention legendary pirate Edward Teach ("Blackbeard"). (You will pass just north of Blackbeard Island and Blackbeard Creek while transiting this inlet.)

Approach: Sapelo Sound Buoy "S" is at N 31° 31.217/W 081° 03.879'.

Navigation: Give both lighted aids and daybeacons a wider berth than usual in this inlet, especially around low tide. Keep track of your markers, running a compass course between distant ones. Many boats have erroneously run for an outlying sea buoy instead of a marker leading into a nearby tributary. Mind the markers at the western end of Sapelo Sound where the ICW route enters the Sapelo River. At low tide approach the whole stretch with caution. Shrimp boats came and go at all hours and often have their outriggers down increasing their beam up to 120 feet, which consumes a large part of the channel.

Current and trustworthy local knowledge required. From the sea buoy, proceed first to red nun buoy "2" and then head slightly south of west to green can buoy "3." Depths will drop from more than 20 feet down to 12 feet MLW along the way. If you see 10-foot MLW depths, you are in trouble and need to reverse course. At green can buoy "5," you will see 20-plus-foot MLW depths return, and it is a simple matter of following the red buoys in until you meet up with the ICW past red nun buoy "10." (Note that some buoys may be off station or missing.)

Cautions & Hazards: Southbound cruisers hoping to avoid the Georgia ICW rarely use this inlet, preferring to jump offshore through the big ship channels at Charleston or Port Royal, SC, or Savannah, GA. This is not the best inlet in rougher weather due to extensive shoals to the north and south of the inlet. Note that low slack water on Sapelo Sound Entrance occurs 30 minutes before it occurs at the Savannah River Entrance.

ICW Connection: Junction of Sapelo Sound and ICW is at Mile 632.

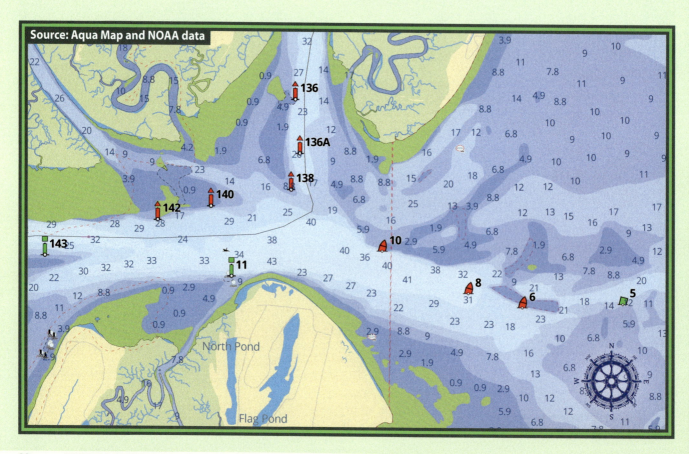

Doboy Sound Entrance, GA

Overview: Uncomplicated inlet with breakwaters that provide some protection from south-setting waves.

Approach: Doboy Sound Lighted Buoy "D" is at N 31° 21.239'/W 081° 11.370'.

Navigation: Heading slightly north of west from the sea buoy, continue in past the breakwaters to the north of red nun buoy "4." The channel shoals to 7 feet MLW approaching green can "3," then deepens again. Continue to red nun "8" on the northerly point of land in 20- to 40-foot depths. Once in the sound, keep an eye out for shoaling.

Cautions & Hazards: Breakwaters to the north and a long easterly shoal on the south side are the main hazards here. Aside from the sea buoy and flashing red "8," all of the aids to navigation in this inlet are unlighted, making it a difficult, if not dangerous, nighttime passage.

ICW Connection: About 2.5 nm from the inlet proper, Doboy Sound intersects the ICW just above Commodore and Doboy Islands at Mile 649. The ICW runs around the north and west sides of Doboy Island.

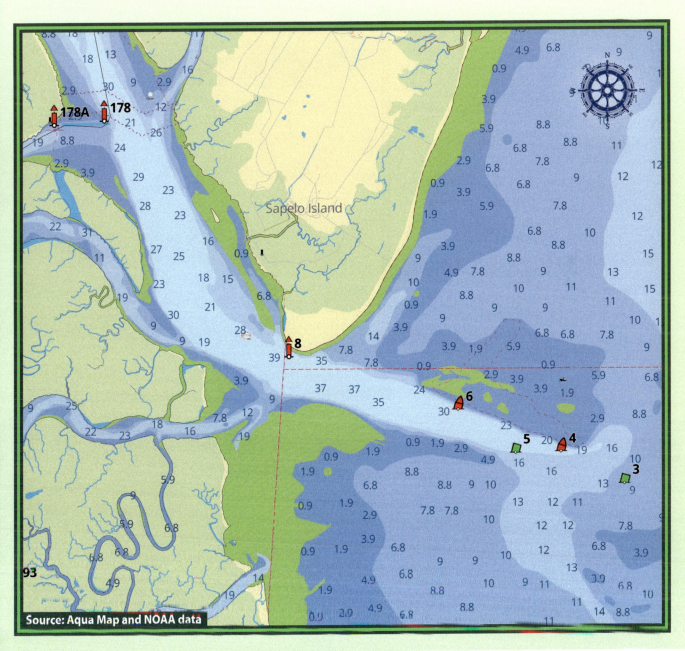

Source: Aqua Map and NOAA data

MID-ATLANTIC EDITION

St. Simons Sound Entrance, GA

Overview: All-weather, wide and deep entrance to the Mackay River leading to Brunswick.

Approach: St. Simons Lighted Buoy "STS" is at N 31° 02.809'/W 081° 14.416'.

Navigation: From the sea buoy, proceed northwesterly to quick flashing red buoy "16" on the range, then turn to port and pick up Plantation Creek Range. Be sure to start from the sea buoy due to shallows that extend quite far from shore. Channel shallows very rapidly outside of the markers, and ebb current is quite strong at the mouth of the inlet.

Cautions & Hazards: Start from the sea buoy due to shallows that extend quite far from shore. Channel shallows very rapidly outside of the markers, and ebb current is quite strong at the mouth of the inlet. Be advised that this inlet can be rough when the wind and current are opposed. This is a busy entrance; keep watch for big ships transiting the inlet.

ICW Connection: The ICW is immediately inside the inlet at Mile 678.

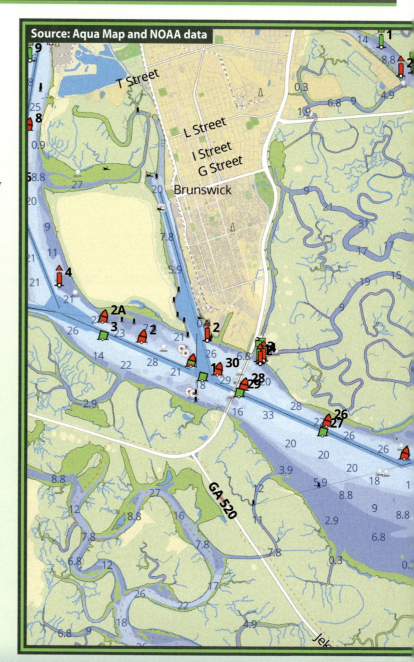

America's Waterway Guide Since 1947

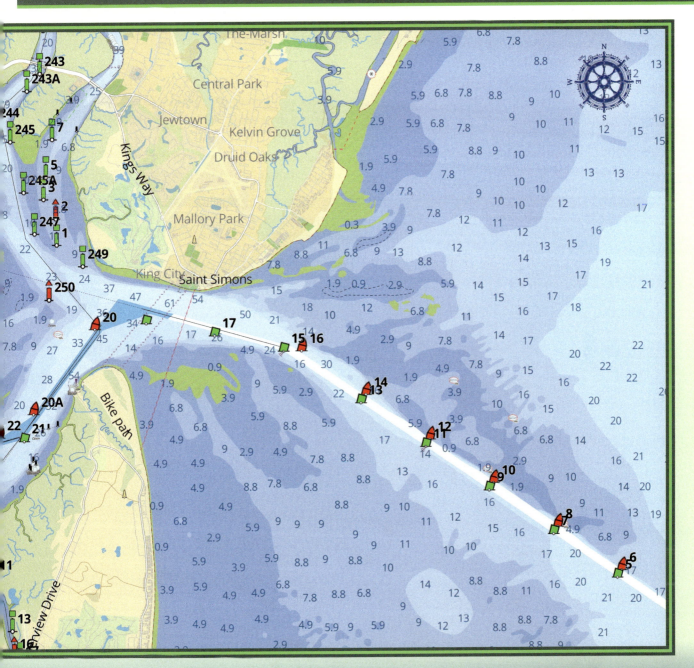

Jekyll Island

MID-ATLANTIC EDITION

St. Marys River Entrance, GA

Overview: Relatively easy entry and exit point conveniently located just off the ICW. The inlet is deep, wide and jettied.

Approach: St. Marys Entrance Lighted Buoy "STM" is at N 30° 42.892'/W 081° 14.652' (2.5 nm seaward of the channel).

Navigation: From the sea buoy, steer to N 30° 42.704'/W 081° 21.526' to access the center of the channel at red marker "10" then proceed due west into Cumberland Sound. There are poorly marked jetties on both the north and south sides that are mostly SUBMERGED at high tide. Don't cut the corner and make sure you account for the single mark at the end of the jetty. Some shoal sections to the north of the channel inside the jetty. The current in this inlet is very strong and dictates appropriate boat handling to compensate. Slower boats are well

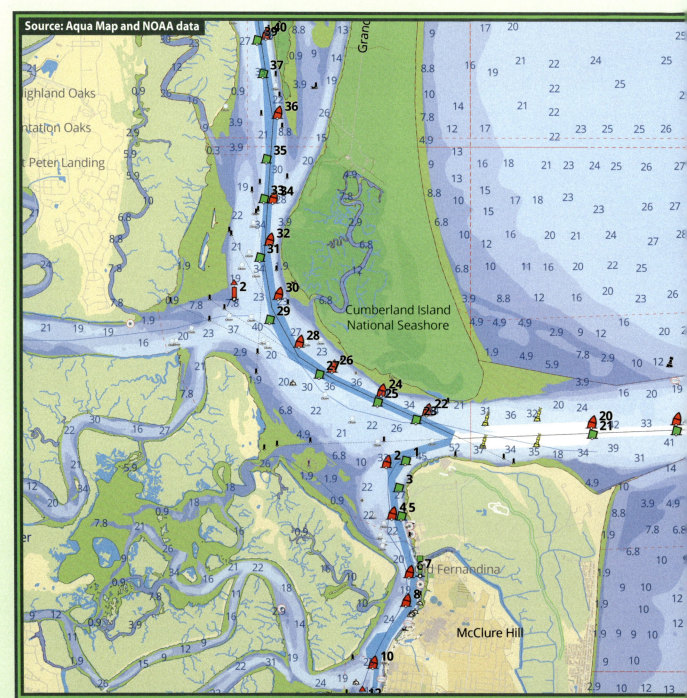

advised to time their passages for slack water or a favorable tide.

Cautions & Hazards: The inlet serves the Kings Bay Submarine Base so be on the lookout for any military craft that might be in the area. the safety and security of submarines, their Coast Guard escorts and the public. No person or vessel may enter or remain within the security zone without the permission of the Coast Guard.

ICW Connection: ICW crosses the inlet at Mile 714. For either north or south, follow the banks, which remain deep outside of the channel.

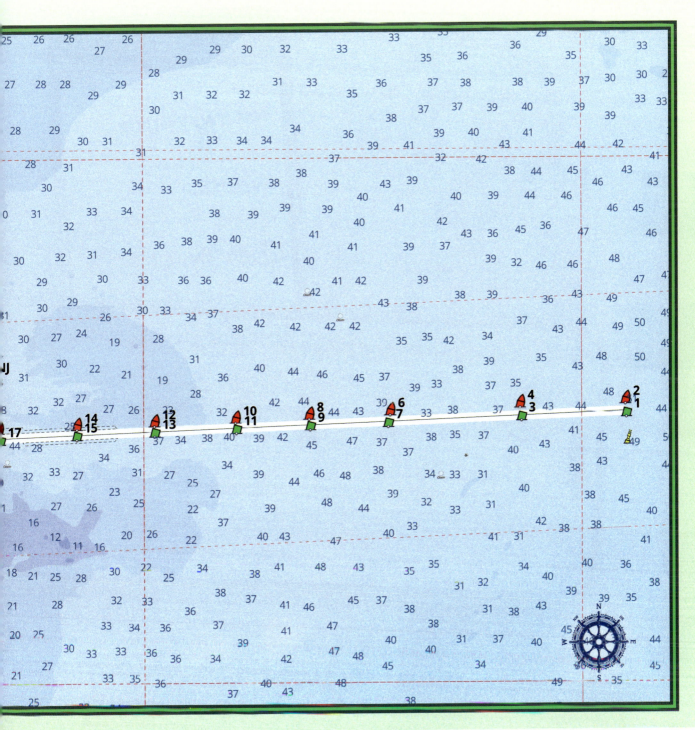

MID-ATLANTIC EDITION   93

Chapter 1: Hampton, Norfolk & Portsmouth, VA

America's Waterway Guide Since 1947 — Chapter 1

Looking South to Hampton Roads from Fort Monroe

HAMPTON ROADS

Strategically situated at Mile Zero, the "official" beginning of the Atlantic Intracoastal Waterway (AICW or ICW), Hampton, Norfolk and Portsmouth offer nearly every type of marine service and equipment and are especially good fitting-out places in preparation for a cruise south or north. They're also exciting places to visit with rejuvenated waterfronts filled with shops, restaurants, hotels, museums and historic sites.

This is also a convenient area for picking up or dropping off guests and for flying in to join a boat crew. Limousine/cab service to and from Norfolk's airport is easy to arrange. If you are in Hampton or Newport News, you should also consider the Newport News/Williamsburg International Airport. It is about 25 minutes north of Hampton on I-64.

The world's merchant fleet loads and unloads cargo at the Hampton Roads and Elizabeth River piers. Colliers fill their holds with 100,000 tons of coal at a time. Even so, the commercial presence is minimal compared to the military presence. Naval Station Norfolk, the largest naval installation in the world, is homeport for the U.S. Navy's Atlantic Fleet encompassing aircraft carriers, cruisers, destroyers, frigates, support ships, nuclear submarines and admiral's barges. The Joint Expeditionary Base at Little Creek is a few miles east over land and is the world's largest amphibious base.

Most of the Navy's operational aircraft are stationed at Naval Air Station Oceana in Virginia Beach. There is also a large Navy training center at Dam Neck and the Army operates Fort Story at Cape Henry. Across Hampton Roads Harbor is Langley Air Force Base. The Marines have several camps in the area. Even NATO has a headquarters in the area. All in all this area is, by far, the largest military complex in the world.

Navigating Hampton Roads

Before you can begin your journey down the ICW, you must traverse the 10-nm stretch through the Hampton Roads area. Hampton Roads Harbor begins at the line between Old Point Comfort on the north shore and Willoughby Spit to the south.

Sitting on a little island in the middle of the harbor's entrance is Fort Wool, which along with Fort Monroe at Hampton's Old Point Comfort, guarded the entry. Hampton Roads is the site of the famous Monitor and Merrimack naval battle of 1862, which ended in a draw between the ironclads and is one of the world's greatest natural harbors.

Mariners must find their way carefully among all the vessels and aids to navigation in this impressive nautical crossroads. Many of us cruising the waters covered by the many editions of *Waterway Guide* will never experience a busier harbor than Hampton Roads. It is just as busy (if not busier) than New York Harbor. Stay tuned to VHF

MID-ATLANTIC EDITION

Chapter 1 — Hampton, Norfolk & Portsmouth, VA

Chesapeake Bay, VA

BUCKROE BEACH		Largest Vessel	VHF	Total Slips	Approach/ Dockside Depth	Floating Docks	Gas/ Diesel	Repairs/ Haulout	Min/Max Amps	Pump-Out Station
1. Southall Landings Marina WiFi	(757) 850-9929	50	16	180	6.5 / 6.5				30 / 50	P
2. Salt Ponds Marina WiFi	(757) 850-4300	110	16	280	6.5 / 8.0	F	GD		30 / 50	P

WiFi Wireless Internet Access
Visit www.waterwayguide.com for current rates, fuel prices, website addresses and other up-to-the-minute information. (Information in the table is provided by the facilities.)

Scan here for more details:

Source: Aqua Map and NOAA data

Channel 16 and VHF Channel 13, the channel on which commercial traffic communicates.

Remember that you are in deep water in this harbor and you can safely run alongside the channel (and outside it) to provide ample space between you and the many 1,000-foot container ships, submarines, aircraft carriers and commercial vessels that move through here.

Twin 3-mile-long bridge-tunnels join the north and south sides of Hampton Roads (from Hampton to Norfolk) between Old Point Comfort and Willoughby Spit (detailed in the Chesapeake Bay edition of *Waterway Guide*). Channels over the tunnels are well marked but they also serve as bottlenecks through which all boat and big ship traffic must pass. Tidal currents are usually strong here.

Proceeding south through Hampton Roads Harbor, give ships at the Norfolk Naval Station a wide berth. This area is constantly patrolled and it is advisable to favor the west side of the channel or even just outside the channel, where there is still adequate water depth. In fact, all military and commercial ships must be given a wide berth–500 yards when possible–as dictated by the Homeland Security Act.

NO WAKE ZONE

This is not a No-Wake Zone but caution should be exercised through this congested area. Before this transit, tie down as if you were going to sea. It will be choppy and confused from the many boat and ship wakes, and you will likely get rocked on your way through by an inconsiderate boater or by residual wakes that you can't avoid.

Side Trip: Salt Ponds

Directly off the Bay, tiny Salt Ponds Harbor at Bloxoms Corner is halfway between Back River and Old Point Comfort.

NAVIGATION: The Long Creek/Salt Ponds channel depths is reported to exceed 6 feet MLW from the entrance to red daybeacon "14." Additional inlet infrastructure work is scheduled, which will include new and lengthened entrance jetties to alleviate beach sand migration into the channel.

Dockage: The 180-slip Southall Landings Marina welcomes transients to 50 feet on their gated piers with very reasonable rates. Resort amenities include a pool and two tennis courts. Many transients who visit here like it so much they become full-time residents. Salt Ponds Marina to the south has floating docks with full-length finger piers and can accommodate catamarans and trimarans on T-heads. The marina has multiple bath houses and laundry facilities plus a well-appointed boaters lounge. Perhaps the best draw is the sandy Chesapeake Bay beach right across the street. Call ahead to confirm channel depths and any dredging or jetty construction. There is no room to anchor here.

City of Hampton

At Old Point Comfort a conspicuous historical brick landmark is the former Chamberlin Hotel (now a senior services community) marking the north side of the entrance to Hampton Roads Harbor. Fort Monroe and Hampton University are on the eastern side of Hampton Harbor.

The City of Hampton, just west of Old Point Comfort, is located on both sides of the short, busy Hampton River. Founded in 1610, Hampton is the oldest English-speaking city in America and is one of Virginia's main seafood packing centers.

A slip on Sunset Creek puts you within walking distance to the Virginia Air & Space Science Center, numerous local restaurants and one of our favorites, Bull Island Brewing, offering pub food and craft beers

NAVIGATION: On the north side of Hampton Roads Harbor, after you cross the twin tunnels of the **Hampton Roads Bridge-Tunnel**, pick up quick flashing green "1HR" marking the start of the dogleg channel into the Hampton River. Take care not to cut the rip-rap too closely at the tunnel's entrance islands; some of the rocks extend out farther than expected.

Chapter 1: Hampton, Norfolk & Portsmouth, VA

HAMPTON, VA

Overlooking the confluence of Chesapeake Bay and the James and Elizabeth Rivers, Hampton is as strategically convenient to traveling boaters in the 21st century as it was to Colonial-era maritime traffic in the 17th century. Entering the Hampton River, you would never know you were approaching what claims to be the longest continuously settled town of English Colonial origin in the United States. Hampton is a good choice for skippers looking to combine a maintenance stop with excursions into Virginia's Lower Peninsula.

Once you successfully cross four-lane Settlers Landing Rd. you will find Hampton's old section, attractively laid out with brick sidewalks and cobbled streets. Restaurants, antique shops and boutiques blend appealingly into the varied architecture and the old-world proportions of the buildings. The Jamestown Settlement, Colonial

ATTRACTIONS

1. **Hampton Carousel**
   Restored 1920s vintage carousel on waterfront next to Virginia Air & Space Science Center at 602 Settlers Landing Rd. (757-727-1102). One of only 170 antique wooden merry-go-rounds still existing in U.S.

2. **Hampton History Museum/Visitors Center**
   Traces town's history from Kecoughtan Indian settlement forward to 20th century. Main visitor center located in lobby at 120 Old Hampton Ln. (757-727-1610).

3. **St. Johns Episcopal Church**
   One of six buildings whose walls still stood after General Magruder's retreating army burned the town in 1861 (100 W. Queens Way, 757-722-2567).

4. **Virginia Air & Space Science Center**
   Gull wing-roofed center is on the waterfront at 600 Settlers Landing Rd. (757-727-0900). In the main hall, real aircraft from biplanes to F-16s hang in mid-air. Serves as the visitor center for Langley Air Force Base and NASA Langley Research Center and offers educational films in an IMAX® theater.

SERVICES

5. **Hampton Post Office**
   89 Lincoln St. (757-722-5543)

6. **Hampton VA Medical Center**
   100 Emancipation Dr. (757-722-9961)

MARINAS

7. **Customs House Marina**
   710 Settler's Landing Rd. (757-636-7772)

8. **The Docks at Downtown Hampton**
   710 Settlers Landing Rd. (757-727-1276)

9. **Hampton Yacht Club**
   4707 Victoria Blvd. (757-722-0711)

10. **Safe Harbor Bluewater**
    1 Marina Rd. (757-723-6774)

11. **Hampton Marina & Dry Storage**
    800 S. Armistead Ave. (757-722-3325)

America's Waterway Guide Since 1947 — Chapter 1

Williamsburg and the battlefields of Yorktown are a short drive away, and you can rent a car in Hampton. There is a car rental office next door to the public docks. If you rent a car, be sure to visit the Mariners' Museum in Newport News, one of the finest maritime museums in the world. A special draw for Hampton is that it can serve as a base from which to explore Virginia's origins and its enduring contribution to American history.

Across the Hampton River, the Hampton University campus has several National Historic Landmark buildings, including the Hampton University Museum (757-727-5308), the oldest African American museum in the country. It is also home to the Emancipation Oak, a National Historic Landmark, that marks the first place in the country where the Emancipation Proclamation was read to slaves.

Chapter 1: Hampton, Norfolk & Portsmouth, VA

Hampton Roads, VA

OLD POINT COMFORT		Largest Vessel	VHF	Total Slips	Approach/ Dockside Depth	Floating Docks	Gas/ Diesel	Repairs/ Haulout	Min/Max Amps	Pump-Out Station
1. Old Point Comfort Marina WiFi	(757) 788-4308	50	16	314	20.0 / 13.0	F	GD		30 / 50	P

WiFi Wireless Internet Access
Visit www.waterwayguide.com for current rates, fuel prices, website addresses and other up-to-the-minute information. (Information in the table is provided by the facilities.)

Scan here for more details:

Source: Aqua Map and NOAA data

The channel into the Hampton River makes a turn to the west at quick flashing red light "6" and green daybeacon "7" and then to starboard at quick flashing green "11" and red daybeacon "12." Despite the curviness the channel is deep and easy to follow. (Shown as "Hampton Creek Approach Channel" on the NOAA chart.) Both commercial and recreational boats frequently use the channel.

All of the marinas are located before the 29-foot fixed vertical clearance **Settlers Landing Bridge**. The tide ranges about 2.5 feet and the current is negligible.

Dockage: Old Point Comfort Marina, which is located at Fort Monroe, offers accommodations for 300 boats to 50 feet including 10 reserved transient slips. The fort is now a National Historic Site rather than an active base. Plans are underway for a 90-room boutique hotel and 500-seat restaurant with expansive outdoor seating areas and waterfront views. Stay tuned.

The first of the facilities are on Sunset Creek, which leads off to the west from the main channel. The well-regarded Safe Harbor Bluewater spans the southwest corner of the Hampton–Sunset Creek fork and features 200 floating slips for vessels up to 200 feet. They offer resort amenities, three separate high-speed fueling stations and complimentary water shuttle service to downtown. Their sister operation, Bluewater Yacht Yards, is located just beyond with world-class marine services. (Bluewater also manages the Bluewater Outer Banks Yacht Yard in Wanchese.)

At the end of the navigable portion of Sunset Creek is the 6-acre Hampton Marina & Dry Storage with over 500 dry slips and 6 acres of dry storage. They also maintain some transient slips for boats to 32 feet.

Hampton River, VA

HAMPTON AREA		Largest Vessel	VHF	Total Slips	Approach/Dockside Depth	Floating Docks	Gas/Diesel	Repairs/Haulout	Min/Max Amps	Pump-Out Station
1. Safe Harbor Bluewater WiFi	(757) 723-6774	200	16	200	12.0 / 12.0	F	GD	RH	30 / 100	P
2. Hampton Marina & Dry Storage WiFi	(757) 722-3325	34	16	495	10.0 / 8.0	F	GD		30	
3. Hampton Yacht Club-PRIVATE WiFi	(757) 722-0711	100		192	10.0 / 8.0	F		H	30 / 50	P
4. Customs House Marina WiFi	(757) 727-1276	50		60	12.0 / 11.0				30 / 50	
5. The Docks at Downtown Hampton WiFi MM 1.5	(757) 727-1276	130	16	27	12.0 / 11.0	F			30 / 100	P

WiFi Wireless Internet Access
Visit www.waterwayguide.com for current rates, fuel prices, website addresses and other up-to-the-minute information.
(Information in the table is provided by the facilities.)

Scan here for more details:

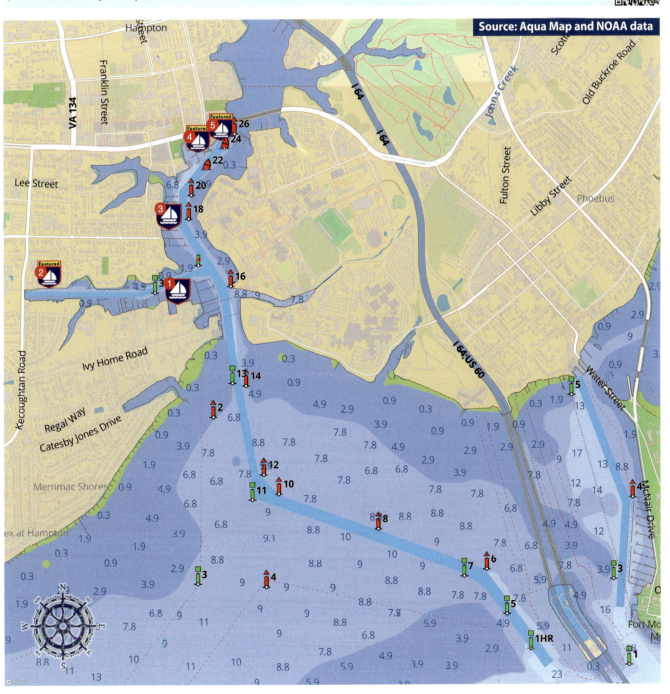

Source: Aqua Map and NOAA data

MID-ATLANTIC EDITION

Chapter 1: Hampton, Norfolk & Portsmouth, VA

Willoughby Bay, VA

WILLOUGHBY SPIT		Largest Vessel	VHF	Total Slips	Approach/ Dockside Depth	Floating Docks	Gas/ Diesel	Repairs/ Haulout	Min/Max Amps	Pump-Out Station
1. Rebel Marina WiFi		(757) 580-6022	100	16	80	10.0 / 9.0	F			30 / 50	P
2. Willoughby Harbor Marina MM 10.7		(757) 583-4150	70	16	271	9.0 / 8.0	F			30 / 50	P

WiFi Wireless Internet Access
Visit www.waterwayguide.com for current rates, fuel prices, website addresses and other up-to-the-minute information.
(Information in the table is provided by the facilities.)

Scan here for more details:

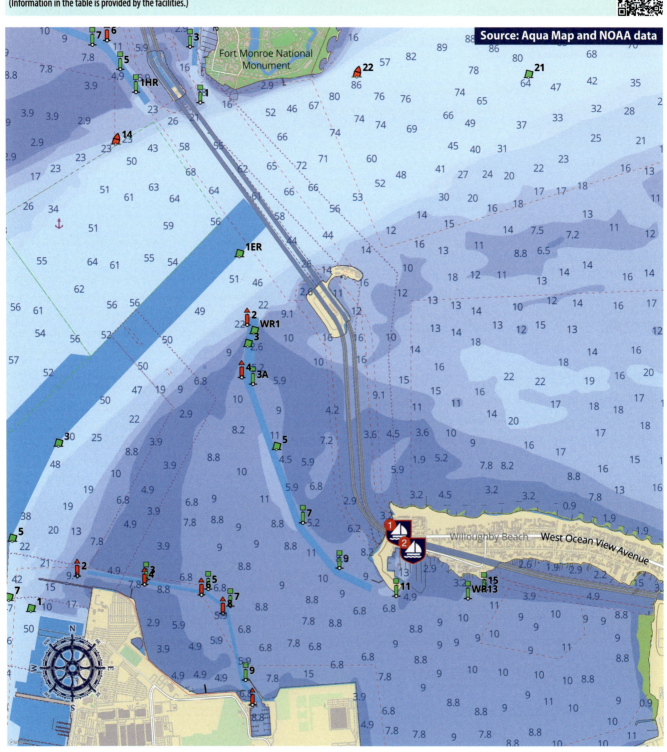

Source: Aqua Map and NOAA data

Back on the Hampton River the private Hampton Yacht Club recognizes reciprocity from other yacht clubs. Call for details. Note that the tour boat to Fort Wool uses the slip next to the Visitor's Center so don't pull in there.

The 60-slip Customs House Marina is convenient to downtown and welcomes transients (if space is available). Next door is the all-transient The Docks at Downtown Hampton. Both offer all the usual amenities plus marine services and supplies on site or within walking distance.

Anchorage: There are several anchorage opportunities on the Hampton River. One is at Cedar Point just north of where Sunset Creek joins the Hampton River at Mile 196.2. The Sunset Creek-Cedar Point anchorage has good holding in 7 to 8 feet MLW in mud but is open to the northeast, south and ICW wakes. Another is opposite the downtown public docks (Hampton River Downtown). Boats may anchor anywhere past red daybeacon "20" on the red-marker side of the channel. Use your depth sounder to find the best spot. Do not block traffic or interfere with the private marina or with the city dock. This is not a "designated anchorage area" so be sure to use appropriate day-shape and anchor lights.

Boats that can get under the 29-foot fixed vertical clearance of the Settlers Landing Bridge at the end of the channel can find good anchorage on the Hampton River north of the 29-foot fixed vertical clearance Settlers Landing Bridge in 8 to 10 feet MLW with good holding and plenty of swing room. As always, exercise caution in shoal areas.

The City of Pheobus on Mill Creek between Fort Monroe and Hampton Roads Bridge-Tunnel has a 96-foot fixed pier with a 60-foot-floating dock to encourage boaters to anchor and then bring their dinghies to shore and visit the downtown area. Shopping, restaurants and a theater are a short walk. The well-established anchorage is open enough to have a breeze in hot weather and protected enough to cut the breeze and waves in a southwest wind.

Willoughby Bay

A less crowded and less protected layover than Hampton is available at Willoughby Bay on the opposite (south) side of Hampton Roads behind Willoughby Spit (where the Hampton Roads Bridge-Tunnel ends).

> NOTE: Helicopters from the highly active Norfolk Naval Air Station airport on the southern shore of Willoughby Bay conduct practice exercises over the water. All mariners are required to remain well clear of the helicopters, the towed devices and the area extending directly behind the aircraft for 400 yards. Do not approach or cross the area directly behind the towed device as a submerged hazard exists regardless of whether the device is in motion or stationary.

NAVIGATION: Two marked channels take you into Willoughby Bay between Willoughby Spit and Sewells Point. The Navy-maintained South Channel by Sewells Point is in a restricted area near the carrier piers. Use the North Channel near the bridge-tunnel to enter Willoughby Bay. Be prepared for strong currents at the entrance by Fort Wool.

When entering the North Channel, stay clear of the lighted green wreck buoy "WR1" and use flashing red "2" as the entrance point. Give the green markers a wide berth, especially green daybeacons "3" through "7." Backsight the channel often as it is shallow to the east and you can easily drift out of line.

> *CAUTION:* The USACE has reported shoaling in Willoughby Channel to 2.6 feet MLW in the vicinity of Willoughby Channel Buoy 3.

Dockage: Rebel Marina and Willoughby Harbor Marina are located on the north side of Willoughby Bay on Willoughby Spit and both have slips reserved for transients. You will need transportation for extensive provisioning or other shopping. (Rebel Marina has a courtesy car.) The biggest draw is the convenient access to the Chesapeake Bay and a spectacular 7-mile stretch of sandy beaches.

Anchorage: Anchor holding in Willoughby Bay past the marina complex (just past the entry on the north side of the bay) is good in approximately 10 feet MLW but watch for submerged, marked pilings and crab markers in the area. In addition to reported debris on the bottom, an unmarked telephone cable crosses this area. Anchor with care.

Chapter 1: Hampton, Norfolk & Portsmouth, VA

NORFOLK & PORTSMOUTH

Norfolk Harbor

NAVIGATION: Even with all its commercial and military activity, navigating through Norfolk Harbor is relatively easy during daylight hours. If southbound from Hampton Roads, pick up the marked channel past Sewells Point at the western end of Willoughby Bay and continue on into the Elizabeth River. Southbound past Sewells Point you will see a great array of naval vessels to the east, from aircraft carriers to submarines. The harbor itself begins at Craney Island (where you should switch to NOAA Small Craft Chart 12206).

No Wake Zones, Idle Speed Zones and various Speed Limit restrictions are in effect throughout the waterways included in this chapter. Exercise diligence in knowing the regulations by observing signs and other markers. Enforcement is always present. As always, be courteous to other vessels and avoid manatees and other marine life.

At night navigation can be a bit more difficult with all the illumination ashore making aids to navigation more difficult to detect. You will be much happier and enjoy the sights a lot more traveling in daylight. As in other large harbors it is recommended you run alongside or outside the marked channel if ship traffic is heavy. Depths alongside the channel are good. The main hazard is flotsam, which can be in the form of wooden planks or piles the size of telephone poles.

If you choose to run outside the channel, use the western side until you are past the Norfolk Naval Base and port operations to the east. Patrol boats and security barriers line the Restricted Area on the eastern side of the channel. From Craney Island southward remain inside the channel to avoid shallows and military or port facilities.

The Western Branch of the Elizabeth River leads off to starboard to the south of the bend in the main channel at Lamberts Point. Note the magenta restricted area on the NOAA chart east of Lovett Point on your approach to Western Branch. The 45-foot fixed vertical clearance **West Norfolk Bridge** located just west of Lovett Point makes it

Elizabeth River, VA

LAFAYETTE RIVER

		Largest Vessel	VHF	Total Slips	Approach/Dockside Depth	Floating Docks	Gas/Diesel	Repairs/Haulout	Min/Max Amps	Pump-Out Station
1. Norfolk Yacht and Country Club-PRIVATE WiFi	(757) 423-4500	100		200	11.0 /	F	GD		30 / 50	P

WiFi Wireless Internet Access
Visit www.waterwayguide.com for current rates, fuel prices, website addresses and other up-to-the-minute information.
(Information in the table is provided by the facilities.)

Scan here for more details:

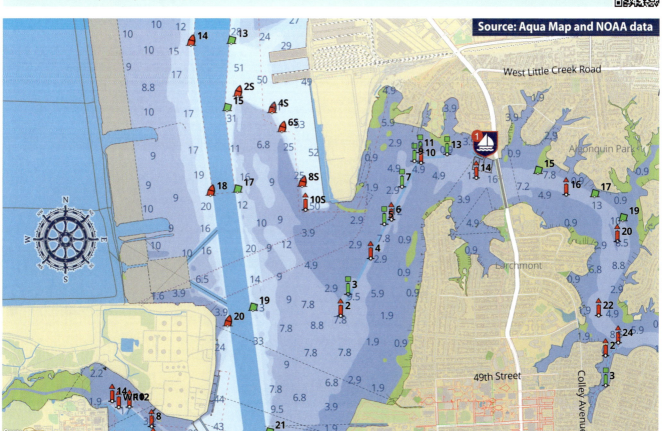

Source: Aqua Map and NOAA data

impossible for some sailboats to pass farther upstream. Those who can clear the fixed bridge will find depths of 15 to 20 feet all the way to the **Churchland (High Street) Bridge** with a 38-foot fixed vertical clearance.

Elizabeth River quick flashing red buoy "32" (which may be shown as "36" on charts) just east of Hospital Point marks Mile 0 and the beginning of the 1,243-mile-long Atlantic ICW. South of the Western Branch junction on the western side of the main Elizabeth River channel is Hospital Point, home to the nation's oldest and largest naval hospital. Beyond that are the sprawling cities of Norfolk and Portsmouth.

The current can be strong here and discourteous boaters may throw a wake that will roll you so be aware and prepared. Expect less current as you proceed from ICW Mile 0 southward. Heavy commercial traffic, bridge schedules and lock openings can also sometimes cause marked delay in arrival time so planning ahead is a good idea before proceeding southward.

Dockage: Norfolk Yacht and Country Club on the Lafayette River is private but recognizes reciprocity from some other clubs. There is a dress code for the dining areas so plan accordingly.

Anchorage: You can drop the hook directly across from Norfolk Yacht and Country Club and just outside the channel between red daybeacons "10" and "14" on the Lafayette River. For boats that can clear a 24-foot fixed vertical clearance Hampton Boulevard Bridges, additional anchorage is available farther up the river in 8 to 9 feet MLW with ample swing room and protection.

MID-ATLANTIC EDITION

Chapter 1: Hampton, Norfolk & Portsmouth, VA

NORFOLK, VA

ATTRACTIONS

1. Armed Forces Memorial
Unique display that tells a story through examples of letters written home by servicemen and women who subsequently died in action. A good time to visit is in late afternoon, when warm light and long shadows highlight the messages, each one borne on cast bronze sheets and displayed as though strewn across the plaza at Town Point Park by the wind.

2. Chrysler Museum of Art
Esteemed museum with broad (30,000 works) collection of ancient to contemporary art including glass and sculpture at 1 Memorial Place (757-664-6200). Also offers demos, talks, performances and classes.

3. Harbor Park Stadium
Home of the Norfolk Tides, a AAA farm team for the Baltimore Orioles known for its outstanding water views from the stands (757-622-2222).

4. MacArthur Center
Three stories of department stores, small shops, restaurants and a theater complex within walking distance to waterfront at 300 Monticello Ave. (757-627-6000).

5. MacArthur Memorial Museum
This learning center and theater celebrates the life and achievements of Gen. Douglas MacArthur and is a tribute to those who served in WWI, WWII and the Korean War. Located downtown next to the MacArthur Center mall at 198 Bank St. (757-441-2965). Admission is free.

6. Nauticus & Battleship *Wisconsin*
Maritime museum at 1 Waterside Dr. with science exhibits, an aquarium and the *Wisconsin BB-64*, an iconic battleship used in World War II and Korean War. Open for public tours and included with admission to museum. The Iowa Class Battleships were the largest and last battleships built before the Navy switched to aircraft carriers. Call 757-664-1000 for operating hours and information.

7. Wells Theater
Restored Beaux Arts landmark that opened in 1913 as a vaudeville theater. Home of the Virginia Stage Company (108 E. Tazewell St., 757-627-1234).

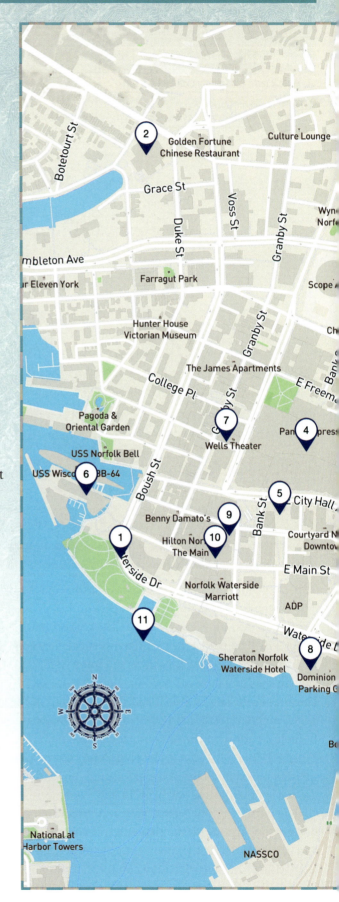

America's Waterway Guide Since 1947 — **Chapter 1**

Norfolk, home of the world's largest naval base, has roots that begin at the waterfront and are entwined with it throughout history. Boaters continue to arrive daily at the waterfront, where they can tie up within walking distance of many of the City's must-see attractions. As in most larger cities, you will have no problem locating and accessing provisions and entertainment. Hampton Roads Transit connects with destinations beyond downtown and with all the cities in the Hampton Roads area via bus, light rail and ferry. Call 757-222-6100 or visit gohrt.com for details.

Public transportation can get you to the Norfolk Botanical Garden, a 175-acre garden filled with over 40 themed gardens and includes a butterfly house, a children's garden and a rose garden (6700 Azalea Garden Rd., 757-441-5830). The Virginia Zoo should also be on your list. This 53-acre zoo is home to over 500 animals from around the world, including lions, tigers, and giraffes (3500 Granby St., 757-441-2374).

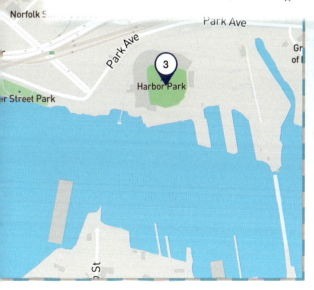

SERVICES

8. Norfolk Post Office
999 Waterside Dr. #114
(757-640-0044)

9. Solver Library
235 E. Plume St. (757-431-7491)

10. Visit Norfolk
232 E. Main St.
(800-368-3097)

MARINAS

11. Waterside Marina
333 Waterside Dr.
(757-625-3625)

MID-ATLANTIC EDITION

Chapter 1: Hampton, Norfolk & Portsmouth, VA

Elizabeth River, VA

NORFOLK		Largest Vessel	VHF	Total Slips	Approach/Dockside Depth	Floating Docks	Gas/Diesel	Repairs/Haulout	Min/Max Amps	Pump-Out Station
1. Waterside Marina WiFi	(757) 625-3625	240	16	50	45.0 / 20.0	F		R	30 / 200+	P
PORTSMOUTH										
2. Portsmouth Boating Center WiFi MM 0.0	(757) 397-2092	80	16	40	8.0 / 10.0		GD	RH	30 / 50	P
3. Tidewater Yacht Marina WiFi MM 0.4	(757) 393-2525	300	16	300	12.0 / 11.0	F	G		30 / 200+	P
4. Ocean Yacht Marina WiFi MM 1.0	(757) 321-7432	350	16	122	45.0 / 30.0	F	GD		30 / 100	P

WiFi Wireless Internet Access
Visit www.waterwayguide.com for current rates, fuel prices, website addresses and other up-to-the-minute information. (Information in the table is provided by the facilities.)

Scan here for more details: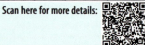

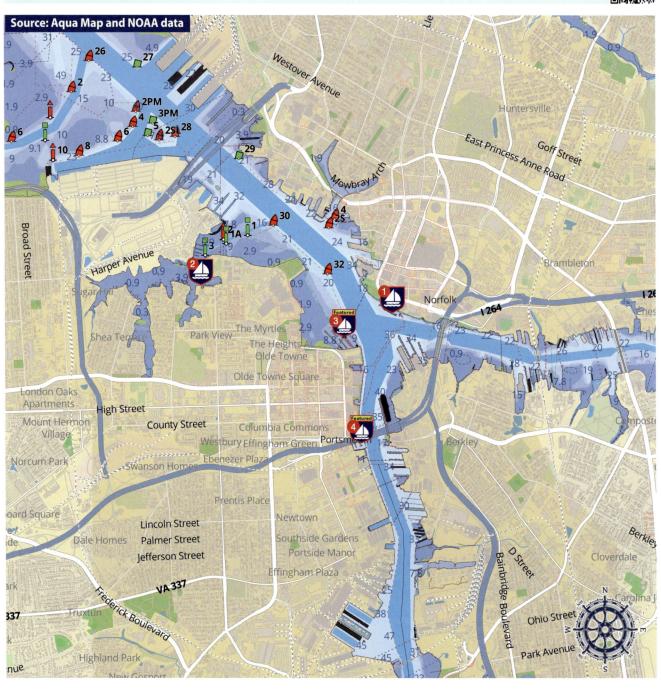

Source: Aqua Map and NOAA data

City of Norfolk

For two centuries Norfolk has been a Navy town and to this day it is flanked on north and south by ships in gray livery. Well before the U.S. Navy was established, merchant ships and sailors called Norfolk home and cargo vessels of all types with international crews still call to load, discharge and undergo repairs.

With a population approaching 250,000, Norfolk is the second largest city in Virginia. (Virginia Beach is the largest with almost 450,000.) It is not surprising that Norfolk supports many of the cultural and recreational outlets associated with bigger cities. It has a symphony orchestra, several museums, professional sports teams and a downtown shopping mall full of high-end retail stores.

Dockage: There is a wave screen directly in front of the 50-slip Waterside Marina to provide protection for vessels moored there. The all-transient facility has floating slips with access to restrooms and showers. Overnight slip holders can get transportation for provisioning arranged by the dockmaster on request. Waterside Marina is part of the City of Norfolk's Waterside District, which has undergone a multimillion dollar renovation. The marina is well protected and within easy walking distance of downtown venues.

You may tie up for 2 hours at no charge at Nauticus if you are visiting the museum. They can only accept vessels to 35 feet that do not exceed 24-foot vertical clearance due to a walking bridge that spans the opening.

City of Portsmouth

Portsmouth has long served as a key point at the beginning or end of a passage through the ICW. For many years before the city began construction on the new face it now presents to the Elizabeth River, it was a place to only to take aboard fuel and provisions before running for the less threatening open spaces of the Bay or the ICW.

Today it is a destination worth exploring for its own sake. The waterfront area has been largely rebuilt and High Street is vibrant with commerce plus several museums and cultural centers.

America's largest warships and support vessels are often berthed in enormous floating dry docks undergoing refits directly across from Portsmouth. Shipyards and industrial piers stretch upstream as far as you can see. Towers of glass and concrete in Norfolk's

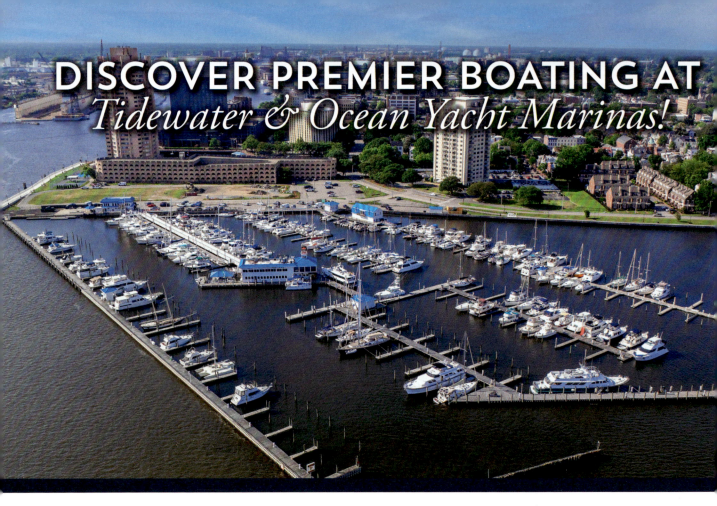

DISCOVER PREMIER BOATING AT
Tidewater & Ocean Yacht Marinas!

**MARINE STORE
ON-SITE RESTAURANT
FUEL DOCK WITH GAS & DIESEL
PUMPOUT FACILITY**

10 Crawford Pkwy.
Portsmouth, VA 23704
N 36° 50.483' W 076° 17.883
(757) 393-2525

Visit Tidewater Yacht Marina and Ocean Yacht Marina, where your boating experience is our top priority. Whether you're docking for a day, a week, or an extended stay, our marinas offer exceptional service and a warm welcome from our experienced, attentive teams. From the moment you arrive until your departure, enjoy top-notch amenities that ensure a safe, comfortable, and stress-free experience on the water!

**MARINE STORE
FUEL DOCK WITH GAS & DIESEL
PUMPOUT FACILITY**

1 Crawford Cr.
Portsmouth, VA 23704
N 36° 49.900' W 076° 17.760'
(757) 656-7644

business district loom above the harbor downstream. The river itself teems with traffic.

NAVIGATION: Located directly on "Mile 0" of the ICW, Portsmouth is a convenient location to regroup for the journey south or to recoup from the rigors of "the ditch" when heading north. Pedestrian ferry service to Norfolk is available at both North Landing Dock and High Street Landing. The 150-passenger Elizabeth River Ferry drops off and picks up every 30 minutes at the Waterside District in Norfolk for $2.00 (one way). There are discounts and multi-day passes available.

Dockage: Scott Creek is home to Portsmouth Boating Center, known for its high-speed diesel pumps and reasonable fuel prices. They offer all types of services, boat storage and brokerage, and slips to 80 feet.

Just to the south and directly opposite Norfolk's Town Point, the full-service Tidewater Yacht Marina welcomes transient boaters at Mile Marker 0. They offer marine facilities and services with an on-site restaurant, 22-acre protected basin, marine store, pump-out services, metered electric, free water, free WiFi and more. Boaters are offered a safe, secure and protected facility with eager staff available for docking.

Ocean Yacht Marina, a sister marina to Tidewater Yacht Marina, is 0.5 miles south with clean facilities, a professional and courteous staff and 122 wet slips that can accommodate vessels up to 250 feet. All slips have water, cable television, electricity hook-ups and boaters have access to showers, laundry room, fuel and pump-out systems.

This facility is adjacent to a large outdoor pavilion where big name entertainers regularly perform and to the Elizabeth River Ferry landing at High Street. The Olde Towne Portsmouth historic district is within walking distance.

Complimentary, short term mooring is available at High Street Landing for vessels 40 feet and under. Boaters are expected to complete the online mooring application before docking. City Code sets a maximum 36 hour limit, not to exceed 72 hours in a 30-day period. Call 757-393-8782 for a recorded message about mooring rules. There are no utilities.

High Street Landing is where the Elizabeth River Ferry drops off and picks up. Note that North Street Landing is no longer open for dockage.

Anchorage: Late arrivals and those who prefer to anchor normally use the harbor's small-boat anchorage (Hospital Point) south and west of the channel at flashing red buoy "36" between the large brick naval hospital and Tidewater Yacht Marina. Anchor in 8 to 9 feet MLW in mud. Holding is only fair so don't skimp on scope. Move to the north side of Hospital Point if strong winds are predicted. The anchorage is popular and usually holds numerous boats and crab pots in season.

The no-wake zone in the harbor keeps you relatively calm (other than occasional tug wakes or inconsiderate boaters) but strong winds in summer storms can funnel down the river.

Dinghy dockage and use of some facilities is available at the Tidewater Yacht Marina on the Portsmouth side for a fee. You can also take the dinghy to Waterside Marina on the Norfolk waterfront and make fast inside (for a small fee) if there is space.

Chapter 1
Hampton, Norfolk & Portsmouth, VA

Goin' Ashore
PORTSMOUTH, VA

Portsmouth was founded as a town in 1752 on 65 acres of land on the shores of the Elizabeth River. The town was founded by William Crawford, a wealthy merchant and ship owner. The 65 acres were part of Colonel Crawford's extensive plantation and were constituted as a town by an enabling act of the General Assembly of Virginia. The town was named after the English naval port of the same name, and many of the streets of the new town reflected the English heritage.

One of our favorite stops is the Bier Garden at 438 High St. featuring home-cooked German cuisine and over 400 beers from around the world. Eat inside or in the enclosed garden (757-393-6022). If you need more distractions, the Elizabeth River Pedestrian Ferry connects downtown Portsmouth across the Elizabeth River to the Norfolk waterfront. The 150-passenger ferry leaves from 1 High St. and from 6 Crawford St. (North Landing) and runs every 30 minutes (757-222-6100).

America's Waterway Guide Since 1947 — Chapter 1

ATTRACTIONS

1. **Children's Museum of Virginia**
   Busy museum offering hands-on exhibits for kids 1-11 exploring cities, space, music, energy and the human body, plus antique trains (221 High St., 757-393-5258).

2. **Commodore Theater**
   Art Deco-style theatre built in 1945 with fully-appointed dining room at 421 High St. Dine while watching first-run movies in this historical building listed on both the National Register of Historic Places and the Virginia Landmarks Register. Call ahead for schedules and reservations (757-393-6962).

3. **Lightship Portsmouth Museum**
   On the waterfront at the foot of High St. (757-393-8591) is a 1915 lightship turned floating museum with displays of historic objects, uniforms, photos and models. Nearby on the waterfront is a first-order Fresnel lens.

4. **Portsmouth Naval Shipyard Museum**
   Offers a unique perspective on U.S. history from Colonial to Civil War times and beyond. Ship models, uniforms, military artifacts and exhibits portray life from the 18th century to present day at 2 High St. (757-393-8591).

5. **Railroad Museum of Virginia**
   Open Friday and Saturday from 10:00 a.m. to 4:00 p.m. Located at Court and Wythe Streets. Call for ticket prices (757-335-2284).

SERVICES

6. **Portsmouth Post Office**
   431 Crawford St. (757-397-5852)

7. **Portsmouth Public Library**
   601 Court St. (757-393-8501)

8. **Portsmouth Visitor Information**
   6 Crawford Pkwy. (757-393-5111)

MARINAS

9. **Ocean Yacht Marina**
   1 Crawford Circle (757-321-7432)

10. **Tidewater Yacht Marina**
    10 Crawford Pkwy. (757-393-2525)

United States Lightship Portsmouth LV-101

MID-ATLANTIC EDITION

Chapter 1: Hampton, Norfolk & Portsmouth, VA

MILE 0: ELIZABETH RIVER

For southbound boats the first 200-mile-long stretch of the ICW between Mile 0 at Norfolk and Mile 205 at Morehead City/Beaufort, NC, presents a diverse array of navigational challenges while offering equally diverse natural beauty, fascinating sights, side trips and ports of call.

The route passes through a lock (or two depending on the route you choose), canals, land cuts and open-water sounds along the way. Some of the open water offers the challenges associated with long fetches, shallow depths and choppy wave action when the wind kicks up. Sailors may consider minimizing motoring time by sailing from sound to sound.

In much but not all of North Carolina (and sporadically in other ICW states) the Army Corps of Engineers has placed signs just outside the channel marking each 5-statute mile increment along the route. Note that the numbers on these signs do not necessarily correspond to the "Mile Markers" on the charts. Some are the same, some are different by a hundred yards or so and some by as much as a mile.

If you are using the actual signs to determine your location in relation to a timed bridge or marina location, you may find yourself a lot closer or farther away than you thought. It is best to use the charts for this information but make sure you have the most current edition.

> Reminder: All mileage on the ICW is measured in statute rather than nautical miles. (1 nm = 1.15 mile).

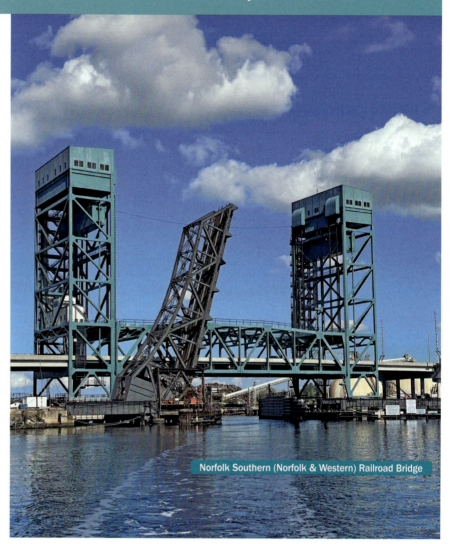

Norfolk Southern (Norfolk & Western) Railroad Bridge

You will traverse five bridges–three railroad bridges that are open unless there is an approaching train, one fixed bridge with a vertical clearance of 145 feet and the Gilmerton Lift Bridge with a closed height of 35 feet.

NAVIGATION: Beyond Mile 0 Town Point on the Norfolk side marks the mouth of the Elizabeth River's Eastern Branch. The Eastern Branch of the Elizabeth River curves around Norfolk's Waterside District to port, while the Southern Branch (ICW) bears to starboard around Portsmouth. Commercial traffic can be heavy in this area with tugs passing through and large commercial vessels maneuvering into and out of the docks. It is a good idea to monitor VHF Channel 13 and to call any tug or other vessel whose intentions are unclear. Sometimes listening is enough. Always yield to commercial traffic in this area.

CAUTION: Before reaching Town Point study your NOAA chart carefully. Many mariners mistakenly continue along the Eastern Branch thinking it is the ICW only to turn around 2 miles later when it dead ends. The ICW route follows the Southern Branch of the Elizabeth River.

Chapter 1
America's Waterway Guide Since 1947

Leave the large shipyard across from Portsmouth to port when heading south on the Southern Branch of the Elizabeth River. The Norfolk Naval Shipyard is farther along, also on the Portsmouth (west) side. As many signs warn, landings are not permitted. Navy and Coast Guard patrol boats guard the naval vessels docked along both sides of the river. (They don't like for you to take photos either.)

Proceeding southward you will encounter a 7-mile-long congested stretch with a 6-mph speed limit (enforced) and six bridges. Be sure to monitor VHF Channel 13, on which all commercial vessels communicate and bridge traffic is handled, as well as VHF Channel 16. Most bridges open promptly except during restricted hours. Northbound vessels leaving the lock at Great Bridge at the same time are usually required to bunch together for openings of all the bridges in this stretch, whether fast or slow, power or sail.

There are two railroad lift bridges on either side of the fixed 145-foot vertical clearance **Jordan Bridge–Belt Line Railroad Bridge** at Mile 2.6 and **Norfolk Southern (Norfolk & Western) Railroad Bridge** at Mile 3.6. Both are usually open but closures do occur. Note that a closed vertical clearance of less than 9 feet has been observed at the railroad bridge despite the published 10-foot clearance. The Belt Line Railroad Bridge is operated remotely and should be open unless a train is approaching.

CAUTION: Do not mistake St. Julian Creek at Mile 4.9 for the ICW. (This is easier to do northbound than southbound when it is just north and to port of the Gilmerton Bridge.) A 45-foot-high overhead power cable also crosses this creek. Beacons warning of the power cable were placed at the mouth of St. Julian Creek after several vessels were dismasted.

The **Gilmerton Bridge** (35-foot closed vertical clearance) at Mile 5.8 opens on signal except from 6:30 a.m. to 8:30 a.m. and from 3:30 p.m. to 5:30 p.m., Monday through Friday (except federal holidays), when the bridge need not open. The adjacent **Norfolk Southern #7 Railroad Bridge** is normally open.

It is important to note that the Gilmerton Bridge will not open unless the railroad bridge is open. Closings of the railroad bridge are announced on VHF Channel 13 and it is operated remotely with light, horn and audio signals when opening and closing. Be sure both bridges are open completely before you start through. There are times when there are multiple rail movements and #7 Railroad Bridge remains closed for long periods of time, even up to an hour or more. Communication with the remote bridgetender is difficult but the Gilmerton Bridge operator is sometimes helpful in providing information.

> **NOTE:** Vessels traveling northbound from Great Bridge Lock will usually be required to group together for the Gilmerton Bridge opening north of the lock.

Plan departures and arrivals carefully to avoid idling in river currents for up to 3 hours while waiting for bridge openings. These bridges are situated on a bend in the river and are hard to see until you are nearly upon them. Yield to commercial traffic and listen to the radio for their intentions. If you have any questions about their movement, contact them using VHF Channel 13 and be clear and direct in your communications.

Those traveling south from Norfolk on the AICW must now choose between two routes into North Carolina: either the Dismal Swamp Canal or the Albemarle–Chesapeake Canal, also known as the Virginia Cut. Each has its advantages, but careful consideration must be given to this decision. Both routes are described in detail in the following chapters.

The online Waterway Explorer, a free interactive web application for navigation, will be a "must have" on the waterways, regardless of which route your choose. Specific marina and anchorage information can be found as well as details on navigation alerts and cruising news. The site provides the ability to make updates, report hazards and read or write reviews on facilities. To help other boaters please take a moment to enter a rating and add any updates when you visit a marina or anchorage. You can also sign up for weekly news and navigation updates, delivered directly to your inbox.

Anchorage: Boats often anchor in 9 to 13 feet MLW all around the Gilmerton Bridge to wait out railroad bridge closures. Some stay all night (safely out of the waterway, of course).

MID-ATLANTIC EDITION   117

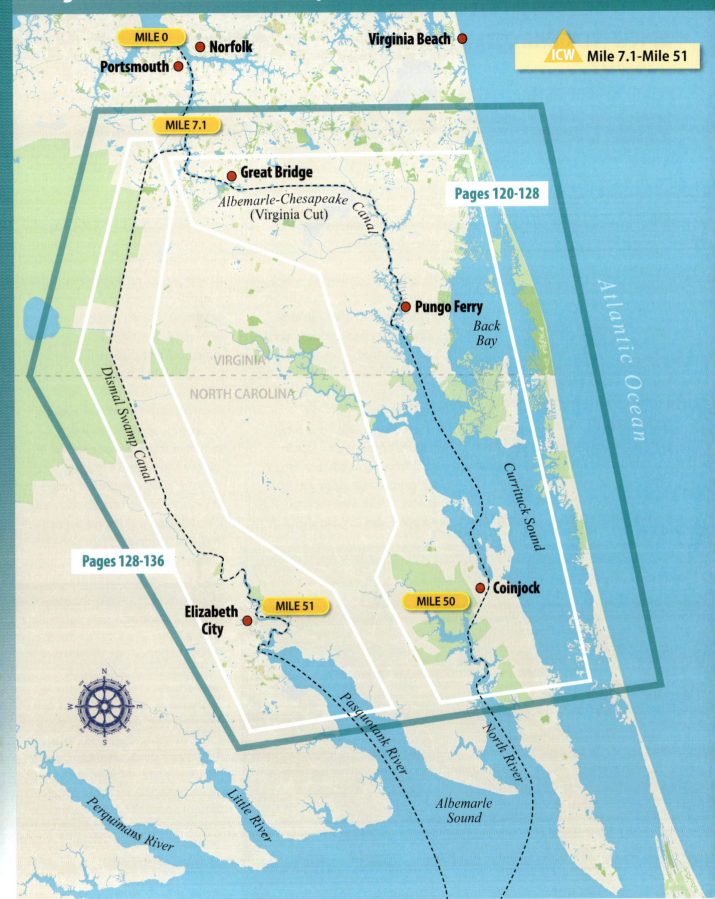

Chapter 2: Virginia Cut & Dismal Swamp Routes, VA/NC

■ ICW (VIRGINIA CUT) ROUTE

Great Bridge to North Landing– ICW Mile 7 to Mile 20

Virginia Cut, the primary ICW route, is well marked and always open for navigation. The Army Corps of Engineers ICW project depth is 12 feet with a channel width of 90 feet. This route begins almost east-west and then turns north-south. The fresh-to-brackish waters have no tide but they may rise or fall with the wind. A strong northerly lowers the water and southerlies can raise it, both by as much as 2 feet, so tie your lines as if you'll have that much tide. Take your time and enjoy the ride.

NAVIGATION: The 65-foot and 100-foot vertical clearance **I-64 Bridges** are at Mile 7.1. An opening for taller vessels requires 24-hours advance notice. The high-rise **Veterans Bridge** at Mile 8.9 has a fixed 95-foot vertical clearance. **The Great Bridge Lock** at Mile 11.7 is the only lock on this route. The lock raises or lowers boats 2 to 3 feet with little turbulence.

Delays can occur at Great Bridge Lock, especially during periods of heavy traffic. Many recreational craft lock through at once when traffic is heavy. Late arrivals should not push ahead if the line is long. The lock opens on the hour for northbound vessels and 20 minutes later for southbound vessels after releasing the northbound vessels. The lock coordinates with the **SR 168 (Battlefield Blvd.) Bridge** just east of the lock, which opens on the hour from 6:00 a.m. to 7:00 p.m. and on request at all other times. (They respond to "Great Bridge" on the VHF.)

The Great Bridge Lock is 600 feet long, 72 feet wide and can handle tows up to 530 feet long. Since commercial traffic has first preference in locking through, it is not a good idea to push ahead of a tug, as you will probably have to wait for the vessel once you arrive. Government and commercial vessels have precedence, while fuel barges and vessels transporting hazardous materials are locked through alone. The lockmaster monitors VHF Channel 13 (or call 757-547-3311) and can provide information on the route ahead if needed.

If the Great Bridge Lock cannot accommodate all the boats waiting and you are left behind, be prepared to wait for the next evolution, which is usually just before the top of the next hour. There is room to maneuver or even anchor short of the lock, but remember that there will be traffic exiting the lock heading towards you before you will be able to move so ensure that the travel way is clear.

Speed is severely limited in this stretch of water but care should be taken when tying up to allow for the surge of heavy commercial barges that sometimes come through this area. If tied up and waiting for the next bridge/lock opening, monitor VHF Channel 13 for instructions.

NO WAKE ZONE

A speed limit of 3 mph (actively enforced by the Virginia Marine Police) applies on the waterway until you are past the lock and bridge. It is a good idea to continue at that speed until you are well past the long face dock at Atlantic Yacht Basin on the south bank, east of the bridge. If you think you are about to miss the opening of the lock and bridge, do not speed. The bridgetender can delay the opening for 10 minutes if notified ahead of time on VHF Channel 13.

SR 168 (Battlefield Blvd.) Bridge

America's Waterway Guide Since 1947 — Chapter 2

The remainder of the canal has no speed limit but the standard rule applies here as elsewhere: You are liable for damage caused by your wake. If yours is a big boat remember to allow for the "canal effect," a tendency of the stern to swing in toward the bank in narrow waters.

The high-rise **Chesapeake Expressway (VA 168 Bypass) Bridge** crosses the channel at Mile 13.0. The **Albemarle & Chesapeake Railroad Bridge** at Mile 13.9 is usually open unless a train is approaching. **Centerville Turnpike (SR 170) Bridge** at Mile 15.2 opens on signal from 6:30 a.m. until 8:30 a.m. and between 4:00 p.m. and 6:00 p.m., Monday through Friday (except federal holidays). From 8:30 a.m. to 4:00 p.m. the draw need only open on the hour and half-hour. The drawtender may delay the opening by up to 10 minutes to accommodate approaching vessels. Call on VHF Channel 13 to announce your intentions.

The 5-mile distance between the Centerville Turnpike (SR 170) Bridge and **SR 165 (North Landing) Bridge** is slightly beyond the speed of most sailboats or slower trawlers to make neatly synchronized openings so you might as well take your time. The aging SR 165 (North Landing) Bridge has experienced numerous closures in recent years due to mechanical and electrical problems. You may want to call the bridge ahead of time at 575-482-3081 to check if it is operational.

Dockage: Transients to 65 feet are welcome at Top Rack Marina north of Veterans Bridge at Mile 8.8. Free mooring is offered for those who dine at the on-site Amber Lantern Restaurant, a fine-dining experience with sunset views from every seat in the house.

If you are heading north towards Norfolk, you can take advantage of Great Bridge Dock #1 on the south side of the canal between SR 168 (Battlefield Blvd) Bridge and the lock while you wait. You can tie up for up to 48 hours here or at Great Bridge Dock #2, which is beyond the bridge going south and on the north side of the canal at the Great Bridge Battlefield and Waterways Park, which pays tribute to the Battle of Great Bridge in 1773. The museum is well worth a visit and the guided trails are also very informative. The park is definitely pet friendly, and there is a Kroger Supermarket about one-quarter mile west on Battlefield Boulevard.

Vessels tied to the face docks on either side of the bridge should be prepared for possible commercial traffic and a rise and fall in the water level from the

Great Bridge: Locking Through

As you approach the lock, you will see either a red or a green signal light. Call the lockmaster on VHF Channel 13 to request an opening, but do not approach closer than 300 feet until the light turns green. Should your VHF call go unanswered, the horn signal for opening is two long and two short blasts. Even in cases where boats are already in line ahead of you for an opening, you should call the lockmaster and give him your boat name so that he knows how many boats are ready to lock through. If there are a lot of boats, he will direct who goes where on the lock walls.

Enter at idle speed with bow and stern lines and fenders ready to moor as directed by the lockmaster. If there are only a few boats to pass through, you will be directed to the north or (more likely) the south side of the lock. The rubber fender system on the south side of the Great Bridge Lock is excellent, which is why the lockmasters are now requesting that all recreational craft choose that side. There are cleats and bollards to loops lines around, but there are no lock attendants to help on this side. When there is an overload of recreational vessels, some will be asked to use the lock's north side. In this case, lock attendants will usually assist in getting your lines looped around the bollards.

Be aware that you will definitely need your own fenders and long dock lines when on the steel and concrete of the north side. Also, be prepared to tend your lines during the locking process, especially the stern lines as the stern may want to swing toward the center of the lock as the water level adjusts.

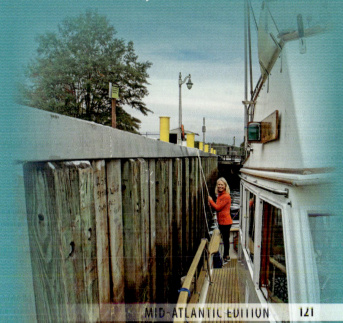

Chapter 2: Virginia Cut & Dismal Swamp Routes, VA/NC

Virginia Cut, VA

GREAT BRIDGE		Largest Vessel	VHF	Total Slips	Approach/ Dockside Depth	Floating Docks	Gas/ Diesel	Repairs/ Haulout	Min/Max Amps	Pump-Out Station
1. Top Rack Marina WiFi MM 8.8	(757) 227-3041	65	16	22	20.0 / 12.0	F	GD	R	30 / 50	P

WiFi Wireless Internet Access
Visit www.waterwayguide.com for current rates, fuel prices, website addresses and other up-to-the-minute information.
(Information in the table is provided by the facilities.)

Scan here for more details: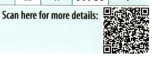

Source: Aqua Map and NOAA data

displacement effect of these vessels. It is not a good idea to leave your boat unattended at these docks. There are no facilities except trash receptacles at Great Bridge Dock #1 between the lock and the bridge.

Atlantic Yacht Basin, Inc. is a full-service boatyard with a well-stocked marine store just east of the SR 168 (Battlefield Blvd) Bridge. This facility's long dock is along the canal (be aware of your wake in this area) and a large, protected work and storage basin is behind the wharf. If the courtesy car is not available, both local supermarkets may give you and your groceries a lift to the boatyard but check with the cashier before you start shopping. There are many restaurants within a short walk from the marina and the town of Chesapeake is very visitor friendly.

GREAT BRIDGE BATTLEFIELD & WATERWAYS MUSEUM

Learn about the first major Revolutionary War armed conflict in Virginia and its impact on our quest for independence. Conveniently located at Mile 12 on the ICW with plenty of new dock space. Guided and Self Guided Tours Available.

Museum Hours:
Wednesday – Saturday
10 AM – 4 PM
Second Sunday of Each Month
1 PM – 4 PM
Sunday – Tuesday (except second Sundays)
CLOSED

Museum Admission:
General Admission - $8
Military (Active, Retired, Reserves) - $7
Seniors (65+) - $7
Youth (ages 6-17) - $5
Children (ages 0-5) - FREE
Rates subject to change.

757-482-4480 • www.gbbattlefield.org
1775 Historic Way, Chesapeake, VA 23320

Virginia Cut, VA

GREAT BRIDGE		Largest Vessel	VHF	Total Slips	Approach/ Dockside Depth	Floating Docks	Gas/ Diesel	Repairs/ Haulout	Min/Max Amps	Pump-Out Station
1. Atlantic Yacht Basin, Inc. WiFi MM 12.2	(757) 482-2141	120	16	200	12.0 / 10.0		GD	RH	30 / 100	P

WiFi Wireless Internet Access
Visit www.waterwayguide.com for current rates, fuel prices, website addresses and other up-to-the-minute information.
(Information in the table is provided by the facilities.)

Scan here for more details:

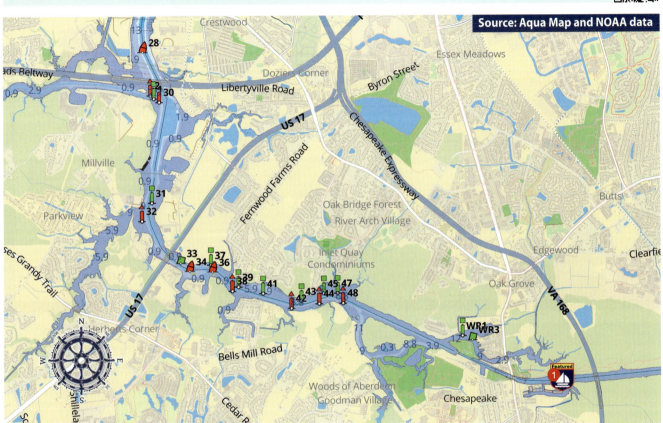

Source: Aqua Map and NOAA data

North Landing River–ICW Mile 20 to Mile 41

About 8 miles beyond Great Bridge the heavily wooded and sparsely populated land cut leads into the headwaters of North Landing River. Recreational boat traffic increases significantly during the transient seasons in fall and spring. The cut is narrow in some areas making it almost impossible for three vessels to pass through at once. Be mindful of other vessels and not just your own schedule. Wakes are especially dangerous in narrow channels.

Over the years wakes have eroded the banks leaving wide shallows off the channel with stumps just below the surface. What looks like a small limb might actually be attached to a tree trunk suspended just below the surface. Give any suspect debris a wide berth. Be aware that barges and tugs use the cut and often travel at night, lighting up the area and leaving behind a rolly wake.

NAVIGATION: The North Landing River winds leisurely southward with a dredged channel cutting through its widening waters. Watch the channel markers in the lower Virginia stretch of the river as shoals tend to encroach from the banks. The route leaves Virginia and enters North Carolina at Mile 34 between flashing green "61" and green daybeacon "63."

Pungo Ferry (SR 726) Bridge has two tide boards on both sides of the bridge showing the charted 65-foot vertical clearance. Some sailboats, however, have reported less than 64-foot clearance here after a south wind. If in doubt contact the authorities or obtain local knowledge before proceeding. (We suggest hailing northbound vessels for tide board readings.)

During the summer the beach north of the bridge is usually full of swimmers, knee-boarders and swarms of personal watercraft so proceed slowly.

Chapter 2: Virginia Cut & Dismal Swamp Routes, VA/NC

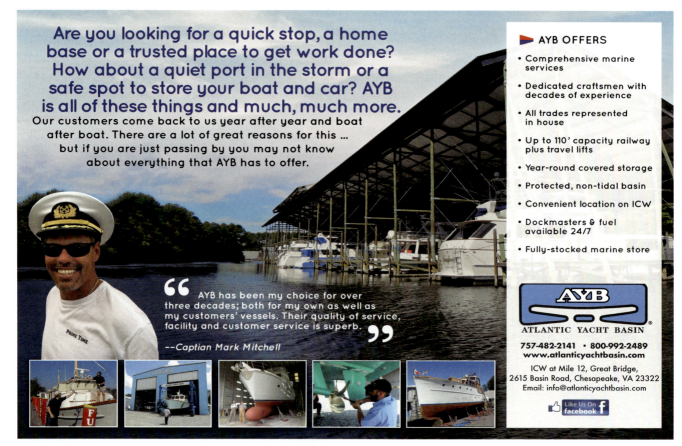

The area on either side of the Pungo Ferry Bridge at Mile 28.7 is a posted No-Wake Zone, from the location of the now-defunct Pungo Ferry Marina immediately north of the spans through the bridge fenders to the south. Be sure to travel through this area at idle speed; it is frequently patrolled by the local authorities.

Anchorage: All along North Landing River to the Pungo Ferry (SR 726) Bridge you will notice side sloughs and bypassed bends of the river, which look like secluded anchorages. Do not be tempted! All these old river loops are either silted in or may have spoil banks, submerged pilings or wrecks across them.

You can anchor at North Landing River just north of red daybeacon "32" and about 50 feet west of the ICW channel. Expect 7 feet MLW immediately outside the channel. Don't anchor too close to the shoal west of the daybeacon.

The old landing has been removed but the piling are still in place and in good condition at Pungo Ferry Landing at Mile 28.5. There is 10 feet MLW at the pilings parallel to the river with 8 feet along the perpendicular pilings. Expect some noise during the daytime when Navy jets fly over from NAS Oceania (Virginia Beach). There is limited space at Pungo Ferry Bridge with 5-foot depths.

Pungo Ferry Landing Park provides shore access via small floating docks and boat ramp. It is located on the east shore in the small channel across from the anchorage.

Just south of Mile 30 to starboard heading south Blackwater Creek offers a fair-weather anchorage with good holding. Enter North Landing River between that tiny marsh island and flashing red "46." A shoal of 4 to 5 feet MLW has been reported at the entrance. The charted point shown on the north side at the entrance is usually under water with just a couple of tufts of grass showing. Favor the southern bank on entering.

If you can navigate the narrow entrance you should find 6- to 10-foot MLW depths once inside and up the creek. Expect local outboard-powered boats rushing up and down the creek on weekends. Winds from the north quadrant can blow the water out of the creek and leave vessels firmly aground. There is little swinging room for boats longer than 35 feet.

Currituck Sound–ICW Mile 42 to Mile 49

NAVIGATION: This stretch is generally placid but Currituck Sound can develop an unpleasant chop. There is little tide but strong winds can affect water levels and create stiff currents. Government snag-boats check the cuts periodically but keep a look-out for floating debris.

Once in Currituck Sound observe intermediate daybeacons carefully. A hedge of submerged pilings on the east side protects the narrow, dredged channel and a beam wind from the west can push you right up on them. These may be closer to the marked channel than indicated by the NOAA chart. This stretch is subject to shoaling. It is important to stay in the center of the channel and to check astern (as well as ahead) to track your progress.

The centerline channel is charted to carry 12 feet MLW. Prolonged strong northerly winds will lower the depths here by as much as 2 or 3 feet but tugs and barges drawing more than 9 or 10 feet regularly transit this sound with few problems.

While the most recent NOAA chart depicts marker "91" (Mile 40) as a daybeacon, it is actually a small can. Also in this area be alert for the ferry from Currituck, which crosses the ICW on its route to Knotts Island. The narrowest and most difficult part of this stretch is between flashing green "111" and flashing red "118." Wind-driven current will also try to push you out of the channel throughout Currituck Sound.

> *CAUTION:* Shoaling to 3 feet MLW has been observed halfway into the channel at Mile 44.6 by flashing green "111." Favor the red side of the channel at the turn by red daybeacon "112" for 10 feet MLW.

Coinjock to Albemarle Sound–ICW Mile 49 to Mile 65

About 1 mile south of shallow Coinjock Bay the quiet hamlet of Coinjock (at Mile 50) is centered on a particularly lonely stretch of the ICW. This is a popular and welcome stop for those in need of a secure place to rest, plug in, take on reasonably priced fuel and restore basic supplies.

Coinjock, named by the Indians for the berries still growing in the area, includes a hardware store, barbershop and Post Office.

Welcome to North Carolina!

You are now in NC waters. Here you will encounter small towns, quiet anchorages and the first of the shoal spots on the ICW. The waters off Cape Hatteras are known as the "Graveyard of the Atlantic" due to the deceptively shallow water offshore here. Cape Lookout and Cape Fear to the south are delightful ports that—like the rest of the Outer Banks—are best visited from the protected inside (ICW) route with its combination of rivers, canals, bays and sounds.

Weather is a critical consideration. The best time to cruise through NC is spring and fall, and you'll have plenty of company. Hurricane season is June 1 through November 30 with a peak from early August through the end of October. Since 1851, a total of 47 hurricanes have made direct hits in the NC coast. As always, be aware of the weather around (and ahead of) you.

Important Note: It is an NC requirement that the owner or operator of a vessel that has a Marine Sanitation Device (MSD) and is in coastal waters that are either designated as a no-discharge zone or are included in a petition to the U.S. EPA to be designated as a no-discharge zone, must maintain a record of each pump-out of the MSD and the location of the pump-out facility. The no-discharge zone begins at New River Inlet and extends to the SC border. It includes the ICW and adjacent and offshore waters. See details at www.deq.nc.gov.

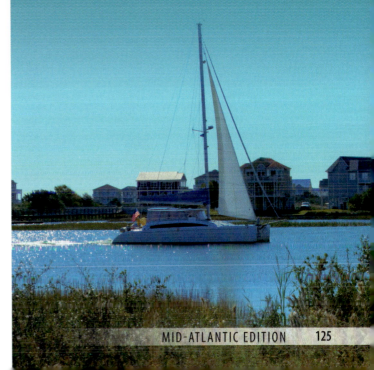

Chapter 2: Virginia Cut & Dismal Swamp Routes, VA/NC

North Carolina Cut, NC

COINJOCK

	Largest Vessel	VHF	Total Slips	Approach/Dockside Depth	Floating Docks	Gas/Diesel	Repairs/Haulout	Min/Max Amps	Pump-Out Station
1. Coinjock Marina & Restaurant WiFi MM 50.0 (252) 453-3271	150	16	24	12.0 / 12.0		GD	R	30 / 100	P

WiFi Wireless Internet Access
Visit www.waterwayguide.com for current rates, fuel prices, website addresses and other up-to-the-minute information. (Information in the table is provided by the facilities.)

Scan here for more details:

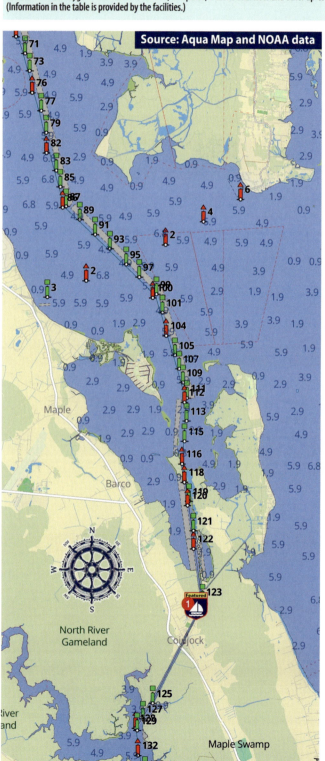

Source: Aqua Map and NOAA data

NAVIGATION: Watch for submerged logs or stumps in the channel in the stretch of Coinjock Bay between Long Point and the entrance to the North Carolina Cut, especially in the narrow cut at Long Point (near quick flashing red "116"). Vessels regularly report obstructions in the vicinity of flashing red "116" at Long Point. The boat ramp on the east side of the North Carolina Cut can be very busy on weekends.

At Mile 49.9 just south of the marinas you pass beneath the **Coinjock (US 158) Bridge**, a high-level fixed span with a 65-foot vertical clearance.

Check the current before tying up at the marinas in Coinjock. Although there is no tidal rise and fall here, the current is wind driven and can be strong. The wind funnels up and down the cut and the strongest current will be with northerly or southerly winds. When leaving, do not forget to check the direction and speed of the current and carefully plan how you are going to leave. It is often more difficult getting off the dock in the morning without issues than it was docking the evening before.

Heavy fog can be an occasional problem in the morning, especially in the fall, although it usually burns off by 9:00 a.m. The route from Coinjock through the upper North River follows a winding but well-marked channel. Be sure to stay in the center of the narrow dredged stretch between flashing red "128" and red daybeacon "132" as it is very shallow outside the channel. Groundings occur here frequently.

Continuing south the river becomes wider and deeper finally reaching Camden Point and the approach to Albemarle Sound. Fish stakes extend from Buck Island southward to flashing green "155."

Dockage: A helpful dock crew will guide you when you tie up at Coinjock Marina & Restaurant. There is a popular restaurant on the premises and an outdoor deck where you can dine with waterfront views. The marina's wide 1,200-foot-long dock provides quiet, secure dockage with all the expected amenities including a modern bathhouse and laundry.

COINJOCK
MARINA & RESTAURANT

Restaurant Dock House

Friendly Service Welcoming the Transient Yachtsman!

- "World Famous" Dockside Restaurant "Home of the 32 oz. Prime Rib"
- Local Fresh Seafood Lounge w/Full ABC Permit Open Lunch and Dinner- Everyday
- Wireless Internet & Buoy Update, email, FedEx Divers, and Airport Transport
- Premium Fuel at Discount Price with high speed pumps
- Best and Most Experienced dock hands on the ICW
- Air Conditioned Bath House
- 1200' Easy Alongside Docking with fast at slip fuel

- Dock with 240/120 Volt 100/50/30 AMP Single and 3 Phase
- Brand new Ships/Grocery Store - charts, clothing, shoes, beer, wine & specialty homemade items - jams, pickles, nuts, etc.
- Laundry and ATM on site
- New covered outdoor seating

(252) 453-3271
for reservations or call on VHF 16
321 Waterlily Road Coinjock, NC 27923

Visit us at www.coinjockmarina.com,
or email us at marina@coinjockmarina.com

Selected The **Best Marina** to Tie Up & Chow Down by POWER & MOTORYACHT

Chapter 2: Virginia Cut & Dismal Swamp Routes, VA/NC

Mechanics are on call. There is also a well-stocked convenience store. Fuel prices here are always competitive.

Marine facilities and secure berths are scarce along this stretch of the ICW so this facility fills up rapidly during the fall and spring transient seasons. Be prepared to be tightly packed in bow to stern and during busy times you may be asked to let a boat tie up alongside. Making an advance call for reservations by phone or on VHF Channel 16 is advised.

Anchorage: Several North River anchorages offer good holding and reasonable protection depending on wind direction. Due east of quick flashing green "153" (around Mile 56.5) there is good shelter during a southerly blow with 7- to 8- foot MLW depths with good holding in mud at Buck Island–North.

Boats drawing more than 5 feet should check charts carefully to avoid shallower areas north of the anchorage area. Southeast of Buck Island there is ample anchorage room in 7- to 9-foot MLW depths with good holding in mud and good protection from the east and northeast (Buck Island–South).

Due west of quick flashing red "164" (Mile 61), North River - Broad Creek affords excellent protection in virtually all conditions and carries 7-foot MLW depths. Once beyond the mouth of the creek boats drawing more than 5 feet should proceed slowly with an eye on the depth sounder as there have been reports of an uncharted shallow spot. In westerly winds it is possible to comfortably anchor off the mouth of Broad Creek if it is crowded or if you are too deep-drafted or large to go all the way in.

> NOTE: From the end of March through the end of October, North River is (in)famous for hatches of "non-biting aquatic midges" locally known as "fuzzy bills." After hatching they cover the entire surface of your boat while making their way into engine spaces through vents. When they die, they leave a greenish goo and desiccated corpses in cracks and crevices, which you will be finding for the rest of your boating life.

Our Cruising Editor, who has encountered the fuzzy bills in this area twice and is still finding carcasses in the engine room and lazarette, suggests tying up at Coinjock Marina and ordering prime rib.

THE DISMAL SWAMP CANAL ROUTE

The Dismal Swamp Canal, steeped in history and natural beauty, offers a tranquil and enchanting route for boaters traversing the Southern Branch of the Elizabeth River at mile 7.1 of the ICW.

George Washington first proposed draining the swamp in 1763 to harvest the timber (cypress for shipbuilding and cedar for shingles) and then farm the land. He and other prominent businessmen purchased 40,000 acres of the swamp land and Washington supervised the digging of the ditch from the swamp to Lake Drummond, today known as Washington Ditch.

In 1909, a lumbering company purchased the swamp land and continued to harvest virgin timber until they cut the last tree down in the 1950s. In 1973, the Union Camp Company donated its swamp holding to create the Great Dismal Swamp National Wildlife Refuge.

Today, recreational boaters cruise past a number of historical sites on the Dismal Swamp Canal. The Dismal Swamp Welcome Center, Dismal Swamp State Park and Dismal Swamp Canal are all recognized as being designated sites on the National Park Service National Underground Railroad Network to Freedom.

It is a beautiful, unspoiled waterway and one of the prettiest on the whole ICW, while also offering the considerable benefit of being easier to transit compared to the narrow, busy, and frequently wind-driven Virginia Cut. The canal is fed primarily by freshwater drainage from Lake Drummond and its feeder system.

> NOTE: Boaters on the Dismal Swamp Canal follow the same course as James Adams' Floating Theatre, which inspired Edna Ferber's 1926 novel, *Showboat*.

Navigation Notes

As you pass under the 65-foot and 100-foot vertical clearance I-64 Bridges southbound, turn right at Deep Creek to begin your journey. A sign on the west side at the entrance of the Dismal Swamp Canal provides essential navigation details such as the lock schedule, controlling depths and operational status. Information about the status of the Dismal Swamp Canal is also available from the Army Corps of Engineers at 757-201-7500 (option 3) or from the Dismal Swamp Canal Welcome Center (877-771-8333).

America's Waterway Guide Since 1947 — **Chapter 2**

Dismal Swamp Canal

CAUTION: The Deep Creek Bridge, located in Chesapeake Virginia at the northernmost point of the Dismal Swamp Canal, is being replaced. The bridge is owned and operated by the Norfolk District Army Corps of Engineers. The repair project is currently scheduled to extend through September of 2026. Various construction operations will be taking place daily adjacent to and within the canal throughout the duration of the replacement project and may impact those transiting the waterway. Additional notices will be released on Waterway Explorer prior to any major impacts. For questions or concerns, please contact the Atlantic Intracoastal Water Way Project Manager, Zack Ware, from the Army Corps of Engineers Norfolk District at (757)633-5749 or Zachary.t.ware@usace.army.mil.

Note that in summer and fall, the Dismal Swamp Canal and Turners Cut channel experience heavy levels of duckweed, a small native aquatic plant that can aggressively spread in the right environmental conditions. The duckweed is located on the water surface in large mats and can be transported from one waterway to another. Duckweed has been known to clog sea strainers, resulting in overheating of marine engines and could possibly cause other mechanical problems.

Vessels that wish to avoid the duckweed should transit the Albemarle and Chesapeake Canal through the Great Bridge Lock in Chesapeake, Virginia. This lock will be open 24 hours per day, 7 days per week. Lock Operators monitor VHF Channel 13.

NO WAKE ZONE

As a rule, skippers using this route are more interested in seeing the magnificent countryside than in making fast time. There is no speed limit here, but you are responsible for your wake. "No Wake" signs are posted in the canal proper in a stepped-up effort to reduce the problem of bank erosion. Regardless of restrictions, common sense dictates slow speed through the canal.

Chapter 2 Virginia Cut & Dismal Swamp Routes, VA/NC

Great Bridge to Turner Cut

NAVIGATION: From the sign at ICW Mile 7.3, the Dismal Swamp route heads off west of the ICW. The Deep Creek land cut leads to Deep Creek itself and the Deep Creek Lock, which introduces you to the Great Dismal Swamp Canal. The distance is approximately 51 miles from Norfolk to Elizabeth City, but the distance does not have to be covered in one day. Birds, reptiles, winged insects and bears inhabit this unique primeval forest. (Use screens and cover up before entering the canal during the summer months.)

Deep Creek Lock (Mile 10.4) raises you 8 feet in elevation, while **South Mills Lock** (at Mile 32.8) lowers you the same amount. At both locks, boats must furnish and tend their own lines. Be sure to have plenty of line and watch your stern, which may want to swing toward the center during the locking process. When the locks are open, the tenders will ask the draft of each vessel and warn those with drafts of more than 5 feet that they may proceed only at their own risk.

Openings at **Deep Creek Bridge** at Mile 11.1 (4-foot closed vertical clearance) are coordinated with the Deep Creek Lock. Vessels are allowed to moor overnight in the canal. If you plan to stay on the newly rebuilt dock between the bridge and the lock, it is courteous to notify the lockmaster on VHF Channel 13 and let him know your intentions.

The locks at Deep Creek opens four times daily (unless low water levels cause restricted openings) at 8:30 a.m., 11:00 a.m., 1:30 p.m. and 3:30 p.m. Boats entering the canal are locked first, meaning at Deep Creek Lock, southbound boats are locked first; at the South Mills Lock, northbound boats are locked first. For boats leaving the canal, the lock openings may be delayed while the entering boats are locked through. Prepare to wait before the bridge, in that case. The lockmasters do double duty as bridgetenders and open the adjacent bridges so you will have to wait for them to drive from the lock to the bridge.

> NOTE: To run the Dismal Swamp Canal in a single day, a boat traveling at a maximum of 6 knots should enter the Deep Creek Lock at either the 8:30 a.m. or 11:00 a.m. opening. The passage to South Mills Lock is 22 miles. Once through South Mills, it is 18 miles to Elizabeth City.

While narrow and unmarked, Deep Creek presents no unusual problems, unless there is an extremely low water, in which case there may be a little over 5-foot depth. Travel at a reasonable speed and do not be misled by the nice-looking side waters; they are extremely shallow. Keep to the center of the main stream and give points a good berth, as shoaling is chronic.

The Army Corps of Engineers has placed small pipe markers, white with a red top, along every mile of the Dismal Swamp Canal, indicating statute mileage from Norfolk. At about Mile 23, there is a sign marking the beginning of a measured nautical mile.

From Deep Creek, the Dismal Swamp Canal reaches south in two arrow-straight stretches. The feeder ditch from Lake Drummond intersects the canal toward the end of the first of these at Mile 21.5. The Dismal Swamp Canal has minimum 6-foot depths as long as there is adequate water in Lake Drummond. This route no longer carries commercial traffic except from below South Mills (Mile 32) to Elizabeth City (Mile 50), so the stretch north of this is not as carefully maintained as it once was.

> *CAUTION:* The Army Corps of Engineers regularly cleans the ICW and clips overhanging tree limbs. Nevertheless, proceed through this area with extreme caution. Report dead heads or obstructions to lockmasters or the Visitor Center and the Corps will get out and tend to them. If you encounter a maintenance barge, you may have a wait, as there is not always ample room to pass.

We have received reports that the farmer who owns land on both sides of the canal at Mile 20.9 has permission to slide a portable steel bridge back and forth to get his livestock and farm equipment across the canal. This bridge (3 feet above the waterline) is normally only in place long enough for the farmer to accomplish his task. Be patient if the waterway is blocked when you get there. For help with this bridge call the Visitors Center (252-771-8333).

> NOTE: At Mile 21.5, the Lake Drummond feeder ditch intersects the canal. If your schedule allows, you can travel the 3 miles up to Lake Drummond in a boat 16 feet or less and with a draft that is less than 3 feet. At the head of the feeder ditch, there is a free rail trolley for carrying boats less than 1,000 pounds (including dinghies) over a small peninsula into Lake Drummond.

There is a pontoon bridge south of the Visitor's Center dock at Mile 28 that allows visitors to access the Dismal Swamp State Park on the opposite side of the canal. **Dismal Swamp Canal Visitor Center Foot Bridge** is generally kept in place for pedestrians to cross and opened whenever a boat approaches. After hours, the bridge is left open for late/early boat traffic. Call 252-771-6593 or VHF Channel 13 should you need an opening. If heading south and planning to stop at the Visitor's Center dock, a courtesy call to the bridgetender will prevent an unnecessary opening.

The fixed **U.S. 17 Hwy. Bridge** crosses the Dismal Swamp Canal at Mile 32.5 with 65-foot vertical clearance. South Mills Lock at Mile 32.5 opens at 8:30 a.m., 11:00 a.m., 1:30 p.m., and 3:30 p.m. and coordinates with the South Mills Bridge at Mile 32.3 (4-foot closed vertical clearance). An average of 2,000 recreational boats pass through the South Mills Lock annually.

Dockage: Inside the canal, on the west side in Deep Creek Lock Pond at Mile 10.7, you will find a long, wooden dock south of the locks and north of the bridge with 8-foot depths (except at the far north end). Known locally as Elizabeth's Dock, this landing is popular with crews wanting to transit the canal the morning after a late-afternoon locking. Restaurants and shopping are nearby.

South of the Deep Creek Bridge at Mile 11.1 is a 75-foot Deep Creek Bulkhead (Chesapeake, VA). An Auto Zone, Food Lion, Arby's (fast food) and 7-11 are short walks from the bulkhead.

Between Miles 18 and 19, the parks department maintains Douglas Landing, a fixed wharf running alongside the canal for 70 feet and then another 30 feet after a jog, as a part of a hike and bike trail. There are restrooms available.

At Mile 21.5, there is a small dock across from the Lake Drummond Feeder Ditch, which is available to cruising mariners, compliments of the Army Corps of Engineers. Rafting is permitted here. There are no recommended anchorages on this route so you may wish to take advantage of these stops.

The Dismal Swamp Canal Welcome Center (Mile 28) offers an 150-foot wharf running parallel to the canal. There are no slips but there is space for three or four boats to tie directly to the dock. Additional boats will raft up so be prepared to have neighbors. Power and water are not available at the dock, but clean restrooms and a water fountain are available. This is a highway rest stop as well as a State Park. The staff monitors VHF Channel 16 or can be reached by phone at 252-771-8333.

You will find a friendly atmosphere here, with charcoal grills and picnic tables, bike trails with rental bikes, and a nature trail. Keep an eye out for bears, bobcats, snakes and other such "locals." If you decide to spend the night here, take time to visit the Dismal Swamp State Park Museum. It is a 3-minute walk from the dock and provides an interesting history and facts on the area (and it's air conditioned).

If you continue on through the South Mills Bridge, you may be able to find an overnight spot along the west bulkhead at South Mills between the lock and the bridge, with about 7-foot MLW depths reported alongside a corrugated steel wall with good cleats along the middle third. There is a convenience store just west of the bridge and a family grocery store about 1 mile farther west.

Dismal Swamp Canal

Chapter 2: Virginia Cut & Dismal Swamp Routes, VA/NC

Turner Cut to the Pasquotank River

South Mills is the place to check your time and decide whether to lock through or to stay put for the night. It is 18 miles to Elizabeth City, and the winding, narrow, unmarked headwaters of the Pasquotank River are hazardous to run after dark. In the daytime, the tall cypress and mistletoe-festooned gum trees give the upper Pasquotank a wild and eerie splendor. Here you will see some of the most undisturbed and natural cruising grounds on the entire ICW.

NAVIGATION: Follow the straight Turners Cut about 3 miles, where it joins the Pasquotank River. About 4 twisty miles farther the river straightens and gradually widens as markers begin to appear. Note that you are now going downstream in a river marked from seaward: Keep green to starboard (markers have yellow triangles).

The first marker, green daybeacon "19," shows up suddenly around a sharp bend near Mile 41. Give all points along this route a fair berth, especially where Turner Cut enters the Pasquotank River and watch for floating debris.

Give tows all the room you can in the narrow, straight area of Turner Cut and in the twisting upper Pasquotank River. When encountering a tow, slow down or stop, hug the bank and allow the tow as much room as possible.

At Mile 47.5, the manually operated Norfolk Southern Railroad Swing Bridge (3-foot closed vertical clearance) is usually left in the open position. If the bridge is closed, the bridgetender will answer to horn signals. The narrow opening is difficult to see until you are almost on top of it.

Anchorage: After transiting the canal, there are several welcome anchorage possibilities on the Pasquotank River before reaching Elizabeth City. The first, at Mile 43, is behind Goat Island - North at green daybeacon "13" with good holding in 8- to 10-feet MLW with room for several boats. There is a small kayak dock nearby where you can land a dinghy.

At Mile 45.8 you can anchor in the Pasquotank River with good holding and ample swing room out of the channel. This scenic anchorage offers easy in and out with very little traffic in morning and evening.

Another anchorage is located in the deep water of Camden Causeway Cove at Mile 48. Depths here are deeper than the 9 feet MLW shown on the charts; it is, however, open to wakes.

Pasquotank River (Elizabeth City)

From the Dismal Swamp Canal Route, you emerge in Elizabeth City. Here you will find convenient dockage, friendly people and lots to see and do.

NAVIGATION: Remember that you are proceeding downstream in a river marked from seaward: Keep green to starboard. (River markers have yellow triangles.) The U.S. 158 Hwy. Bridge ((locally known as the Elizabeth River Bridge) at Mile 50.8 opens on signal, except from 7:00 a.m. to 9:00 a.m. and from 4:00 p.m. to 6:00 p.m., Monday through Friday, when the draw need only open at 7:30 a.m., 8:30 a.m., 4:30 p.m., and 5:30 p.m. if vessels are waiting to pass. Call the bridgetender on VHF Channel 13 once the fast-opening bridge comes into view.

NO WAKE ZONE

The No-Wake Zone along the city is strictly enforced with a 6-mph speed limit.

Dockage: Well-protected Lamb's Marina at Mile 47.2 on the Dismal Swamp Canal north of Elizabeth City has the only fuel in the area. They also have an on-site convenience store and a café. PVC pipes mark the entrance channel and fairway leading to the turning basin next to the fuel docks.

Mid-Atlantic Christian University has slips with short finger piers as well as a 150-foot dock with 20-foot depths for side ties and is free for up to 48 hours. Wind, wake, and wave protection is excellent. There is potable water available but no power. Call Dan (336-681-0575) for slip availability. The school opens its facilities to boaters including on-campus meals at very reasonable prices. This area is often used as an alternative to the Elizabeth City town docks when strong east to south winds make those docks uncomfortable.

Jennette Brothers' Bulkhead is a food distribution company with a dock with room for about four boats. Sign a release in the office. They request that you patronize a local restaurant in exchange for free dockage. (This should not be a problem.)

Depending on your direction, the town docks in Elizabeth City at Mile 51 mark the beginning or end of your trip through the Dismal Swamp Canal. Mariners' Wharf, Elizabeth City is right in the downtown area with 14 transient slips offered on a first-come, first-served basis.

Pasquotank River, NC

ELIZABETH CITY AREA

		Largest Vessel	VHF	Total Slips	Approach/Dockside Depth	Floating Docks	Gas/Diesel	Repairs/Haulout	Min/Max Amps	Pump-Out Station
1. Lamb's Marina WiFi MM 47.2	(252) 202-4150	65		60	8.0 / 8.0		GD		30 / 50	

WiFi Wireless Internet Access
Visit www.waterwayguide.com for current rates, fuel prices, website addresses and other up-to-the-minute information.
(Information in the table is provided by the facilities.)

Scan here for more details:

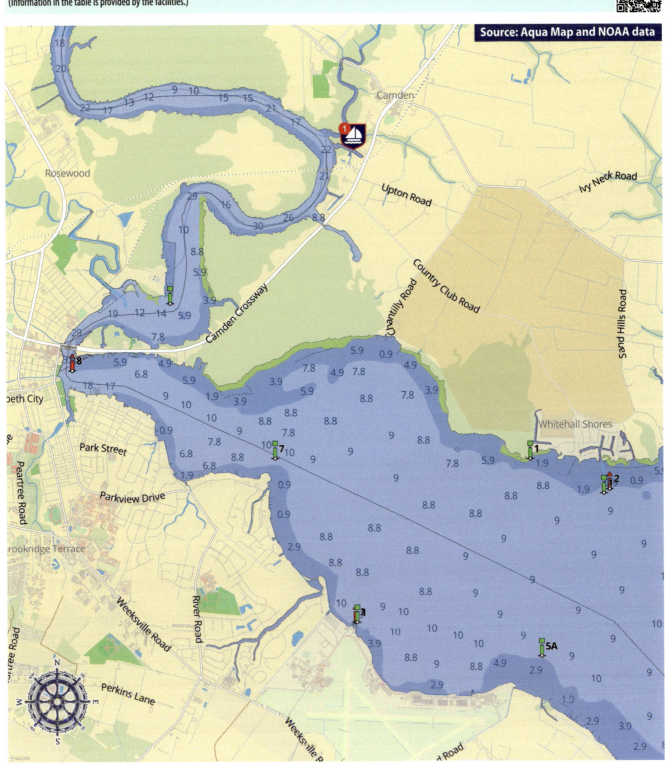

Source: Aqua Map and NOAA data

Chapter 2: Virginia Cut & Dismal Swamp Routes, VA/NC

GOIN' ASHORE

ELIZABETH CITY, NC

ATTRACTIONS

1. **Arts of the Albemarle**
   Showcases fine art and traditional crafts from both regional and local artists at 516 E. Main St. (252-338-6455).

2. **Downtown Waterfront Market**
   Held weekly May through July on Saturdays (plus some weekends in September). Great place to pick up lunch and enjoy the waterfront view at Mariners' Wharf Park (252-330-8050).

3. **Ghost Harbor Brewing Co.**
   Housed in an early 1900s era horse stable on historic Pailin's Alley (602 E. Colonial Ave., 252-340-4643). Serving a variety of beer brewed on site with names like Blood Magick (cherry mango gose) and Time in the Sun (American IPA). They do not serve food but encourage guests to bring to-go orders from local restaurants.

4. **Moth Boat Park**
   Pays tribute to the Moth Boat, an 11-foot one-design sailboat designed here on the corner of Water St. and Main St. Moth Boat Regatta takes over the city's harbor in September.

5. **Port Discover**
   Interactive science center for kids of all ages at 611 E. Main St. Call for hours and fees (252-338-6117).

6. **Visitor Information/Museum of the Albemarle**
   Located in the Museum of the Albemarle (501 S. Water St., 252-335-1453). Over 700 artifacts, covering 400 years of local history and stories of the Native Americans, colonists, farmers and fishermen who settled in the Albemarle region (501 S. Water St., 252-335-1453).

SERVICES

7. **East Albemarle Regional Library**
   100 E. Colonial Ave. (252-335-2473)

MARINAS

8. **Mariners Wharf**
   707 E. Fearing St. (252-335-5330)

America's Waterway Guide Since 1947 — Chapter 2

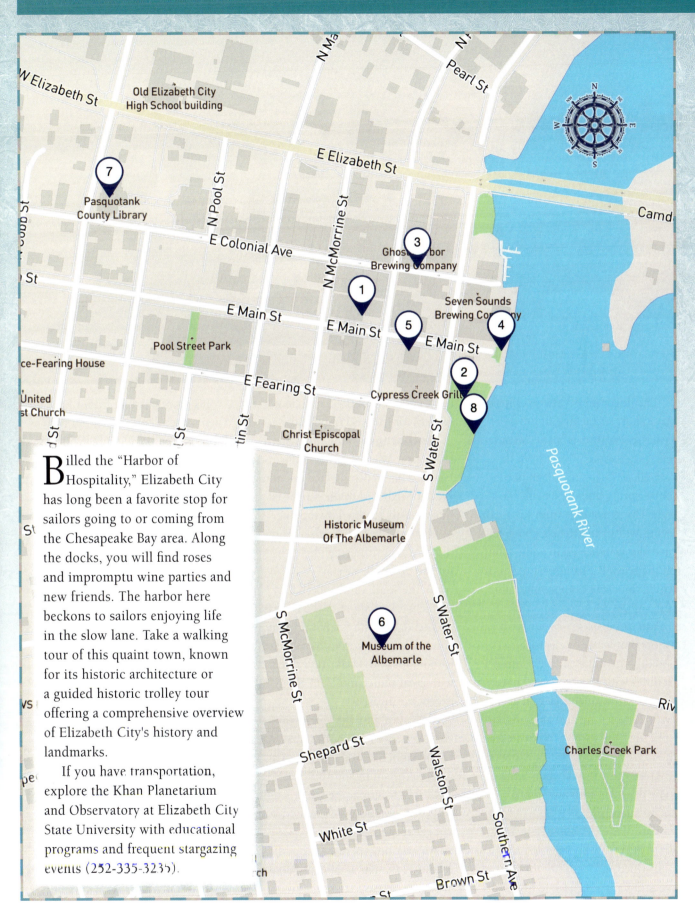

Billed the "Harbor of Hospitality," Elizabeth City has long been a favorite stop for sailors going to or coming from the Chesapeake Bay area. Along the docks, you will find roses and impromptu wine parties and new friends. The harbor here beckons to sailors enjoying life in the slow lane. Take a walking tour of this quaint town, known for its historic architecture or a guided historic trolley tour offering a comprehensive overview of Elizabeth City's history and landmarks.

If you have transportation, explore the Khan Planetarium and Observatory at Elizabeth City State University with educational programs and frequent stargazing events (252-335-3235).

Chapter 2: Virginia Cut & Dismal Swamp Routes, VA/NC

Pasquotank River — Elizabeth City

The finger piers between slips are quite short so backing in provides easier access from a boat. The outer pilings are about 35 feet from the seawall, so larger boats will need to use spring lines to stay off the wall. The slips range from 11 to 18 feet in width, and the clearance for each slip is indicated in white paint on the seawall. Strong east to south winds can cause an uncomfortable surge at the dock.

You can dispose of your trash ashore, but water or electrical hookups are not available. Comfort facilities with restrooms and hot showers are available as well as free WiFi. Bicycles are available on loan from Visit Elizabeth City, located at the nearby Museum of the Albemarle (400 S. Water St.). There is a place to tie dinghies, although there are no attendants.

East of the city slips there is a short steel seawall dedicated to the U.S. armed services with the flags of every branch of service flying. Boats docking here will need sufficient fenders for the steel bulkhead.

Anchorage: Along the eastern shore near Mile 49 is Machelhe Island. This well-protected anchorage is a little exposed to the northeast that is easily rectified by moving to the north side of the river. Some minor wakes from small boats headed up and down the river.

To the south of Elizabeth City on the western shore of the river is an anchorage with 8 feet MLW and good holding at Forbes Bay. There is room for 6 to 8 cruising vessels with great protection from any wind except northeast.

Directly across the Pasquotank River is a cove at Chantilly that is just within sight of Elizabeth City. This is open to the south and southeast but a good spot to stop if the wind is light and you need more breeze than you can get at the free docks.

An easy dinghy ride to the Mid-Atlantic Christian University docks makes for an easy walk into town.

It's a straight shot from Elizabeth City to the Albemarle Sound with a few fair-weather anchorage options along the Pasquotank River including Bateman Shores just south of the Elizabeth City Coast Guard Air Station (west shore) and Wharf Bay on the east shore at Mile 64. This anchorage offers 8 to 11 feet MLW with good holding and some protection from the north and east. The river's mouth is spacious, with fair holding in hard mud and makes a good stop when winds are from the east or west.

Because of the long fetch, anchorages could be choppy in a strong southeast wind, especially near the mouth of the river. Make sure your anchor is set well. You will be accompanied by a lot of crab pots and the friendly crabbers who stop by to check them. Depths are suitable for anchoring in the coves upriver and the scenery is lovely for those who don't mind the long trip to the upper reaches.

Side Trip: The Albemarle & Roanoke Sounds, NC

Chapter 3

Chapter 3 — Side Trip: The Albemarle & Roanoke Sounds, NC

■ THE ALBEMARLE SOUND

The Albemarle Sound runs east to west and covers 50 miles from Kitty Hawk on the Outer Banks to Edenton at the mouth of the Chowan River. This is a delightful sailing and boating destination with many small towns along the numerous rivers and creeks.

It is important to note that an east or west wind can stir the relatively shallow waters of Albemarle Sound into a short, nasty chop, making conditions uncomfortable and sometimes dangerous. Many a prudent skipper has holed up on either side of Albemarle Sound for days waiting for the weather and seas to calm down before making the crossing.

Albemarle Sound compensates by offering some picturesque and peaceful cruising waters in the tributaries along its banks. Several of these are deep and easy to enter with many good anchorages.

> NOTE: Many of the marinas and municipal docks participate in the Albemarle Loop promotional campaign, which offers free dockage at several of these facilities for up to 48 hours. Call ahead for details.

Perquimans River (Hertford)

The Perquimans River is home to historic Hertford, NC. A port of entry as early as 1701 Hertford's records go back to a 1685 deed book. You can visit the restored Newbold-White House said to be one of North Carolina's oldest brick houses as well as other historical sites.

Learn more at the Hertford with an informative Visitor Center, impressive museum honoring professional baseball player Jimmy "Catfish" Hunter and a corner drug store with double dips of ice cream at the fountain. See more at Visit Perquimans.

NAVIGATION: Four miles to the west of green daybeacon "1L" at the mouth of Little River lies the Perquimans River and historic Hertford. Navigation is fairly straightforward up the well-marked Perquimans River. Start your approach at flashing red "2P" just south of Reed Point and then head northwest into the river, making sure to honor the markers positioned at most of the points. Eight- to 11-foot MLW depths prevail in the river proper.

The US 17/NC 37 Bridge just east of town on the Perquimans River is locally referred to as the Jim "Catfish" Hunter Bridge. The fixed 33-foot vertical clearance bridge is followed by the North Church Street (Bus 17) Swing Bridge (7-foot closed vertical clearance), which opens on request. Call on VHF Channel 13 or 252-426-7241 from 8:00 a.m. to midnight (seasonal hours).

Dockage: Adjacent to the public boat ramp the 9-slip Hertford Bay City Dock can accommodate transient vessels to 35 feet. Free electric, pump-out service and water are available with dockage. The marina is located one block from the historic downtown with restaurants, shops, a hardware store and a convenience store with groceries. The town manager suggests that boaters contact the town office prior to arrival at the marina at 252-426-1969.

Anchorage: About 8 miles west of the Pasquotank River Entrance Light flashing green "1PR" (or 14 miles from flashing green "173" at the North River), off the north side of Albemarle Sound, you will find the entrance to Little River. Little River is easy to enter. The entrance is marked by green daybeacon "1L" and there is a platform to its northwest. Watch for fish net stakes. Depths in the river run 8 to 10 feet MLW but be wary of the shoals that extend from Mill and Stevenson Points at the entrance. The remainder of the river is unmarked.

The abundance of good anchorages makes Little River a natural place where groups of boaters can rendezvous. There is a good anchorage (despite a southeast exposure and a lot of crab pots) about 1 mile past Mill Point on Little River. The holding ground is fair in 7 to 9 feet MLW in the Perquimans River, less than halfway between the river entrance and Hertford, and you can dinghy ashore. Here you will find 9 to 11 feet MLW with a soft mud bottom.

Yeopim River

NAVIGATION: The Yeopim River is 6 miles west of the mouth of the Perquimans River. Enter the river from flashing green "1" and then follow the private aids northward to Albemarle Plantation. The approach to the dock is easy but pay attention to the marks. Also be aware that there are lots of crab pot buoys in the area.

Dockage: Albemarle Plantation Marina off the entrance channel to the Yeopim River welcomes boaters to visit this beautiful boating and golfing community. The 166-berth marina sells competitively priced gas and diesel and amenities include a free laundry, saltwater pool and fitness center.

America's Waterway Guide Since 1947

Chapter 3

Albemarle Sound, NC

PERQUIMANS RIVER		Largest Vessel	VHF	Total Slips	Approach/ Dockside Depth	Floating Docks	Gas/ Diesel	Repairs/ Haulout	Min/Max Amps	Pump-Out Station
1. Hertford Bay City Dock	(252) 426-7805	35		9	11.0 / 11.0				30 / 50	P
YEOPIM RIVER										
2. Albemarle Plantation Marina **WiFi** 10.0 mi. W of MM 75.0	(252) 562-1087	92	16	166	6.0 / 7.0		GD		30 / 50	P

WiFi Wireless Internet Access
Visit www.waterwayguide.com for current rates, fuel prices, website addresses and other up-to-the-minute information.
(Information in the table is provided by the facilities.)

Scan here for more details:

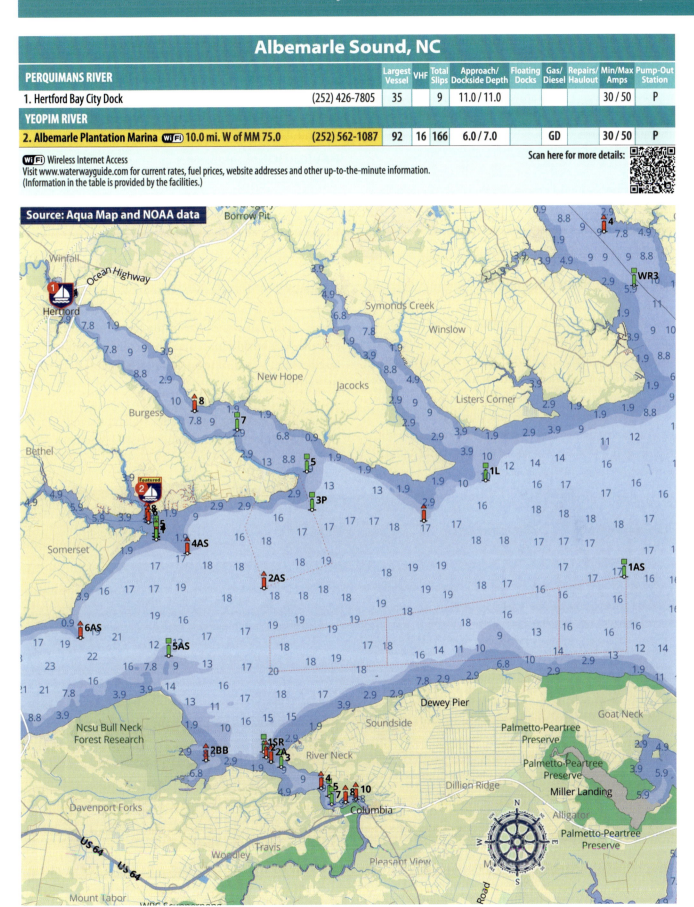

Source: Aqua Map and NOAA data

MID-ATLANTIC EDITION   139

Chapter 3 — Side Trip: The Albemarle & Roanoke Sounds, NC

Clubhouse Restaurant offers fine dining and beautiful views. The more casual Dockside Café has a large deck with both screened and open areas and the menu includes wood-fired pizza. The award-winning Sound Golf Links are open to visiting boaters. Call 252-426-5555 to arrange a tee time.

Anchorage: The Yeopim River offers a good anchorage in protected waters (from all directions except east). Tuck in behind Drummond Point for protection from all but east winds. Water depths are 5 to 7 feet MLW once you have cleared the well-marked entrance channel. Mind the depth sounder carefully.

The Chowan River (Edenton)

Edenton is a delightful side trip from the ICW. Largely unscathed through the Revolutionary and the Civil Wars, Edenton maintains many historic colonial buildings while also being a thriving small town. There's a nice trolley tour as well as a well-designated walking tour and a Visitor's Center, located next to the marina, is a great place to start your exploration. The welcoming atmosphere and short entrance makes this a good destination while exploring the western reaches of the Albemarle Sound.

Three miles west of Edenton Bay the wide mouth of the Chowan River opens up with the picturesque river swinging northward for many undeveloped miles. The shores with their high wooded banks are especially scenic. These inland freshwater rivers offer many miles of delightful cruising.

NAVIGATION: Cruising west on Albemarle Sound toward Edenton you will pass under the fixed high-rise **Albemarle Sound Bridge** (65-feet fixed vertical clearance). Overhead power lines farther upriver have a 94-foot minimum vertical clearance in the marked channel.

Once you have passed the power lines, watch for flashing red "2" leading into Edenton. Reedy Point on the west side of Edenton Bay hosts submerged fish stakes as well as the taller ones seen throughout the area. The entrance is a broad funnel and the channel here is well marked with a controlling depth of 5.5 feet MLW past the turning basin.

Should you feel like exploring, the Chowan River carries 12-foot depths for 80 miles beyond the high-rise **U.S. 17 Bridge** at Emperor Landing and Edenhouse

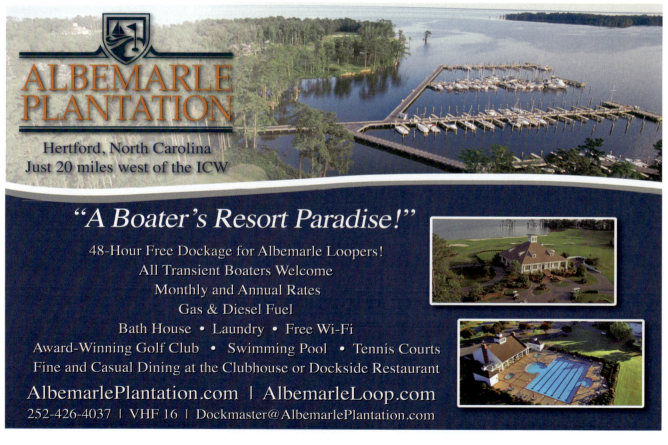

Albemarle Sound, NC

EDENTON		Largest Vessel	VHF	Total Slips	Approach/Dockside Depth	Floating Docks	Gas/Diesel	Repairs/Haulout	Min/Max Amps	Pump-Out Station
1. Edenton Harbor (WiFi)	(252) 337-4488	130	16	10	7.5 / 7.5				30 / 100	P
2. Edenton Marina	(252) 482-7421	85		107	6.0 / 8.0		GD		30 / 50	

(WiFi) Wireless Internet Access
Visit www.waterwayguide.com for current rates, fuel prices, website addresses and other up-to-the-minute information.
(Information in the table is provided by the facilities.)

Scan here for more details:

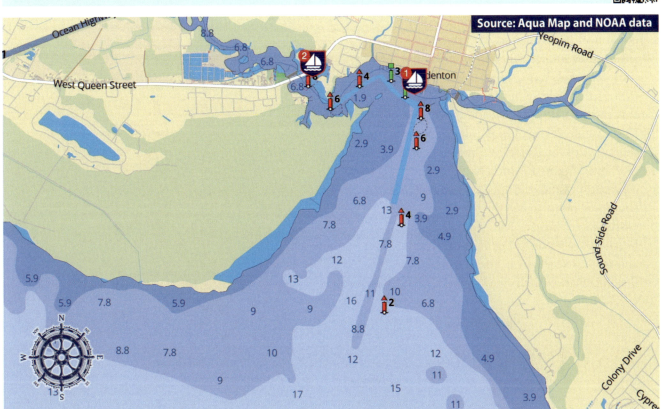

Source: Aqua Map and NOAA data

Point. It is interrupted by a 33-foot fixed vertical clearance U.S. 13 Bridge located 32 miles upriver at the town of Winton. Snags dictate caution, especially in the bend around Holiday Island.

Beyond Winton, near the mouth of the Meherrin River, skippers need to exercise caution in the Parker's Ferry area. Do not pass any cable ferry until it has reached the other side of the river and its cables have dropped.

There is no public dockage but there is a boardwalk that can accommodate dinghies. A short walk will bring you to the courthouse, restaurants, banks and convenience stores. The real attraction is the journey–beautiful scenery, abundant wildlife and quiet anchorages. Look for old ballast piles at creek entrances from the days that the Chowan River was a major trading link.

Dockage: At green daybeacon "1" the municipal Edenton Harbor has a total of 10 slips so reservations are strongly recommended. The marina has just completed a complete rebuild (2023) and is reported to be in full working order for boats up to 60 feet in length. Located in the heart of the historic downtown, this is a stop not to be missed.

Dockage is also available at Edenton Marina up Pembroke Creek before the 5-foot fixed vertical clearance W. Queen St. Bridge. The approach seems daunting due to the shallow water depths, but it's straight forward. Stay in the middle for best depths (over 6 feet MLW).

Anchorage: While you may see small boats anchored in or near Edenton Harbor, we cannot recommend it due to shoal water outside the channel and poor protection outside the harbor.

Chapter 3

Side Trip: The Albemarle & Roanoke Sounds, NC

Goin' Ashore
EDENTON, NC

Sailing into Edenton Harbor is a voyage back in history. Standing on the broad-columned porch of the Penelope Barker House, you can look across Edenton Bay at a row of Revolutionary War cannons supplied by France. The Edenton Battery protects stately homes nestled among cypress trees and serves as a reminder that the town on Queen Anne's Creek began a cultural revolution that changed the future of the Colonies. From a bluff overlooking Edenton Bay and the Albemarle Sound, the open windows of shops and homes catch the full effect of the water's breeze. The 45-minute Edenton Trolley Tour highlights this and more. Tickets are available at the Penelope Barker Welcome Center.

If you are in town the first weekend in June, check out the annual Edenton Music and Water Festival, a community-wide celebration featuring live bands, parades, food vendors, animal exhibits and local artwork and crafts. You can take a ghost tour any time of the year to learn about the haunted history of this historic locale.

ATTRACTIONS

1. Chowan County Courthouse
Oldest and most intact Colonial courthouse in the country (built in 1767) recognized as a National Historic Landmark. Host to a gala reception for President James Monroe in 1819 (101 S. Broad St., 252-368-5000).

2. Cupola House
Named for octagonal tower perched on roof. National Historic Landmark built in 1758 and restored in 1967 as a museum with formal, lush gardens. Features gorgeous reproduction woodwork. Call for hours and fees (408 S. Broad St., 252-482-2637).

3. Edenton Bay Trading Company
Expansive selection of specialty wines and global craft beer with a lush and serene "secret" courtyard patio. Vinyl night every Saturday and Trivia Night on Wednesdays are especially popular (407 S. Broad St., 252-482-4045).

4. Edenton Cotton Mill Museum of History
Located in over-100-year-old Cotton Mill at 420 Elliott St. Mill Village consist of the historic mill, an office, 70 houses and multiple out buildings. Open every Saturday from 11:00 a.m. to 2:00 p.m. and Sunday from noon to 3:00 p.m.

5. Edenton Farmers Market
Outdoor market held every Saturday from April through December with local crafts, artisan soaps, organic fruits and vegetables, meat, eggs, cheese, honey and baked goods. Also features live music at 200 N. Broad St.

6. James Iredell House
Circa 1800 home of James Iredell, an attorney appointed (at age 39) to the first Supreme Court by President George Washington. House is two-story, "L"-shaped frame dwelling with Georgian and Federal style design elements (107 E. Church St., 252-482-2637).

7. Penelope Barker House (Welcome Center)
Built in 1782 and home to Edenton Historical Commission and famous Edenton Tea Party. Serves as Welcome Center with exhibits and gift shop (505 S. Broad St., 252-482-7800). Open daily from 10:00 a.m. to 5:00 p.m.

8. Roanoke River Lighthouse
Fully restored furnished lighthouse built in 1886 available for tours (7 Dock St., 252-482-2637). Lighthouse's original fog bell is on display in Queen Anne Park.

SERVICES

9. Edenton Post Office
100 N. Broad St. (252-482-2611)

10. Shepard-Pruden Memorial Library
106 W. Water St. (252-482-4112)

11. Vidant Family Medicine–Edenton
300 Court St. (252-482-2116)

MARINAS

12. Edenton Harbor
621 W. Queen St. (252-482-7421).

13. Edenton Marina
510 S. Broad St. (252-337-4488)

Chapter 3: Side Trip: The Albemarle & Roanoke Sounds, NC

Albemarle Sound, NC

PLYMOUTH		Largest Vessel	VHF	Total Slips	Approach/ Dockside Depth	Floating Docks	Gas/ Diesel	Repairs/ Haulout	Min/Max Amps	Pump-Out Station
1. Plymouth Landing Marina WiFi	(252) 217-2204	55	19	9	12.0 / 7.5				30 / 50	P
2. Mackeys Marina	(252) 793-5031	35			/	F	GD	H	30 / 50	

WiFi Wireless Internet Access
Visit www.waterwayguide.com for current rates, fuel prices, website addresses and other up-to-the-minute information. (Information in the table is provided by the facilities.)

Scan here for more details:

Should you choose to explore the upper reaches of the Chowan River north of the high-rise Albemarle Sound Bridge, there is a well-protected anchorage at Rockyhock Creek with 7 to 14 feet MLW with fair holding in soft mud. It is exposed to the south.

Father north, off the north bank of the Chowan is Bennett's Creek, which carries 11 feet MLW and offers all-around protection. Turn into the creek just beyond green flashing daybeacon "13."

Roanoke River (Plymouth)

Across from Edenton around Black Walnut Point, the Roanoke River leads to the southwest. The lower reaches are marked and the upper reaches are deep. There is still some commercial traffic on the river, which keeps it open.

Plymouth, located 6 miles upriver, is a quaint town perfect for a diversion from the ICW or a day trip. There are restaurants within walking distance of the marina and two fine museums: Port O' Plymouth Museum (252-793-1377), which is housed in a 1923 Atlantic Coast Line train depot, and the Roanoke River Lighthouse and Maritime Museum (252-217-2204), a perfect replica of the second Roanoke River Lighthouse. Nearby the Davenport Homestead (252-797-4336) was built around 1790 and is the oldest surviving homestead open to the public in the region.

NAVIGATION: The Roanoke River is much narrower than the Chowan River but is generally deep (about 10-foot MLW depths) and well marked. Shoaling has been observed in the area of red daybeacons "8" to "12" along Rice Island so proceed with caution. The fixed **Roanoke River Bridge** (50-foot vertical clearance) crosses the river about 2.5 miles upstream.

Dockage: Plymouth Landing Marina has fixed and floating docks with water, power and showers plus laundry and pump-out service (for an extra fee). The docks are located at the base of the lighthouse and are

Albemarle Sound, NC

SCUPPERNONG RIVER		Largest Vessel	VHF	Total Slips	Approach/Dockside Depth	Floating Docks	Gas/Diesel	Repairs/Haulout	Min/Max Amps	Pump-Out Station
1. Columbia Marina	(919) 495-1028	45		10	9.0/				30/50	
2. Columbia Municipal Dock WIFI	(252) 796-2781	72		7	10.0/20.0				30/50	P

WIFI Wireless Internet Access
Visit www.waterwayguide.com for current rates, fuel prices, website addresses and other up-to-the-minute information.
(Information in the table is provided by the facilities.)

Scan here for more details: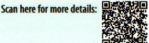

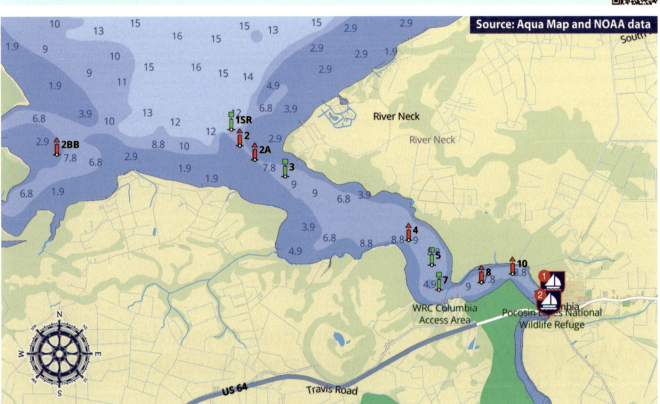

parallel to the current so plan accordingly. Clean facilities including laundry are located at the maritime museum. A Post Office, groceries, shopping and restaurants are nearby along Hwy. 64. Ask the dockmaster at the marina about transportation.

Mackeys Marina, farther east on Kendrick Creek, is a local working marina that is usually full, but there is usually a spot on their bulkhead. Water is very deep (17 feet MLW) and the approach is well marked, but pay attention. It will look as if you are going to run into the trees ashore. Lunch at the on-site restaurant makes this a worthwhile stop.

Anchorage: You can anchor almost anywhere along the cypress shores and marshes of Rice Island. There is a good anchorage before the Roanoke River Bridge with 10-feet MLW depths and all-around protection.

In the southwest corner of the Albemarle Sound is Batchelors Bay at the confluence of the Roanoke and Cashie Rivers. This somewhat open bay has a channel with at least 7 feet MLW all the way to the 16-foot fixed vertical clearance Cashie River Bridge. The channel is narrow and there is more swing room near the mouth but less protection. You can anchor closer to the western shore in 7 to 9 feet MLW with protection from all but the northeast through east.

Scuppernong River (Columbia)

Broad, open Bull Bay forms the entrance to the scenic Scuppernong River located along the Albemarle Sound's southern shore between the Alligator River and Laurel Point. About 4 winding, well-marked miles upriver is the town of Columbia, once an important shipping point and now popular as a boating center.

Sportsmen use Columbia as a year-round base to fish the waters of Albemarle Sound and the improved waterfront provides access to downtown shops and

Chapter 3 — Side Trip: The Albemarle & Roanoke Sounds, NC

restaurants. Within a few blocks of the municipal marina there are an array of restaurant choices as well as a pharmacy, banks (with ATM), a hardware store and a Post Office.

Take the boardwalk under the highway to the large Tyrrell County Visitor Center to get situated. Just to the south is the 110,000-acre Pocosin Lakes National Wildlife Refuge and the beginning of the Scuppernong River Interpretive Boardwalk. The raised boardwalk takes you into the pristine bottomland swamp and makes a 0.75-mile loop complete with signage to explain the blackwater ecosystem.

NAVIGATION: All sailing vessels have reached the extent of their Scuppernong excursion at the town dock due to three low bridges that cross the Scuppernong River. The first (12-foot closed vertical clearance) is immediately after the municipal Columbia Municipal Dock, while the other two are further upriver (one at Cross Landing with a 5-foot fixed vertical clearance and the other at Creswell, a removable span with an overhead cable limiting vertical clearance to 25 feet). Be aware that the projected depths upstream are just 3 feet MLW.

Dockage: The municipal Columbia Municipal Dock has 7 transient slips (with 72 feet being the largest) available right downtown. Dockage is available for boats up to 45 feet; the pilings, however, are no more than 25 feet from the seawall. Shore power is available for a fee. Restrooms, showers and water are on site. Call the town office at 252-796-2781 for reservations.

The 10-slip Columbia Marina has limited transient space to 45 feet. Call ahead for slip availability. Note that an uncomfortable chop can develop here in a heavy northwest wind.

Anchorage: You will find several good anchorages in the Scuppernong River with 7 to 10 feet MLW and a mud bottom. The town of Columbia is easily accessible by dinghy. The cypress swamps of the river's upper reaches warrant exploration by dinghy or the town of Columbia's guided boat tours.

After exploring the western end of Albemarle Sound, it's decision time again. The Alligator River and the ICW proper head south and west, but the distant outline of rising dunes to the east heralds the beginning of the Outer Banks and the shorter route south.

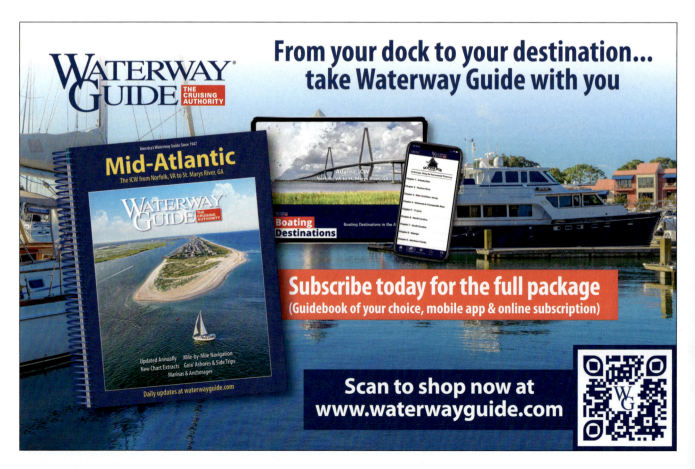

THE ROANOKE & CROATAN SOUNDS

Roanoke Sound

Originally an instrumental route for the East Coast's first English settlers and still a popular destination for water lovers of all varieties, the Roanoke Sound separates the central Outer Banks from Roanoke Island.

On the western side of the sound lies the towns of Manteo and Wanchese, which can be accessed by the Washington Baum Bridge (better known as the Manteo/Nags Head Causeway or vice versa), which stretches across the Roanoke Sound. Because Roanoke Island is bordered by two sounds–the Croatan Sound, which separates it from the mainland, and the Roanoke Sound, which separates it from the beaches– the little waterfront community is surrounded by water.

Manteo (pronounced "man-knee-oh" if you want to sound like a local) is on the northern and western sides of Shallowbag Bay off Roanoke Sound and is often overlooked by cruisers moving along the ICW but it is well worth the side trip. It is just a 5-minute taxi ride to the Outer Banks beaches and the town itself has a friendly air and much to offer.

At the south end of Roanoke Island is a real commercial fishing and boat building village that is home base for several fishing companies that receive and ship the catch for the substantial oceangoing fleet that operates from here. Wanchese is the home base for the reality show "Wicked Tuna–Outer Banks" as well as several custom sportfishing boat manufacturers. You will find few amenities for recreational boaters.

Silting has been an ongoing problem in the harbor so proceed cautiously.

NAVIGATION: From ICW Mile 70 cruise east on Albemarle Sound, setting a course to lighted "MG" at the head of Croatan and Roanoke Sounds.

CAUTION: Vessels that cannot clear the 44-foot fixed vertical clearance **US 64 Bridge** crossing Croatan Sound can reach Manns Harbor and other Croatan Sound points via Roanoke Sound (crossed by the 64-foot vertical clearance **Washington Baum Bridge**).

To proceed to Manteo on Roanoke Sound, it is necessary to head south from light "MG" to Croatan Sound flashing green "3CS," approximately 4 miles to the south-southeast to avoid shoals. Continue to flashing red "42" and the well-marked Roanoke Sound channel. Proceeding southward keep the red lights and daybeacons on your port side.

Use caution. It is winding and aids are not as prevalent south of Shallowbag Bay, which can be confusing, especially farther down at Oregon Inlet.

South of the Manteo entrance the Roanoke Channel is crossed by the 65-foot fixed vertical clearance Washington Baum Bridge.

Manteo Waterfront Marina

Roanoke Marshes Lighthouse

Chapter 3 — Side Trip: The Albemarle & Roanoke Sounds, NC

Goin' Ashore
MANTEO, NC

Manteo is the last year-round community before the Outer Banks beaches and the hub of Roanoke Island's shopping and dining. It was a mere 400 years ago that the island was the landing site of the first travelers to the New World, and the subject of the Lost Colony Outdoor Drama. The outdoor theater production tells the story of the first English colony in America, which was established on Roanoke Island in 1587. (Take your bug spray.) Also located within the Fort Raleigh National Historic Site is the Elizabethan Gardens featuring the world's largest bronze statue of Queen Elizabeth I. Another "must see" is the NC Aquarium on Roanoke Island, where you can experience live animal encounters, feedings, a 285,000-gallon shark tank, interactive exhibits, films and more (252-475-2300). Transportation is required to visit these locations from the Manteo waterfront but that shouldn't be an issue. A helpful local will likely give you a ride.

America's Waterway Guide Since 1947 — Chapter 3

ATTRACTIONS

1. **Bluegrass Island Trading Co.**
   Home of free Pickin' on the Porch concerts held throughout the summer. Owners host annual Outer Banks Bluegrass Island Festival and sell tickets, CDs, records and bluegrass-related souvenirs in the Phoenix Shops on Budleigh St. (252-423-3039).

2. **Roanoke Island Festival Park**
   Located on 25 acres and including re-creations of the first English settlement and a Native American town. On-site adventure museum allows guests of all ages to experience life as original 1500s settler. Costumed interpreters show how colonists lived, worked and played. Replica of 16th-century ship Elizabeth II is anchored here (1 Festival Park, 252-475-1500).

3. **Roanoke Island Maritime Museum**
   Nautical museum located on waterfront in George Washington Creef Boathouse featuring famous shad boats built here over 100 years ago. Eclectic collection of small boats includes circa 1883 shad fishing boat, New England Beetle Cat, Hampton Bay One Design and 1950s vintage outboard hydroplane. Admission is free (104 Fernando St., 252-475-1750).

4. **Roanoke Marshes Lighthouse**
   Replica of 1877 screwpile lighthouse once found at Croatan Sound that includes history exhibits and a vintage Fresnel lens. Located at the end of a pier at 104 Fernando St. (252-475-1750).

5. **Manteo Weather Tower**
   Weather tower on the waterfront boardwalk that originally flew flags to warn locals, fishers and sailors about oncoming weather. Weather messages came in by telegraph, so Manteo's first telegraph operator, Adelphus P. Drinkwater, was the first to telegraph news to the world of the Wright Brothers' first flight. One of only five weather towers still used by NOAA to fly weather flags during the day (lights up at night).

6. **Pioneer Theater**
   Nostalgic theater dating back to 1918, making it the oldest continually running theater that is family-owned in the US. One showing every night (without trailers) with extremely affordable prices including popcorn and beverages (113 Budleigh St., 252-473-2216).

SERVICES

7. **Dare County Library**
   700 U.S. 64 (252-473-2372)

8. **Manteo Post Office**
   212B U.S. Hwy. 64/264 (252-473-2534)

9. **Outer Banks Family Medicine–Manteo 604**
   Amanda St. (252-473-3478)

10. **The Wash House**
    Laundromat at 114 U.S. 64 (866-825-6052)

MARINAS

11. **Manteo Waterfront Marina**
    207 Queen Elizabeth Ave. (252-473-3320)

12. **Marshes Light Marina**
    301 Dartmoor Ln. (252-305-4737)

13. **Shallowbag Bay Marina**
    1100 N. Bay Club Dr. (252-305-8726)

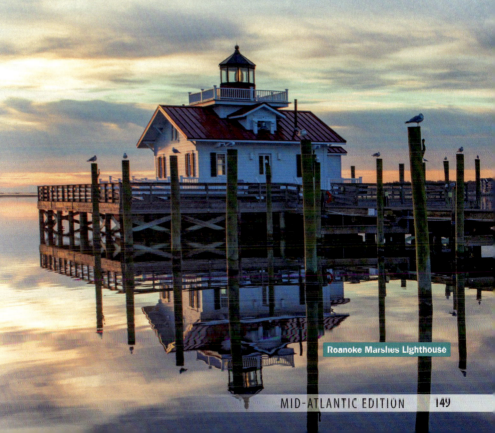

Roanoke Marshes Lighthouse

MID-ATLANTIC EDITION

DON'T JUST CROSS THE ALBEMARLE, TAKE TIME OUT TO DISCOVER AMERICA'S BEGINNING...

Manteo Waterfront Marina

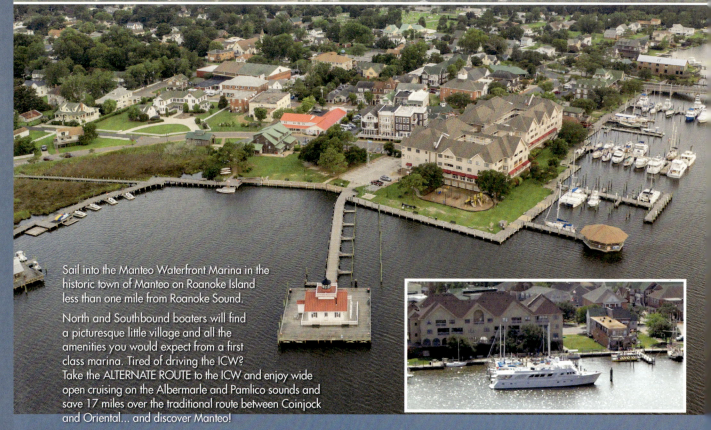

Sail into the Manteo Waterfront Marina in the historic town of Manteo on Roanoke Island less than one mile from Roanoke Sound.

North and Southbound boaters will find a picturesque little village and all the amenities you would expect from a first class marina. Tired of driving the ICW? Take the ALTERNATE ROUTE to the ICW and enjoy wide open cruising on the Albermarle and Pamlico sounds and save 17 miles over the traditional route between Coinjock and Oriental... and discover Manteo!

Just off our docks is a town with shops, restaurants, inns, arts and all the history of the first settlement in the New World...The Lost Colony founded in 1587!

You'll find most everything you need within a few hundred feet of the docks, and a full shopping center with grocery, post office, hardware is less than 1/2 mile away.

Approach depths from Roanoke Sound are 7ft.+ except in unusual conditions, but if you have a deep draft vessel, give us a call and we'll be happy to help you navigate in. We can accommodate vessels up to 100 ft. and the small harbor has excellent protection from the weather.

If you're not in a big rush, stick around and explore the Outer Banks beaches, less than 5 miles away, visit the NC aquarium with the kids, or the Elizabethan Gardens and our outdoor Lost Colony play which is in its 75th year of performances! We may have lost a colony...but you'll find a big welcome in the town of Manteo. For more information or reservations call 252-473-3320. For reservations please go to dockwa.com

- Transient, weekly, and monthly rates
- 30 amd 50 amp outlets at each slip
- 53 slips, accommodating boats to 140'
- A small, deep and well-protected harbor
- Modern air-conditioned showers & laundry
- WiFi and cable TV
- Adjacent to great shopping, fine dining, and elegant accommodations in Old Town Manteo

P.O. Box 246, Manteo, NC 27954-1328
252-473-3320   VHF 16 & 9
www.manteonc.gov

Chapter 3

America's Waterway Guide Since 1947

> ⚠️ **CAUTION:** Be advised that maintenance on the Washington Baum Bridge will continue daily from 7:00 a.m. to 5:30 p.m. and 7:00 p.m. to 7:00 a.m. through September 15, 2025. During work hours, under-bridge access trucks will be in the navigational channel, reducing the vertical clearance of the bridge to approximately 55 feet. Vessels that can safely transit through the bridge during periods with a reduced vertical clearance may do so at any time.

Vessels that cannot safely transit through the bridge during periods of reduced vertical clearance may transit through the bridge, if at least a 30-minute prior notice is given to the project foreman. Maintenance personnel, equipment and vessels will relocate from the movable span and navigable channel, upon request.

The project foreman can be reached at 703-231-8589 or 703-865-1041. Safety vessels may be reached on VHF Channels 13 and 16. Mariners should use caution navigating through the area.

Approach depths into Manteo are 7 to 12 feet MLW, despite what is noted on the latest charts. The *Elizabeth II* replica, which draws 8 feet, transits the channel frequently. Shoaling does occur at the entrance to Shallowbag Bay so slow down, mark the buoys and daybeacons carefully, and keep an eye on your depth sounder. Some chartplotters fail to show all the buoys unless zoomed in tight.

> **NOTE:** It is helpful to know that all markers with numbers in the 20s and 30s are for the main Roanoke Bay channel, while the markers with numbers starting at "2M" belong to the Shallowbag Bay Channel.

From either direction wait to turn west to the Shallowbag Bay Channel until just north of the red "30A." Give red buoy "2M" lots of room and keep a sharp lookout for additional buoys that may have been added to mark recent shoaling. After your turn hug green daybeacons "5" and "3" for deep water. The channel broadens until red "8," where it turns west to red daybeacon "10."

Dockage: North of red daybeacon "10" the 50-slip Manteo Waterfront Marina can accommodate vessels to 100 feet. The marina is run by the town of Manteo and has climate-controlled showers and laundry, shore power and a pump-out facility. The town uses www.Dockwa.com for

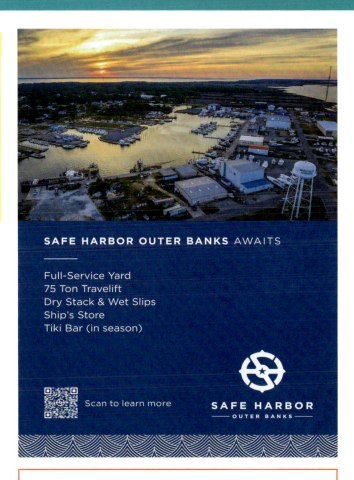

SAFE HARBOR OUTER BANKS AWAITS

Full-Service Yard
75 Ton Travelift
Dry Stack & Wet Slips
Ship's Store
Tiki Bar (in season)

Scan to learn more

SAFE HARBOR — OUTER BANKS —

SKIPPER BOB
Publications

Updated Annually

ATLANTIC AND GULF ICW GUIDES
- Anchorages Along The Intracoastal Waterway
- Marinas Along The Intracoastal Waterway
- Cruising the Gulf Coast

CANAL AND INLAND RIVER GUIDES
- Cruising the New York Canal System
- Cruising the Rideau and Richelieu Canals
- Cruising the Trent-Severn Waterway, Georgian Bay and North Channel
- Cruising From Chicago to Mobile

PLANNING GUIDES
- Cruising America's Great Loop
- Bahamas Bound

Published by

WaterwayGuide.com

Available in Print and the Waterway Guide App

804-776-8999 • skipperbob.net

MID-ATLANTIC EDITION

Chapter 3: Side Trip: The Albemarle & Roanoke Sounds, NC

Roanoke Island, NC

MANTEO		Largest Vessel	VHF	Total Slips	Approach/ Dockside Depth	Floating Docks	Gas/ Diesel	Repairs/ Haulout	Min/Max Amps	Pump-Out Station
1. Manteo Waterfront Marina WiFi	(252) 473-3320	100	16	53	7.0 / 7.0				30 / 100	P
2. Marshes Light Marina WiFi	(252) 573-8452	60	16	60	10.0 / 9.0				30 / 50	P
3. Shallowbag Bay Marina WiFi	(252) 305-8726	100	16	75	7.0 / 7.0	F	GD	R	30 / 50	P
4. Pirate's Cove Marina WiFi	(252) 473-3906	90	78	195	10.0 / 13.0		GD		30 / 100	

WiFi Wireless Internet Access
Visit www.waterwayguide.com for current rates, fuel prices, website addresses and other up-to-the-minute information.
(Information in the table is provided by the facilities.)

Scan here for more details:

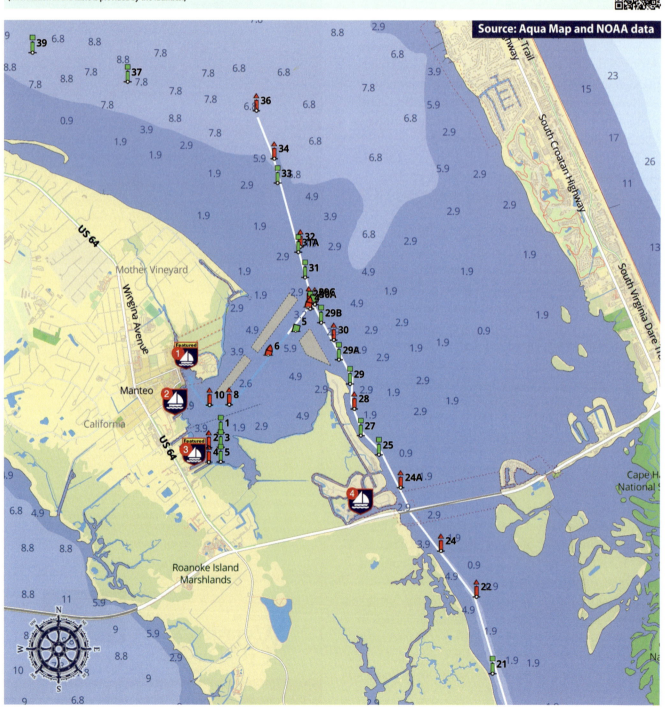

Source: Aqua Map and NOAA data

A Superb Marina in the Heart of Manteo

- Floating Slips
- Pump out
- Walk to Town
- Ship Store
- Fitness Center
- High Speed Fuel Pumps
- Short & Long-term Leases Available
- Bike Rentals

10% OFF at Stripers for boaters

The renowned Stripers Restaurant

(252) 305-8726

1100 b South Bay Club Drive Manteo. North Carolina 277954
Longityude: W-75 39' 54.90" / Latitud: N+35 54' 02.23"   cmckenney1979@yahoo.com

Award Winning Food

Stripers Bar and Grille is an award winning service oriented 3 floor restaurant with every seat overlooking the water. The extensive food menu is enhanced by a large variety of wines, beers, cocktails and specialty drinks.

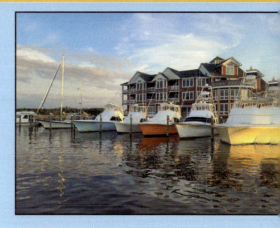

1100A South Bay Club Drive
Manteo, NC 27954
www.stripersbarandgrille.com

Chapter 3: Side Trip: The Albemarle & Roanoke Sounds, NC

Roanoke Island, NC

WANCHESE		Largest Vessel	VHF	Total Slips	Approach/ Dockside Depth	Floating Docks	Gas/ Diesel	Repairs/ Haulout	Min/Max Amps	Pump-Out Station
1. Safe Harbor Outer Banks	(252) 473-5344	80	67	45	14.0 / 14.0	F	GD	RH	15 / 50	
2. Bayliss Boatworks WiFi	(252) 473-9797	100	16	7	11.0 / 20.0	F	GD	RH	30 / 100	P

WiFi Wireless Internet Access
Visit www.waterwayguide.com for current rates, fuel prices, website addresses and other up-to-the-minute information. (Information in the table is provided by the facilities.)

Scan here for more details:

dockage reservations. The dockmaster will confirm your reservation through Dockwa and send an email with your slip assignment. The marina is adjacent to many shops, inns, restaurants and the 1-mile-long town boardwalk.

The town of Manteo also provides free overnight tie-up with no services on a space available basis with room for 3 to 4 boats on the docks between the lighthouse and the town gazebo. There is a pump-out service available and a public restroom at the nearby maritime museum.

Marshes Light Marina is part of a waterfront community and offers some transient dockage on protected canals for (mostly power) vessels to 60 feet. They offer few amenities and it can be difficult to enter in an east wind. Call ahead for slip availability.

A set of private markers to the south lead from the red daybeacon "10" into Shallowbag Bay Marina, which accommodates vessels up to 100 feet on floating docks and boasts multiple fueling stations providing "in-slip" fueling to most boats. They also have an on-site restaurant, pool, hot tub and laundry facilities.

If you have any interest in a day of offshore fishing there are over 20 large charter boats based here that can make the run to the offshore canyons in comfort.

Pirate's Cove Marina, located just on the north side of the Washington Baum Bridge on Roanoke Island, is part of a large residential development and offers transient slips to 90 feet. They mostly cater to sportfishing vessels. Amenities include a pool, a tiki hut with entertainment and daily specials and an on-site restaurant and raw bar with a fantastic view overlooking the marina.

If you need your boat fixed, Wanchese at the south end of Roanoke Island is the place. There are several

America's Waterway Guide Since 1947 — Chapter 3

yards with large travel lifts, prop shops, canvas shops, metal fabricators and engine shops including Bayliss Boatworks, a custom sportfishing boat dealer that maintains some transient space.

Your best bet is Safe Harbor Outer Banks with a state-of-the-art service facility, featuring drystack and floating docks with slips to 70 feet. You can also book a dolphin cruise or a fishing charter on site or stock up on supplies at the ship store.

Anchorage: The anchorage area at Manteo is a triangle created by three points: the red daybeacon "10" to the south, the lighthouse to the northwest and the brown gazebo to the northeast. Anchor in hard mud and sand in 6 to 8 feet MLW with no tide (only wind-driven changes in depth). Protection is excellent from the north and west but strong south or east winds can kick up a chop. Farther west the bottom shoals swiftly and a charted pipe restricts anchoring to the south. You can take the dinghy to the town dock for land access.

Side Trip: Oregon Inlet

NAVIGATION: A well-defined channel with 9- to 10-foot MLW depths leads south from Wanchese, 6 miles down to Oregon Inlet. It is crossed by the fixed high-rise **Marc Basnight Bridge** (70-foot vertical clearance). The inlet is used by one of the East Coast's largest sportfishing fleets. Having said this, Oregon Inlet is considered the most changeable of all the East Coast inlets.

Be aware that aids to navigation change frequently at the Oregon Inlet intersection. This inlet regularly experiences severe shoaling and is NOT a recommended inlet. Proceed with an abundance of caution and always obtain accurate local information before attempting this inlet as it can be quite dangerous, even in calm conditions. Follow one of the local charter or fishing boats

MID-ATLANTIC EDITION

Chapter 3: Side Trip: The Albemarle & Roanoke Sounds, NC

Roanoke Sound, NC

OREGON INLET		Largest Vessel	VHF	Total Slips	Approach/ Dockside Depth	Floating Docks	Gas/ Diesel	Repairs/ Haulout	Min/Max Amps	Pump-Out Station
1. Oregon Inlet Fishing Center	(252) 441-6301	65	69	55	6.0 / 6.0		GD		50	

WiFi Wireless Internet Access
Visit www.waterwayguide.com for current rates, fuel prices, website addresses and other up-to-the-minute information. (Information in the table is provided by the facilities.)

Scan here for more details:

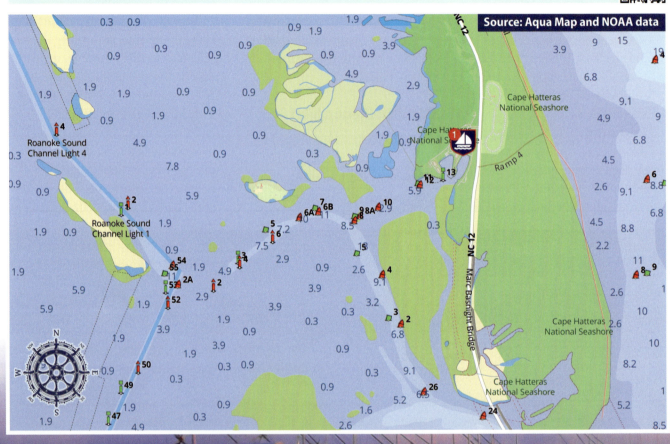

Source: Aqua Map and NOAA data

America's Waterway Guide Since 1947 — Chapter 3

in or out of the inlet if possible. Do not try to run the inlet in foul weather.

> ⚠️ **CAUTION:** Shoaling has been located throughout Oregon Inlet. Water depths as low as 2 feet MLW have been observed.

Dockage: Oregon Inlet Fishing Center sits north of the inlet offering transient berths and is a good resource on the Oregon Inlet channel. They mostly cater to sportfishing vessels and is home to the largest fishing fleet on the Eastern Seaboard. Charter boats come and go from here for inshore, near shore, offshore and headboat fishing.

Anchorage: Nearby House Channel Islands offers great holding in 15 feet MLW in sand between two large islands. There is a high reversing current so let out plenty of scope and a good quality anchor is a must. There is beach access to either island for exploring or dog walks, but this is a bird sanctuary so no dogs are allowed on shore in summer months. Expect several small fishing boats to pass through in the daytime.

Croatan Sound

Many power vessels use the Croatan Sound Route to the Pamlico Sound to circumvent the ICW and slower vessels. This open water route starts at Mile 66 after entering the Albemarle Sound from the North River and ends at Mile 169 in the Neuse River.

NAVIGATION: Boats that can clear the 44-foot fixed **U.S. 64 Bridge** can run 4 miles down Croatan Sound (western side of Roanoke Island) from flashing green Croatan Sound Light "3CS" to Manns Harbor (no transient facilities) on the mainland side just before the 66-foot fixed **Virginia Dare Memorial Bridge**. Check water levels carefully if your mast approaches this height.

> ⚠️ **CAUTION:** According to local knowledge, the U.S. 64 Bridge actually has a vertical clearance of between 42 and 44 feet.

After clearing both bridges in Croatan Sound heading south, your next waypoint will be Roanoke Marshes flashing white 20-foot "RM." The well-marked channel carries 7- to 8-foot MLW depths. Red aids are to the west (starboard when heading south on the ICW).

Chapter 3 — Side Trip: The Albemarle & Roanoke Sounds, NC

Roanoke River Lighthouse

Your subsequent waypoints from the southern end of Croatan Sound, through Pamlico Sound and ending with the Neuse River are as follows: Stumpy Point (27-foot flashing white "N"), Long Shoal (15-foot flashing red "2LS"), Bluff Shoal (18-foot flashing white "BL"), Brant Island Shoal (40-foot flashing white "BI") then Neuse River (24-foot flashing white "NR"). A licensed boat captain and long-time user of this route reported to us that it shaves 18 miles off the trip north or south.

Vessels that cannot clear the 44-foot fixed U.S. 64 Bridge crossing Croatan Sound can reach Manns Harbor and other Croatan Sound points via Roanoke Sound, which is crossed by the 65-foot-fixed vertical clearance Washington Baum Bridge. Old House Channel carries at least 7-foot MLW depths from Oregon Inlet west into Pamlico Sound. The channel is well marked. Carry the red lights and daybeacons on the starboard side from this point south to Pamlico Sound.

The buoys change here and they can be confusing. Slow down here and sort it out before proceeding or you may find yourself aground. The dredged channel runs east of Roanoke Island, rounds the island via Old House Channel in Pamlico Sound, then heads north up Croatan Sound. Note that aids to navigation reverse between flashing red "4" and flashing green "OH" in Old House Channel. Also, aids to navigation are frequently relocated and there may be uncharted piles and pipes in this area.

Whether you choose to take the Roanoke Sound or Croatan Sound route, both converge in Pamlico Sound leaving you poised to continue north to the Chesapeake Bay or south on the ICW.

Albemarle Sound to the Neuse River, NC

Chapter 4

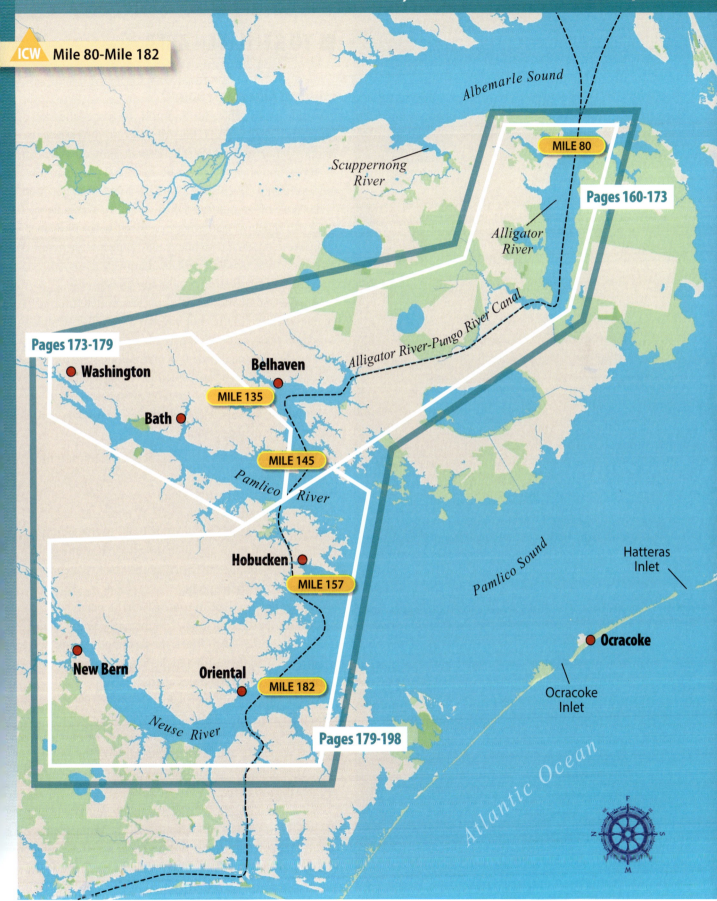

Chapter 4: Albemarle Sound to the Neuse River, NC

Belhaven, NC: Birthplace of the ICW

Poised on the estuary of the Pamlico Sound up the Pungo River at the mouth of Pantego Creek, Belhaven is a delightful destination for day boaters and cruisers who will find small town hospitality and history throughout the treelined streets and waterfront marinas.

In September 1928, the Alligator River–Pungo River Canal was completed and opened. This was the last remaining link to complete the 1,090-mile Atlantic Intracoastal Waterway from Norfolk to Miami. 20,000 people descended on the tiny town of Belhaven for the dedication ceremonies. The Navy sent two seaplanes, the Coast Guard dispatched several cutters and the Army hovered a blimp to join officials from Washington, DC, who were present for the festivities. On the 75th anniversary of the canal's completion in 2013, Belhaven was designated "The Birthplace of the ICW" by the Atlantic Intracoastal Waterway Association. The town celebrates this distinction and the waterway's completion with an annual ICW Celebration that includes a chowder tasting, street festival, flotilla with antique boats and traditional Blessing of the Boats ceremony.

Belhaven's restaurants and businesses have garnered great reviews from cruisers and visitors who appreciate the ambience and character of the small North Carolina town. A landmark that has stood since 1904 is the historic River Forest Manor and Grand Manor Marina, once a must-visit destination for celebrities and politicians including Dean Martin, Frank Sinatra, James Cagney and Walter Cronkite. In 2023, new owners purchased the manor and marina, which are being transformed back to its former glory. The marina and the manor's famous River Room lounge and restaurant have been completely renovated and are once again a must-visit destination for all transient boaters.

Consider a visit to Belhaven, whether by boat or by land. The beautiful harbor town, local marinas and River Forest Manor & Marina are off the beaten path but well worth exploring.

■ TO BELHAVEN AREA

Crossing Albemarle Sound

Traveling south Albemarle Sound is the first of the few sometimes challenging bodies of water on the Norfolk to Miami section of the ICW. The 14-mile-long crossing can be very sloppy because winds from almost any quarter tend to funnel either up or down the long, straight sound.

Because of its uniformly shallow depth, even a light wind can quickly create rough, confused seas. To further complicate matters, crab buoys may appear anywhere, including the narrowest parts of channels.

VHF Weather Radio provides forecasts for the Albemarle Sound and the Alligator River, including a characterization of the chop present in the river. Should wind and sea conditions appear unfavorable for an Albemarle crossing, prudent boaters should remain in or return to their last port, whether that be Coinjock or Elizabeth City for those coming down the ICW, or Columbia or Albemarle Plantation for those who opted to see more of Albemarle Sound.

NAVIGATION: Camden Point is about 19 miles from southeast Elizabeth City along the Pasquotank River. When crossing Albemarle Sound you can save a couple of miles by deserting the chart's ICW course to make for flashing green "1PR" east of Wade Point in the mouth of the Pasquotank River and then directly to flashing green "1AR" at the entrance to the Alligator River. Watch for crab pot buoys off the point.

Along the Virginia Cut route two lighted aids to navigation set the course across Albemarle Sound from the mouth of the North River: the flashing 6-second white isophase "N" to the north and flashing 4-second white "S" to the south (about 6.5 miles apart).

As the course from the Dismal Swamp Canal Route from the Pasquotank River across Albemarle Sound converges with the Virginia Cut Route, the second marker, flashing 4-second white "S," will lie close to the course. It is another 3.5 miles to flashing green "1AR" at the mouth of the Alligator River.

Should you decide to cross Albemarle Sound when the wind is up, it is a good idea to call the bridgetender of the Alligator River (U.S. 64) Bridge at Mile 84.2 for a situation report (252-796-7261). The bridge opens on signal except during unsafe conditions (in wind speeds of 34 mph or greater) when the bridge need not open. You should be aware of this potential obstacle before beginning your crossing.

> NOTE: The bridge operator may request your registration or documentation number. Be sure to have these numbers close by when approaching the bridge. If not documented, your visible registration number will suffice.

> **CAUTION:** A proposal is in place to replace the existing swing-span Alligator River Bridge with a 65-foot fixed bridge just north of the current bridge. Construction is slated to begin in the fall of 2024. A copy of Public Notice D05PN-03-2024, which describes the proposal in detail, can be obtained by calling 757-398-6227 and at NC DOT. Stay tuned to Waterway Explorer for updates.

If the wind comes up en route and the bridge is closed, you have the option of ducking into Alligator River Marina just before the bridge for protection or anchoring as described in the next section. If the wind is as little as 15 mph out of a westerly direction the resulting waves can make for a very unpleasant crossing of the sound.

The Alligator River

NAVIGATION: This heavily marked channel for the Alligator River is confusing, even to veteran ICW travelers, so be sure to slow down and take time to sort out the markers. Just before Mile 80 is the entrance marker for the Alligator River, flashing green "1AR." Next in line to the south is quick flashing green "3," which is difficult to see approaching from either direction but is in the location of the Mile Marker 80 sign.

> **CAUTION:** There have been numerous groundings by vessels missing flashing green "3" and heading straight to flashing green "5." The board for flashing green "5" is visible only when approached from the correct direction.

Long Shoal Point at the mouth of the Alligator River is popular with the local hunting crowd and can be thick with duck blinds, boats and shotguns during duck season.

In late fall, migrating whistling swans settle onto the shallows in large flocks, a sight that is beautiful to behold.

Red daybeacon "6" is just north of Long Shoal Point and quick flashing red "8" marks the shoal southeast of Long Shoal Point. Long Shoal seems to get longer with each passing year.

Flashing green "7" is just east of quick flashing red "8" and marks the eastern boundary of the ICW channel here. Make sure you honor both marks, favoring the green side. The pole from the charted former white "Danger" beacon is still on the shoal but has no boards. Favor the east side of the channel between flashing green "7" and green daybeacon "9."

As you approach lighted red buoy "8A" located between green daybeacon "9" and flashing red "10" stay near the red side of the channel. From here set your course for the opening span of the Alligator River (U.S. 64) Bridge at Mile 84.2.

Always follow the markers but especially in this area as the markers are moved frequently. Up-to-date charts are a necessity for accurate navigation but even then, markers may have moved. Any departure from the main channel carries the risk of prop damage or worse. Do not shortcut points and do not hug the banks too closely.

The **Alligator River (U.S. 64) Bridge** (14-foot closed vertical clearance) normally opens on signal but it cannot open in winds stronger than 34 knots and at the discretion of the bridgetender may remain closed in winds of lesser velocities. In either case look for a good spot to hole up in should it become necessary.

Southbound boats might want to check weather conditions at the bridge and call the bridgetender on VHF Channel 13 before crossing the Albemarle. You certainly don't want to make this crossing only to find the bridge closed due to high winds.

Drought conditions and prolonged strong winds can lower the water level throughout the Alligator River. A north or south blow can kick up 6-foot waves and make this transit very uncomfortable. While the Alligator River continues wide and deep almost to its head, snags are frequent outside the channel and boaters should follow the markers carefully.

The most snags have been observed between quick-flashing red "WR24" and quick-flashing green "37." An extra pair of eyes is always helpful in this area. Snags and obstructions are often partially submerged and difficult

Chapter 4: Albemarle Sound to the Neuse River, NC

Alligator River, NC

ALLIGATOR RIVER		Largest Vessel	VHF	Total Slips	Approach/Dockside Depth	Floating Docks	Gas/Diesel	Repairs/Haulout	Min/Max Amps	Pump-Out Station
1. Alligator River Marina WiFi 1.5 mi. W of MM 84.0	(252) 796-0333	155	16	29	5.7 /		GD		30 / 100	

WiFi Wireless Internet Access
Visit www.waterwayguide.com for current rates, fuel prices, website addresses and other up-to-the-minute information. (Information in the table is provided by the facilities.)

Scan here for more details:

Source: Aqua Map and NOAA data

to see and you may hear other skippers reporting them to the Coast Guard on VHF Channel 16 and making Sécurité calls.

South of the Alligator River (U.S. 64) Bridge the east bank of the river is primitive with side streams worth exploring but only by dinghy. Milltail Creek, east of the bend in the channel at quick flashing red "18" (about Mile 88), is pristine but hard to locate. Five miles upstream are the turning basin and the decaying town wharf of Buffalo City. The creek is narrow and fallen trees may lie across the creek in areas.

Dockage: At the northwestern end of the Alligator River (U.S. 64) Bridge is Alligator River Marina with a well-protected harbor and the only fuel available along the 82 miles on the Virginia Cut Route between Coinjock (Mile 50) and Dowry Creek Marina (Mile 132). This friendly marina accepts transients of all sizes and offer all the usual amenities plus a convenience store and early morning breakfast and short-order favorites at the on-site restaurant. (The fried chicken is outstanding.) It is easily recognizable by its candy cane-striped lighthouse.

Anchorage: Sandy Point on the Alligator River offers limited protection on the east side of the river north of the bridge, especially in any northerly or easterly wind. There is 6 feet MLW and fair holding behind Mill Point near the mouth of the Little Alligator. It is not a spot to wait out a cold front passage nor is it a comfortable refuge if the Alligator River (U.S. 64) Bridge cannot open because of strong winds when southbound.

If planning to stay north of the bridge for weather reasons, it is better to head further off the track to the east and anchor to the southwest side of Durant Island-South, the common entrance to East and South Lakes. Here you will find good shelter from northeast winds among the numerous crab pots.

Just past Briery Hall Point at the mouth of Broad Creek on South Lake offers some protection. Venture carefully into south Lake or East Lake if you draw more than 5 feet; the channel is unmarked and narrow. Although both carry 8- to 10-feet MLW depths, they shallow to 3 to 5 feet MLW just outside of the channel. Both anchorages have good holding and wind protection.

If you are northbound and there is a bridge closure, you will need to find a spot close to the southwestern end of the bridge to drop the hook and wait it out. This is not a good anchorage in a north or northeast wind so when in doubt contact the bridge. A better bet is Catfish Point at Mile 94.3, which is an excellent all-around anchorage in clay with 6- to 14-foot MLW depths.

The Alligator River in the proximity of Mile 100 is wide so choose a location that provides wind protection. In season there may be plenty of bugs and fisherman traffic early morning. It is recommended that a trip line be used when anchoring in the Alligator River due to the many snags on the bottom.

Anchoring options include Swan Creek, an open anchorage that is convenient and easy access from the ICW. Others include Newport News Point at Mile 101 with good holding in 7 to 8 feet MLW (exposed to the north) and Deep Point at Mile 102 with good holding in 7- to 8-foot MLW depths in mud (exposed to the east). When anchoring position yourself as far out of the channel as possible to stay away from maneuvering tugs and barges in this vicinity and show anchor lights at night.

Tuckahoe Point (Mile 104) just before the entrance to the 20-mile-long Alligator River-Pungo River Canal offers the best all-around protection in 6- to 10-feet MLW depths. Turn to the north off the ICW at green daybeacon "49" and then proceed slowly to Tuckahoe Point. Do not get too close to the point; the area is foul with tree stumps. Holding, swing room and protection are good.

If you have four-legged crew, you might prefer to be closer to the Gum Neck Boat Ramp. Be careful going in and out, as there are submerged stumps and it is shallow, although the locals have marked most obstructions with white poles. It is also a long dinghy ride from the deep water where you anchor to the boat ramp.

Alligator River–Pungo River Canal– ICW Mile 105 to Mile 126

The 21-mile-long Alligator River-Pungo River Canal runs northeast to southwest. It is scenic and heavily wooded at its upper end. Do not be in a hurry or you might miss deer snacking near the shore or a black bear swimming across the channel. The occasional alligator has been spotted here as well. Farther on are areas that have burned in the past but now have their second growth.

The canal is relatively narrow and boats dragging huge wakes have a tendency to damage the banks. Each year more and more trees topple into the water. Proceed slowly.

The Fairfield Canal at Mile 113.8 leads to Lake Mattamuskeet, which is part of the Mattamuskeet Wildlife Refuge. The refuge is popular with hunters and naturalists from November through May when huge flocks of water birds gather in the lake and marshes. Arrangements to visit the refuge can be made in Belhaven.

NAVIGATION: While enjoying the scenery and wildlife keep a lookout for stumps and snags outside of the channel. This is another area where deadheads have been spotted in the channel. Keep a watchful eye on the water when transiting this canal.

It is a good idea to stick to the center of the channel and maintain a radio watch; tugs and recreational boats will frequently point out possible hazards with Sécurité calls on VHF Channel 16. Channel markers in the vicinity of the Fairfield (NC 94) Bridge at Mile 113.9 and farther west will help you maintain your mid-channel position in those areas.

The Alligator River-Pungo River Canal's controlling depth is 12 feet MLW; however, keep a close eye on the depth sounder, stick to the center of the channel and squeeze to the side carefully if you must pass another boat.

Fairfield Canal crosses the ICW just before the fixed **Fairfield (NC 94) Bridge** at Mile 113.9. The bridge has a charted 65-foot vertical clearance but we have received reports of it being closer to 64 feet. Tree stumps line both sides of the channel and there can be considerable current present here.

Boats have been observed anchoring here with lines tied to shore and anchors astern. This is not a recommended anchorage except in an emergency situation.

ICW 136 Downtown Belhaven, North Carolina!
Phone 252-944-0066, VHF 16/9, belhavenmarina.com

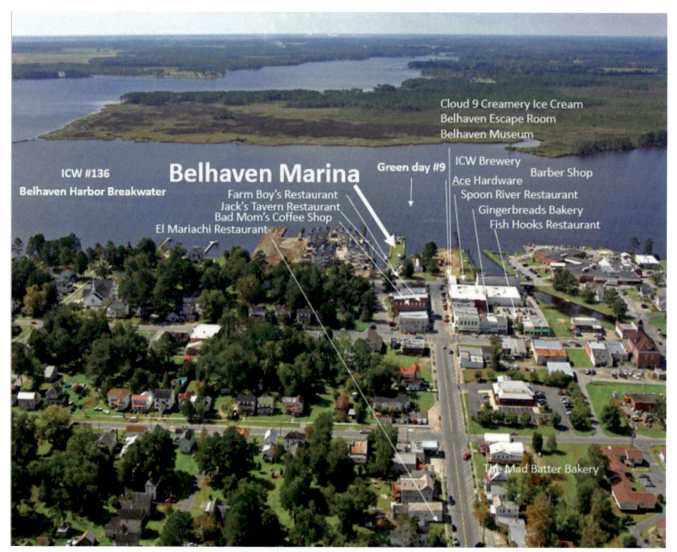

- Location, Location, Location!
- All restaurants and shops directly across the street from marina
- In slip fueling 90NE Gas & Diesel
- Pump out
- Full bar with upper deck overlooking harbor + much more

At Mile 125.8 you will pass under the high-level **Wilkerson (U.S. 264) Bridge** (also known as the Walter B. Jones Bridge), which has a fixed vertical clearance of 64 feet at mean high water.

> ⚠️ *CAUTION:* Sailboats with masts over 60 feet should know their exact mast height with antennas and exercise extreme caution when passing under the Wilkerson (U.S. 264) Bridge. The slight tidal range here may or may not provide the extra clearance required for safe passage. If the tide boards are missing from this bridge, check locally for information.

Pungo River (Belhaven)–ICW Mile 126 to Mile 145

Belhaven (which translates as "beautiful harbor") is a popular rest stop for ICW travelers. The town sits among old forests and wide creeks, good anchorages and dark water. It offers the charm of an historic small town life with pastoral views and many opportunities to observe wildlife.

Drop anchor or tie up at the town dock or one of the marinas and take a short walk into town where you will find shops, restaurants and the museum. You will pass beautiful Victorian homes along Belhaven's tree-lined streets, many with their windows open to catch the river breeze.

NAVIGATION: Flashing green "59AR" east of the Wilkerson (U.S. 264) Bridge is the last ICW marker before the Pungo River marking system takes over. Green daybeacon "27PR" is the first Pungo River marker with red daybeacon "28" just to its south. The river is easy to follow, although floating logs and submerged obstacles require caution.

During periods of extreme low water the tips of several submerged pilings are sometimes visible along the channel between the Wilkerson Bridge and quick-flashing green "23" on the north edge of the channel.

Heading southwest on the Pungo River stay in the channel and give flashing green "21" a wide berth to avoid the chronic shoaling extending from the western bank. The channel is well marked up to Belhaven's entrance channel, which is reached by heading northwest from quick-flashing red "10" in the Pungo River.

RIVER FOREST
BOATYARD/SHIPYARD

THE FINEST HAUL-OUT & MECHANICAL SERVICES AVAILABLE!
Specializing in QUICK prop and shaft repair, hull painting, electrical repairs and all types of marine overhauls.

30, 50 Amp • Propeller and Engine Shop • 40-ton TraveLift
Pumpout • WiFi • Laundry • Complimentary Golf Carts
Full-time Mechanic & Diver Services • Airport Transportation
Nearby Restaurants • Truck Vessel Transport Service

River Forest

24/7 Towing, Ungrounding, Salvage & Pollution Control

office. **252-943-2151** • mobile: **252-945-5579**
axson@riverforestshipyard.com • www.riverforestshipyard.com
843 East Pantego Street, Belhaven, NC 27810

Chapter 4: Albemarle Sound to the Neuse River, NC

Goin' Ashore: BELHAVEN, NC

ATTRACTIONS

1. **ICW Brewery**
   Downtown business offering craft beer brewed on site plus wine at 211 Pamlico St. (252-489-6646). Self-pour taps make it easy to try multiple brews and inside and outdoor seating are available. They also have fun special release celebrations plus game and movie nights.

2. **Riddick & Windley Hardware**
   Old-fashioned hardware store carrying just about everything, including great wine selection, ice and a nice selection of stainless fasteners for marine use (235 Pamlico St., 252-943-2205).

3. **River Bend Cultural Arts Center**
   Community arts center with yoga classes, local art and even dinner theater at 467 Pamlico St. (252-495-8671).

4. **Spoon River Artworks and Market**
   Farm-to-fork style restaurant with menus that change seasonally, weekly, and even daily, based upon what's available locally. Also sells artwork and antiques as well as local specialty foods at 263 Pamlico St. (252-945-3899).

SERVICES

5. **Belhaven Chamber of Commerce**
   293 E. Water St., Ste. 202 (252-943-3770)

6. **Belhaven Post Office**
   614 W. Old Country Rd. (252-943-2364)

7. **Belhaven Public Library**
   333 E. Main St. (252-943-2993)

8. **ECU Health Multispecialty Clinic-Belhaven**
   598 W. Old County Rd. (252-943-0600)

MARINAS

9. **Belhaven Marina**
   332 E. Water St. (252-944-0066)

10. **Belhaven Town Docks at Wynne's Gut**
    268 E. Water St. (252-944-0066)

11. **River Forest Boatyard/Shipyard**
    843 E. Pantego St. (252-945-5579)

12. **Grand Manor Marina (formerly River Forest Manor and Marina)**
    738 E. Main St. (252-943-0320)

13. **TJ's Marina & Boatyard**
    774 East Pantego St. (252-943-3333)

America's Waterway Guide Since 1947 — Chapter 4

When Daniel Latham built a hunting and fishing camp in 1868 on what is now the River Forest Manor, Jack's Neck was little more than a small settlement inhabited by a few farmers and fishermen. In time, the town changed its name to Belhaven and with the addition of a rail spur from the Norfolk and Southern Railroad, and the port's location near the Pamlico Sound, the town became a vital transportation artery for the distribution of goods throughout eastern North Carolina. Today, the town's businesses mainly serve the surrounding farming communities, the local residents and tourists. Many of the grand homes built in the late 1800s and early 1900s remain standing today, the largest of which is River Forest Manor (circa 1904), which was recently renovated.

This small town really knows how to host a celebration! If you visit on the 4th of July, be sure to attend the annual Belhaven Waterfront Festival featuring live music, food vendors, and arts and crafts booths, as well as boat tours and a fireworks display.

MID-ATLANTIC EDITION

Chapter 4: Albemarle Sound to the Neuse River, NC

Pungo River, NC

		Largest Vessel	VHF	Total Slips	Approach/Dockside Depth	Floating Docks	Gas/Diesel	Repairs/Haulout	Min/Max Amps	Pump-Out Station
PUNGO CREEK (NORTH)										
1. Dowry Creek Marina WiFi MM 132.0	(252) 943-2728	200	16	73	9.0 / 11.0		GD	R	30 / 200+	P
BELHAVEN										
2. TJ's Marina & Boatyard WiFi	(252) 943-3333			40	6.5 / 6.5			RH	30 / 50	P
3. River Forest Boatyard/Shipyard WiFi 1.6 mi. W of MM 136.0	(252) 943-2151	75	16		6.0 / 6.0			RH	15 / 50	
4. Grand Manor Marina NC WiFi MM 136.0	(252) 943-0030	140	16	31	9.0 / 9.0		GD	R	30 / 100	P
5. Belhaven Marina WiFi 0.25 mi. W of MM 136.0	(252) 944-0066	150	16	34	9.0 / 9.0		GD		30 / 50	P
6. Belhaven Town Dock at Wynne's Gut WiFi MM 136.0	(919) 880-1183	40	16	5	7.0 / 7.0				30	P

WiFi Wireless Internet Access
Visit www.waterwayguide.com for current rates, fuel prices, website addresses and other up-to-the-minute information.
(Information in the table is provided by the facilities.)

Scan here for more details:

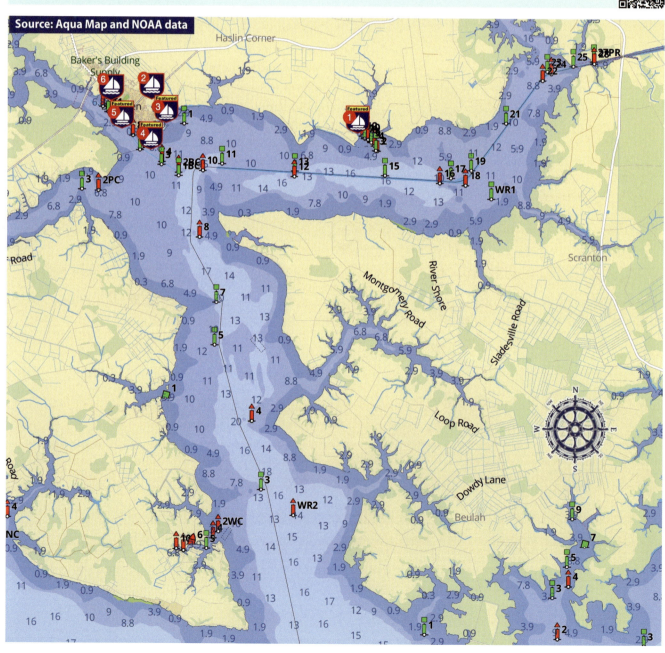

Source: Aqua Map and NOAA data

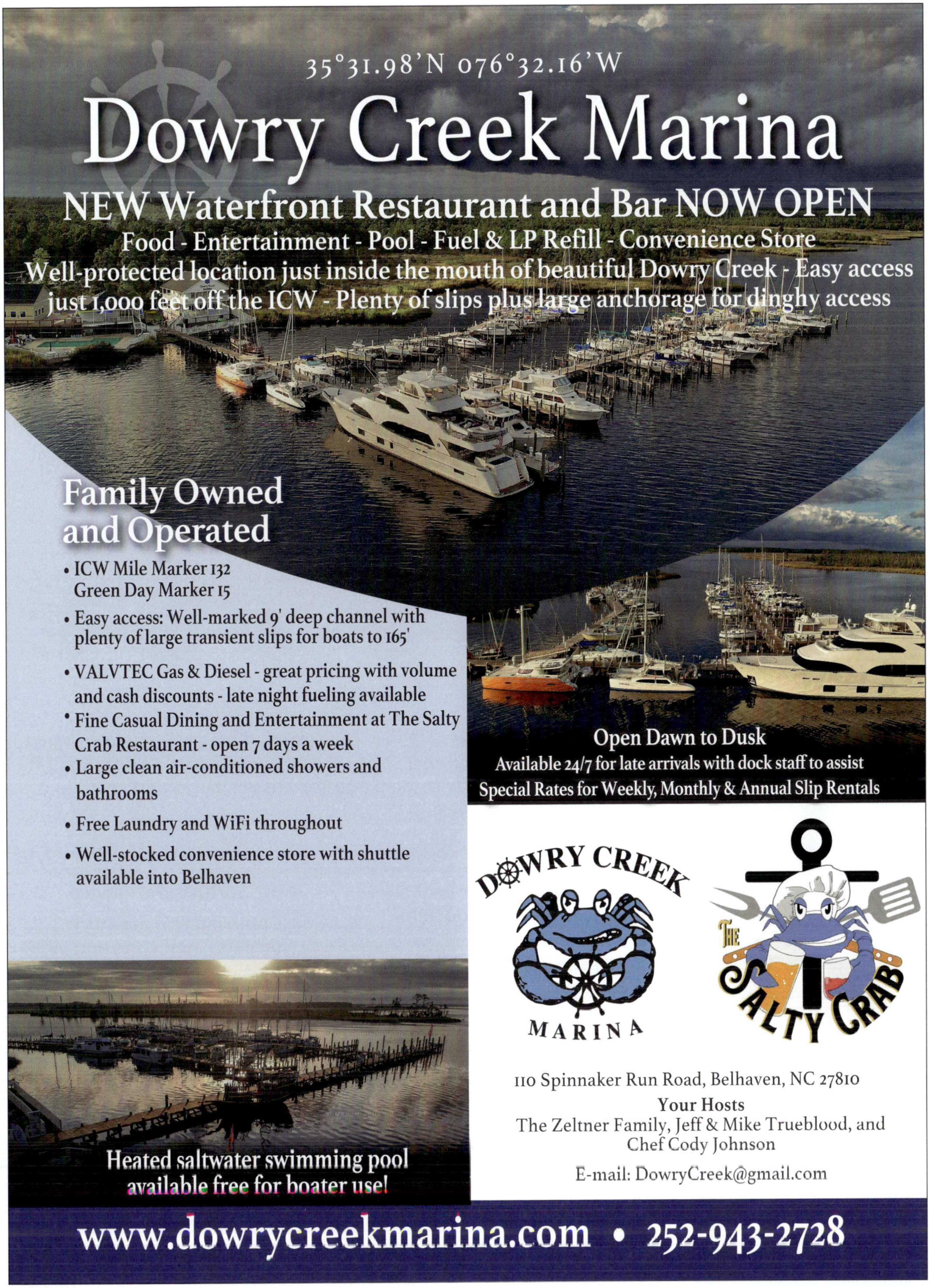

35°31.98'N 076°32.16'W

Dowry Creek Marina

NEW Waterfront Restaurant and Bar NOW OPEN

Food - Entertainment - Pool - Fuel & LP Refill - Convenience Store
Well-protected location just inside the mouth of beautiful Dowry Creek - Easy access just 1,000 feet off the ICW - Plenty of slips plus large anchorage for dinghy access

Family Owned and Operated

- ICW Mile Marker 132 Green Day Marker 15
- Easy access: Well-marked 9' deep channel with plenty of large transient slips for boats to 165'
- VALVTEC Gas & Diesel - great pricing with volume and cash discounts - late night fueling available
- Fine Casual Dining and Entertainment at The Salty Crab Restaurant - open 7 days a week
- Large clean air-conditioned showers and bathrooms
- Free Laundry and WiFi throughout
- Well-stocked convenience store with shuttle available into Belhaven

Open Dawn to Dusk
Available 24/7 for late arrivals with dock staff to assist
Special Rates for Weekly, Monthly & Annual Slip Rentals

Heated saltwater swimming pool available free for boater use!

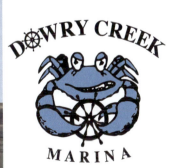

110 Spinnaker Run Road, Belhaven, NC 27810

Your Hosts
The Zeltner Family, Jeff & Mike Trueblood, and Chef Cody Johnson

E-mail: DowryCreek@gmail.com

www.dowrycreekmarina.com • 252-943-2728

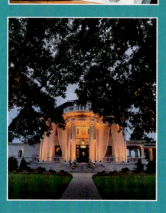

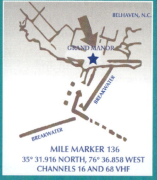

THE RIVER FOREST MANOR AND GRAND MANOR MARINA ARE LOCATED ON THE BEAUTIFUL BELHAVEN COASTLINE on the Pantego Creek inside the breakwall, just off the Pungo River. The Marina offers a protected harbor with dockage for vessels large and small and the amenities cruisers seek.

AMENITIES:

- 13 deep-water transient slips with 300' of face dock for yachts up to 150'
- 39 total slips with 17 slips for vessels up to 55'
- Daily, monthly, annual slip leases available
- Pump-out and mobile mechanic
- 30/50/100 amp service
- Complimentary laundry facilities, golf carts and Wi-Fi
- Climate-controlled restrooms and showers
- Premier wedding and event venue

738 East Main Street, Belhaven, NC 27810
Tel: 252.943.0030
grandmanormarina@gmail.com
www.grandmanormarina.com

The approach to the full-service marinas and boatyards of Belhaven is easy and well marked. On approach to Pantego Creek reduce your speed and wake just beyond green daybeacon "3" and red daybeacon "4." The channel carries 9-foot MLW depths along the centerline. At Belhaven the Pungo River makes a 90-degree turn to the south for the 10-mile run to the Pamlico River.

> NOTE: Heading south into the Pungo River the buoys suddenly reverse with green aids to starboard but still with the familiar ICW yellow triangles and squares marking the boards to signify they are ICW markers. This is because you are going downstream here on the Pungo River, which is marked from seaward.

> CAUTION: Beware the artificial reef located due east of green daybeacon "5," off Quilley Point in the Pungo River at Mile 140.

Dockage: After exiting the Alligator River-Pungo River Canal the well-regarded Dowry Creek Marina is just north of the channel at green daybeacon "15" (Mile 131.6). The marked entrance channel has a minimum depth of 8 feet MLW. Experienced and accommodating deckhands will help you dock.

The marina offers transient slips with amenities such as clean bathroom and private showers, WiFi, a laundry, a saltwater swimming pool, tennis courts and a courtesy car. They have a restaurant under construction (opening soon). There is also a good place to walk pets. Late night arrivals are welcome.

Just north on Battalina Creek is River Forest Boatyard/Shipyard, a full-service shipyard specializing in prop and shaft repair, hull painting, electrical repairs and all types of marine overhauls. They have a full-time mechanic and diver, plus a 40-ton lift. DIY boaters are welcome. Rental cars are available and they have complimentary golf carts for getting around town.

Also on Battalina Creek is the family-owned and -operated TJ's Marina & Boatyard, which welcomes transients and offers full amenities including clean bathrooms and showers, efficient washers and dryers, and courtesy golf carts and a vehicle. They also offer a wide range of marine services.

Immediately inside the charted Belhaven storm barrier to the right (via a marked channel) is Grand Manor Marina. The marina's slips have been renovated and features a newly built marina store. Located on the grounds of the iconic River Forest Manor, the marina offers transient, seasonal and annual dockage with water and power, plus complimentary laundry and electric golf carts to tour beautiful Belhaven.

Belhaven Marina is to the north with over 1,000 feet of transient dockage accommodating boats up to 150 feet. They are known for their clean heads and showers with soap and towels. Other amenities include free laundry, outdoor grills and numerous land-based entertainment options such as corn-hole, croquet, a putting green, beach volleyball, a basketball court and a large gazebo.

Immediately to the north are the Belhaven Town Docks At Wynne's Gut with power (30 amp) and water. A nice boater lounge, restrooms and showers are only available when the Chamber of Commerce is open (closed Saturday, Sunday and Monday). Payment for the town docks can be made by calling the dockmaster at Belhaven Marina (252-944-0066). He will come to you or you can go to him. There is a maximum 72-hour stay.

Also owned by the town is Belhaven Town Docks at Cooperage Landing just past red daybeacon "12" on Pantego Creek. The fixed docks (no water or electrical service) are complimentary and available on a first-come, first-served basis with a maximum stay of 72 hours.

Anchorage: When the wind is up the best protection in the area can be found in the headwaters of the Pungo River at green daymarker "23" just north of the lower end of the Alligator River-Pungo River Canal in 7 to 10 feet MLW among crab pots. Mind the depth sounder and pick your way for some distance into the river. The bottom is uneven, soft and given to hump-like shoals even in the center channel. This anchorage gets high marks for its protection, and there is a sandy beach for shore access for the dog.

Scranton Creek on the south side of the Pungo River at Mile 129.5 has good holding in mud in 8 to 10 feet MLW. It is exposed to the west. Local knowledge advises that you stay in the middle of the creek due to sunken pilings beneath the surface along both sides.

Satterthwaite Point at Mile 130 has good holding. The views are nice and you are unlikely to ever have anyone anchor on top of you. Northbound and westbound tugs can be disconcerting until you adjust to them bearing down on you before making the turn in the ICW. Wakes are not an issue as they dissipate before reaching anchored boats.

Chapter 4: Albemarle Sound to the Neuse River, NC

Blackbeard the Pirate

You will find many references to Edward Teach (also known as Blackbeard) in this guide. The Pamlico Sound and River were his home waters and the scene of much of his pirating on his flagship, the *Queen Anne's Revenge*.

Supposedly born in Bristol, England, Teach had friends in high places, was quite the lady's man (with as many as seven wives) and had great successes as a pirate. He became a renowned pirate, known for his thick black beard and fearsome appearance; it was reported that he tied lit fuses under his hat and into his beard to frighten his enemies.

Blackbeard's pirate forces terrorized the Caribbean and the southern coast of North America and were notorious for their cruelty. Sometime in June 1718, Blackbeard and at least 20 members of his crew passed through Ocracoke Inlet, NC, entered Pamlico Sound and headed for the town of Bath on the Pamlico River. There he met with Governor Charles Eden who agreed to pardon Blackbeard on behalf of England in exchange for a share of his sizable booty and a promise that he would stop pirating.

When Teach began pirating again, Governor Alexander Spotswood of Virginia dispatched a British naval force under Lieutenant Robert Maynard to North Carolina to deal with Blackbeard. On November 22, Blackbeard's forces were defeated, and he was killed in a bloody battle of Ocracoke Island. Rumor has it that his treasure is buried at Springers Point on Ocracoke. This is now a National Park Service Preserve, so you need not bring your metal detector or shovel.

Another anchorage is available across the river in the center of Upper Dowry Creek (Mile 131.6), north of Dowry Creek Marina. The creek carries 5- to 6-foot MLW depths for about a 0.25 mile north of the mouth. Secure holding in clay and a short fetch make this location a favorite retreat for local skippers when even the most severe storms approach. You can arrange for facilities use with Dowry Creek Marina for a modest daily fee.

Several smaller side creeks along the Pungo River have adequate depths for anchoring shallow-drafted boats.

Once inside the storm barrier at Belhaven you can anchor northwest of the channel in Pantego Creek in 7- to 9-foot MLW depths with fair holding. This is a popular spot despite considerable wave action when the wind picks up, as it often does in the afternoon. This is not a good anchorage in wind from any southerly quadrant. Care should be taken to avoid a shoal in front of the (closed) hospital.

To access the dinghy landing, follow Wynn's Gut past Belhaven Town Docks At Wynne's Gut and under the Water Street Bridge (7-foot fixed vertical clearance, depending on tide). The Belhaven Mainstreet Landing is to starboard with 130 feet of dockage suited for dinghies or small powerboats visiting downtown sites.

If you are not planning on going ashore, Persimmon Tree Point is an excellent alternative to anchoring inside Belhaven Harbor. Turn west of the ICW between green marker "1BC" and green daybeacon "7." Head west to red "2PC" at the entrance to the creek. Once around the corner pick an anchorage based on the wind protection. There is plenty of space with 8- to 9-foot MLW depths and good holding around the entire basin.

After rounding the Persimmon Tree Point, Pungo Creek widens and carries no less than 9 feet MLW for about 1.5 miles. The entire south shore and half of the north will provide good anchoring and shelter from winds and waves from any direction. Simply choose your spot for the expected winds.

Five miles south off the Pungo River and to the south and east of flashing red "4" at Mile 140 is Jordan Creek, another anchoring possibility. The entrance is marked but has a bar and should not be attempted without local knowledge if you draw more than 5 feet. (You will see large sailboats inside.) Favor the green side of the channel. A well-marked 6-foot channel leads to safe anchorage with excellent holding from all but strong easterly winds. Best holding can be found in main bowl or to north at the fork.

Directly across the river is Allison Creek, which is a great spot to avoid wind and weather from most directions, except west or northwest. Watch for the sunken boat and shoaling on the northern side of the Slade Creek Inlet. If more shelter is desired, there are more opportunities farther up Slade Creek.

■ SIDE TRIP: PAMLICO RIVER

Sixty-five miles (via the ICW) south of Albemarle Sound lays the northwestern prong of Pamlico Sound, which reaches up to meet the Pamlico River. The Pamlico River is wide and easily navigable to Washington, NC, where the Pamlico River becomes the Tar River. This wide, beautiful river is lined with wooded banks and one industrial site–a phosphate mine on the south side of the river a little more than 10 miles from the ICW.

NAVIGATION: If you are southbound, the entrance to the Pamlico River from the ICW is around the junction of flashing red "PR" (Mile 145.7), which is marking the shoal off Wades Point at the mouth of the Pungo River. Do not attempt to cut inside the marker unless you are very familiar with the area. Take care not to hit the unmarked, unlighted Mile 145 marker on the east side of the Pungo River prior to Wades Point.

CAUTION: The Pamlico River ferry runs year-round between Aurora (on South Creek) and Bayview (north shore) at 6:30 a.m., 8:00 a.m., 10:15 a.m., 11:45 a.m., 2:45 p.m., 5:00 p.m. and 6:15 p.m. Be alert and give way. Keep your eyes open and stay out of its way.

South Creek

South Creek lies just west of the small charted Pamlico River - Indian Island on the south shore of the Pamlico River. Deep and well marked all the way to the town of Aurora, this is an excellent creek for exploration or anchorage, but be aware that there are no facilities for transient boaters. Dinghies can tie to the former town docks, which are now leased by North Carolina Fish and Wildlife.

Downtown Aurora is about three blocks from the waterfront. The Aurora Fossil Museum (400 Main St., 252-322-4238) located near the head of South Creek off the Pamlico River is well worth a visit. It houses a collection of shark teeth, whalebones and other fossils. Visitors can sift through fossil bed soil (compliments of the nearby phosphate mine) and find their own souvenir shark teeth, free of charge.

NAVIGATION: When approaching Aurora the channel narrows and depths shoal to 5 to 7 feet MLW. Follow the daybeacons carefully and save any shallow-water exploration for your dinghy.

Anchorage: South Creek offers numerous anchorage possibilities off of the well-marked channel but has no protection from the east or west. Nearby Bond Creek to the south (at the town of South Creek) has good holding in soft mud with 7 to 9 feet MLW.

North Creek

Just off the north side of the Pamlico River and directly across from South Creek is peaceful North Creek. About 6 miles to the east is the ICW, running across the mouth of the Pamlico Sound. About 25 minutes to the west is Washington, NC, where you will find many marine supply stores to meet your boating needs.

NAVIGATION: It can be difficult to spot the entrance to North Creek but once inside, the channel is well marked. Proceed about 0.5 miles up North Creek, turning into the western branch (Ashon Gut) at red daybeacon "4" to reach the marine facilities. Don't try to turn in a red daybeacon "2," which leads to a shallow (1- to 2-foot MLW) cove. The East Fork continues upriver a short way northeast past daybeacon "4" to Ross Creek and carries at least 6 feet MLW. (The western branch to the marina carries closer to 5 feet MLW.) Expect lots of local boat traffic on both branches.

Dockage: The slips at Potter's Marine at Cradle Point are well protected from the windy Pamlico River. This is a quiet location with a few amenities and no nearby amenities. They maintain 4 transient slips to 50 feet. (Transportation required to visit Bath.)

Anchorage: Anchor in North Creek according to wind and wave protection. Expect to share the space with ski boats on weekends.

Chapter 4: Albemarle Sound to the Neuse River, NC

Pamlico River, NC

NORTH CREEK		Largest Vessel	VHF	Total Slips	Approach/ Dockside Depth	Floating Docks	Gas/ Diesel	Repairs/ Haulout	Min/Max Amps	Pump-Out Station
1. Potter's Marine WiFi	(252) 945-0189	50		25	8.0 / 6.0				30 / 50	P

WiFi Wireless Internet Access
Visit www.waterwayguide.com for current rates, fuel prices, website addresses and other up-to-the-minute information.
(Information in the table is provided by the facilities.)

Scan here for more details:

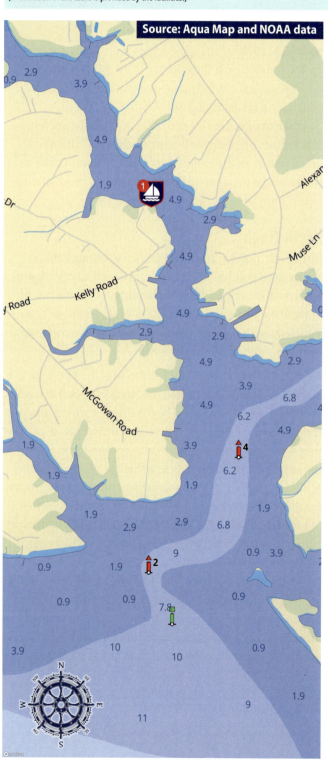

Source: Aqua Map and NOAA data

Bath Creek

The waterfront at the little historic town of Bath on the north shore of the Pamlico River is well worth a visit, especially if you are a history buff. Founded in 1696 and established in 1705 it is listed as the oldest town in North Carolina. Bath's most notorious citizen was Edward Teach, also known as Blackbeard (the pirate). Standing in front of the historic Bonner House and looking south across the bay it is easy to see why Blackbeard selected Bath and Plum Point as his base of operation: privacy. That much has not changed. You can find information about Blackbeard and Bath at the Historic Bath Visitor Center (252-923-3971) between Main St. and Harding St. just one block from the water.

NAVIGATION: You can set a northerly course into Bath Creek beyond the ferry crossing and 3 miles northwest of flashing red "4" off Gum Point. Avoid the fish stakes at the entrance and be wary of any possible submerged pilings after clearing flashing green "1" at the entrance. The harbor is easy to enter if you mind the NOAA chart and watch out for the crab pots around flashing green "1" and red daybeacon "2" (Archbell and Plum Points).

Dockage: Pass green daybeacon "3" and flashing red "4" to reach dockage at Bath Harbor Marina just to the south of the **NC 92 (Bath Creek) Bridge** (13-foot fixed vertical clearance) and have at least 6-foot MLW approach depths. (Bridge clearance has been observed to be closer to 14.5 feet.) The marina has slips for vessels to 60 feet and hotel rooms to rent. (Hint: Boat slip is free if you book a room.)

There are no utilities at the Harding's Landing Marina, Bath State Dock but dockage is complimentary for 72 hours (with permission from Harbor Master).

Anchorage: Back Creek (to starboard off Bath Creek) provides a protected anchorage with good holding and depths of 6 to 7 feet MLW up to the fixed NC 92 (Back Creek) Bridge (7-foot vertical clearance). Ice cream, cold beer and a casual grill (burgers, hot dogs, shrimp burger)

Pamlico River, NC

BATH CREEK

		Largest Vessel	VHF	Total Slips	Approach/ Dockside Depth	Floating Docks	Gas/ Diesel	Repairs/ Haulout	Min/Max Amps	Pump-Out Station
1. Bath Harbor Marina WiFi	(252) 923-5711	60	16	43	6.0 / 8.0				30 / 50	

WiFi Wireless Internet Access
Visit www.waterwayguide.com for current rates, fuel prices, website addresses and other up-to-the-minute information.
(Information in the table is provided by the facilities.)

Scan here for more details:

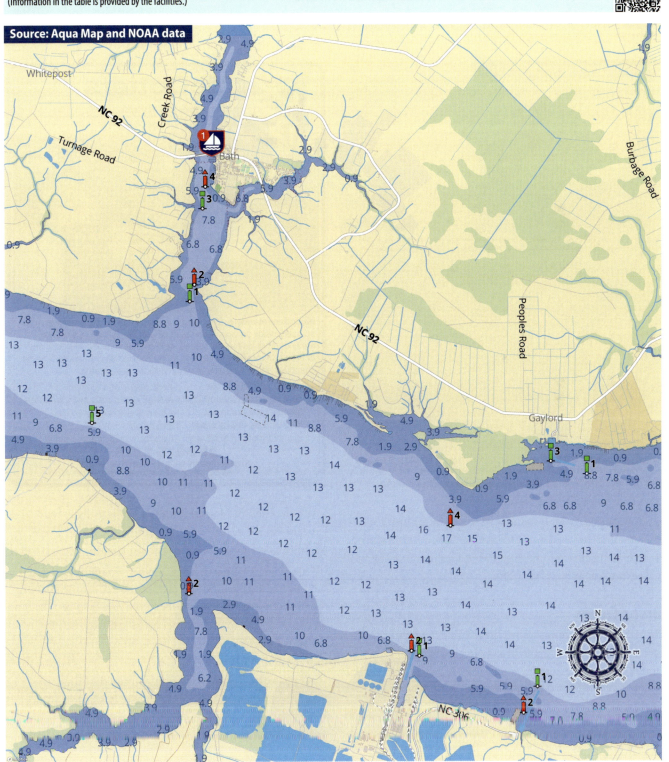

Source: Aqua Map and NOAA data

Chapter 4: Albemarle Sound to the Neuse River, NC

Pamlico River, NC

BROAD CREEK		Largest Vessel	VHF	Total Slips	Approach/Dockside Depth	Floating Docks	Gas/Diesel	Repairs/Haulout	Min/Max Amps	Pump-Out Station
1. Broad Creek Marina	(252) 946-4924	38		100	4.0 / 4.0				30	P
2. McCotters Marina & Boatyard WiFi 20.7 mi. W of MM 146.0	(252) 975-2174	65	16	180	6.0 / 6.0			RH	30 / 50	P
3. Washington Yacht & Country Club-PRIVATE WiFi	(252) 402-5153	55		177	6.0 / 6.0		GD		30 / 50	P

WiFi Wireless Internet Access
Visit www.waterwayguide.com for current rates, fuel prices, website addresses and other up-to-the-minute information. (Information in the table is provided by the facilities.)

Scan here for more details:

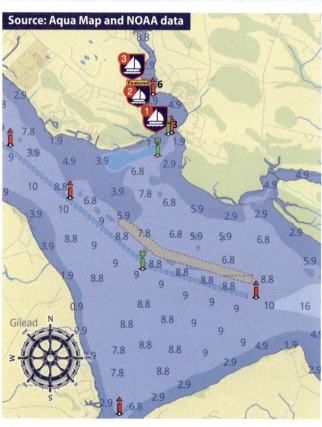

McCotters Marina & Boat Yard is a full service marina complete with an outstanding service department able to handle any type of boat repair or modification. We are located on the protected western shore of Broad Creek off the north side of the Pamlico River. In addition to our chandlery and the usual marina services we also provide:

- canvas and sail repair
- custom canvas fabrication
- holding tank pump out
- slips and on land storage
- gas and diesel mechanics
- boat riggers and restorers
- marine electricians and carpenters
- expert in gelcoat application and repair
- experts in polyurethane paint

252-975-2174
mark@mccottersmarina.com
McCottersMarina.com

are at Quarterdeck Marina by the bridge. Gas is also available for shallow-draft boats.

You can drop the hook inside Archbell & Plum Pt. on the east and west sides of the creek at the mouth. Expect 4- to 6-foot MLW depths and pull in far enough to be out of the way of any passing traffic.

Broad Creek

Broad Creek is 7 miles to the west of Bath. Several hundred sail and powerboats make Broad Creek their home port and it is the main boating center for Washington located 7 miles farther to the north-northwest.

NAVIGATION: Broad Creek's entrance is well marked and easy to negotiate from the east. Steer in a northwesterly direction from flashing green "7" (in the main Pamlico River channel off Maules Point) until flashing green "1" is visible to the north and then follow the Broad Creek channel to green daybeacon "3" and flashing red "4." Note the spoil areas south of the entrance. If coming from the west steer east past the red daybeacon "8" before turning north then turn northwest once on a line between flashing green "7" in the main channel and flashing green "1" in the Broad Creek channel. There is no room for anchoring in this small harbor.

Dockage: To starboard you will see the Pamlico Plantation private docks (no transient dockage). To port is Broad Creek Marina, a small-boat marina with 4-foot approach and dockside depths that can accommodate boats to 38 feet.

Pamlico River, NC

WASHINGTON		Largest Vessel	VHF	Total Slips	Approach/ Dockside Depth	Floating Docks	Gas/ Diesel	Repairs/ Haulout	Min/Max Amps	Pump-Out Station
1. Moss Landing Marina WiFi	(252) 623-1314	60	16	52	10.0 / 15.0	F			30 / 50	P
2. Washington Waterfront Docks WiFi	(252) 940-1231	80	16	36	14.0 / 18.0				30 / 50	P

WiFi Wireless Internet Access
Visit www.waterwayguide.com for current rates, fuel prices, website addresses and other up-to-the-minute information.
(Information in the table is provided by the facilities.)

Scan here for more details: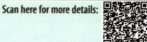

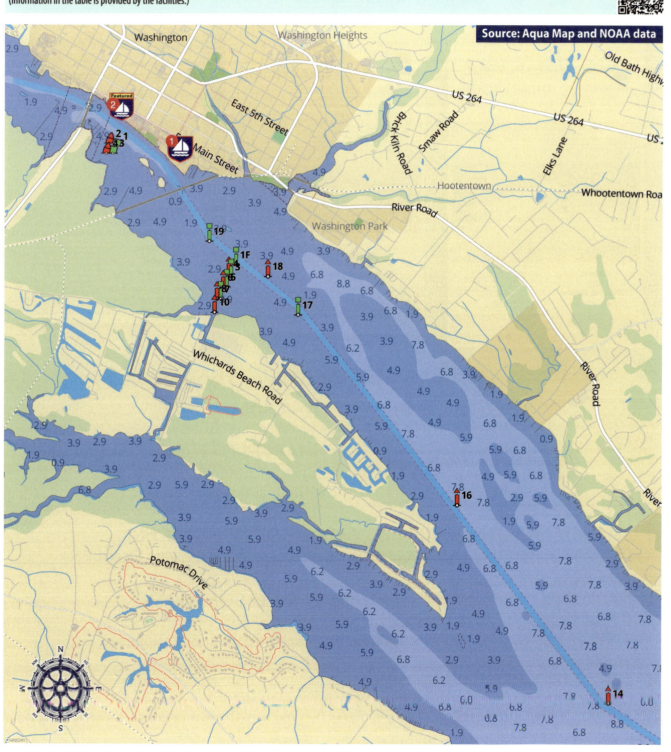

Source: Aqua Map and NOAA data

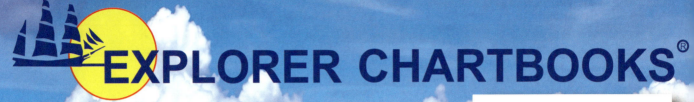

THE ONLY ALL-IN-ONE BAHAMAS CHARTS AND CRUISING GUIDE

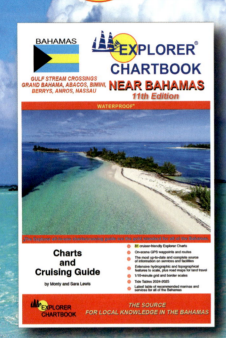
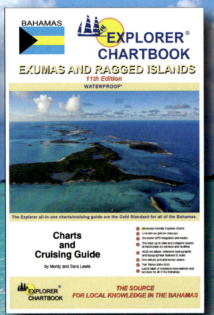
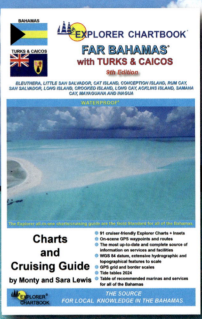

EXPLORER® ELECTRONIC CHARTS AVAILABLE FROM:

CHARTPLOTTERS
B&G • Furuno • Lowrance • Raymarine
SIMRAD • Standard Horizon

MOBILE DEVICES (APPS)
AquaMap • Embark • iNavX • TZ iBoat • OpenCPN

MAC & PC SOFTWARE
C-Map
MaxSea: MapMedia, TimeZero, Nobeltec
RosePoint: Coastal Explorer

Contact providers directly to tailor Explorer data for your nav station needs

Don't leave the dock without The Explorer!

Locally-owned and operated McCotters Marina & Boatyard dates back to the 1950s and was originally the regional Chris Craft Dealership. Today the facility has modern haul-out facilities and can handle repairs and upgrades, storage and boat sales. Their canvas department can fabricate custom dodgers, biminis, enclosures, awnings and sail covers, plus restore upholstery and cushions. They maintain 15 transient slips to 65 feet. Call ahead.

The private Washington Yacht & Country Club is beyond red daybeacon "6." (Give the marker good clearance.) The club offers transient dockage and amenities to members of reciprocating clubs and features a championship 18-hole golf course, fine dining and tennis courts.

Washington

This small community of just under 10,000 residents has a maritime culture all its own with dozens of colorful crab statues lining the downtown streets, hundreds of boats–both big and small–lining the waterfront and miles of open Tar and Pamlico River views extending in virtually every direction. Here you will find a sprawling waterfront with stores, businesses and the historic haunts of pirates.

NAVIGATION: The NOAA chart shows plenty of water in the Pamlico River even outside the channel until flashing red "14." From here markers "16," "17," "18" and "19" lead to the **Norfolk Southern Railroad Bridge**. The bridge has 7-foot closed vertical clearance and is usually open, however, it may be closed between 7:30 a.m. and 10:30 a.m. on weekdays and Saturday. Past the bridge is the Washington riverfront located to starboard before the **US 17 Business Bridge** (6-foot closed vertical clearance), which will open with 24-hour notice. This bridge marks the confluence of the Pamlico River and the Tar River and the river actually changes names at this point. When approaching the town keep Castle Island to port and stay within the 9-foot MLW channel.

Dockage: Moss Landing Marina is part of an upscale condo complex. They offer deeded slips in a gated facility but may be able to accommodate you. Do call ahead.

Transient slips with electricity, water and WiFi are available at Washington Waterfront Docks. Reservations are accepted. The lighthouse building has climate-controlled heads and showers and a laundry (fee charged). Short-term docking is also available for a fee.

Cypress Landing Marina to the south at Chocowinity Bay is private. (No transient slips.)

Anchorage: Boats anchor off the waterfront bulkheads at Washington when slips are full but there is no protection here; it is completely open to wind and wakes. Be sure to stay out of the channel. A floating dinghy dock is located at the west end of the waterfront near the lighthouse building. Boats anchored in the harbor may use the dinghy dock and the heads and showers once registered with the Washington Waterfront Docks attendant.

TO THE NEUSE RIVER

Pamlico River Crossing

The ICW follows the broad lower reach of the Pungo River to the junction of the Pamlico River. (Markers are still reversed, green to starboard going south; continue running the yellow squares and triangles.) The markers in the lower Pungo River are spaced far apart and sometimes difficult to locate but the river is wide and adequately deep.

NAVIGATION: The Pamlico River crossing is straight and is usually an easy run; however, conflicting currents meet at the junction of the Pungo and Pamlico Rivers. When easterly or westerly winds are strong and gusty the crossing of the Pamlico River can be rough and wet. Confused seas are common, especially within a mile or so of Wades Point flashing red "PR," which is located around Mile 145.7. It can be difficult to locate, especially if northbound from Goose Creek.

The Neuse River–ICW Mile 162
NAVIGATION:

CAUTION: After crossing the Pamlico River to Goose Creek, aids to navigation return to the ICW configuration of red-to-starboard running south. This is especially important when entering Goose Creek, where red daybeacon "4" marks the southeastern edge of a 3-foot MLW shoal and submerged piles. There is also shoaling between green daybeacons "5" and "7" so be sure to stay in the middle of the channel.

Chapter 4: Albemarle Sound to the Neuse River, NC

Goin' Ashore: WASHINGTON, NC

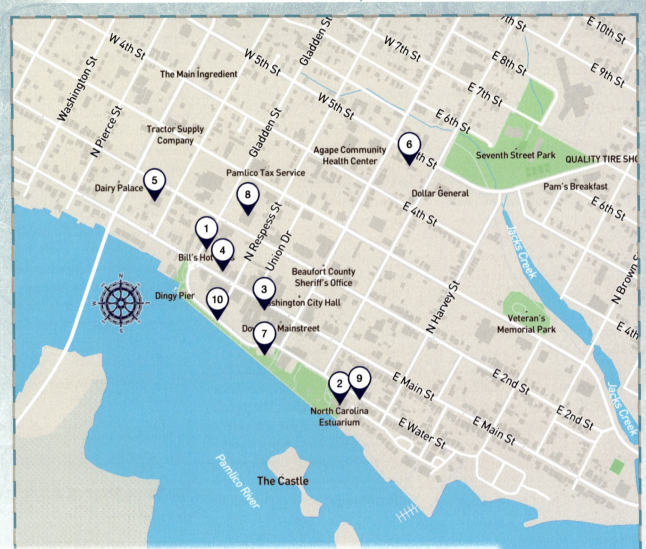

First called Forks of the Tar, the city name was changed in 1776 in honor of Gen. George Washington. Because it was America's first city to be named for Gen. Washington, it is sometimes referred to as "The Original Washington" or "Little Washington" to avoid confusion. "Little" does not, however, describe the amenities here. A large living aquarium, historic homes, antiques galleries, quaint waterfront restaurants, a waterfront park (with swings) and even a sailing school coexist here. The entire Washington waterfront is listed in the National Register of Historic Places. The Pamlico River provides a scenic backdrop for a variety of activities including boating, kayaking and fishing. Other outdoor activities include hiking, biking and birdwatching.

The Beaufort County Arts Council hosts a variety of events and exhibits throughout the year, showcasing local artists and performers. The town also hosts several annual festivals and events, including the annual Summer Festival held in June and the Smoke on the Water BBQ Competition in October.

America's Waterway Guide Since 1947

Chapter 4

ATTRACTIONS

1. **Bill's Hotdog Stand**
   Listed here for historic and gastronomic reasons. Washington Institution since 1928 serving "no frills" hotdogs served plain or "all the way" (how we prefer it) with spicy chili, onions and mustard at 109 Gladden St. (252-946-3343). This is the original; there's a second location farther inland.

2. **North Carolina Estuarium**
   Aquarium with unique exhibits about the Pamlico-Tar River System featuring over 200 exhibits, living aquariums and a gift shop (223 E. Water St., 252-948-0000). Special programs throughout the year. River tours of the estuary (seasonal) require reservations.

3. **River Walk Gallery**
   Offering a variety of fine art and high quality craft from local artists including jewelry, ceramics, metal work, paintings and fabric arts. Also hosts classes and events at 139 E. Main St. (252-974-0400).

4. **Washington Wine and Gourmet**
   Fun to visit and with provisioning possibilities including wine, craft beer, gourmet food, cheese and vinegars and olive oil at 220 W. Main St. (252-974-2870).

SERVICES

5. **Brown Library**
   122 Van Norden St. (252-946-4300)

6. **The Wash House**
   123 E. 5th St. (866-825-6052)

7. **Washington-Beaufort Chamber of Commerce**
   102 W. Stewart Pkwy. (252-946-9168)

8. **Washington Post Office**
   222 W. 2nd St. (252-946-0128)

MARINAS

9. **Moss Landing Marina**
   227 E. Water St. (252-944-3045)

10. **Washington Waterfront Docks**
    301 W. Stewart Pkwy. (252-940-1231)

MID-ATLANTIC EDITION

Chapter 4 — Albemarle Sound to the Neuse River, NC

Neuse River, NC

HOBUCKEN		Largest Vessel	VHF	Total Slips	Approach/ Dockside Depth	Floating Docks	Gas/ Diesel	Repairs/ Haulout	Min/Max Amps	Pump-Out Station
1. R. E. Mayo Seafood Marine Supply 157.3	(252) 745-5331	90	16		12.0 / 6.0		GD		30	

WiFi Wireless Internet Access

Visit www.waterwayguide.com for current rates, fuel prices, website addresses and other up-to-the-minute information. (Information in the table is provided by the facilities.)

Scan here for more details:

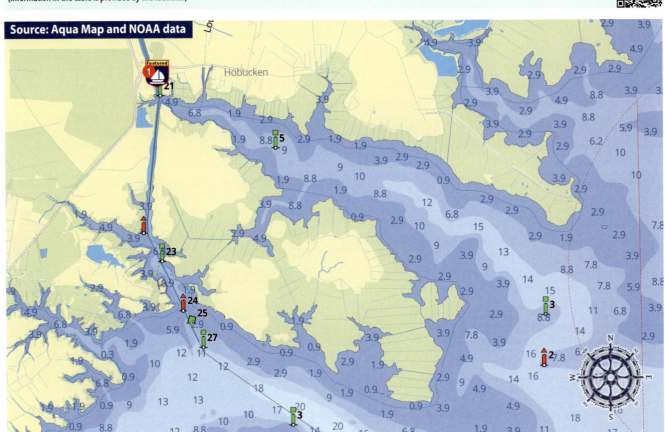

Source: Aqua Map and NOAA data

At Mile 157.2 the area surrounding the Hobucken (NC 33/304) Bridge and the Coast Guard Station is a No-Wake Zone. The bridge is concrete and the underside arches slightly towards the center. There are no bridge boards. The bridge is charted at 65-foot fixed vertical clearance but is closer to 64 feet at mean high water. There can be a considerable wind-driven current here.

At about Mile 159 the land cut (canal) ends at Gale Creek, an arm of the Bay River. Use caution in transiting Gale Creek, which is naturally winding though the channel is charted as arrow-straight.

Be on the lookout for crab pot floats that may be present in the channel between green buoy "25" and quick-flashing green "27" at the end of the cut before Bay River. From Gale Creek the ICW cuts 5 miles down Bay River to Maw Point and Maw Point Shoal (near Mile 165), which continues to build out into the Neuse River. The Hobucken Coast Guard station can give you information on conditions around Maw Point (252-745-3131). When strong winds blow down the Bay River wave action can be almost as bad as on the much larger Neuse River.

Southeast along the Bay River, Pine Tree Point is marked by flashing green "3" to starboard (Mile 162.4) and then by flashing green "1," which marks the shoaling off Deep Point. Do not pass too close to flashing green "1" as shoaling has been reported to extend slightly into the channel from the marker.

Like the Pungo River, the marking system for the Bay River is numbered from seaward (i.e., the colors of the markers are reversed with green on starboard going south until the Neuse River Junction).

Neuse River, NC

BAYBORO		Largest Vessel	VHF	Total Slips	Approach/Dockside Depth	Floating Docks	Gas/Diesel	Repairs/Haulout	Min/Max Amps	Pump-Out Station
1. Hurricane Boatyard WiFi	(252) 745-3369	60		17	8.0 / 6.5	F		RH	30	P

WiFi Wireless Internet Access
Visit www.waterwayguide.com for current rates, fuel prices, website addresses and other up-to-the-minute information. (Information in the table is provided by the facilities.)

Scan here for more details:

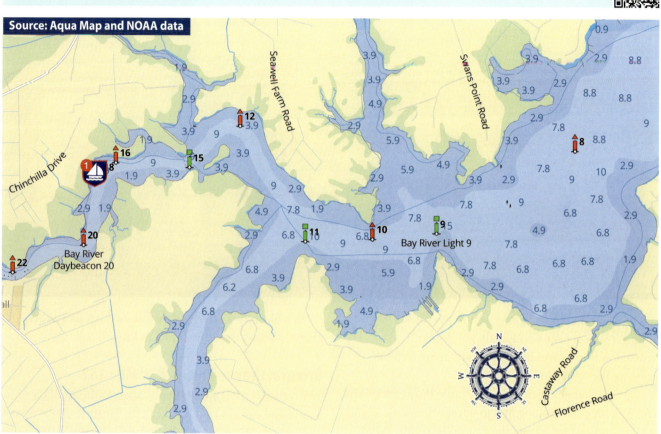

Source: Aqua Map and NOAA data

Maw Point and the Neuse River are often easier to run in the morning just after dawn when surface winds may be lighter so anchoring in Bay River the night before is a good idea. Adequate depths run well upriver to the quaint and quiet towns of Vandemere ("village by the sea") and Bayboro. To reach Bayboro proceed past Vandemere continuing to follow the markers carefully, especially green daybeacon "11" and red daybeacon "12."

Dockage: The commercial facilities at R. E. Mayo Seafood Marine Supply are on the south side of the Hobucken (NC 33/304) Bridge (Mile 157.2). They carry boat parts and have an excellent marine supply store and welcome transients when they have space. Amenities are limited, and the restrooms are in the ship store and are only available when the store is open. This is working shrimp dock and they will pack fresh and fresh frozen seafood in any quantity you like.

Hurricane Boatyard in Bayboro has a great DIY boatyard. They can also provide full or partial service if needed. Transients have access to clean showers and a small but well-stocked chandlery.

Anchorage: Goose Creek abounds with anchorages. Anchor according to wind direction at Snode Creek or Eastham Creek in east winds or Campbell Creek in west winds.

You can anchor west of Gale Creek R22 (approximately Mile 159) in 4- to 6-foot MLW depths. An underwater electric cable runs from the mainland to the Jones Island Club, a private lodge on the island shore just east of green daybeacon "23." A sign in the bay warns "Danger High Voltage" so do not anchor here. When leaving Gale Creek do not mistake the Bay River markers that lead west to Vandemere for those leading southeast to the Neuse River.

Chapter 4: Albemarle Sound to the Neuse River, NC

Oriental Marina and Inn

There is another anchorage just to the south at Mile 159.6 at Gale Creek with 360 degree protection from waves and is a good staging area for crossing the Neuse River.

One convenient anchorage is in Little Bear Creek (Mile 160.8) with good holding in 8 to 9 feet MLW with a mud bottom and exposure from the east to the south. Wind current will keep you in the same position all night.

Although there are no amenities, you can anchor off Vandemere village dock on Bay River with exposure from the southeast to the southwest. Stay clear of the channel because shrimp boats use it. Steer toward the village docks from flashing green "5" and drop the anchor in 9 to 10 feet MLW. An east to southeast wind can create rough conditions. Show an anchor light at night and always ask permission to tie up the dinghy if you go ashore.

There is a good anchorage to the south in Long Creek at Bonner Bay. To reach Bonner Bay exit the ICW at quick flashing green "27" (Mile 161) and head southwest. Feel your way in via the unmarked channel with the depth sounder and go up Long Creek (the left fork) to anchor in 9 to 11 feet MLW with good holding in mud. It is a beautiful secluded anchorage with no structures in sight but it can be buggy in the summer months.

In a blustery westerly blow, follow the 8-foot MLW channel across the Bonner Bay to Riggs Creek.

Oriental (Neuse River)–ICW Mile 182

The Neuse is a large river that is open to the Pamlico Sound and can get rough. Check the weather and proceed with respect. First-timers should run compass courses and use radar or GPS whenever possible.

A southwest wind can make the 18-mile run to Oriental at Mile 182 a very wet ride. A fall northwester, however, will leave the river calm with the wind coming from the shore. At those times the wide, lovely Neuse River can be a pleasant change from the narrow land cuts of the ICW, especially for sailors who want to shake out the sails.

Oriental has become widely known as the "Sailing Capital of North Carolina" and locals claim sailboats outnumber people three to one, although boating facilities in the area also attract visiting power boaters. The sheltered creeks provide immediate access to the country's second largest estuary and sailing, cruising and gunkholing areas.

Local marinas welcome transients and offer supply and repair capabilities to handle virtually any requirement.

RIVER DUNES
ORIENTAL, NORTH CAROLINA

DISCOVER A NEW COASTAL RETREAT

Book your next ICW stop at an award-winning protected marina with overnight dockage up to 130', Fuel and Deep Water Slips. Enjoy the thriving Harbor Village, pool, waterfront dining, bikes and the big water of the Pamlico Sound & Neuse River.

WATERFRONT HOMESITES | NEW HOMES | SLIPS | LODGING | OVERNIGHT DOCKAGE
DINING | BOATERS LOUNGE | WIFI | PICKLEBALL | TENNIS | WATERSPORTS

Southern Living
INSPIRED COMMUNITIES

(800) 348-7618 | ICW MM 173 | RIVERDUNES.COM

Chapter 4: Albemarle Sound to the Neuse River, NC

Goin' Ashore

ORIENTAL, NC

Life moves slowly in this welcoming village. The harbor is the heart of Oriental, with scenic views of the water, boats and marinas. It's a great place to relax and enjoy the peaceful surroundings. Boats and bikes rest against dock pilings and porch railings. Talking and walking may not be considered official recreational activities in most towns but in Oriental, they fit with the feel of a quaint waterfront town where biking, sailing, kayaking, fishing, and boating are popular pastimes. Long known as the "Sailing Capital of North Carolina," Oriental is blessed with wide waters, steady winds and easy access to dozen of creeks and estuaries. The town lives up to its moniker with numerous boating options

ATTRACTIONS

1 Down East Canvas & Gallery
Located at the foot of the bridge, this is a combination canvas shop and art gallery (301 Broad St., 252-249-1004). Open Tuesday through Saturday (year-round).

2. Inland Waterway Provision Company
Marine supplies, including some that can be ordered in advance, as well as local meats, eggs, dairy and produce and beer and wine. They also offer a Cruisers Corner, where visitors can chill out or warm up with free WiFi and a swap bookcase (305 Hodges St., 252-249-1797).

3. Nautical Wheelers
Cruiser favorite with locations in Oriental and New Bern offering nautical gift items, clothing, shoes and jewelry. They also sell wine and frequently host wine tastings on the porch at 411 Broad St. (252-249-0359).

America's Waterway Guide Since 1947

Chapter 4

for boating services and supplies including a West Marine at 1104 Broad St. (252-249-3200) and sail repair, cleaning and canvas work close to Town Dock at 603 Hodges St., 252-249-0739). Village Marine Hardware has some marine supplies and great customer service at 804 Broad St. (252-249-1211).

The annual Croaker Festival is a celebration of Oriental's fishing heritage and includes live music, food, arts and crafts, and a parade. It is held the last week in June. The oriental Boat Show in held in April. This annual event draws thousands of visitors to Oriental each year, with hundreds of boats on display, vendors and live music. As a nod to the town's mascot, dragon boat races are held every August. (Dragons lurk throughout the village.)

4. Oriental's History Museum
Displays model skiffs, oyster scoops, the bronze porthole from its namesake, *S.S. Oriental*, a Wurlitzer juke box and much more documenting Oriental's history at 802 Broad St. (252-249-3340). Pick up a Historic Walking Tour brochure and follow the route past over 70 historical buildings and sites.

5. The Silos
A local and boater favorite located in a pair of reclaimed silos about a 15-minute walk from the Town Dock (1111 Broad St., 252-249-1050). Offering a specialty pizza and pasta menu. "Open Mike Night" every Wednesday. On-site Red Rooster outdoor bar and stage offers casual outdoor venue with frequent live concerts.

6. The Village Gallery
Eight rooms of works in oil, pastels, acrylic, photography, jewelry, watercolor, pottery, glass and more, which you can buy directly from the juried artists (300 Hodges St., 252-249-0300).

SERVICES

7. CCHC Oriental Medical Center
901 Broad St.
(252-249-2888)

8. Oriental Post Office
809 Broad St.
(252-249-0454)

9. Oriental Town Hall
507 Church St.
(252-249-0555)

10. Oriental Village Veterinary Hospital
407 Broad St.
(252-249-2149)

MARINAS

11. Clancy's Marina
309 Midyette St.
(252-675-1410)

12. Oriental Harbor Marina
518 S. Water St.
(252-671-9692)

13. Oriental Marina & Inn
103 Wall St.
(252-249-1818)

14. Sailcraft Service
1400 Tosto Circle
(252-249-1754)

15. Whittaker Point Marina
5001 Maritime Dr.
(252-249-1750)

16. Whittaker Creek Yacht Harbor
415 Whittaker Point Rd.
(252-670-3759)

MID-ATLANTIC EDITION

Chapter 4: Albemarle Sound to the Neuse River, NC

Neuse River, NC

BROAD CREEK		Largest Vessel	VHF	Total Slips	Approach/Dockside Depth	Floating Docks	Gas/Diesel	Repairs/Haulout	Min/Max Amps	Pump-Out Station
1. River Dunes Marina at Grace Harbor WiFi MM 173.0	(252) 249-4908	125	16	400	7.0 / 9.0	F	GD		30 / 200+	P
2. Marine Craft WiFi	(252) 571-9980	80		32	7.0 / 7.0			R	30	P
3. Ensign Harbor Marina WiFi	(910) 508-6696	40		29	5.5 / 6.0				30	P

WiFi Wireless Internet Access
Visit www.waterwayguide.com for current rates, fuel prices, website addresses and other up-to-the-minute information. (Information in the table is provided by the facilities.)

Scan here for more details:

Source: Aqua Map and NOAA data

This is a popular place and space is limited so reservations are recommended.

NAVIGATION: Maw Point Shoal introduces you to the Neuse River. Follow the magenta line carefully as you make the 90-degree turn around the Neuse River Junction Light "NR," a 15-foot flashing (2 + 1) red light at 6-second intervals. Use special caution here. The three red flashing lights (uncharted) in the prohibited area of Rattan Bay can be confused with the entrance light. More importantly, there are 30 miles of open water between Maw Point and the Outer Banks. Winds out of the east make it rough and if you are not careful, you could be set onto the shoal.

If on station, flashing green "1" (off Deep Point) and flashing red "2" (off Maw Point Shoal) make a shortcut inside the Neuse River junction light but do not use it if brisk winds make Maw Point Shoal a lee shore. Even though depths are at least 8 feet along this shortcut route, crab traps are scattered throughout the area and require attention. From Bay River flashing green "1" off Deep Point run a course that will put you at least 0.25 mile off flashing red "2" and then head for flashing red "4" off the tip of the shoal extending from Piney Point (at Mile 171.4) on a south-southwesterly course.

If heading west to the Neuse River from Pamlico Sound through the Brant Island Slue, be aware that shoaling to 3 feet MLW has been reported in the area off the southeast tip of the charted shoal across from flashing green "1."

There has been ongoing discussion about extending the existing Marine Corps bombing range to include Brant Island Shoals. This would effectively prevent all vessels from crossing Brant Island Shoal through the Brant Island Slue, forcing them to go all the way around the end of Brant Island Shoal. Stay tuned for updates at Waterway Explorer.

Northbound boats will appreciate the anchorages in Broad Creek (ICW Mile 173) off the Neuse River's western shore. This is also home to the amenity-rich River Dunes Marina at Grace Harbor, a destination in itself.

The white marker "Danger Shoal" guides skippers bound for Broad Creek around the extending shoal south of Piney Point. Shoals at Piney Point and Gum Thicket Shoal continually build out. The danger beacon marks the tip of the shoal between flashing red "4" and the warning daybeacon platform. Do not mistake the more dilapidated white warning daybeacon for flashing red "4" off Piney Point. Depths inshore of the platform are less than 2 feet MLW in spots. All markers off Piney Point should be left well to the north.

Boats bound for Broad Creek should exit the ICW halfway between flashing red "4" and "6" on the Neuse River and follow the markers into Broad Creek. Give green daybeacon "3" a wide berth. Be on the lookout as there may be numerous crab pot floats in the creek.

Marine facilities at Oriental begin at Mile 180.5 where a marked entrance leads to Whittaker Creek. There are more markers here than shown on the NOAA chart and they make it easy to stay on the range (not charted), which can be picked up on entry. Be sure to give green buoy "5" a wide berth before turning left into the facility-lined creek. Depths of 8 feet MLW are reported for the channel; nevertheless, southwesterly winds can lower this depth, and some shoaling persists in the area around and south of green buoy "5."

Boats coming from the north can head straight for the 15 foot high flashing red "6" and join the channel there. It is best to call ahead to the marina of your choice to check for current depths and steering directions at time of entry. Mind the crab traps and do not be surprised to see them in mid-channel. Oriental has no tide to contend with, only the wind-driven ups and downs of eastern and western storms.

Just to the southwest of the entrance to Whittaker Creek on the Neuse River a well-marked channel carrying 8.5 feet MLW leads to the basin confluence of Smith Creek and Greens Creek immediately beyond the fixed **Oriental Road (NC 1308) Bridge** spanning the junction.

> *CAUTION:* Oriental Road (NC 1308) Bridge is not on the ICW and only has a vertical clearance of 45 feet. Do not attempt to navigate up Greens Creek to the anchorage or marina if your vessel's air draft exceeds 40 feet. Also, the charted depths in these creeks can be misleading. Wind and weather can raise (as well as lower) the water level appreciably in this area. If winds have been out of the west or southwest for any length of time, a drop in water levels of as much as 3 feet is possible. Sound your way in.

Dockage: River Dunes Marina at Grace Harbor is reached by heading northwest from the ICW halfway between flashing reds "4" and "6" and then following the marked channel into Broad Creek. Give the markers at least 50 yards as you pass. The marina is on the port side of the creek at red daybeacon "4."

Entry is through a private, well-maintained and marked, bulkheaded channel with charted 8-foot MLW depths. Unless you have the latest updates on your electronic charts you will not see the channel marked so follow the private markers. The floating docks at River Dunes Marina at Grace Harbor have full-length finger piers and 8 feet MLW. They offer resort-type amenities including croquet on the green, tennis and billiards. A courtesy car is available for the 10-mile trip into Oriental and its many services and amenities.

A well marked and maintained channel to the north on Brown Creek leads directly to Marine Craft. They have slips up to 80 feet on fixed docks in good repair. There are 1.5 acres of dry storage space for rent off season. The location provides great protection nearly 360 degrees. The clubhouse is a great place to watch the sunsets.

Also on Brown Creek is the 29-slip Ensign Harbor Marina, which welcomes transients to 40 feet with 5-foot approach depths.

Whittaker Pointe Marina is located at the mouth of Whittaker Creek on the east side of the entrance. They have a wave attenuator for southwest protection and the marina welcomes transients (including catamarans) in a quiet, park-like setting. They will loan you a courtesy van to provision after helping you settle in.

Nearby 140-slip Whittaker Creek Yacht Harbor is immediately visible just inside the point. Call ahead for slip availability.

Zimmerman Marine-Oriental offers full boat repair services from rigging to mechanical and electrical and including carpentry and fiberglass. Zimmerman's has other yards in Holden Beach, NC; Southport, NC; Deltaville, VA; Mobjack Bay, VA; Herrington Harbour, MD; Solomons, MD; and Charleston, SC.

Chapter 4: Albemarle Sound to the Neuse River, NC

Neuse River, NC

		Largest Vessel	VHF	Total Slips	Approach/ Dockside Depth	Floating Docks	Gas/ Diesel	Repairs/ Haulout	Min/Max Amps	Pump-Out Station
WHITTAKER CREEK										
1. Whittaker Pointe Marina WiFi MM 181.0	(252) 249-1750	100	16	53	8.0 / 9.0				30 / 50	
2. Whittaker Creek Yacht Harbor WiFi 1.7 mi. NW of MM 181.0	(252) 670-3759	140	16	140	7.0 / 8.0			R	30 / 50	
3. Sailcraft Service WiFi MM 181.0	(252) 249-0522	65	16	12	8.0 / 7.0			RH	30 / 50	
4. Zimmerman Marine - Oriental WiFi MM 181.0	(252) 249-1180	65	16	29	7.0 / 7.0			RH	30 / 50	P
ORIENTAL HARBOR										
5. Oriental Marina & Inn WiFi 1.9 mi. NW of MM 181.5	(252) 249-1818	100	16	27	8.0 / 6.5		GD		30 / 50	
6. Oriental Harbor Marina WiFi MM 182.0	(252) 249-0777	100	16	110	8.0 / 6.0				30 / 50	P
SMITH CREEK										
7. Clancy's Marina WiFi	(252) 675-1410	60		17	6.0 / 5.0	F			30 / 50	P
8. Blackwell Point Marina WiFi MM 182.0	(252) 340-7459	50	16	10	6.0 / 6.0	F			20	
WINDMILL POINT										
9. Pecan Grove Marina-PRIVATE WiFi	(252) 249-2532			222	/				30 / 100	P

WiFi Wireless Internet Access
Visit www.waterwayguide.com for current rates, fuel prices, website addresses and other up-to-the-minute information.
(Information in the table is provided by the facilities.)

Scan here for more details:

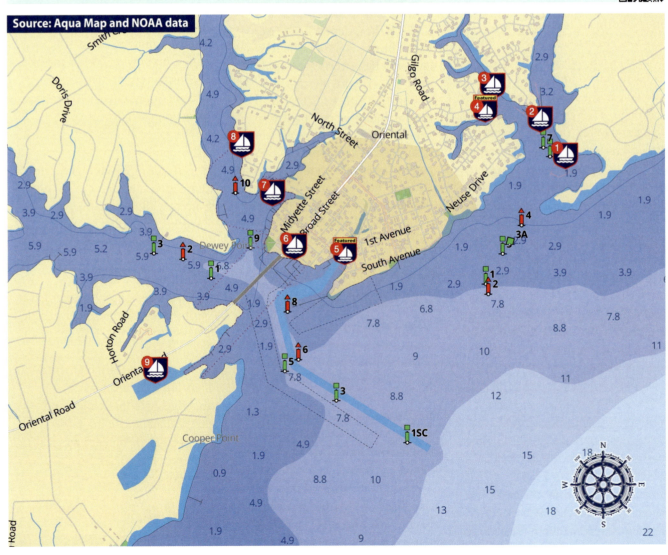

America's Waterway Guide Since 1947 — Chapter 4

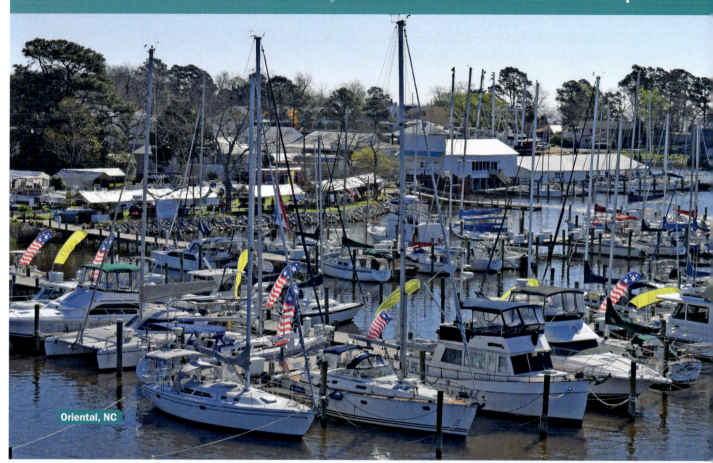
Oriental, NC

Inland Waterway Provision Company

- Marine Supplies
- Fishing Gear
- Safety Gear
- Inflatable Boats
- Kayak Rentals
- Gifts
- Fresh Local Produce & Meats, Beer & Wine

Located at ICW MM 182 in Oriental, NC
252-249-1797 • iwpc@dockline.net
InlandWaterwayProvisionCompany.com

Oriental Marina & Inn
Your Best Stopover
Oriental, North Carolina

All Suite Inn
- Nightly Rates
- 1, 2, 3 Bedroom & ADA
- Kitchenettes
- All Waterfront Balconies

Transient Boat Slips
- Per Foot Charge
- Up to 105' X 25'
- Water, Power
- Wireless Internet

• Flotillas Welcome • Fuel Dock • Pool • Laundry • Showers
• Tiki Bar • Toucan Grill and Fresh Bar • ALL ABC PERMITS
• We now have additional slips • 440' Face Dock — Vessels to 150'

252-249-1818 • MM 182 ICW VHF 16 • www.orientalmarina.com

Search **Waterway Explorer**® for navigation advice, destinations, fuel prices and more.

Use this QR code

WATERWAY GUIDE — THE CRUISING AUTHORITY
www.waterwayguide.com

MID-ATLANTIC EDITION

Chapter 4: Albemarle Sound to the Neuse River, NC

Oriental's harbor (known locally as Raccoon Creek) lies immediately to starboard after passing flashing red "8" at the end of the rock jetty south of Whittaker Point. This harbor is tight with the distance between the north and south shores being not much more than a generous fairway. The breakwater here only minimally protects the harbor from a bouncy and uncomfortable chop when the winds blow over 10 knots across the 5-mile fetch of the Neuse River.

To reach the amenity-rich Oriental Marina & Inn follow the dredged channel past the private Oriental Yacht Club to the north and proceed straight ahead to the marina. This is actually a complex of facilities consisting of docks, an inn and lounge, a swimming pool with a tiki bar and the on-site Toucan Grill & Fresh Bar (252-249-2204), famous for fresh seafood meals (open for lunch and dinner). All 27 slips are reserved for transients so there is usually space.

Oriental Marina & Inn also manages the 110-slip Oriental Harbor Marina. They offer boat repair and cleaning and can accommodate vessels to 100 feet. The face docks are immediately adjacent to the channel under the bridge going upriver, which gets considerable traffic, especially on weekends. Unfortunately this is NOT in a "No Wake" area resulting in bumpy conditions on the face dock.

There are two town docks in Oriental Harbor on either side of Oriental Marina & Inn. Oriental Town Dock #1 has approximately 80 feet of dockage and is complimentary for up to 48 hours and in any 30-day period (except during red drum season, when it becomes a free 2-hour per day tie-up). There is a free pump-out station on this dock. There is no shore power or water but there are clean restrooms next to the dock and you may pay for use of the showers at Oriental Marina & Inn.

Directly at the end of the harbor channel is a second public pier (Oriental Town Dock #2) with 70 feet of two-sided dock with pump-out service. This is directly across the street from The Bean, a popular coffee shop and gathering place (252-249-4918). Boaters will appreciate the newly restored Sergeant House next to Town Dock #2, which acts as a self-service welcome center. It is climate controlled, has free WiFi, a book exchange and is a great place to sit, relax and maybe catch up on emails and such.

The small Clancy's Marina is an option for those who can fit under the fixed 45-foot vertical clearance Oriental Road (NC 1308) Bridge to access Smith Creek. It is about three blocks from downtown Oriental in a residential area. (The marina is adjacent to the owner's home.) They welcome transients.

The well-protected Blackwell Point Marina is just past red daybeacon "10" in Smith Creek. There are on-site bike rentals for getting to town. They only have 10 total slips so do call ahead for slip availability.

Across from Oriental south of Windmill Point is the private Pecan Grove Marina with over 300 slips. None, unfortunately, are for transients.

Anchorage: If the free town docks are full you can anchor in soft mud with 5- to 8-foot MLW depths in the Oriental anchorage. This is a small anchorage. There is only room for about six boats if the channel is to remain clear and even that is tight.

Keep in mind that the shrimp boats will leave and arrive at all hours so do not block their ability to get to their docks. Behind the breakwater is protected from all directions but closer to the bridge is exposed from SE to SW. If your air draft allows, the anchorage on the other side of the bridge is better protected.

There are two nice dinghy docks, one close to the anchorage and one at the free docks.

In settled weather you will find more anchoring room in Outside east of the navigation channel. This offers good holding but no wind protection from any direction. What it does have is lots of swing room (and lots of crab pots). It's an easy dinghy ride to the free docks.

Anchorage is possible in Greens Creek if you can travel beyond the 45-foot vertical clearance of the fixed Oriental Road (NC 1308) Bridge. There is good holding and a nearby dinghy dock. The length of the creek is open to southerly winds. Should you choose to explore the side creeks be aware that depths may be less than charted due to shoaling. Proceed slowly and sound your way in.

Side Trip: Upriver to New Bern

The Neuse River provides a delightful side trip for anyone with the time and inclination. The southwestern prong of Pamlico Sound leads up the Neuse River to New Bern where the Trent River comes in.

A trip upriver can be a great time or a real challenge, depending on wind direction. The wind's direction and strength (not the moon) cause the tide fluctuations in the upper Neuse River. No tables or regular schedules can be established but water depths change by a foot or two in each direction. Overall, the depth is adequate for all drafts but pay attention to your charts.

The Cherry Point Marine Corps Air Station occupies the Hancock Creek and Slocum Creek areas on the south side of the river.

New Bern is 21 miles from flashing green "1AC," which is near ICW Mile 183.5 at the mouth of Adams Creek. The town offers visitors hospitality and Southern charm with the best of modern conveniences. New Bern's greatest assets are its natural resources: abundant water, steady winds and a vibrant waterfront.

This is a river town, not a coastal city. In New Bern you will find park benches and city sidewalks, restaurants and brick storefronts adorned with polished brass. This is the home of Pepsi-Cola and best-selling author Nicholas Sparks. It is the state's first capital and the final port of call for those seeking small-town living without the big-box feel.

NAVIGATION: The channel up the Neuse River to New Bern is well marked and easy to navigate. The lighted clock tower on City Hall is an excellent landmark. The 65-foot fixed vertical clearance **US 17/NC 55 Bridge** (also known as the Neuse River Bridge) to the south of New Bern is visible for about 10 miles. Be aware that strong northeasterly winds can raise the water level resulting in reduced bridge clearance.

Alfred Cunningham (US 70) Bridge at Mile 0 in the Trent River has 14-foot closed vertical clearance and opens on the hour and half hour, Monday through Friday (except holidays), from 6:00 a.m. to 10:00 p.m., except from 7:30 a.m. to 8:30 a.m. and from 4:30 p.m. to 6:00 p.m. when the draw need not open. It will open on signal at all other times.

The **Norfolk & Southern Railroad Bridge** (5-foot closed vertical clearance) also crosses the Trent River. This bridge is usually open except for during the infrequent train crossings. Two thousand feet upstream are the twin fixed US 17/U.S. 70 Hwy. Bridges (45-foot vertical clearances). Note that winds may affect water levels and there may be less than the charted 45-foot clearances.

Dockage: About 7 miles up the Neuse River from Oriental at Minnesott Beach is Wayfarers Cove Marina & Boatyard offering a well-protected alternative to a stopover in Oriental. They offer slips, have boatyard facilities (including DIY) and boasts a private, sandy beach. Call ahead for slip availability.

Closer to New Bern (4 miles southeast) is the well-protected Northwest Creek Marina. The marina has 274 slips and can accommodate yachts up to 60 feet with the usual amenities. Adjacent to the marina is the Broad Creek Recreation Center with a fitness center, indoor and outdoor pools, tennis, basketball and volleyball courts, miniature golf, billiards, ping-pong, horseshoes, bicycle rentals and movies. There is also a dog walk area.

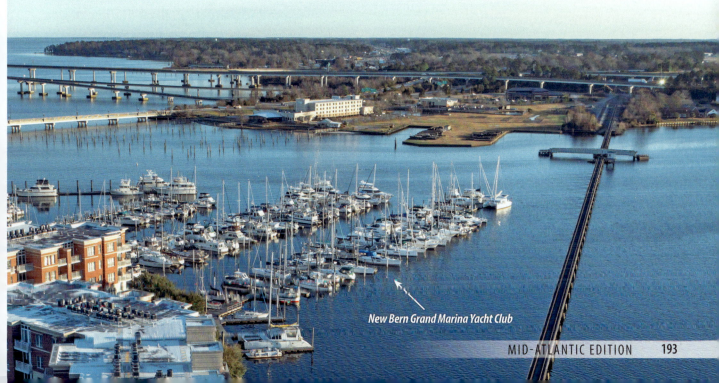

New Bern Grand Marina Yacht Club

Chapter 4: Albemarle Sound to the Neuse River, NC

Goin' Ashore: NEW BERN, NC

ATTRACTIONS

1. **Birthplace of Pepsi-Cola**
   Former pharmacy where Caleb Bradham created Pepsi-Cola in 1898. Now a soda fountain, museum and gift shop at 256 Middle St. (252-636-5898).

2. **Craven Arts Council & Gallery Bank of the Arts**
   Features monthly exhibits of painting, sculpture, photography and pottery (317 Middle St., 252-638-2577).

3. **Nautical Wheelers**
   Nautical home decor and gift items, clothing, shoes and jewelry plus specialty wines at 202A Craven St. (252-514-2553) with a second location in Oriental.

4. **New Bern Firemen's Museum**
   Dedicated to the Great Fire of 1922, which destroyed more than 1,000 buildings in the town. Relics are on display as well as a brass sliding pole, early steam pumpers and an extensive collection of other early fire-fighting equipment (408 Hancock St., 252-636-4087).

5. **Surf, Wind and Fire**
   Sip a craft beer while you shop at outfitter offering camping and outdoor gear with an in-store bar (Surfing Pig Tap Room) at 230 Middle St. (252-288-5823).

6. **Tryon Palace Historic Site and Gardens**
   The 13-acre estate includes the palace (a mansion), the George W. Dixon House, the John Wright Stanly House, stables, a series of landscaped gardens and the Academy Museum. Demonstrations of the period include cooking, blacksmithing and weaving. Originally built between 1767 and 1770, Tryon Palace was the first permanent capitol of the Colony of North Carolina and a home for the Royal Governor and his family. Adjacent to Tryon Palace is the North Carolina History Center, a large and impressive museum with many interactive exhibits. One price gets you into the museum (a must-see) and the Tryon Palace (610 Pollock St., 252-639-3500).

SERVICES

7. **Craven-Pamlico-Carteret Library**
   400 Johnson St. (252-638-7800)

8. **New Bern-Craven County Convention & Visitors Bureau**
   203 S. Front St. (252-637-9400)

9. **New Bern Post Office**
   233 Middle St. #101 (252-638-6921)

MARINAS

10. **Galley Stores Marina**
    300 E. Front St. (252-633-4648)

11. **New Bern Grand Marina Yacht Club**
    101 Craven St. (252-638-0318)

12. **River Station Marina**
    804 E. Front St. (269-591-5441)

New Bern is a town of firsts. It was North Carolina's first capital, and the home of the state's first printing press, as well as its first publicly chartered school, its first motion picture theater, and was also the first town to hang electric Christmas lights above city streets. It is also the birthplace of Pepsi-Cola. Be aware that New Bern residents are quick to point out that Caleb Bradham's soda pop has a better kick than the "other" brand.

America's Waterway Guide Since 1947 **Chapter 4**

From the downtown marinas you can walk along the streets of New Bern's historic downtown of New Bern, which is filled with beautiful homes and buildings from the 18th and 19th centuries. Spread among the houses and businesses are splendidly dressed fiberglass bears–a nod to the town founder who was from Bern, Switzerland, which has a bear on its Coat of Arms. The 300-year-old town is also home to a haunted history, which you can "see" for yourself on a ghost walk tour, which takes you through the city's most haunted spots. Don't feel like walking? Consider a guided trolley tour that takes you through the Historic District and other important landmarks.

New Bern hosts several festivals throughout the year, including the MumFest, a two-day event held in October with music, food and the New Bern ArtWalk, a self-guided tour of local art galleries.

Tryon Palace Historic Site and Gardens

Chapter 4: Albemarle Sound to the Neuse River, NC

Neuse River, NC

MINNESOTT BEACH

		Largest Vessel	VHF	Total Slips	Approach/Dockside Depth	Floating Docks	Gas/Diesel	Repairs/Haulout	Min/Max Amps	Pump-Out Station
1. Wayfarers Cove Marina & Boatyard WiFi MM 185.0	(252) 249-0200	55		150	6.5 / 7.0			RH	30 / 50	P

WiFi Wireless Internet Access
Visit www.waterwayguide.com for current rates, fuel prices, website addresses and other up-to-the-minute information.
(Information in the table is provided by the facilities.)

Scan here for more details:

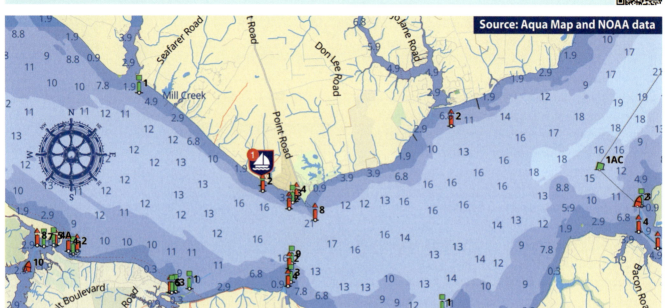

Source: Aqua Map and NOAA data

Beyond the marina is Fairfield Harbour, a private community on a deepwater canal.

Just before the US 17/NC 55 Bridge is Duck Creek Marina & Boatyard, located up Duck Creek on the eastern shore of the river. Although the approach looks tight, it is properly marked and has a minimum of 5.6 feet MLW, which is defined as a 0 foot reading on the NOAA water level gauge for New Bern. Well protected and quiet, it offers an excellent place to leave a boat for an extended period as well as an excellent place for both DIY and yard managed repairs.

Across the Neuse River from New Bern and before the Neuse River Railroad Bridge (usually open) is Bridgeton Harbor Marina has over 1,000 feet of dockage available and additional transient slips inside a well-protected basin. They also offer dinghy/tender tie-up space for a nominal fee. They are a bit off the beaten path but have all the usual amenities in a quiet and secure residential neighborhood.

River Station Marina is part of an upscale home community, which is centrally located and convenient to shopping and restaurants. They welcome transients to 60 feet.

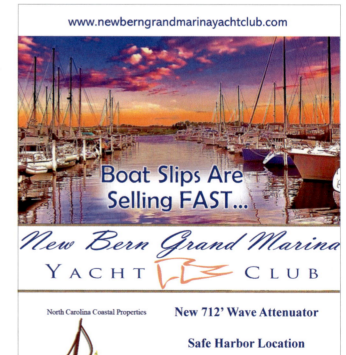

Neuse River, NC

NEW BERN AREA

		Largest Vessel	VHF	Total Slips	Approach/Dockside Depth	Floating Docks	Gas/Diesel	Repairs/Haulout	Min/Max Amps	Pump-Out Station
1. Northwest Creek Marina WiFi MM 185.0	(252) 638-4133	60	16	274	8.0 / 12.0		GD		30 / 50	P
2. Duck Creek Marina & Boatyard	(252) 638-1702	45		60	7.0 / 6.0			RH	30	
3. Bridgeton Harbor Marina WiFi	(252) 628-8010	150	16	145	8.0 / 8.0	F			30 / 100	P
4. Galley Stores Marina WiFi MM 185.0	(252) 633-4648	100	16	25	/	F	GD		30 / 50	P
5. New Bern Grand Marina Yacht Club WiFi	(252) 638-0318	200	16	223	12.0 / 12.0	F			30 / 100	P

WiFi Wireless Internet Access
Visit www.waterwayguide.com for current rates, fuel prices, website addresses and other up-to-the-minute information.
(Information in the table is provided by the facilities.)

Scan here for more details: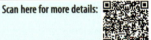

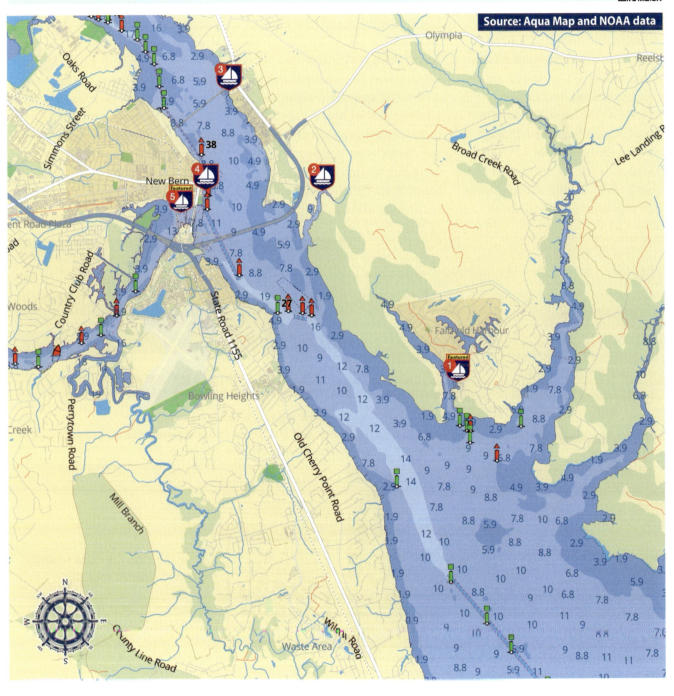

Source: Aqua Map and NOAA data

Chapter 4: Albemarle Sound to the Neuse River, NC

The all-transient Galley Stores Marina is located directly on the channel on the Neuse River, north of the Trent and Neuse River intersection. This facility has more than 400 feet of day dockage and 400 feet of transient dockage with 25 slips for boats to 100 feet and offers walkable access to town. The on-site gourmet and provisioning market features wine, beers and specialty items.

Marine facilities on the Trent River (west of the restricted Alfred Cunningham (US 70) Bridge are also convenient to all the amenities of New Bern. The friendly New Bern Grand Marina Yacht Club located between the bridges has 223 slips to 65 feet plus side-tie dockage for larger vessels inside a protected breakwater. This is a convenient location for crew changes or for accommodating visiting family and friends. They welcome transients and also offer free day dockage.

While there is a no wake zone here locals appear to ignore it and law enforcement seems to be nonexistent. On weekends you will rock and roll due to wakes. It's easy to stay off the boat should the wakes kick up. Extensive shopping, restaurant and bars and an excellent market are nearby. Across Front Street from Union Point is a convention center, which hosts the Visitor Center.

Anchorage: There are places all along the Neuse River to tuck in and several good creeks on both side. Sound your way in and anchor according to wind direction. Off Union Point Park is a great anchorage with plenty of room. Holding is good soft mud. Free floating docks are located right on the edge of the park. There is space for about six boats. Signage indicates a 4-hour limit, which is just enough time to dock and visit New Bern without contending with the bridges.

Across the river at the Town of Bridgeton, the entire area along the shoreline from Bridgeton Boatworks to Bridgeton Marina is suitable for anchoring in 5 to 9 feet MLW. Charts are accurate in this area. We do not recommend anchoring south of the boatyard as the old bridge from Bridgeton to New Bern was located here and the possibility of fouling your anchor on debris exists. This is a good anchorage in north to east winds, when the New Bern side of the river may become quite choppy.

NORTHWEST CREEK MARINA

AN OASIS EXPERIENCE

VISIT US TODAY!

Enjoy top-notch amenities including:
- Our Fuel Dock with gas and diesel
- Updated Boater's Lounge
- Ship Store with snacks, drinks and boat parts
- Free WiFi & more!

Liveaboards welcome!

Call or scan the QR code to learn more and reserve your slip!

104 Marina Dr, New Bern, NC
(252) 638-4133

Chapter 5: Side Trips: The Pamlico Sound & Outer Banks, NC

■ PAMLICO SOUND

Pamlico Sound, the second largest ICW estuary after the Chesapeake Bay, is 65 miles south of Albemarle Sound (via the ICW) and deserves the same amount of respect. The afternoon sea breeze, combined with prevailing southwesterlies, can often produce winds in excess of 20 knots and a short, steep chop that can fairly be called "vicious."

In November migratory waterfowl transiting the Atlantic Flyway visit the refuge area halfway between Englehard and Swanquarter. Swanquarter is the seat of Hyde County and the trading center for this area. It is also an embarkation point for ferries crossing Pamlico Sound to Ocracoke Island.

NAVIGATION: If you are southbound, the entrance to the Pamlico River from the ICW is around the junction flashing red (2+1) "PR" (Mile 146) marking the shoal off Wades Point at the mouth of the Pungo River. Do not attempt to cut inside the marker unless you are very familiar with the area. Take care not to hit the unmarked, unlighted Mile 145 marker on the east side of the Pungo River prior to Wades Point.

Pamlico Sound markers are generally 5 to 15 miles apart so we strongly recommend that you run compass courses or GPS routes between them. Currents, often set up by the wind, can cause you to drift 10 to 15 degrees off course. Where these currents begin and end is impossible to predict but they are indeed there so check your position continually. Pamlico Sound, like any large sound, is a good area in which to use the GPS.

> An alternative route to the ICW via the Croatan and Roanoke Sounds is covered in "Side Trip: The Albemarle & Roanoke Sounds, NC."

Anchorage: The many bays west of Swanquarter Bay look good on the NOAA chart but they are low marsh, have soft bottoms and offer little protection. Large commercial trawlers use this entrance so be especially diligent here.

Wysocking Bay to the south beyond Far Creek has a hard mud bottom and marshy borders with protection from chop except from the south to southeast. From July to April this harbor is likely to be busy with commercial fishing boats. Groceries, a hardware store and a hotel are to the north in the town of Englehard.

Juniper Bay, the next bay to the west, can be followed upriver to good protection and 6-foot MLW depths in soft mud. This location can be buggy on still summer nights.

The Long Shoal River to the north offers anchorage in 6 to 8 feet MLW in hard mud with a bit of wave break due to the encroaching shoals at the south entrance but no protection from the north. The next harbor to the north is Stumpy Point with good holding in around 6 to 8 feet MLW. This is a remote, peaceful area.

■ THE OUTER BANKS

North Carolina's Outer Banks, a long strip of barrier islands, are unlike any other islands along the Mid-Atlantic coast. Vulnerable to wind and wave, they extend in a crescent from the Virginia state line bending farther and farther out to sea until Cape Hatteras and then abruptly sweep back west, leaving an exposed and dangerous cape. They finally meet with the mainland at Cape Lookout near Morehead City and Beaufort.

The Outer Banks enclose Currituck, Albemarle, Roanoke, Croatan, Pamlico and Core Sounds (in that order). As an alternative to the better-protected ICW route that cuts across Albemarle and Pamlico Sounds, this route offers higher speeds, more opportunity to sail and some of the most pristine and wild scenery on the East Coast should you choose to go ashore.

Currituck and Core Sounds, at the two extremes, are narrow, shoal and suitable only for small or shoal-draft craft with local knowledge.

The northern end of the Outer Banks has been a popular summer resort for generations with many cottages, condominiums and commercial services. Below Nags Head the Cape Hatteras National Seashore stretches the length of the barrier islands to meet Cape Lookout National Seashore at Core Sound beyond Ocracoke. The wild beaches, dunes, marshes and woodlands are preserved as National Seashores and are interrupted in only a few places by villages and private property holdings.

The Outer Banks are truly one of our nation's natural treasures and well worth your time to explore and enjoy. The best way to see the Outer Banks is from the inside (not from the Atlantic) and the best time is summer when the sounds are relatively placid. The waters in the sound is often shoal and channels near inlets shift rapidly. Although channels are marked, they may not be entirely reliable after a storm. Off-channel waters are sprinkled with crab floats and fishnet stakes, which warrant a wide berth.

For those who would like to avoid the wide-open waters of Pamlico Sound but also wish to see more of North Carolina's treasures, the Pamlico and Neuse Rivers both offer excellent waters, anchorages and historic towns for exploration. These waterways are described in the "Albemarle Sound to the Neuse River, NC" section.

Hatteras Island

Hatteras Island is the longest of the barrier islands, stretching from Oregon Inlet south and around the elbow of Cape Hatteras to Hatteras Inlet. Occupied since the 1700s by European settlers, the community has always lived off the sea. In 1846 a hurricane opened Hatteras Inlet to the ocean and the community began to thrive. Damage from various storms has at times separated Hatteras Village from the remainder of Hatteras Island.

While there is still a commercial fishing industry here, charter sport fishing is the lifeblood of the community. It is a short run from the island out to the deep waters of the Gulf Stream where the marlin, swordfish and sailfish wait to be caught.

Start your visit at the north end of town in the old Weather Station, which has been restored and now serves as the Hatteras Visitor Center. This was an active weather station from 1901 until 1946 and issued the first hurricane warnings ever in the U.S. Its radio operator happened to pick up the SOS from the *Titanic* the night she sank. A guided tour of Hatteras Village includes 20 historic sites and markers.

Since the 1500s more than 600 ships have wrecked along the treacherous coastline surrounding Cape Hatteras. The Graveyard of the Atlantic Museum at Hatteras Village features displays on shipwrecks and North Carolina's maritime history.

Do not fail to visit the circa 1870 Cape Hatteras Lighthouse (10 miles from Hatteras Village). To protect it from beach erosion, it was moved 2,900 feet inland in 1999. (It is the largest structure of its kind ever moved.) The view from its top toward famous Diamond Shoals is an unforgettable sight. It is 268 steps to the top but definitely worth the effort. Climbing hours are 9:00 a.m. to 4:30 p.m. daily. Tickets (available on site for a fee) are required.

Graveyard of the Atlantic

The treacherous waters off the NC Outer Banks have earned the nickname "Graveyard of the Atlantic" due to the over 600 shipwrecks scattered across the ocean floor here. So many shipwrecks occurred that the government eventually required that lifesaving stations be built every 7 miles along the coast of the Outer Banks. These stations and their personnel would later become the U.S. Coast Guard.

From the Outer Banks north to the southern entrance of Chesapeake Bay off the Virginia coastline, two forces collide to create stormy, dangerous seas on a regular basis. One of those forces is the Labrador Current, which is an arctic stream of icy water that originates off the coast of Greenland. The other is the Gulf Stream, which contains warm waters from the Caribbean. When these two forces collide, rough seas and dense fog are usually the result.

In addition to severe weather, these areas have strong currents that can cause sandbars to shift, making it hard to navigate. It is believed that Blackbeard the Pirate used these factors to his advantage to keep from being captured. There is no doubt that this section of the Atlantic Ocean is extremely dangerous.

The first recorded shipwreck in the area occurred in 1526 at the mouth of the Cape Fear River. Explorers were attracted to the area because it was wild and new. It quickly became known as a dangerous spot for mariners, though, as ships began to encounter the deadly conditions often present in the area. Legend has it that the wild Spanish mustangs of the Outer Banks got there by swimming ashore from sinking colonial ships.

The Graveyard of the Atlantic Museum, located in Hatteras Village at 59200 Museum Dr. (252-986-0726), focuses on the history of this area and features many artifacts recovered from area shipwrecks. Blackbeard's ship, *Queen Anne's Revenge*, was discovered here in 1996. Parts of the ship are on display at the North Carolina Maritime Museum in Beaufort, NC.

Chapter 5 — Side Trips: The Pamlico Sound & Outer Banks, NC

Pamlico Sound, NC

HATTERAS ISLAND		Largest Vessel	VHF	Total Slips	Approach/Dockside Depth	Floating Docks	Gas/Diesel	Repairs/Haulout	Min/Max Amps	Pump-Out Station
1. Hatteras Boatyard	(252) 995-4331	55	7	9	6.0 / 6.0			RH	30	

WiFi Wireless Internet Access
Visit www.waterwayguide.com for current rates, fuel prices, website addresses and other up-to-the-minute information. (Information in the table is provided by the facilities.)

Scan here for more details:

Source: Aqua Map and NOAA data

NAVIGATION: The Pamlico Sound side of the island is shoal for a considerable distance out from the shore. Approach Hatteras Village from Pamlico Sound (flashing red "42 RC") via long, well-marked Rollinson Channel. Leave red markers to port.

The Pamlico Sound is big, open water and can get rough. If you are going to venture to the Outer Banks and visit Hatteras and Ocracoke, check your weather window carefully. This is one of those places you can get stuck for many days if bad weather blows in. (There are much worse places to get stuck in our opinion.)

Be sure to call ahead and check the status of transient dockage before making your way to Hatteras Village.

CAUTION: A navigational inlet was established in 2022 north of the old inlet. The Coast Guard monitors the new inlet and positions aids to navigation to mark the safest water. Mariners are advised to continue exercising caution while transiting this channel as shoaling remains present in several areas. Buoys have been removed from the South Ferry Channel to avoid confusion.

Dockage: The facilities here cater to sportfishing vessels but welcome all. The 9-slip Hatteras Boatyard offers slips and professional boatyard services and a comfortable and casual place for DIY boat owners. They also maintain 3 transient slips.

Chapter 5

Pamlico Sound, NC

HATTERAS ISLAND		Largest Vessel	VHF	Total Slips	Approach/ Dockside Depth	Floating Docks	Gas/ Diesel	Repairs/ Haulout	Min/Max Amps	Pump-Out Station
1. Oden's Dock	(252) 986-2555	75	1	25	6.0 / 10.0		GD		30 / 50	
2. Village Marina Hatteras WiFi	(252) 986-2522	70	1	23	7.0 / 6.0		G		30 / 100	
3. Hatteras Harbor Marina WiFi 72	(800) 676-4939	60	1	44	7.0 / 6.0		D		30 / 100	
HATTERAS ISLAND SOUTH										
4. Teach's Lair Marina Inc. WiFi	(252) 986-2460	70		85	6.0 / 6.0		GD		30 / 50	
5. Hatteras Landing Marina WiFi	(252) 986-2077	90		37	9.0 / 9.0		GD		30 / 50	P

WiFi Wireless Internet Access
Visit www.waterwayguide.com for current rates, fuel prices, website addresses and other up-to-the-minute information. (Information in the table is provided by the facilities.)

Scan here for more details:

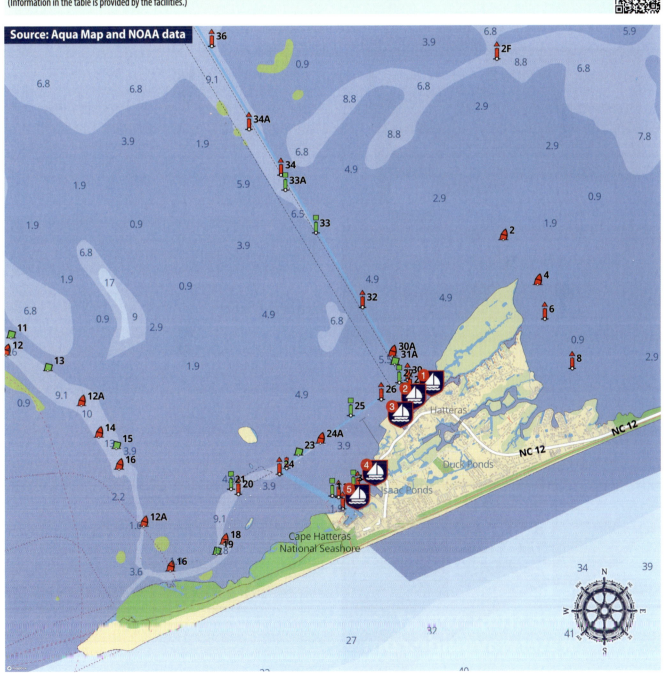

Source: Aqua Map and NOAA data

MID-ATLANTIC EDITION

Chapter 5 — Side Trips: The Pamlico Sound & Outer Banks, NC

Hatteras Basin to the south is breakwater protected and the facilities here cater to sportfishing vessels. Call ahead for slip availability. Hatteras Marlin Club is a private social club but report that they have some reserved transient space.

The full-service Oden's Dock has all the necessary amenities and offers quick access to Breakwater Restaurant (252-986-2733) as well as many other Hatteras Village businesses.

Also in Hatteras Basin is Village Marina Hatteras with slips to 70 feet and an on-site restaurant (Dinky's). The full-service Hatteras Harbor Marina has a 20 boat charter fleet as well as deep-water transient slips to accommodate boats to 60 feet.

In a separate basin to the south Teach's Lair Marina Inc. has ample transient space and serves as the base of several fishing charters. They will even prepare your catch for cooking at their fish-cleaning station. This facility is managed by the same folks who run Hatteras Landing Marina in the next basin to the south, where you will find a community of fine stores and eateries as well as extensive boardwalks to the ocean and sound.

> NOTE: Keep an eye out for the car ferries that run in and out of this basin from 5:00 a.m. until midnight. The schedule changes seasonally. See details at NC Dept. of Transportation.

Ocracoke Island

Ocracoke Island is the last link in the Cape Hatteras National Seashore and is about as close as you can get to out-island cruising in North Carolina. The anchorage is well protected, bordered by beautiful beaches with a marine forest and an ancient lighthouse.

Although motels, cottages, shops and restaurants cater to a large number of tourists, most of the island's longtime residents strive to preserve the small-town atmosphere and staunchly defend its merits. The road wasn't paved until 1957 when regular ferry service began. Geography is also a contributing factor.

Ocracoke Island has a road but no bridge so access is by boat or aircraft only. Motorists must take a ferry from Swan Quarter, Cedar Island or Hatteras Island. A car ferry and a passenger-only ferry runs between Hatteras and Ocracoke Islands with a seasonal schedule. See more at NC Dept. of Transportation.

America's Waterway Guide Since 1947 — **Chapter 5**

NAVIGATION: Big Foot Slough Channel, routinely used by the large car ferries coming from the mainland, carries minimum depths of 10 feet MLW. It is the obvious choice for deep-draft vessels and those lacking current local knowledge. The channel shoals constantly and portions are frequently dredged.

> **CAUTION:** Ocracoke Inlet should not be attempted under anything but the most benign conditions and only with local knowledge. Although protected from the north, shoaling is constant and breakers on both sides are evident in nearly all conditions. Check with Coast Guard Sector North Carolina via VHF Channel 16 for current conditions before using the inlet at or near low tide.

Dangers in this area are not restricted to shoaling. Dredges work just outside the temporary buoys and ferry traffic is a regular and serious hazard. If possible, time your trip to enter the channel after any exiting ferry traffic or to follow incoming ferries.

> **CAUTION:** Be careful not to confuse the Nine Foot Shoal Channel markings for the Big Foot Slough Channel. The most confusing spot is where the Big Foot 6-second flashing red "8" marking the channel into Ocracoke appears close by the Nine Foot 2.5-second flashing red "4." Heading toward the "4" may put you hard aground. Shoaling has been observed throughout the area; proceed with caution.

Ocracoke's harbor, known as Silver Lake (or Cockle Creek by locals), is entered using a secondary channel that heads north from a junction marker. The marker has a 6-second flashing (2+1) red light and a red-over-green "SL" board. Once south of the junction marker head north along the entrance channel, which is well marked and straightforward, keeping reds on the starboard side. Stay in the middle of the channel but watch for ferries. Prop thrust from the ferries can cause a considerable current inside Silver Lake.

Dockage: The Silver Lake Marina (Ocracoke NPS Docks) are located near the Park Service offices on the port side of the Silver Lake entrance between two ferry

MID-ATLANTIC EDITION

Chapter 5: Side Trips: The Pamlico Sound & Outer Banks, NC

Goin' Ashore

OCRACOKE ISLAND, NC

ATTRACTIONS

1. Books To Be Read
Housed in 1898 cottage with selection of books, handcrafted items and unique gifts (34 School Rd., 252-928-3936).

2. British Cemetery
Four British sailors who perished in the sinking of the *HMS Bedfordshire* are buried here. Tradition dictated that they be buried on British soil, so the small graveyard was leased to Great Britain in perpetuity. It is cared for by the U.S. Coast Guard (234 British Cemetery Rd., 252-473-2111).

3. Down Point Decoys
Housed in the former Post Office with historic wooden deoys along with contemporary, decorative birds at 340 Irvin Garrish Hwy. (252-928-3269).

4. Ocracoke Lighthouse
Lighthouse overlooking Silver Lake and the Pamlico Sound. The first light station was built on the island in 1803, but 20 years later was destroyed by lightning and replaced with the current lighthouse (360 Lighthouse Rd., 252-473-2111).

5. Ocracoke Preservation Society Museum
Museum at 49 Water Plant Rd. (on National Park Service property) displaying photographs, artifacts and exhibits pertaining to island life and culture (252-928-7375). A small gift shop exhibits works from local artists. Upstairs is a small research library.

SERVICES

6. Ocracoke Library
225 Back Rd. (252-928-4436)

7. Ocracoke Island Visitor Center
38 Irvin Garrish Hwy. (252-475-9701)

8. Ocracoke Post Office
1122 Irvin Garrish Hwy. (252-928-4771)

9. Zillie's Island Pantry
Bar and retail shop with large selection of global wines, craft beers, gourmet snacks, cheeses and gift items (538 Back Rd., 252-928-9036). Features wine and beer tastings and a relaxed deck.

MARINAS

10. Anchorage Inn & Marina
205 Irvin Garrish Hwy. (888-295-1128)

11. Down Creek Marina
260 Irvin Garrish Hwy. (901-491-0111)

12. Ocracoke National Park Service Docks
Hwy. 12 (252-928-5111)

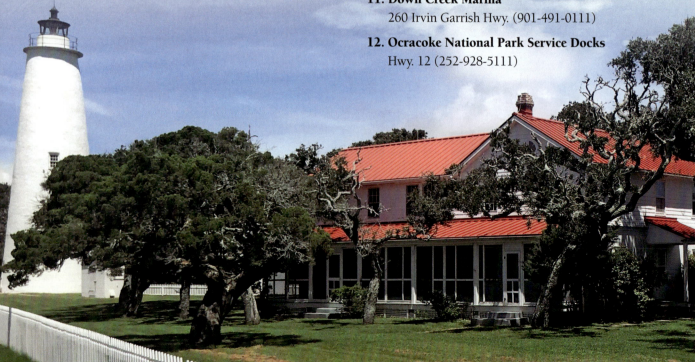

Exuding a Cape Cod ambiance, Ocracoke Island is peppered with pirate legends and a rich nautical heritage. You will hear Ocracokers speaking with an old English "brogue," a unique dialect passed down from the early settlers of the Outer Banks. (Remember that to the locals, you are the one speaking with an accent!)

Ocracoke Island is accessible only by ferry, and taking a ride on the ferry is a great way to see the island and surrounding waters. A one-way trip takes about 70 minutes. With few cars on the island, biking is a popular way to get around and explore the island's natural beauty. The village occupies only 4 square miles and the remaining 13 miles or so are part of Cape Hatteras National Seashore and offer miles of pristine beaches, perfect for swimming, sunbathing and surfing. Or visit the 120-acre Springer's Point Nature Preserve, home to a diverse range of plant and animal life as well as historic sites dating back to the 1700s.

Chapter 5: Side Trips: The Pamlico Sound & Outer Banks, NC

Pamlico Sound, NC

OCRACOKE		Largest Vessel	VHF	Total Slips	Approach/ Dockside Depth	Floating Docks	Gas/ Diesel	Repairs/ Haulout	Min/Max Amps	Pump-Out Station
1. Silver Lake Marina (Ocracoke NPS Docks)	(252) 475-8316	60		15	7.0 / 7.0				30 / 50	
2. Anchorage Inn & Marina WiFi	(252) 928-6661	100	16	35	10.0 / 9.0		GD		30 / 50	

WiFi Wireless Internet Access
Visit www.waterwayguide.com for current rates, fuel prices, website addresses and other up-to-the-minute information.
(Information in the table is provided by the facilities.)

Scan here for more details:

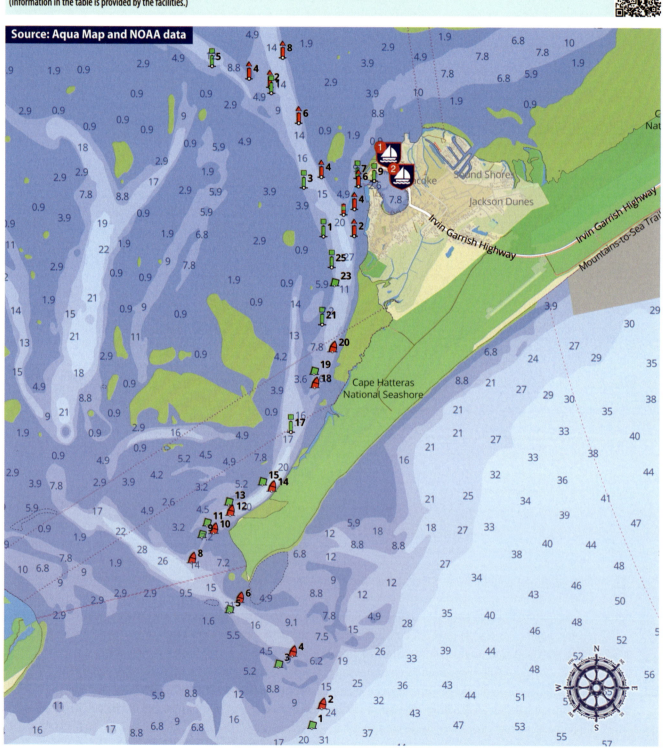

Source: Aqua Map and NOAA data

docks. Rates are reasonable with discounts for senior citizens possessing a Park Service "Golden Age Passport." The two fixed transient docks are located between two clusters of huge pilings. Tie up alongside the sturdy piers faced with large, widely spaced bollards (originally built for PT boats during World War II). In the summer the maximum allowable stay here is two weeks. There is room for about a dozen transients on a first-come, first-served basis. Expect some surge here as the ferry enters and departs.

The 35-slip Anchorage Inn & Marina has ample space for transients plus a swimming pool and bike rentals. This can be a busy place during in-season weekends; it is best to call ahead for reservations. (Note that there is a no laundry service on the island.)

Anchorage: Silver Lake is a perfectly protected harbor with anchoring depths of 7 to 13 feet MLW, except in the shallow cove to the southwest. Holding is good but watch for a weedy bottom, which can give a false sense of security. There are also reports of debris on the bottom. Make certain you set your anchor well. There is ample room for those who want to drop a hook, even on summer weekends. Be sure to anchor away from the ferry channel and dock.

There are two dinghy docks–the National Park Service dock and a community dock. These provides easy access to groceries, restaurants and shops. Many restaurants and coffee shops offer outdoor seating and are pet friendly. Note that many of the restaurants and stores are closed between November and March.

To Cape Lookout

One of the most beautiful anchorages of the Carolinas, Lookout Bight offers a secure place to set the hook in all but the most inclement weather within the protective arm and elbow of the cape. Miles of unspoiled, dune-backed beaches of the Cape Lookout National Seashore provide the perfect setting to search for shells of the giant whelk or watch the antics of laughing gulls, a variety of terns, willets, dunlins, cavorting oystercatchers and the inimitable working patterns flown by resident black skimmers.

Look for the wild horses on nearby Shackleford Banks, where they have roamed since the 1500s when a failed colony released the horses. They have fended for themselves and prospered ever since. Cape Lookout Lighthouse has been a landmark for the coast since 1812. For a grand view, climb to the top of the lighthouse (open through late September).

Cape Lookout

Chapter 5: Side Trips: The Pamlico Sound & Outer Banks, NC

NOTE: The distinctive black-and-white diamond pattern on the Cape Lookout Lighthouse helps you locate your position. Black diamonds indicate you are north or south of the light, while white diamonds indicate you are east or west.

While arriving in Cape Lookout Bight on your own vessel is the better way to see the bight, you can also go by passenger ferry from Beaufort or Harkers Island. The Harkers Island Visitor Center at the east end of the island serves as home to the National Park Administrative Offices and Headquarters (1800 Island Rd., 252-728-2250). They have an interactive map of the Cape Lookout National Seashore Park, exhibits and seasonal programs. The Island Express Ferry runs daily (year round). The schedule is seasonal.

NAVIGATION: Cape Lookout is best accessed from the ocean from Beaufort Inlet, although it can be accessed in a shoal-draft vessel via Back Sound, which leads between Shackleford Banks (part of Rachel Carson Reserve) and Middle Marsh. This is strictly small-boat territory. Seek local knowledge.

CAUTION: Barden Inlet has shoaled to an average channel depth of less than 3 feet MLW. Under the current condition of the inlet, the aids to navigation can no longer be configured to safely mark a passable channel and the aids to navigation have been discontinued. "Danger Shoal" buoys are at each end of the removed section. Mariners are advised to use extreme caution while navigating this area.

At the eastern end of Cape Lookout a dredged channel leads to Lookout Bight and Cape Lookout. Coming from the ocean, the entrance buoy to the Bight (flashing red "4") is located 6.2 miles from flashing red "6" on Beaufort Inlet, NC on an east-southeasterly course coming from the inlet.

Beaufort Inlet is discussed in more detail in the chapter "Beaufort to Southport, NC."

On some charts the stone jetty at the entrance to Lookout Bight is not well marked. Most of it is submerged at high tide. At low tide it is mostly, but not all exposed. If running by dinghy from the bight to the tip of the cape you need to be aware of this jetty.

Anchorage: During summer months most skippers anchor just east of Power Squadron Spit at Lookout Bight, taking advantage of prevailing southwesterly breezes with a short fetch. Holding is excellent in thick mud at depths ranging from 8 to 26 feet MLW. Anchor for up to 14 days within the boundaries of Cape Lookout National Seashore.

Section 2: Beaufort, NC to Isle of Palms, SC

Chapter 6: Beaufort to Southport, NC   **Chapter 7:** Lockwoods Folly, NC to McClellanville, SC

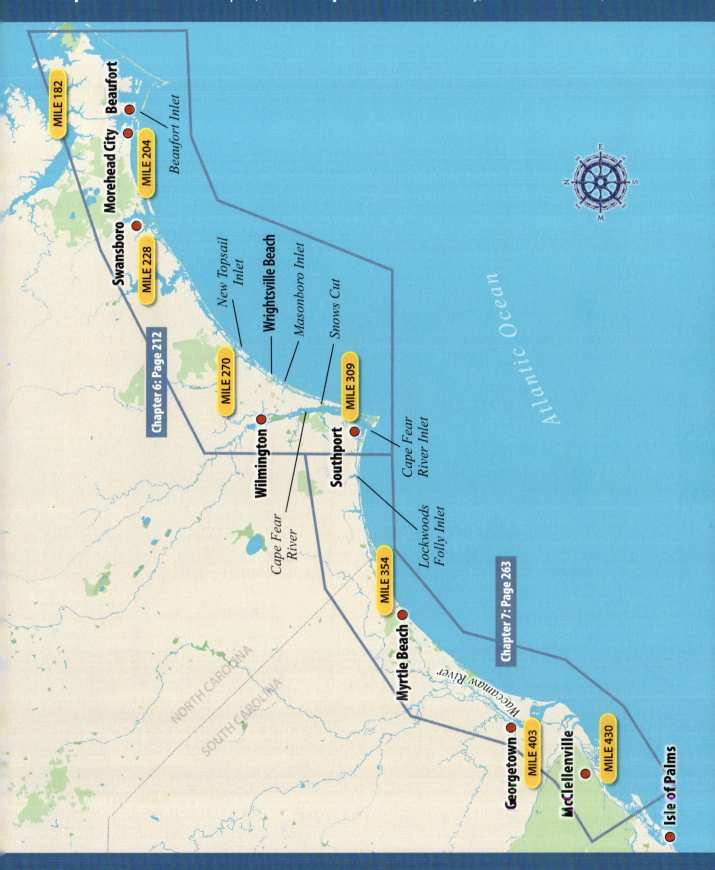

TO BEAUFORT & MOREHEAD CITY

Roughly 265 miles along the ICW from Bogue Sound in North Carolina to Charleston, SC, this passage will slowly reveal different kinds of waterways and scenery. The wide, deep waters of the North Carolina sounds are behind you and the route now follows a succession of dredged channels through small sounds, shallow sloughs and salt marshes, all connected by a series of land cuts.

Halfway along the passage North Carolina gives way to South Carolina and you begin to enter the aptly named "Lowcountry."

Cruising Conditions

This section of the ICW has more than its fair share of bridges, particularly in the stretch between Swansboro and Georgetown (SC). Seventeen of these are fixed high-level bridges. Some bridges open only once an hour and your trip may be delayed by their schedules.

CAUTION: Boats with masts taller than 65 feet must run outside from Beaufort Inlet, NC, to Georgetown or Charleston, SC, both of which have safe big-ship entrances.

Shoaling continues to be an issue in some sections of this stretch of the ICW. While we cover these areas in detail in this section, certain areas require your utmost attention and are noted in the guide by "navigation alerts." When shoaling becomes a problem the Army Corps of Engineers does its best to survey these areas and frequently gives specific GPS waypoints that you can use to avoid the shoals. Be aware that conditions may change between the survey date and the time you pass through.

While the mile marker figures do not change, aids to navigation are frequently relocated and additional aids added to reflect the current deep part of navigable channels especially near inlets. If a marker or two on your chart appears to be on the wrong side of the magenta line, don't be alarmed. In most cases the marker has been moved as conditions have changed and is in the correct position on the chart.

It is our recommendation that you always follow the markers and not the magenta line unless you have extremely reliable local information. Also check the *Local Notice to Mariners* (Fifth District) and Waterway Explorer (www.waterwayexplorer.com) for possible changes in the markers.

Bridge Openings

ICW bridges will not delay openings if boats are already waiting so you must know your speed and calculate your transit carefully; slow boats may not be able to synchronize their passages with the openings. Bridges in VA and NC respond on VHF Channel 13, while SC and GA bridgetenders monitor VHF Channel 09. It is a good idea to monitor both.

Tidal Currents

Keeping an eye on tidal currents is important in this area. Beginning at Morehead City you suddenly encounter tide and tidal current conditions quite different from those on the run down from Norfolk. The 3-foot tidal fluctuation becomes progressively greater and peaks at 9 feet in Georgia. It is important to have accurate tide and current information available when traveling this portion of the ICW. NOAA offers tidal information online at www.tidesandcurrents.noaa.gov.

Tidal currents grow stronger as you head south and are strongest around inlets, bridges and converging waterways, which have a side-sweeping effect. Try to visualize beforehand which way the current might push (or pull) your boat and consider how an ebb or flood tide might affect the situation. Learn to check your course astern from the relative position of the markers and steer to compensate. Places where the side-setting effect of the current can be serious are detailed in the text.

When approaching a bridge with the current have your boat under control and do not move in too close while waiting for the bridge to open. There is no regulation on these waters as to which boat has the right-of-way passing through bridges, but it is generally accepted that a boat going against the current should yield to one going with the current. It is foolish and dangerous to contest the channel with another boat under any circumstance.

Be careful to follow the marked channel, particularly on a falling tide as going aground then can be serious. Your boat might wind up high and dry, allowing for the possibility of a swamping when the tide begins to rise.

Chapter 6: Beaufort to Southport, NC

Adams Creek, NC

MITCHELL CREEK		Largest Vessel	VHF	Total Slips	Approach/ Dockside Depth	Floating Docks	Gas/ Diesel	Repairs/ Haulout	Min/Max Amps	Pump-Out Station
1. Bishop's Marina and RV Park WiFi	(252) 444-1805	50	16	103	8.0 / 6.5		GD		30 / 50	P
ADAMS CREEK CANAL										
2. Sea Gate Marina WiFi MM 193.3	(252) 728-4126	60	16	70	6.0 / 6.0		GD		30 / 50	P
3. Bock Marine WiFi MM 196.0	(252) 728-6855	75	16	7	8.0 / 8.0			RH	15 / 50	
4. Safe Harbor Jarrett Bay WiFi MM 198.0	(252) 728-7100	125	16	15	12.0 / 9.0	F	GD	RH	15 / 100	P

WiFi Wireless Internet Access
Visit www.waterwayguide.com for current rates, fuel prices, website addresses and other up-to-the-minute information.
(Information in the table is provided by the facilities.)

Scan here for more details:

Source: Aqua Map and NOAA data

Adams Creek to Beaufort, NC–ICW Mile 185 to Mile 200

Beaufort and its sister city, Morehead City, are two of the most popular stopovers between Norfolk and Florida. Beaufort is well known as a transient stop with numerous marinas and service facilities that can handle the needs of cruisers, both power and sail. Morehead City is a renowned commercial and sportfishing center with a large fishing charter fleet year-round. Note that tides and currents now begin to be a major consideration as you proceed south on the ICW in close proximity to the coast.

NAVIGATION: The ICW route leaves the Neuse River at Mile 185 and enters Adams Creek. Do not be tempted to cut inside Garbacon Shoal flashing green "7" in the Neuse River (Mile 180.6) when approaching Adams Creek. The fishermen's markers off Winthrop Point indicate nets just below the surface. Follow the magenta line on the NOAA chart around flashing green "1AC" (Mile 183.4), which marks the entry to Adams Creek, and make a dogleg approach. You will then be on a range for 1.5 miles.

The aids to navigation along Core and Adams Creeks are located 30 to 35 feet outside the channel limits. Although the chart shows 8-foot MLW depths in Adams Creek opposite marker "9," cutting this corner puts you in 6-foot MLW depths.

In general the marks are widely spaced here. Quick-flashing red "8A" helps with this. Where you have a green on one side and a red a long way farther along, go almost to the green before changing course for the red. Unlike the common practice of marking the inside edges of turns and shoals, the channel markers are usually set on the outside edge. This makes it tempting to cut the corners but it is safer to follow the legs to their full natural extensions before making your turns.

Flashing red "18" at Mile 191.1 is the last marker before the canal, which is unmarked but holds good 12-foot MLW depths. Keep to the center of the channel except when passing other boats or being passed. This area was last dredged in 2019.

Adams Creek is connected to Core Creek at Mile 195.8 via the Adams Creek Canal, a 5-mile-long land cut that ends at the headwaters of Core Creek below the Core Creek (NC 101) Bridge. Adams Creek Canal is mostly undeveloped. Keep an eye out for deer, eagles and other wildlife along the way. Adams and Core Creeks as well as the canal may have floating debris so keep a close eye on the course ahead.

There is a huge residential development on the Adams Creek Canal north of the Core Creek (NC 101) Bridge with numerous docks extending toward the ICW channel. Tidal currents from the Beaufort Inlet begin to appear in the vicinity of the bridge. Currents are particularly strong around the bridge, at Bock Marine just below the bridge and at the outside docking area at Safe Harbor Jarrett Bay.

Strong wind-driven currents can be felt as well in the Adams Creek Canal and into lower Adams Creek in certain conditions. From the Core Creek (NC 101) Bridge to the Morehead City/Beaufort area at Mile 205, ebb current provides strong assistance to southbound craft.

At Mile 199.3 the ICW route turns to the southeast after flashing red "24." From there follow the Newport River as it makes several dogleg turns. At Mile 200.7 you can continue on the ICW to Morehead City or to take a side trip to Beaufort, using the channel to port and keeping red daymarker "2" to starboard.

> **CAUTION:** The split between the ICW and the channel to Beaufort causes much confusion. As you head south, many of the markers are oriented such that it is hard to determine the correct path. On the ICW heading south, pass red daybeacon "28" and red daybeacon "30" to starboard then green/red marker "RS" to port and green nun buoy "29A" to port.

There may be additional uncharted buoys between quick-flashing green "29" and green daybeacon "31." To further complicate matters, shoaling to 5 feet MLW has been observed in this area. Mariners are advised to use extreme caution while navigating this area.

Dockage: Just before Adams Creek Canal on the Neuse River is Bishop's Marina and RV Park at Mitchell Creek. This is part of a campground and RV park and has six reserved transient slips.

At Mile 193.3 Sea Gate Marina is located on the west side of the Adams Creek Canal just 1.5 miles north of the Core Creek (NC 101) Bridge. This friendly marina is part of a neighborhood association and offers transient slips with the usual amenities plus a well-stocked convenience store. It is an excellent "hurricane hole" located at the end of a 75-yard-long protected channel dredged to 6 feet MLW.

Chapter 6: Beaufort to Southport, NC

Just beyond the Core Creek (NC 101) Bridge at Mile 195.8, family-run Bock Marine has repair and service capabilities and welcomes DIY boaters. They maintain some transient slips and welcome liveaboards. The tidal flow can make docking demanding but you will find plenty of helping hands.

The next group of facilities are in the Jarrett Bay Marine Industrial Park at Mile 198 on Core Creek including the large Safe Harbor Jarrett Bay, a Down East Carolina custom builder and full-service boatyard. With a 175-acre yard, a 200-ton lift and a 12-foot-deep basin, their service department can handle virtually any project on vessels up to 130 feet in length or a draft of up to 10 feet. Transient dockage is available for vessels up to 125 feet including nine 22-foot-wide slips fronting the ICW. A well-stocked ship store is on site.

Adjacent to Jarrett Bay is Western Branch Diesel-Beaufort, one of the largest power dealers on the East Coast. They have a fully stocked parts department and respond to after-hour emergencies. In the same marine industrial park are Gregory Poole Marine Power (offering engine repair), Bluewater Yacht Sales-Beaufort (boat brokerage) and Banks Boatworks (full-service boatyard).

Anchorage: Sandy Huss Creek is an easy access stop if time doesn't allow transiting the Neuse River or heading south to Morehead City. This open area offers some protection from the north to east and is far enough off the ICW to avoid wakes. Barges do run through this area at night so make sure you are well off the waterway.

Just beyond the straight stretch of the first range in Adams Creek and behind quick flashing green "9" is the mouth of Cedar Creek (Mile 187.6), a good anchorage for vessels with drafts of 6 feet or less with more room than you might think from the chart. The secret is to go farther in where you get good protection from a south wind.

Anchor towards the south shore and east of the 5-foot line as shown on the charts. There is about 7 feet MLW as you snug up behind the point of land to protect you from a south wind. There is a strip of sand on the south shore for pet relief. Be sure to pick up when done.

Shrimp boats leave this harbor at all hours (day and night) in season. Many years ago a sailboat sunk in this anchorage. The wreck of a sailboat is approximately 150 to 200 yards to the east-northeast of flashing green "9A" and is marked by white PVC poles.

America's Waterway Guide Since 1947 — Chapter 6

Just 1.5 miles south of Cedar Creek is Back Creek providing excellent protection from southwest and northeast winds and wakes from the ICW for boats drawing 4.5 feet or less. There are no other protected anchorages until you reach Beaufort and Morehead City.

Beaufort, NC–ICW Mile 200

Founded in 1709 the charming city of Beaufort, NC (pronounced "BO-fort" not "BEW-fort" as in the SC town) preserves traces of its nautical history as a backdrop to a thriving modern boating center.

Beaufort is home to yachts of all descriptions year-round, either moored out or tied up along the town side of the waterfront channel. During the fall passage-making sailboats dominate the scene with preparations for ocean voyages from this major jumping-off point for trips to the Caribbean.

Long hailed as the "Gateway to the Caribbean," Beaufort is often cooled by a brisk sea breeze. Then in the fall, as the western edge of the Gulf Stream veers to within 40 miles of the inlet, fresh northwest winds carry eager sailors into the Atlantic. It is a four-day sail to the Bahamas and one day more to Bermuda.

This close proximity to the Atlantic trade routes was not lost on the early settlers and to this day Beaufort is still receiving cargo and sailors from afar. It is a great walking town with eclectic shops, good restaurants and a waterfront full commercial fishing vessels, shrimp boats, kayaks and paddleboards as well as pleasure boats of all sizes.

NAVIGATION: Southbound vessels heading for Town Creek should depart the ICW by passing daybeacon "28," red daybeacon "30," flashing green (2+1) junction marker "RS" and red daybeacon "2" to starboard (Mile 200.8) then follow the Russell Slough Channel east of the ICW and west of Russell Creek.

Favor the green side of the channel at red daybeacon "4" and after making the turn to starboard at flashing green "5" plot a course to green daybeacon "7." Quick-flashing "6A" beyond red daybeacon "6" assists you in reaching green daybeacon "7." In addition to red nun "8," there is now a lighted junction marker, flashing (2+1) "RG" with red at the top and green at the bottom of its board.

Once past green daybeacon "7" turn immediately to port toward red daybeacon "10" and continue southeast on Gallants Channel to quick flashing red "12."

> NOTE: The 65-foot fixed vertical clearance U.S. 70 Bridge (also known as Gallant Channel Bridge) replaced an old bridge to the south, which has been removed.

The Town Creek channel, located south of the **U.S. 70 Bridge**, is marked by lighted junction buoy (red and green) "TC" followed by red daybeacons "2" and "4." Be cautious of shoaling south of the reds (between the channel and Homer Smith Docks and Marina).

Southbound vessels on the ICW headed to Taylor Creek can bear south and follow the Russell Slough Channel markers to the Beaufort waterfront. (Note that Russell Slough Channel is known locally as "Gallants

Chapter 6: Beaufort to Southport, NC

Goin' Ashore

BEAUFORT, NC

ATTRACTIONS

1. Beaufort Historic Site
Beaufort Towne (circa 1713) comprises a 12-block area listed in the National Register of Historic Places that includes Carteret County Courthouse (oldest wood-framed courthouse in NC); Old Jail with 28-inch-thick walls and legends of active ghosts; and Apothecary & Doctors Office, housing a unique collection of medicinal and pharmaceutical artifacts. Welcome Center and gift shop located at 130 Turner St. (252-728-5225).

2. Harvey W. Smith Watercraft Center
Watch boat builders at work in this active workshop where volunteers preserve signicant examples of NC's rich history in wooden boatbuilding (326 Front St, 252-504-7790).

3. North Carolina Maritime Museum
Features active boatbuilding program and environmental education programs (315 Front St., 252-504-7740). Maritime store carries nautical and coastal books, gifts, prints and souvenirs. Annex facility on Gallants Channel (next to Town Creek Marina) features exhibit on North Carolina shipwrecks. Photographs and artifacts include from wreck of *Queen Anne's Revenge*, Blackbeard's flagship.

4. Old Burying Ground
Beneath the shade of live oak trees at 400 Ann St. (252-728-5225), weathered tombstones chronicle the heritage of Beaufort and the surrounding coast. Deeded to the town in 1731 and listed on the National Register of Historic Places. Union soldiers, Confederate soldiers, freed African-Americans and slaves all rest together here.

America's Waterway Guide Since 1947 — Chapter 6

In Beaufort, the town is the culture and its seascape the canvas. A flourishing arts community of painters, photographers, sculptors and writers reside here, as evidenced by the numerous galleries, all within walking distance of the docks. The best way to see the town is by bicycle. Pedal through 300 years of history, past 18th and 19th century homes nestled behind white picket fences. To see the town from a different point of view, the popular Beaufort Ghost Walk covers approximately nine blocks and lasts around one hour. You will be entertained by pirate guides, who will regale you with an enjoyable assortment of chilling stories about ghost ships and haunted houses. Tours start at 108 Middle Ln. (252-772-9925).

For a change of scenery, take the dinghy to Rachel Carson Reserve for hiking and a chance to see a variety of wildlife and bird species including wild horses. Or take island Express Ferry Service (252-728-7433) to Cape Lookout or Shackleford Banks.

SERVICES

5. Barbour's Marine Supply
Chandlery and machine shop catering to commercial and sport fishermen, boat yards and DIY individuals at 410 Hedrick St. (252-728-2136). Celebrated 100 years of service in 2019.

6. Seaside Family Practice
407 Live Oak #1 (252-728-2328)

7. The General Store
Just what the name implies: Enjoy ice cream, fudge (32 flavors) and other treats while you shop for Guy Harvey, Simply Southern and Columbia Sportswear, as well as toys and souvenirs. They also have a coin-operated laundry (515 Front St., 252-728-7707).

MARINA

8. Beaufort Docks Marina
500 Front St. (252-728-2503)

9. Beaufort Yacht Basin
103 Cedar St. (252-504-3625)

10. Gallants Channel
293 West Beaufort Road Ext. (252-728-2762)

11. Homer Smith Docks and Marina
101 Cedar St. (252-728-2944)

12. Town Creek Marina
114 Town Creek Dr. (252-728-6111)

SAFE HARBOR JARRETT BAY AWAITS

Largest Full-service Facility Between Norfolk, VA & Savannah, GA
Custom Built Jarrett Bay Boats
Mobile Service & Parts
Complete Repair & Refit Services
Fully Stocked Marine Parts Store Onsite
24/7 Fuel Dock

Scan to learn more

Channel" where it passes Gallants Point and leads towards the bridge.)

If northbound on the ICW and bound for Beaufort, turn southeast from the turning basin into the Morehead City Channel. Heading toward the inlet round the southern tip of Radio Island and follow the well-marked channel to Taylor Creek and the Beaufort waterfront. (This is the same approach if traveling north from Beaufort Inlet.)

Remember that the numerous range markers for the entrance from the Beaufort Inlet are different from the red or green ICW lateral system or the lateral markers for the inlet. Some boats have mistaken these range markers (especially at night) for other navigation aids in this area, realizing the error only once they have run aground.

Dockage: There are several great marinas in the Town Creek area. Gallants Channel is an annex of the North Carolina Maritime Museum. Although it is a bit removed from the facilities of Beaufort (1 mile from the waterfront), it does have attractive transient pricing. It offers floating docks with water and power but no heads, showers or other facilities.

The full-service Town Creek Marina is located on Town Creek Basin at Mile 202, where you can find transient dockage or take on gas or diesel in-slip or at their fuel docks. This is a major repair facility with state-of-the-art floating docks and premiere amenities. The popular City Kitchen restaurant is above the marina office and is a great spot for catching the sunset. The marina provides a courtesy car for trips to provision or the Beaufort waterfront.

Beaufort Yacht Basin may have space for you on their floating docks. They cater to sportfishers, powerboats and sailboats in an attractive and comfortable environment. The approach can be a little tricky so examine their website prior to entering. The friendly staff will help you get in.

Homer Smith Docks and Marina maintains 10 transient slips to 100 feet and offers many attractive cruiser amenities including washers/dryers (free) and a courtesy car. The well-kept facilities and helpful dock hands make this a great stop. Be aware that there is a 40-foot minimum as well as an additional wide-beam fee for vessels with over 18-foot beam (which are placed on the T-head).

The largest and most convenient marina to town is Beaufort Docks Marina on Taylor Creek, where

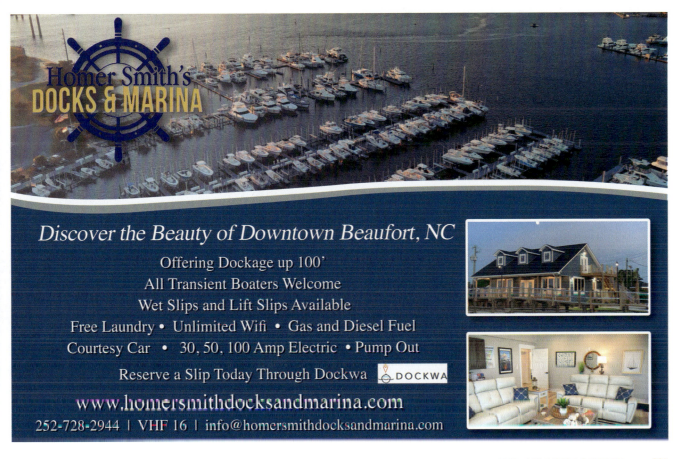

Chapter 6: Beaufort to Southport, NC

Beaufort, NC

TOWN CREEK AREA		Largest Vessel	VHF	Total Slips	Approach/ Dockside Depth	Floating Docks	Gas/ Diesel	Repairs/ Haulout	Min/Max Amps	Pump-Out Station
1. Gallants Channel	(252) 728-2762	100		20	12.0 / 12.0	F			30 / 50	
2. Town Creek Marina WiFi 1.3 mi. S of MM 202.0	(252) 728-6111	180	16	71	10.0 / 10.0	F	GD	RH	30 / 100	P
3. Beaufort Yacht Basin WiFi	(252) 504-3625	100	16	74	7.0 / 5.5	F			30 / 50	P
4. Homer Smith Docks and Marina WiFi	(252) 728-2944	150	16	95	10.0 / 8.0	F	GD		30 / 100	P
TAYLOR CREEK										
5. Beaufort Docks Marina WiFi MM 202.0	(252) 728-2503	250	16	98	16.0 / 16.0	F	GD	R	30 / 100	P
6. Loggerhead Marina - Boathouse Marina WiFi MM 202.0	(252) 838-1524	60		70	15.0 / 12.0	F	GD		30 / 50	P

WiFi Wireless Internet Access
Visit www.waterwayguide.com for current rates, fuel prices, website addresses and other up-to-the-minute information.
(Information in the table is provided by the facilities.)

Scan here for more details:

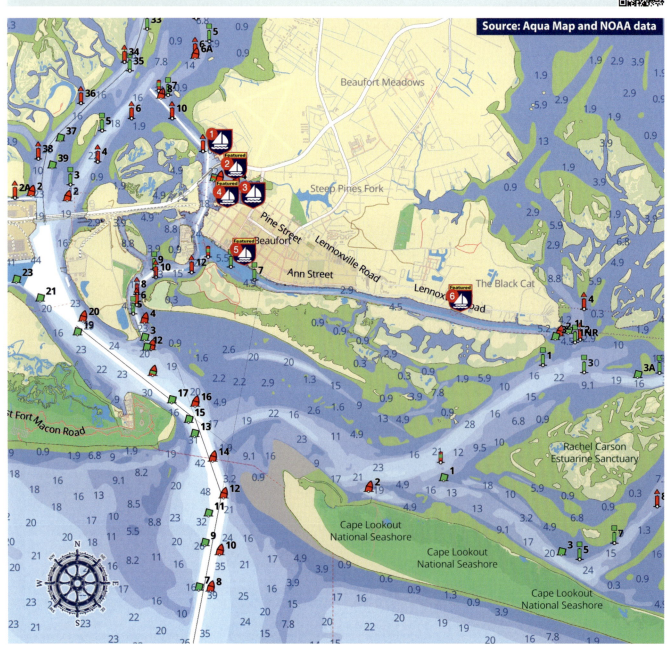

Source: Aqua Map and NOAA data

the marina slips along Front St. are adjacent to the sights, sounds and activities of downtown Beaufort and convenient to all the waterfront attractions, businesses and services. The marina has 98 slips with floating piers maintained solely for transients.

There are 25 restaurants and ample shopping within a short walk and the marina offers free WiFi and an adjacent laundry. The marina has diesel fuel available in-slip and multiple courtesy cars for trips around town.

Loggerhead Marina - Boathouse Marina at Front Street Village bills itself as "part boat storage facility, part yacht club." They offer a variety of amenities and have a complete ship store and wine shop. The on-site 34° North Restaurant (252-838-7250) is open to the public and offers a weekend brunch menu on Saturday and Sunday (reservations recommended). There is also a boutique hotel on site. Trolley service into Beaufort is available.

Anchorage: Boats sometimes anchor to the northwest of Town Creek Marina in 6 to 12 feet MLW. Anchorage space is minimal, however, due to the remains of sunken boats in the anchorage and a few private moorings. The holding is poor and the anchorage is exposed to the northwest.

Anchoring space here is further limited by the docks and shoreside activities at the North Carolina Maritime Museum. You can, however, land your dinghy on the small sandy beach to the southwest.

The anchorage in Taylor Creek is very limited; you may not be able to find space to drop the hook. Keep this in mind as you plan ahead. The swift tidal current and the close quarters dictate that you use caution when anchoring. Anchor only on the southern side of the channel and consider using a Bahamian moor. Be mindful of the precipitous shoaling along the southern side of the anchorage.

Large excursion vessels use the channel at all hours to get to their docks upstream and the Coast Guard frowns on anchored boats that encroach upon the channel. Be mindful of the precipitous shoaling along the southern side of the anchorage.

The town dock across the street from the Post Office has a convenient floating dinghy dock; look for the gazebo at the shore end. The bathhouse at the western end of the Beaufort Docks Marina is available for a modest charge. There is a second dinghy dock two blocks away at the foot of Orange Street.

BEAUFORT DOCKS
MARINA
Explore North Carolina's third oldest town!

Beaufort Docks is one of the most popular stops for yachtsmen on the waterway. Located in the heart of Beaufort NC, the marina is immersed in history with shops, restaurants, bars, museums, and everything else you would expect from a historic portside town.

Nestled just inside a well-marked deep water inlet, it's an excellent stop for fuel-and-go vessels and is convenient to the ICW. It's also an annual destination for transient boaters heading north and south.

The marina is an all-transient facility with 98 berths, all of which are floating docks. Fuel is available in most slips. Other amenities include water, electricity, 100 AMP single-phase and three-phase, multiple courtesy cars, showers, adjacent laundromat, general supplies, block and crushed ice, dive service, electronic & engine repairs, sail repairs, charts, plus it's only 2 miles from an airport with private charters.

252-728-2503 * VHF-16 * BeaufortDocks@Gmail.com
500 Front St, Beaufort, NC 28516

Beaufort Inlet

Beaufort Inlet, NC is a big ship inlet that is wide, deep and very well marked. From the Beaufort Inlet area you can take the dinghy and do some real exploring. The long dinghy trip east through Taylor Creek out into Back Sound past Harkers Island and down to Cape Lookout provides a glimpse of North Carolina that transients do not often witness. This trip is for anyone with a large, sturdy, fast and reliable dinghy or shoal-draft cruiser and time on their schedule to play.

On the return trip, follow Shackleford Banks on the inside from Middle Marsh to the inlet. There is some beautiful, clear water with many deserted sandy islands, quaint shoreline and plentiful wildlife including birds, fish and turtles. Be especially alert for the herd of over 100 wild horses that occupies Shackleford Banks. Be sure to leave time to explore Cape Lookout.

NAVIGATION: To reach the Beaufort Inlet from Taylor Creek head west out of the creek following the marked channel that swings to port past Radio Island and then joins the Morehead City and inlet channels. The inlet channel leads south past Shackleford Banks then southsouthwest out to sea.

Lights on the Beaufort Inlet range markers at night are bright green (white during the day) and skippers should identify them when making a night entry through the inlet. The range markers are much brighter than channel markers and have different characteristics.

An offshore jaunt to the south from Beaufort Inlet to Masonboro Inlet at Wrightsville Beach is approximately 73 miles, while the inside route is about 70 miles. Radio Island Marina is private, as is Olde Towne Yacht Club on the east side of the island.

Morehead City–ICW Mile 204

Like its sister city, Beaufort, Morehead City is a strategic spot on the southeast coast and it has become a favorite for offshore skippers heading north to avoid the rigors of Cape Hatteras and with ICW boaters heading south and looking forward to some free travel along the open Atlantic. Thus, a large marine community serving both commercial and recreational boats flourishes here.

All repairs–from electronics and propellers to diesel engines–are available at Morehead City and the waterfront is packed with restaurants to feed the crew. It is also the first of a string of towns with easy access to gorgeous Atlantic beaches.

NAVIGATION: Southbound vessels heading for Morehead City on the ICW pass red daybeacon "28," red daybeacon "30," flashing green (2+1) junction marker "RS" and continuing on the well-marked Newport River channel.

The ICW channel that leads down the Newport River to the bridges at Mile 203.6 is holding its depths (12 feet MLW) but has a very strong crosscurrent (1 to 2 knots). The shoal to the west near flashing red "38" is bare at low tide (rather than 2 feet MLW as indicated on the NOAA chart) so be sure to stay in the channel. There may be additional uncharted buoys in this area.

Proceed under the **Beaufort Channel (U.S. 70) Bridge** (65 foot fixed vertical clearance) and adjacent **Beaufort Channel Railroad Bridge** (4-foot closed vertical clearance, usually open) between Beaufort and Morehead City (Mile 203.6). The horizontal opening at the Beaufort Channel (U.S. 70) Bridge is very narrow with strong current and is made more difficult by the narrow opening of the railroad bridge on the other side. This is a "one boat at a time" passage.

> **NO WAKE ZONE**
> Local authorities and the Coast Guard enforce a No-Wake Zone here 24 hours a day. Since currents run swiftly at 1 to 2 knots through the harbor cut, skippers of underpowered or slow-turning craft should pick a slack tide for docking duties.

As a peninsula Morehead City has two waterfronts. Morehead City Yacht Basin is the only facility for recreational vessels on the back (north) side of the Morehead City waterfront. From the north leave the ICW about 0.25 mile north of the Beaufort Channel (U.S. 70) Bridge and adjacent Beaufort Channel Railroad Bridge, turning west at Mile 203.5 into Calico Creek at red nun "2," the next red marker south of the flashing red "38." Do not confuse this buoy with the red nun buoy on Chimney Island Slough north and east of the bridges. Leave red markers to starboard on the way in.

The Morehead City waterfront proper (on the south side of the peninsula) is approached from the ICW by taking a sharp turn to the west around the Port Terminal Turning Basin (at Mile 204.2) before reaching the junction light "MC" at Mile 204.9 (where the marker

Chapter 6: Beaufort to Southport, NC

Goin' Ashore: MOREHEAD CITY, NC

ATTRACTIONS

1. **Carolina Artist Gallery**
   Features the work of local artists and hosts events and workshops throughout the year at 1702 Arendell St. (252-726-7550).

2. **Carteret County Curb Market**
   On the corner of 13th and Evans Streets is the oldest continuously operating curb market in North Carolina. Stalls open each Saturday through Labor Day at 7:30 a.m. Come and pick from fresh vegetables, local seafood, cut flowers and baked goods.

3. **History Museum of Carteret County**
   Houses a collection of local artifacts from NC coast and an excellent research library with over 10,000 books and publications at 1008 Arendell St. (252-247-7533). Museum store offers books on wide variety of subjects and unique gifts for children and adults.

4. **King Neptune Statue**
   Great photo-op near Olympus Dive Center at 800 Shepard St.

5. **Olympus Dive Center**
   For an up close look at history, try deep sea diving. Depending on conditions, you may be able to dive on an 18th-century schooner, cargo ship, British fishing trawler, World War I gunboat or German submarine. The dive shop is located at 713 Shepard St. (252-726-9432).

6. **Tightlines Pub & Brewing Company**
   Brewery and restaurant with 30 craft beers on tap and serving lunch and dinner, including shareables. Live music in the outdoor beer garden the third Saturday of every month (April through October) at 709 Arendell St. (252-773-0631).

SERVICES

7. **Ace Marine Rigging & Supply**
   Hardware store specializing in marine hardware and supplies with knowledgeable staff. Located at 600 Arendell St. (252-726-6620).

8. **Almost Southern Marine**
   Specializing in marine hardware and other boating/trailer needs at 410-C Arendell St. (252-622-4074).

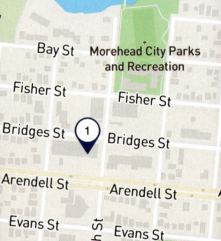

America's Waterway Guide Since 1947 **Chapter 6**

9. Carteret County Chamber of Commerce
801 Arendell St. #1 (252-726-6350)

10. Webb Memorial Library and Civic Center
812 Evans St. (252-726-3012)

MARINAS

11. Morehead City Transient Docks
807 Shepard St. (252-725-5025)

12. Morehead City Yacht Basin
208 Arendell St. (252-726-6862)

13. Morehead Gulf Docks
611 Evans St. (252-726-5461)

14. Portside Marina
209 Arendell St. (252-726-7678)

15. Russell Yachts
903 Sheppard St. (252-240-2826)

16. Sanitary Fish Market and Restaurant
501 Evans St. (252-247-3111)

Morehead City was originally called Shepherd's Point and marked the confluence of Newport River, Bogue Sound and Beaufort Inlet. Governor John Motley Morehead envisioned a great commercial hub, so he designed a town built around city blocks with a system of alleys between each block in the form of an "H." In this way, all houses and businesses could be serviced from the alleys. Each block contained 16 lots, and much of that "Philadelphia plan" remains today.

This is home to numerous fishing charters offering deep-sea adventures. Wahoo, tuna, bluefish, king mackeral and the coveted blue marlin are sought here. Since the 1950s the town has hosted the annual Big Rock Blue Marlin Tournament, one of the oldest and largest charity tournament in the country. Speaking of fish, don't miss a visit to Sanitary Fish Market, which opened in 1938 as a 12-stool restaurant with a small 2-kerosene burner stove. It is as popular today as it was then so expect to wait for a table in "high season." Offers daily specials (usually whatever has just come in off the fishing boats) and specializes in broiled and fried seafood (501 Evans St., 252-247-3111). There are several other fine restauarnts and markets here....Just ask a local!

Just across the Atlantic Beach Bridge from Morehead City are several beautiful beaches and Fort Macon State Park. And if you are lucky, your visit will coincide with a Morehead City Marlins baseball game at Big Rock Stadium. (Transportation required.)

MID-ATLANTIC EDITION   227

Chapter 6: Beaufort to Southport, NC

Morehead City, NC

MOREHEAD CITY		Largest Vessel	VHF	Total Slips	Approach/ Dockside Depth	Floating Docks	Gas/ Diesel	Repairs/ Haulout	Min/Max Amps	Pump-Out Station
1. Morehead City Yacht Basin WiFi MM 203.5	(252) 726-6862	200	16	88	12.0 / 8.0	F	GD		30 / 100	P
2. Portside Marina WiFi MM 205.0	(252) 726-7678	150	16	25	35.0 / 10.0	F	GD	RH	30 / 100	P
3. Dockside Yacht Club-PRIVATE WiFi MM 203.9	(252) 247-4890	80	16	75	14.0 / 14.0	F			30 / 50	P
4. Sanitary Fish Market & Restaurant MM 204.9	(252) 247-3111	55		15	12.0 / 12.0					
5. Morehead Gulf Docks MM 204.9	(252) 726-5461	130	16	9	14.0 / 14.0	F	GD		30 / 50	
6. Morehead City Transient Docks WiFi	(252) 725-5025	50	16	10	8.0 / 8.0	F			20 / 50	

WiFi Wireless Internet Access
Visit www.waterwayguide.com for current rates, fuel prices, website addresses and other up-to-the-minute information. (Information in the table is provided by the facilities.)

Scan here for more details:

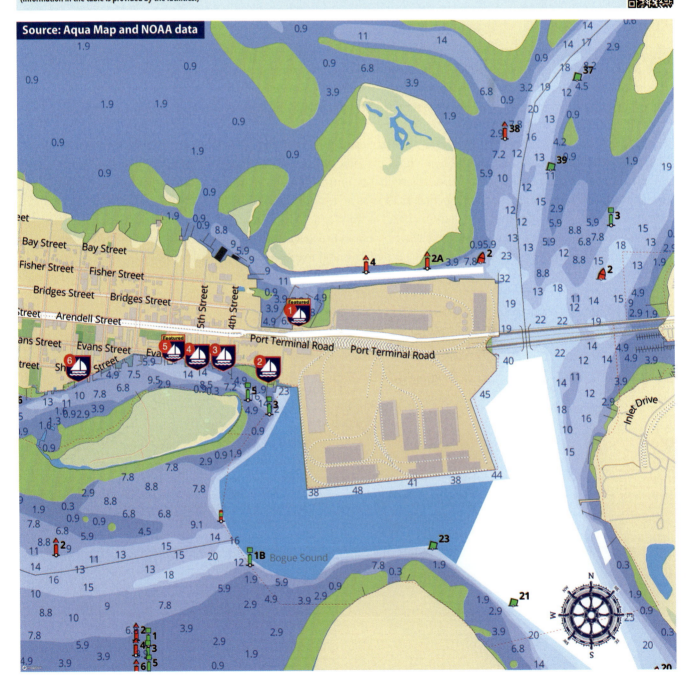

America's Waterway Guide Since 1947 — **Chapter 6**

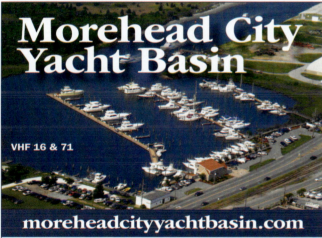

Morehead City Yacht Basin

VHF 16 & 71

moreheadcityyachtbasin.com

Located on the ICW just 2 miles from Beaufort Inlet offering the following conveniences:

- First and Oldest Marina in the County
- Remodeled in 2004 with Floating Docks
- Convenient and Clean Buildings and Bathrooms
- Short Walk to Over 20 Restaurants
- Laundromat
- Gas and Diesel Available
- Private Club House
- Safe Protected Harbour with Light to No Current

208 Arendell Street, • Morehead City, NC 28557
Phone (252) 726-6862 • Fax (252) 726-1939
Reservations by Phone or Email
dockmaster@moreheadcityyachtbasin.com

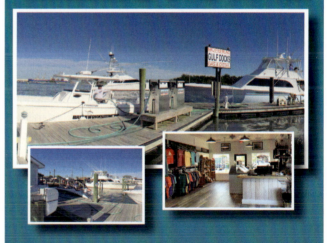

MOREHEAD GULF DOCKS

Located in the Heart of Morehead City!

- Transients Welcome
- Vessels up to 130'
- 13' MLW Dockside
- Ship's Chandlery
- Commercial Fuel Rates
- High-Speed Pumps
- High-Sulphur Diesel
- Non-Ethanol Gas

MoreheadGulfDocks.com
Docks: 252-726-5461 • After Hours: 252-723-3178

MID-ATLANTIC EDITION

Chapter 6: Beaufort to Southport, NC

numbers start over). Stay well off the bulkhead and be alert for ship and tug traffic around the terminal.

The channel between Sugar Loaf Island and Morehead City carries at least 7 feet MLW to the west end where it shallows dramatically. A channel is shown on some charts leading back to the ICW to the west but depths reach as low as 5 feet MLW in spots. At low tide or in a deep-draft vessel, returning to the ICW via the channel east of Sugar Loaf Island is the safer, if slower, option.

> **CAUTION:** High-speed reversing tidal currents rip through this area. Ebb tide begins at the Beaufort Channel Bridge and the adjacent railroad bridge (Mile 203.6) 11 minutes after the times given for Charleston Harbor. If you leave Morehead City southbound at low water slack, you can carry the flood tide south to around Mile 220. This is especially advantageous for smaller and slower boats.

Dockage: The "back way" into Morehead City's north side (above the Beaufort Channel (U.S. 70) Bridge) has a well-marked canal, Calico Creek, which holds 9.5-foot MLW depths and leads directly to the well-protected Morehead City Yacht Basin. The facility has been around since 1947 and has played host to Ernest Hemingway, along with legions of other renowned sportsmen, and is the original home of the Big Rock Blue Marlin Tournament.

Transient dockage on well-maintained floating docks and in-slip fueling is available. Amenities include an on-site laundry facility, clean restrooms and spacious showers plus a comfortable lounge/office area overlooking the harbor.

Proceeding under the Beaufort Channel (U.S. 70) Bridge and then entering Morehead City's waterfront from the Turning Basin, you will encounter a large number of establishments including marinas, commercial docks and seafood restaurants. The uninhabited Sugar Loaf Island and marshland to port strike a natural counterpoint.

Keep in mind the high-speed reversing tidal currents that rip through this area. All of these facilities can pose a docking challenge when the tidal current is running at 3 to 4 knots. Check with the dockmaster before you approach.

Traveling west from the Turning Basin (on the south side) Portside Marina is the first facility to starboard behind a protective breakwater. They have deep-water slips and dockage for vessels up to 125 feet with full amenities. Dockside Yacht Club in the next basin is private.

Sanitary Fish Market & Restaurant, a large retail seafood market and popular restaurant, offers inexpensive face-dock moorage (without service or dockside amenities) on a first-come, first-served basis. Do take the time to stop and eat here; the portions are huge and the food (mostly seafood) is fresh. Sugarloaf Island Deli & Yellowfin Pub are located next door.

The full-service Morehead Gulf Docks are in the heart of Morehead City and can accommodate vessels to 130 feet on their face dock with 13-foot MLW dockside depths. They have a well-stocked chandlery, where in addition to tackle and clothing, they also sell coffee, ice cream, snacks and some groceries. They are often full so call ahead.

Morehead City Transient Docks are to the west. The municipal dock is managed by Morehead City Parks and Recreation Department. They have 10 slips for vessels to 50 feet with 8- to 10-foot MLW dockside depths. Make reservations through Dockwa. (Cash and checks not accepted.)

Anchorage: Swing room is limited but anchoring is possible in the lee of Sugar Loaf Island with good holding in 7 to 8 feet MLW (despite the 3.5 feet MLW designated on the charts). Several vessels appear to be permanently anchored fore-and-aft, decreasing the amount of space available and requiring some careful consideration of placement in order to remain distant from the non-swinging boats.

You can also anchor on the opposite side at Sugar Loaf Island (south) with good holding, but it is exposed to ICW traffic. Great swing room.

TO NEW TOPSAIL INLET

Cruising Conditions– Bogue Sound

Below Morehead City the ICW follows Bogue Sound almost 25 miles to Swansboro (Mile 229), the port for Bogue Inlet. The ICW channel to Swansboro is marked with daybeacons and lights; green and red are staggered with few exceptions.

The Bogue Sound route is by no means monotonous. Covered with tall pines and windswept oaks, the high mainland side is dotted with beautiful homes, many with private docks along the sound. Dolphins often frequent the sound's lower portion and goats sometimes appear on the spoil islands. You can also expect to see people digging for clams (although clamming is banned in some places so check before you join them).

Opposite the mainland Bogue Banks stands in stark contrast. From the ICW this long barrier island no longer appears as a dense growth of scrub pine and myrtle. More and more, however, vacation homes, condominiums and resorts are covering the sand dunes.

Farther down Bogue Sound waters alongside the channel turn shoal with the bottom just inches below the surface. Commercial watermen sometimes wade rather than work from their boats and often the workboats are deliberately grounded on tiny islets.

If your vessel draws 4 feet or more and you want to continue southbound down the ICW from Morehead, go back east around Sugar Loaf Island to the Morehead City Harbor's entrance then follow the buoys carefully to rejoin the ICW channel. The western exit of the Morehead basin, which is adequately marked, has been sounded at depths from 12 to 4.5 feet MLW in different portions of the channel and carries a raging current.

Currents and tides are something to contend with here. Be aware of tides and the timing of their occurrences; you can use them to your advantage with proper planning. However, where there are ocean inlets the currents will change at and between each one. Fast boats will see many floods and ebbs on any given day. Slower boats may be able to use a flood to find the turnaround point then take the ebb to the next inlet.

The channel through Bogue Sound is narrow so it is a good idea to set your depth sounder alarm at 8 feet. If it sounds and the depth continues to decrease, slow down. This method helps you stay in the channel and spot shoal areas. With its sometimes scattered shoaling and shallow water outside the channel, Bogue Sound is a good place to use this technique.

The aids to navigation in Bogue Sound on to New River and then to the Cape Fear River are located 30 to 35 feet outside the channel limits. This is yet another good reason never to cut marks too closely. Many areas between Morehead City and Swansboro are subject to shoaling, despite frequent dredging.

Encroaching shoals are frequently marked with temporary floating aids to navigation until dredging can correct problems. If you see a stationary beacon and a temporary floating marker of the same identification (sometimes the temporary marker will be designated with an "A" or a "B"), honor the temporary marker. Additionally, if the original marker was lighted, it will be extinguished and the light on the temporary marker should be honored. Of course, it is always advised to travel in the safety of daylight whenever possible and use the most recent (print-on-demand) NOAA charts.

Another hazard of Bogue Sound is that a strong wind on your beam can set you on the often-hard edge of the dredged channel. Watch behind you and be sure to steer toward the windward side of the channel so if you go aground the wind will help push you off. Keep current with the *Local Notice to Mariners* regarding shoaling in this stretch.

Bogue Sound

Chapter 6: Beaufort to Southport, NC

Bogue Sound to Swansboro–ICW Mile 206 to Mile 228

NAVIGATION: At Mile 206 the markers to the side channels in Atlantic Beach become very confusing. Be sure to sort them out before proceeding along the ICW or up one of the side channels. To reach the westernmost of Morehead City's services from Bogue Banks, follow the marked ICW channel through the Atlantic Beach Bridge at Mile 206.6 (65-foot fixed vertical clearance). (Note that the tide boards and cruisers consistently report 2 to 3 feet less than the charted 65-foot fixed vertical clearance at this bridge.)

> **CAUTION:** Do not mistake the "Resume Speed" sign just before (east of) the bridge for green daybeacon "3A." The sign is in shallow water and boats have gone aground here by making that mistake. You may see small powerboats taking this marked side channel through Money Island Bay (south of ICW green buoy "3") but it carries just 1.5-foot MLW depths. This is strictly small-boat territory.

Peletier Creek at Mile 209.2 is a couple of miles west of Morehead City and considered part of the city. The Peletier Creek marinas and anchorage are popular with locals and transients who can handle the 3-foot MLW approach depths. Once inside, the depths increase some, making the creek accessible to deeper boats that can time their arrival and departure for higher tides. Leave the ICW just east of green daybeacon "7."

One mile west of Peletier Creek on the ICW nice homes and docks surround the large basin at Spooner Creek (or "Spooners Creek" as it is referred to by locals). A marked entrance channel off the ICW at flashing green "9" leads to the marked entrance channel, which is reported to be 7 feet MLW but is prone to shoaling. Watch for crosscurrents when entering channel. High tide is approximately 2.5 hours later here than at Beaufort.

Currents in Bogue Sound occasionally run swiftly at velocities up to 1 to 2 knots. Slow boats leaving Morehead City during the last part of the flood tide usually catch the first of the ebb tide at about Mile 220.

A fair tide carries to the point where Bogue Inlet meets at Swansboro a few miles below the B. Cameron Langston Bridge (65-foot fixed vertical clearance), which is known locally as either the Cedar Point or the Emerald Isle Bridge. From here to Mile 290 current reversals at the various inlets work to cancel each other out.

Favor the mainland side when crossing Bogue Inlet, since the area is subject to shifting bars and shoaling. This is a difficult passage with winds of 15 knots or greater as there is wave action coming between the two islands to the south to push you off track, not to mention on-coming boats in the narrow passage.

Anchorage: It is possible to drop the hook in 4 to 8 feet MLW depths (once past the 3-foot MLW entrance) in Peletier Creek. Boats sometimes anchor in the middle of the widest part of Spooner Creek but the area offers poor holding in soft mud and is tight. Nearby Spooners Creek Marina does not accept transients.

Go past the condominium development and anchor in the basin. You will see a boat ramp and small floating dock. These are private and should not be used to go ashore. Numerous private docks on Spooner Creek reduce anchorage space.

Swansboro–ICW Mile 228

Popular with inland anglers Swansboro also has a sizable charter fishing fleet of considerable commercial importance because of its inlet. Swansboro is a friendly little town with a few good dining spots, convenient provisioning and numerous small antiques shops all making it increasingly popular as a tourist destination.

NAVIGATION:

> **NO WAKE ZONE**
> Local boaters traditionally considered the area from red daybeacon "44" to flashing red "48" (Mile 227 to Mile 229) a No-Wake Zone; however, the signs have been removed and there are no speed/wake restrictions. There are two marinas in the area, however, and (as always) you should control your wake.

In approaching Swansboro be wary of crosscurrents and their side-setting effect, particularly on the ebb. Here and at other places like it the flow out of the river accelerates the current. Stay to mid-channel favoring the mainland side between green can "45A" and red daybeacon "46B" and keep an eye on the depth sounder. This area is regularly dredged but is a persistent shoaling problem.

Chapter 6

Swansboro Area, NC

SWANSBORO AREA		Largest Vessel	VHF	Total Slips	Approach/ Dockside Depth	Floating Docks	Gas/ Diesel	Repairs/ Haulout	Min/Max Amps	Pump-Out Station
1. Dudley's Marina WiFi MM 228.7	(252) 393-2204	35	16	26	6.0 / 4.0	F	GD	RH	30 / 50	
2. Church St. Town Dock WiFi MM 229.0	(910) 326-2600	100		10	8.0 / 8.0	F			30 / 100	P
3. Casper's Marina WiFi MM 229.3	(910) 326-4462	180	16	20	16.0 / 14.0		GD		30 / 50	

WiFi Wireless Internet Access
Visit www.waterwayguide.com for current rates, fuel prices, website addresses and other up-to-the-minute information.
(Information in the table is provided by the facilities.)

Scan here for more details:

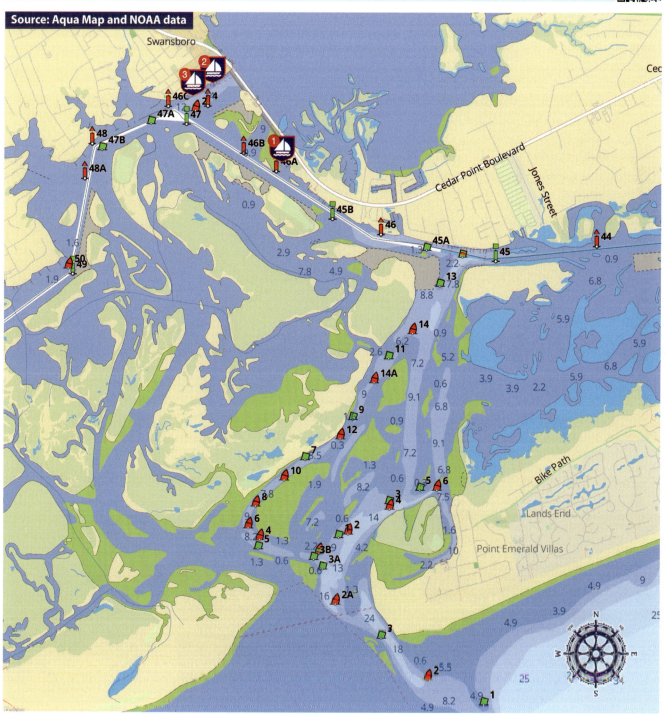

Source: Aqua Map and NOAA data

MID-ATLANTIC EDITION

Chapter 6: Beaufort to Southport, NC

Goin' Ashore: SWANSBORO, NC

ATTRACTIONS

1. **Bake Bottle & Brew**
   Sells wine, beer, coffee and sweets at 147 N. Front St. (910-325-7550).

2. **Bicentennial Trail**
   Best way to see Swansboro's historic downtown, the Croatan National Forest, Hammocks Beach State Park and other historic landmarks is to bike along the 25-mile Bicentennial Bicycle Trail, which starts at harborside Bicentennial Park. While there, check out the statue of Capt. Otway Burns, an American privateer during the War of 1812 and later an NC State Senator born in Swansboro.

3. **Poor Man's Hole**
   Enjoy a nautical treasure hunt at this antique store filled with historic articfacts and handcrafted furniture at 131 Front St. (252-671-0020).

4. **Riverview Park**
   Dog-friendly park with boardwalks and interpretive signage, plus observation shelters and picnic tables at 310 W. Corbett Ave. (910-326-2600).

SERVICES

5. **Bayshore Animal Hospital**
   623 E. Sabiston Dr.
   (910-939-5298)

6. **Med First Primary & Urgent Care**
   718 W. Corbett Ave.
   (910-326-5588)

7. **Swansboro Post Office**
   664 W. Corbett Ave.
   (910-326-5959)

MARINAS

8. **Casper's Marina**
   301 S. Water St.
   (910-326-4462)

9. **Church St. Town Dock**
   137 Front St. (910-326-2600)

10. **Dudley's Marina**
    106 Cedar Point Blvd.
    (252-393-2204)

America's Waterway Guide Since 1947 — Chapter 6

Located along the shoreline where the White Oak River joins the ICW, this "Friendly City by the Sea" is a walkable waterfront community with a rich, maritime history dating back to the 1700s. Recent years have also brought tourism to this quaint town but its maritime history and quiet waterfront remain the same. While there is a relaxed pace to this small, seaside town, finding something fun to do in the warm coastal sun is as easy to do as finding the perfect seafood dinner with a view. We recommend Saltwater Grill (with public slips) for locally caught seafood and upscale fare for lunch, dinner or drinks at 99 Church St. (910-326-7300). Closed on Mondays.

If you have the time, visit nearby Hammocks Beach State Park, an Island retreat with seasonal ferry service, a beach, campsites, outdoor showers and a snack bar.

MID-ATLANTIC EDITION

Chapter 6: Beaufort to Southport, NC

Directly off the ICW at the mouth of the White Oak River is Swansboro. The ICW turns abruptly west and the turn is marked on its outside corner by quick-flashing red "46C." If bypassing Swansboro while heading south pass green daybeacon "47" and continue toward flashing red "46C" until green can buoys "47A" and "47B" are lined up then turn west.

> **CAUTION:** The entrance to the secondary channel to Swansboro is marked by red nun buoy "2," which should be left to starboard on entry. Do not miss the nun buoy and head straight for red daybeacon "4." Although clearly charted these marks seem to confuse newcomers. An immediate grounding awaits those who attempt to go between these markers.

Dockage: Approaching Swansboro, cruising boaters can tie up comfortably or have most hull and engine repairs handled at Dudley's Marina, which has a large-boat marine railway at Mile 228.7. They also offer a well-stocked bait and tackle store and a courtesy car. They maintain 8 transient slips to 35 feet.

Church St. Town Dock is run off-site by Swansboro Parks & Recreation and has 10 total slips to 100 feet. Customers are responsible for docking their own vessels; staff assistance is not available.

You will have plenty of help docking at the friendly Casper's Marina, located adjacent to Swansboro's Historic District. This family-owned facility has 20 slips (10 reserved for transients) and room for larger vessels on an outside wall. A short-term tie-up for breakfast or lunch is available for a small fee.

Anchorage: Anchoring near Swansboro is tricky due to intense currents and traffic. Try outside the channel at Swansboro Marker 45B in 7 feet MLW. Quiet at night but expect wakes during the day.

Snug in farther behind the spoils island for a more protected anchorage. Wind and current may cause you to swing a bit in this narrow area so anchor accordingly. There are beaches on the island for walking the dogs a short dinghy ride away.

Some boats anchor near the town at Swansboro. The current is strong but the holding is good. Just be sure your anchor is dug in. There is a free dinghy dock at the end of Main Street.

To New River Inlet–ICW Mile 246

NAVIGATION: Departing from Swansboro the ICW zigzags its way southwest with two noteworthy bends– one at quick flashing red "48" and another at quick-flashing green "49" at Mile 230.2. Neither marker is on the exact edge of the turn so exercise care not to cut or overshoot the channel.

Around Mile 231.7 a narrow marked channel leads southeast to Hammocks Beach State Park at Bear Island. Watch for shoaling on the northwest side of flashing green "55" off Sanders Creek starting at Mile 233.5. There is less than 7 feet MLW.

Note that the chronic shoaling at Browns Inlet (Mile 238.2) has been alleviated due to frequent dredging and the markers have been moved to mark the newly dredged channel.

From Mile 235 to the New River at Mile 246 the ICW cuts through the U.S. Marine Corps' Camp Lejeune military reservation where signs along the way prohibit landing. Camp Lejeune extends about 18 miles upstream on the New River, almost to Jacksonville.

> **NOTE:** The ICW through Camp Lejeune is occasionally closed for artillery, small-weapons firing and beach-landing exercises. The affected area is from just south of red daybeacon "58" (Mile 235.1) to Mile 240 north of the Onslow Beach Swing Bridge. Prominent lighted signs stand at both ends of the range area.

All navigable waters between the south bank of Bear Creek and the north bank of Browns Inlet are strictly off-limits due to highly sensitive unexploded ordnance in the area. Boaters may proceed through the inlet (without stopping) during periods of non-military use.

> **CAUTION:** The Onslow Beach Swing Bridge (12-foot closed vertical clearance) at Mile 240.6 is under construction with a project completion date of February 2025. There are new (somewhat complicated) opening schedules for the old and new bridges, which are detailed at www.waterwayexplorer.com. The horizontal clearance of the bridge with the work barge in the navigation channel will be reduced to approximately 20 feet. Barge and other work vessels may be reached on VHF Channel 13 and 16 when operating the area. The on-site project foreman may be contacted at 910-520-1319. Mariners should navigate the waterway with extreme caution.

This **Onslow Beach Swing Bridge** is owned and operated by the Marine Corps. It is very slow to open (openings usually take about 8 to 10 minutes). Use the northwest side, which swings away from boats heading south. Note that sails must be furled during a bridge opening. All vessels, and especially those with wider beams, should exercise extreme caution.

Even though you have passed the danger area when through the bridge there can be heavy military activity along the sides of the ICW to the south, where the Marines practice amphibious landings.

There is a three-way junction at Mile 246 where the ICW, New River and New River Inlet channel meet. Be prepared for strong side currents and favor the ocean side. Take time beforehand to sort out markers as the upriver channel buoys can be confusing. Note that red buoys are used to mark inshore shoals at the junction of the ICW and inlet channels. These are moved as required to show deep water limits.

CAUTION: At this junction, the New River heads off sharply to starboard toward the inlet. Significant shoaling exists throughout the New River Inlet Channel. Aids to navigation may be unreliable and not marking the best water. Mariners are advised to use extreme caution while navigating this area.

It is possible to journey up the New River to the north to the Marine Corps training base, Camp Lejeune, and on to the City of Jacksonville. Some areas of the New River including its intersection with the ICW are shoal. Seek local knowledge before heading up this river.

Anchorage: The large dredged basin in Mile Hammock Bay at Mile 244.5 offers a popular anchorage with room for 10 or so boats. The entrance channel has adequate depths (10 to 12 feet MLW) for deep-draft vessels to enter and anchor inside. Do not go too far east of the eastern wharf where depths are only 1 to 2 feet MLW. Except for a few soft spots, holding is very good in the area. Stay clear of the docks; an Army Corps of Engineers dredge often ties there.

NOTE: This is Marine Corps property and civilians are prohibited from going ashore. Frequent military activity and exercises in this basin can sometimes be interesting to observe. Note that a helicopter, Osprey aircraft or Inflatable full of well-armed marines may buzz you.

Chapter 6: Beaufort to Southport, NC

To Topsail Beach–ICW Mile 270

In this stretch to Topsail Beach and beyond a wide expanse of channel and slough-threaded marsh separates the ICW from barrier beaches. Most of these small waterways dead-end inside the barrier beach dunes. (Watch for side-setting currents and shoaling where these meet the ICW.) Others provide access to small inlets and some are even deep enough for anchoring if you feel adventurous.

A Coast Guard patrol boat may check on you if you anchor near the channel. The bottom is very sandy here and currents can run swiftly. Because of increased hurricane activity over the past decade, last year's good anchorage may be too shallow this year or a formerly shoaled entrance channel may have been scoured deep. The ICW channel tends to shoal near small inlets. Deep-draft boats should proceed cautiously in such areas.

The countryside begins to change in this section. Inlets appear with more frequency and the high wooded shores gradually become lined with year-round houses and vacation cottages. Because this is popular fishing and boating territory, most homes have their own boats at docks snuggled up side creeks or in dredged private channels. Some of these small communities have landings but they are not set up to handle transients.

NAVIGATION: Once you pass New River, the ICW doglegs and the marina facilities at Swan Point (Mile 246.7) become visible. Just north of red daybeacon "4" you will find a mix of local recreational boats, small-scale commercial fishermen and cruisers.

The route from Swan Point runs southwest along a mostly straight dredged path for about 10 miles to the NC 210 Hwy. Bridge (64-foot fixed vertical clearance) at Mile 252.3.

All the remains of the old swing bridge have been removed and the area has been dredged at the fixed 65-foot Surf City (NC 50) Bridge at Mile 260.7.

At junction flashing green "BC" at Mile 263.7 a marked channel makes off to the southeast and meanders along the backside of the barrier island, past Topsail Beach to New Topsail Inlet. Used extensively by locals this scenic side trip is suitable only for shallow-draft boats (despite depths shown on the NOAA chart).

> **CAUTION:** New Topsail Inlet is primarily used by local fishermen. The Coast Guard has reported significant shoaling throughout the inlet. Several aids to navigation have been discontinued and any remaining are unreliable. Mariners should use extreme caution while navigating this area.

Surf City (NC 50) Bridge

New River, NC

SNEADS FERRY

		Largest Vessel	VHF	Total Slips	Approach/Dockside Depth	Floating Docks	Gas/Diesel	Repairs/Haulout	Min/Max Amps	Pump-Out Station
1. Swan Point Marina WiFi MM 247.0	(910) 327-1081	100	16	40	8.0 / 5.0			RH	30 / 50	

WiFi Wireless Internet Access
Visit www.waterwayguide.com for current rates, fuel prices, website addresses and other up-to-the-minute information. (Information in the table is provided by the facilities.)

Scan here for more details:

Source: Aqua Map and NOAA data

Dockage: There are several boatyards along this route but few transient slips. Swan Point Marina at Mile 247 remains open, but is under construction so there is no fuel and limited power and water. The store is also closed. They do have a few transient docks and boaters are asked to call first. (Note that Topsail Island Marina at Mile 261 no longer accepts transients.)

A channel at Mile 267 on the mainland side leads into the well-maintained Harbour Village Marina, which is private but will rent a slip to you if available. You must call ahead (at least one day in advance). They will provide a drone video of the approach and marina, written directions for tie up and a picture of the marina layout. This is a convenient stop in a pet-friendly neighborhood setting.

Anchorage: On the way south you will pass several loading basins used by pulpwood barges many of which are abandoned and shoaled so we do not recommend anchoring there. For a proper anchorage leave flashing green "BC" to starboard to head for Sloop Point.

Shoal-draft vessels can drop the hook at Sloop Point G21 in 5 feet MLW or continue following the channel markers and anchor in sand between Sloop Point G13 and green daybeacon "15" in 6 feet MLW.

At the foot of Humphrey Ave. is a small public beach. You can land a dinghy and walk across the peninsula to the ocean beach.

Chapter 6: Beaufort to Southport, NC

Topsail Island Area, NC

HAMPSTEAD		Largest Vessel	VHF	Total Slips	Approach/Dockside Depth	Floating Docks	Gas/Diesel	Repairs/Haulout	Min/Max Amps	Pump-Out Station
1. Harbour Village Marina Inc. WiFi MM 267.0	(910) 270-4017	100	16	192	8.0 / 7.0	F	GD		30 / 50	P

WiFi Wireless Internet Access
Visit www.waterwayguide.com for current rates, fuel prices, website addresses and other up-to-the-minute information. (Information in the table is provided by the facilities.)

Scan here for more details:

Source: Aqua Map and NOAA data

■ TO SNOWS CUT & WILMINGTON

Wrightsville Beach–ICW Mile 283

Wrightsville Beach is a burgeoning water-oriented community and for the ICW traveler it is well worth a visit. The ICW itself is only part of what Wrightsville Beach has to offer. Motts Channel has more marinas, while Banks Channel offers secure, if busy, anchorages as well as a public (during daylight only) group of floating docks.

NAVIGATION: Continuing from New Topsail Inlet at Mile 270 to Wrightsville Beach at Mile 283 the ICW channel is straight, well marked and easy to run. Note that several previous areas of concern along this stretch have been remedied by recent dredging.

Figure Eight Island Swing Bridge at Mile 278 (20-foot closed vertical clearance) opens on the hour and the half-hour, 24 hours a day. The bridge will not open when the sustained wind is stronger than 30 miles per hour and can remain closed at the discretion of the bridgetender in bad weather.

In the 5 miles between the Figure Eight Island Swing Bridge and the SR 74 Bridge at Mile 283.1, the route is straightforward, although aids to navigation are fewer and farther apart. When the marshes flood at high tide it is hard to make out the channel. At such times monitor your chart plotter closely and run compass courses between marks.

Going through Middle Sound after mid-afternoon watch for commercial mullet fishermen with their nets stretched across the channel. (Middle Sound is hard to identify even on the most up-to-date charts but extends from around Mile 278 to Mile 283.) Ordinarily fishermen tend to the nets and promptly lower them so that approaching boats can pass over them. To be on the safe side boaters should travel at a reasonable speed and allow ample time for the nets to reach the bottom. The Coast Guard at Wrightsville Beach has stated that the nets are to be at least 6 feet below the surface and always tended.

> NOTE: The Mason Inlet area at Mile 280.2 has been dredged and green nun "121A" and green daybeacon "121" may not be correctly displayed on charts due to relocation.

At Mile 283.2 **SR 74 Bridge** (also known as Wrightsville Beach Bridge) has a published clearance of 19 feet MHW (center spane). Due to heavy road traffic, the bridge only opens on the hour.

If you are northbound it is best to wait at least a 0.5 mile short of the bridge, especially with a following tidal current. Any closer will put you in constrained waters with considerable boat traffic that will complicate your wait.

The current picks up as you approach the SR 74 Bridge and then reverses just south of the bridge making it difficult for slower vessels to correctly time arrivals at the bridge.

Sailboats and slower trawlers have a difficult time making the 5 miles between this and the Figure Eight Island Swing Bridge to the north. Currents are particularly strong directly at the bridge and at the marinas adjacent to the ICW below the bridge. Exercise care in holding for this bridge on either side.

You may receive instructions to bunch with other boats during the unrestricted hours. Traffic from a busy launching ramp just north of the SR 74 Bridge adds to the congestion. Boats waiting on the south side of the bridge will also see congestion from marina traffic and Motts Channel.

Motts Channel is south of the SR 74 Bridge at Mile 284 and runs east from the ICW at green daybeacon "25" (not an ICW number) to Banks Channel, which extends southwest to Masonboro Inlet.

> NOTE: When you use these channels you are off the ICW and away from its marking system. Refer to the NOAA chart for buoy information before leaving the ICW. The area is wide with good water depths.

Deep-draft boats can enter the Banks Channel anchorage area via Shinn Creek (10- to 15-foot MLW depths) at Mile 285.1. The Coast Guard maintains dockage on Banks Channel just north of Masonboro Inlet and responds quickly to emergency calls.

The channel from the inlet to Shinn Creek is marked and readily passable. On summer weekends, however, this area resembles Fort Lauderdale and is packed with boats of all types.

When turning off the ICW into Shinn Creek, watch for current set and treat ICW green can "129" (Mile 285.1) as a green marker for the ICW as well as for Shinn Creek, which is marked with red on the right coming from the sea. Cut halfway between green can "129" and the sandy north shore of Shinn Creek for 8 feet MLW. Check the most recent Army Corps of Engineers survey for Shinn Creek Crossing.

Just south of Mile 285 on the ICW strong crosscurrents can make it difficult to maintain a mid-channel course. Favor the ocean side of the main channel on the flood tide and the mainland side on the ebb. Tidal range is from 3 to 4 feet.

At Mile 287.5, there is shoaling in the middle of the channel about 500 feet north of green daybeacon "135." Move over to the red side of the channel. Continue to favor the red side to green daybeacon "137" (Mile 288.4) to avoid shoaling on the green side.

Dockage: Several marinas are right on the ICW after the SR 74 Bridge and navigation is straightforward. Just south of the bridge on the mainland side Bridge Tender Marina has a 350-foot floating dock making overnight dockage convenient and easily accessible. Note that restrooms are only available when the restaurant is open so not early in the morning or late in the evening. The venerable on-site Bridge Tender Restaurant offers fine dining. Reservations are recommended (910-256-4519).

Across the waterway is the full-service Wrightsville Beach Marina on Harbor Island. There are always plenty of hands to help as you approach this full-service facility. Be sure to follow marina docking instructions here regarding the current. The Bluewater Waterfront Grill (910-256-8500) is adjacent to the marina and several others are within one block.

The well-maintained Seapath Yacht Club & Transient Dock is located farther east on the northern side of the channel. Floating docks include 190 slips and 600 feet of face dock. Call ahead for reservations (No online reservations.)

Chapter 6: Beaufort to Southport, NC

Wrightsville Beach, NC

WRIGHTSVILLE AREA		Largest Vessel	VHF	Total Slips	Approach/Dockside Depth	Floating Docks	Gas/Diesel	Repairs/Haulout	Min/Max Amps	Pump-Out Station
1. Bridge Tender Marina WiFi MM 283.3	(910) 256-6550	200	16	65	18.0 / 18.0	F	GD		30 / 100	
2. Wrightsville Beach Marina WiFi MM 283.3	(910) 256-6666	200	16	100	15.0 / 15.0	F	GD		30 / 100	P
3. Seapath Yacht Club & Transient Dock WiFi MM 284.0	(910) 256-3747	150	16	190	8.0 / 10.0	F	GD		30 / 50	P

WiFi Wireless Internet Access
Visit www.waterwayguide.com for current rates, fuel prices, website addresses and other up-to-the-minute information. (Information in the table is provided by the facilities.)

Scan here for more details:

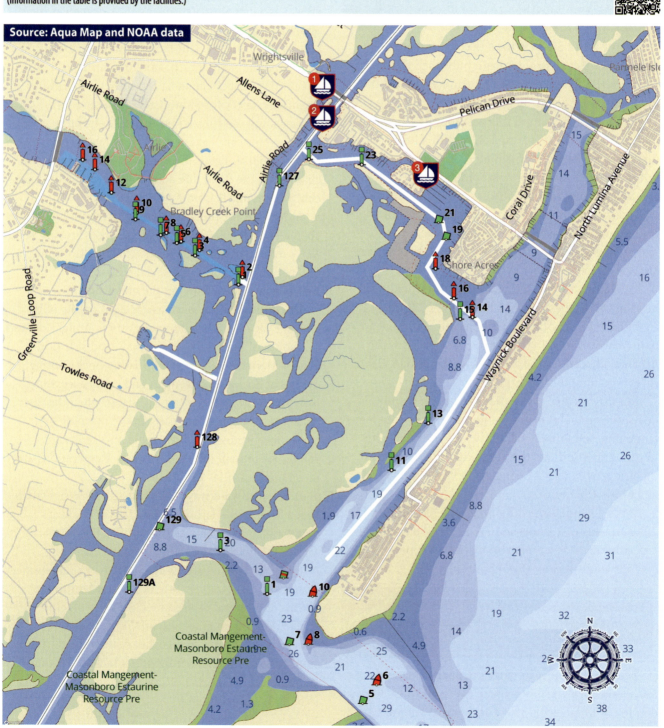

Source: Aqua Map and NOAA data

Masonboro Inlet at Wrightsville Beach

Anchorage: A favorite (but busy) anchorage is in the bight just southwest of the Motts Channel junction with Banks Channel (south flashing red "15") inside the protective arm of Wrightsville Beach (Motts/Banks Channel Bight). There are 12- to 15-foot MLW depths with a fine sand ("mucky") bottom, which will require you to back down hard on your anchor for a good set. This is exposed to wakes and wind from the southwest. Expect lots of traffic even at night so leave the lights on–both anchor and navigational, if possible.

An equally good anchorage lies northeast of Motts Channel and south of Causeway Drive Bridge (8-foot fixed vertical clearance) between Harbor Island and Wrightsville Beach. This anchorage has a varied type of bottom in 10-foot MLW depths. The shallower parts have a very hard bottom with poor holding, while the deeper areas have a softer bottom and usually will hold with some extra work in backing down.

In both anchorages boats will swing, sometimes rather wildly, with the current rather than the wind unless the wind is quite strong. Those dropping the hook here should plan accordingly. Expect lots of boat traffic. You can dinghy to the municipal docks located just south of the bridge on the beach side. There is a grocery store and other amenities nearby.

Masonboro Inlet

Masonboro Inlet, NC is the first major inlet south of Beaufort and is popular with sportfishing vessels. It is an uncomplicated entrance protected by jetties on both sides and has good depths within. Depths are maintained at 12 feet in the 400-foot-wide channel running midway between the jetties. The uncharted buoys in Masonboro Inlet are frequently relocated.

Once inside, if you are heading to Wrightsville Beach, bear to starboard at green and red daybeacon "WC" into Banks channel and then turn to port at Motts Channel bit farther up. For Masonboro, continue straight to the ICW.

Dockage: Five miles south of Wrightsville Beach at Whiskey Creek (Mile 288.2), the Masonboro Yacht Club and Marina is visible to starboard. A limited number of slips are available for rental, long-term and transient dockage. The deep water wet slips include metered power, dock boxes and water. Their two-story clubhouse has a fantastic view, along with showers and laundry facilities. This is home to an exceptional community of active sailors and recreational boaters.

Anchorage: To the west at Mile 286.6 there is a quiet spot for an overnight anchorage at Masonboro Island. This provides easy dinghy access to the island for pets. Trails to the beach are reportedly wet but worth the effort.

Chapter 6: Beaufort to Southport, NC

GOIN' ASHORE
WRIGHTSVILLE BEACH, NC

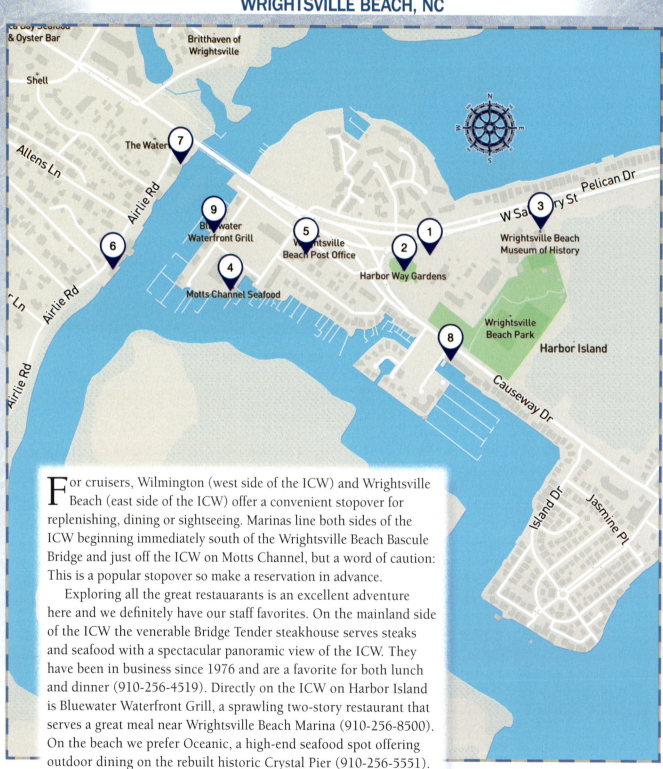

For cruisers, Wilmington (west side of the ICW) and Wrightsville Beach (east side of the ICW) offer a convenient stopover for replenishing, dining or sightseeing. Marinas line both sides of the ICW beginning immediately south of the Wrightsville Beach Bascule Bridge and just off the ICW on Motts Channel, but a word of caution: This is a popular stopover so make a reservation in advance.

Exploring all the great restauarants is an excellent adventure here and we definitely have our staff favorites. On the mainland side of the ICW the venerable Bridge Tender steakhouse serves steaks and seafood with a spectacular panoramic view of the ICW. They have been in business since 1976 and are a favorite for both lunch and dinner (910-256-4519). Directly on the ICW on Harbor Island is Bluewater Waterfront Grill, a sprawling two-story restaurant that serves a great meal near Wrightsville Beach Marina (910-256-8500). On the beach we prefer Oceanic, a high-end seafood spot offering outdoor dining on the rebuilt historic Crystal Pier (910-256-5551). Transportation required.

ATTRACTIONS

1. Farmers Market
Held from May 15 to October 30 from 8:00 a.m. to 1:00 p.m. on Mondays with fresh, locally grown produce at the Wrightsville Beach Municipal Complex (910-256-7925).

2. Harbor Way Gardens
Located on west end of Wrightsville Beach Park with arbors at all four entry points and a fifth that opens into the center where there is a recirculating water fountain feature. Paths made from bricks and pavers and other water features are among the many features (910-297-4674).

3. Wrightsville Beach Museum of History
Located in the 1909 Myers Cottage at 303 W. Salisbury St. (910-256-2569) the museum preserves and shares the history of Wrightsville Beach. Exhibits include a shell collection, maps from the 1920s and a scale model of Wrightsville Beach circa 1910 with a running trolley car.

SERVICES

4. Motts Channel Seafood
This wholesaler will be happy to put together a seafood sampler of fresh shrimp, fish steaks and scallops. You are likely to find locally grown produce out front to accompany your meal (120 Short St., 910-256-3474).

5. Wrightsville Beach Post Office
206 Causeway Dr. (910-256-0159)

MARINAS

6. Dockside Restaurant and Marina
1308 Airlie Rd. (910-256-2752)

7. Bridge Tender Marina
1418 Airlie Rd. (910-256-6550)

8. Seapath Yacht Club & Transient Dock
330 Causeway Dr. (910-256-3747)

9. Wrightsville Beach Marina
6 Marina St. (910-256-6666)

Chapter 6: Beaufort to Southport, NC

Snows Cut Area, NC

MASONBORO		Largest Vessel	VHF	Total Slips	Approach/Dockside Depth	Floating Docks	Gas/Diesel	Repairs/Haulout	Min/Max Amps	Pump-Out Station
1. Masonboro Yacht Club and Marina WiFi MM 288.2	(910) 791-1893	60	16	103	7.0 / 7.0	F		H	30 / 50	

WiFi Wireless Internet Access
Visit www.waterwayguide.com for current rates, fuel prices, website addresses and other up-to-the-minute information. (Information in the table is provided by the facilities.)

Scan here for more details:

Source: Aqua Map and NOAA data

To Snows Cut–ICW Mile 298

Below Wrightsville Beach the route follows a dredged channel through a succession of marshy sloughs for about 12 miles to Snows Cut (Mile 295), the connecting link with the Cape Fear River. Continuing straight in Myrtle Grove Sound at Mile 295 will take you to Carolina Beach. This is one of the state's busiest (and oldest) summer resorts with an iconic boardwalk.

The 761-acre Carolina Beach State Park is home to Flytrap Trail, where Venus flytraps grow freely among the pines. While flytraps are cultivated throughout the world, they are native to only a small area of the coastal plain in North and South Carolina.

NAVIGATION: Through Masonboro Sound and Myrtle Grove Sound the route runs straight and narrow. Shoaling frequently occurs here, especially at the many junctions where side creeks cross the ICW and temporary buoys are placed to mark the shallow areas. Caution and local knowledge are advised. There is a known area of shoaling to 6 feet MLW located at Mile 292.9.

Note that Carolina Beach Inlet (Mile 293.5) is closed due to shoaling to 2 feet MLW. The Coast Guard has pulled all the navigational aids until further notice. This is a local knowledge, small-boat inlet in the best of conditions and should be avoided until the buoys are reset after dredging (date undetermined). Mariners should use extreme caution while navigating this area.

At Mile 295 immediately before the ICW turns to enter Snows Cut a deep, well-marked channel leads to Carolina Beach and the marinas. Frequent dredging provides a straight and deep channel in Snows Cut; however, shoaling is an ongoing problem for vessels and passage should be researched in advance. Pass green daybeacon "161A" by 100 to 150 feet off to avoid shoaling.

A word of advice: In general, if you have a current on the stern in Snows Cut, it will be against you in the Cape Fear River. There can be exceptions at the beginning of reversals in the currents, per the tide tables, so transit cautiously as you may encounter strong tidal eddies in the narrow channel.

The high-rise Carolina Beach Road (US 421) Bridge (65-foot vertical clearance) and the overhead power cables (68-foot vertical clearance) just west of the bridge at Mile 295.7 should provide enough room for most. Exercise care here, however, as the current runs strong at the bridge and eddies can make boat handling difficult. On top of that, be prepared for a lot of local boat traffic.

CAUTION: At the southeast end of Snows Cut, shoaling has been observed on the red side of the channel between red daybeacons "168" and "170" and also between red daybeacons "172" and "174." The Coast Guard has placed movable red nuns ("172A" and "172B") where there is shoaling and a sand bar (visible at low tide). Exercise caution in this area.

Snows Cut Area, NC

CAROLINA BEACH AREA

		Largest Vessel	VHF	Total Slips	Approach/Dockside Depth	Floating Docks	Gas/Diesel	Repairs/Haulout	Min/Max Amps	Pump-Out Station
1.	Inlet Watch Yacht Club - PRIVATE WiFi	(910) 392-7106	45			/	F				P
2.	Carolina Beach Yacht Club & Marina WiFi MM 295.0	(910) 458-5053	100	16	69	6.0 / 6.0	F	GD		30 / 50	P
3.	Carolina Beach Marina and Mooring Field	(910) 386-1492	55			30.0 / 14.0	F				P
4.	Mona Black Marina WiFi MM 295.0	(910) 520-5242	60		24	20.0 / 20.0	F			30 / 50	P
5.	Federal Point Yacht Club Marina WiFi	(910) 458-4201	90		110	15.0 / 25.0	F			30 / 50	P
6.	Carolina Beach State Park MM 297.1	(910) 458-7770	48	16	54	5.0 / 4.0	F	GD		30 / 50	

WiFi Wireless Internet Access
Visit www.waterwayguide.com for current rates, fuel prices, website addresses and other up-to-the-minute information. (Information in the table is provided by the facilities.)

Scan here for more details:

Source: Aqua Map and NOAA data

Chapter 6: Beaufort to Southport, NC

Dockage/Moorings: At the north entrance to Snows Cut (Mile 295) you will find Carolina Beach Yacht Club & Marina to port with transient and long-term slips with minimal amenities. (It is also home to a Freedom Boat Club.) Be aware that the fuel and transient dock is just off the ICW beyond flashing green "161" and should be passed without a wake. Nearby Inlet Watch Yacht Club is private but may have space for you. Call ahead.

Although this is a 2-mile dinghy ride from the "business end" of Carolina Beach, there are good bus service connections into Wilmington (6 miles away).

More marine services and facilities are available on the channel south of the north entrance to Snows Cut including the popular Carolina Beach Marina and Mooring Field. The 10 well-maintained moorings are located beyond green daybeacon "5" and the small grassy island beyond and can accommodate boats to 55 feet. A dinghy dock is located to the south of the mooring field (near mooring number 1). Additionally, there are three transient slips on the west side of the marina. There is a beach across the street with public restrooms and outside showers.

The municipal marina at the south end of the channel has three transients boat slips. Amenities include water, electric, public restrooms and a pump-out station. Located in the heart of Carolina Beach, the marina is easy walking distance to restaurants and the Boardwalk District.

Nearby Mona Black Marina may have space for you but do call ahead. This is a small, family-owned facility.

The well-appointed Federal Point Yacht Club Marina offers transient slips to 50 feet with full amenities including dock boxes and a pool. It is located within a neighborhood of beautiful homes and is within walking distance to restaurants and shopping. They also have bikes on site for rental.

In a protected basin at the southeast end of Snows Cut is the 54-slip Carolina Beach State Park with a secluded camping area and miles of hiking trails. Fishing and camping supplies are available at the marina store along with restroom and laundry facilities. Transient slip reservations can be made online at ReserveAmerica or by calling 1-877-722-6762.

Anchorage: The entire bight at Carolina Beach (south of Snows Cut and behind the beach) has more than adequate water off the marked channel except where specifically noted on the NOAA chart. Be aware of sharp shoaling and submerged pilings in the harbor near red daybeacon "4." North of green daybeacon "5" and the grassy island it marks, a deep, 30-foot hole provided long-scope anchorage for boats with plenty of rode (Carolina Beach-North).

South of green daybeacon "5" and north of the large moorage area sign, there is room for several boats in 14 feet MLW (Carolina Beach-South). Boat traffic, particularly on summer weekends, is intense. Holding is fair here but be prepared for an eddy effect under certain wind and tide conditions. From here it is easy to get an early morning start through Snows Cut and down the Cape Fear River.

Side Trip: To Wilmington (Cape Fear River)

While you could use a rental car to drive from Wrightsville Beach to Wilmington, the 15-nm trip upriver on the deep, well-marked shipping channel provides an easy passage with interesting features. Renting a car from Wrightsville Beach might still be your best bet if you want to see the surrounding area.

NAVIGATION: Do not be tempted by the channel shown on the NOAA chart that runs northwest from Snows Cut (just after red nun "162A") and joins the shipping channel farther north. Local commercial fisherman and towing companies indicate this has silted in to less than 2 feet MLW.

From Snows Cut set a course southwest to join the main Cape Fear River shipping channel at flashing green "33" then turn north toward Wilmington. The main shipping channel is wide and well marked with several charted ranges.

The easiest way to make this upriver run is to go with the flood tide but be prepared for a rough chop if the wind is against the current. Conditions will improve in the upper reaches where the river narrows but currents will be strong during the ebb tide.

Cape Fear Memorial Bridge crosses the river south of the marinas. It has 65-foot closed vertical clearance and opens on signal (except during special events) for large ships. The bridgetender monitors VHF Channel 18.

Cape Fear River, NC

WILMINGTON		Largest Vessel	VHF	Total Slips	Approach/ Dockside Depth	Floating Docks	Gas/ Diesel	Repairs/ Haulout	Min/Max Amps	Pump-Out Station
1. Wilmington Marine Center WiFi 7.0 mi. N of MM 297.0	(910) 395-5055	100	16	130	5.5 / 5.0	F	GD	RH	30 / 50	P
2. Port City Marina WiFi	(910) 251-6151	250	16	86	25.0 / 6.5	F	GD		30 / 200+	P
3. Sawmill Point Marina WiFi 14.0 mi. N of MM 297.0	(910) 772-9277	50		50	40.0 / 20.0	F			30 / 50	
4. Cape Fear Marina WiFi 14.4 mi. N of MM 297.0	(910) 762-1256	175	16	75	40.0 / 20.0	F			30 / 100	P

WiFi Wireless Internet Access
Visit www.waterwayguide.com for current rates, fuel prices, website addresses and other up-to-the-minute information.
(Information in the table is provided by the facilities.)

Scan here for more details:

Source: Aqua Map and NOAA data

Chapter 6 — Beaufort to Southport, NC

Wilmington Marine Center
Marina ★ Marine Service

Marina: 910.395.5055
Service: 910.395.5016
WilmingtonMarine.com

Refresh Old Faded Gel Coat With a Respray. 16' - 70'. Competitive Pricing.

Our safe, secure and scenic marina has a slip waiting for you and our friendly, professional staff is eager to host your stay with us. Our high-quality floating docks, affordable rates, professional management, and fabulous sunsets make for an unbeatable destination!

- NC Clean Marina
- Current-free Enclosed Basin
- Floating Slips 15'-100'
- Full Yacht Repair Service
- Diesel, Non-Ethanol Gas, and Ice
- 400-Ton Railway for Commercial Use

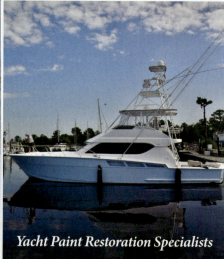

Yacht Paint Restoration Specialists

Certified North Carolina Clean Marina/Service Center

Wilmington Marine Center • 3410 River Road Suite 201 • Wilmington, NC 28412
34 10.15 North • 77 56.56 West

To the north is **Isabelle Holmes Bridge** with 40-foot closed vertical clearance. The draw opens on signal, except from 6:00 a.m. to 6:00 p.m., when the draw only opens at 10:00 a.m. and 2:00 p.m. for waiting vessels.

Dockage: Upriver at flashing green buoy "59" (approximately 7 nm north of ICW Mile 297) a well-marked channel leads off to starboard to Wilmington Marine Center. Yard capabilities include bottom painting, electrical, plumbing, fiberglass repair and complete yacht painting services. What they do not offer is transient slips.

Port City Marina to the north can accommodate boats up to 250 feet with a 10-foot dockside depth on concrete floating slips. They welcome all–from superyachts to smaller vessels–in a prime location. The adjacent outdoor music venue is a great place to catch a show and a beautiful public park when not in use.

Continuing north, Sawmill Point Marina has floating docks for vessels to 50 feet with water and power at each slip and offers direct access to the Wilmington Riverwalk.

A short distance upriver beyond the Isabelle Holmes Bridge (40-foot closed vertical clearance) you can find transient slips on floating docks at Cape Fear Marina. The facility is located in a rural area that is restricted to residential and recreational use (no charter fishing boats, tour boats or scuba dive boats). They cater to larger sailboats and motor yachts with slips to 175 feet. Boat slip rentals include membership to a gated, secure dock with full amenities.

Free day dockage is available at the Wilmington City Docks north of the Cape Fear Memorial Bridge. There are two sets of docks: Market Street Landing and Hotel Ballast. Overnight dockage is not allowed. There are public restrooms and a laundry nearby.

The docks are located downtown in the center of the Historic District with museums, shops, restaurants and nightlife all within walking distance.

Anchorage: This is a good place to plan to take a slip but if you are determined to anchor, try north of green daybeacon "59" on the intersecting Brunswick River. Depth shouldn't be an issue here (at least 10 feet MLW) and the mud bottom holds well. Anchor closer to the junction with the Cape Fear for easier dinghy access to the free docks located upriver.

Boardwalk along the Cape Fear River in Wilmington, NC

■ TO SOUTHPORT

Snows Cut to Southport–ICW Mile 298 to Mile 309

Back on the ICW the route to Southport leads through Snows Cut and down the Cape Fear River. A good procedure along this 12-mile downstream run to Southport is to run compass courses for each leg to assist in identifying the navigational aids that mark the course. The color of the marks changes from side to side and also the numbering changes as you continue down the Cape Fear River. Studying your charts before departure is, as always, a very wise decision.

NAVIGATION: South of Snows Cut additional buoys have been added in the Cape Fear River, increasing the ease of maintaining a visual ICW channel course from the helm. The numerous ranges used by the large ships in the Cape Fear River may not correspond with those on your NOAA chart.

> **CAUTION:** Between flashing green "33" (Mile 299.2) and flashing green "19" (Mile 307.7) you will be in the ship channel going up the Cape Fear River to Wilmington and the buoys are set with "Red Right Returning". All marks still carry the appropriate yellow ICW symbols.

Between Mile 299 and 302 on the west side of the Cape Fear River you will pass the Army's Military Ocean Terminal at Sunny Point with its three large piers. This is a restricted area protected by a security barrier marked by a (charted) series of flashing yellow warning boundary lights. This is the largest ammunitions port in the U.S. and is patrolled by smaller vessels. Steer clear of this area.

Also of note in navigating the Cape Fear River is the Fishers Island Ferry, which makes regular runs across the river between Federal Point (Mile 303.5) and the Ferry Terminal just north of Price Creek (Mile 306.5). You may also encounter large ships going to and from the port of Wilmington.

The Cape Fear River is unprotected water and wind will build up big waves quickly; especially with an adverse current. If well timed in good weather, the trip is pleasant, but a poorly timed trip in bad weather is best avoided. Because the Cape Fear River flows down from inland with a long tidal reach, there is a large disconnect between high and low tide and actual tidal current change.

Chapter 6: Beaufort to Southport, NC

GOIN' ASHORE
WILMINGTON, NC

ATTRACTIONS

1. U.S.S. Battleship North Carolina
Permanently moored battleship that fought in every major offensive naval engagement in the Pacific during World War II. Tour main deck, interior rooms and 16-inch gun turrets and learn about history of the ship and role it played in the war. Aso features a gift shop, visitor's center and picnic area at 1 Battleship Rd. (910-399-9100).

2. Bellamy Mansion Museum
Great example of antebellum architecture that dates from after the fall of Fort Fisher in 1865, when Federal troops used the home as their headquarters. Four stories with 22 rooms of history. Carriage and walking tours begin out front at 503 Market St. (910-251-3700).

3. Cape Fear Museum of History and Science
Oldest history museum in North Carolina (circa 1898). Learn about history and culture of the region through interactive exhibits and artifacts. Features include 20-foot-tall Giant Ground Sloth skeleton, a miniature recreation of the second battle of Fort Fisher and a room dedicated to native son and basketball great Michael Jordan (814 Market St., 910-798-4370).

4. Lower Cape Fear Historical Society
Historical society and museum housed in the 14-room Victorian Italianate Latimer House featuring period furnishings (126 S. 3rd St., 910-762-0492).

5. Old Wilmington City Market
Collection of eclectic and unique merchandise offered by local artists, vendors and specialty shops. Originally established in 1880 (120 Front St., 910-399-3674).

6. Thalian Hall
Venerable performing arts venue dating to 1858 with two stages for films, concerts and live theater at 310 Chestnut St. (910-632-2285).

7. The Cotton Exchange
At the turn of the century, cotton was still king and one of the largest and busiest cotton export companies in the world was located in Wilmington. Today, eight restored buildings, connected by brick walkways and open-air courtyards, house 30 unique specialty shops and restaurants, each a charming reflection of the style and feel of Wilmington's 19th-century working port days (321 N. Front St., 910-343-9896).

America's Waterway Guide Since 1947

Chapter 6

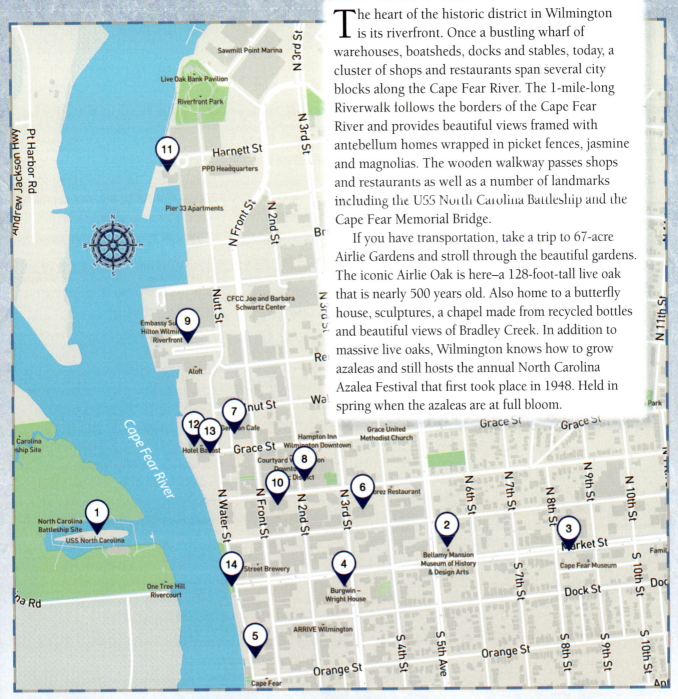

The heart of the historic district in Wilmington is its riverfront. Once a bustling wharf of warehouses, boatsheds, docks and stables, today, a cluster of shops and restaurants span several city blocks along the Cape Fear River. The 1-mile-long Riverwalk follows the borders of the Cape Fear River and provides beautiful views framed with antebellum homes wrapped in picket fences, jasmine and magnolias. The wooden walkway passes shops and restaurants as well as a number of landmarks including the USS North Carolina Battleship and the Cape Fear Memorial Bridge.

If you have transportation, take a trip to 67-acre Airlie Gardens and stroll through the beautiful gardens. The iconic Airlie Oak is here–a 128-foot-tall live oak that is nearly 500 years old. Also home to a butterfly house, sculptures, a chapel made from recycled bottles and beautiful views of Bradley Creek. In addition to massive live oaks, Wilmington knows how to grow azaleas and still hosts the annual North Carolina Azalea Festival that first took place in 1948. Held in spring when the azaleas are at full bloom.

SERVICES

8. New Hanover County Public Library
201 Chestnut St. (910-798-6300)

9. Wilmington and Beaches Convention and Visitors Bureau
505 Nutt St., Unit A (910-341-4030)

10. Wilmington Post Office
152 N. Front St. (910-313-3293)

MARINAS

11. Port City Marina
10 Harnett St.
(910-251-6151)

12. Wilmington City Docks - Coastline
Wilmington River Walk
(910-341-7852)

13. Wilmington City Docks - Hotel Ballast
301 N. Water St.

14. Wilmington City Docks - Market Street Landing
Market St. (910-520-6875)

MID ATLANTIC EDITION 253

Chapter 6: Beaufort to Southport, NC

Side Trip: Cape Fear River Entrance

The Cape Fear River Entrance, NC is the first port south of Morehead City suitable for all sizes of oceangoing vessels via a major deepwater channel. This is a well-marked channel that is protected from the north and an easy entrance day or night. This is one of several good inlets for snowbirds heading south should conditions deteriorate.

NAVIGATION: If you wish to exit the ICW and continue on the outside, bear south at flashing red "18" between Southport and Battery Island and follow the well-marked channel for the Cape Fear River Entrance, NC.

For those headed north it is wise to stay on the ICW to avoid a significant detour around Frying Pan Shoals, which extend 30 nm out into the Atlantic. Because of Jay Bird Shoals, buoys on Cape Fear's main shipping channel should be observed and the Western Bar Channel should be avoided. Older charts may still show the old entrance channel to the west of the new channel that replaced it. Follow the markers.

The current is very strong; time your entrance to take advantage of the tides. Northbound slower boats would be well-advised to check the tides before attempting the Cape Fear Rivers strong currents. This is a busy inlet so keep a constant watch posted for big ships.

Side Trip: Bald Head Island

Bald Head Island on the northeastern shore at the mouth of the Cape Fear River offers a destination marina and shore development well worth the 2-mile diversion off the ICW. Its remoteness (accessible only by water), 14 miles of wide, unspoiled beaches and magnificent dunes, alongside meandering creeks through diverse forests and waving marsh grass makes this natural barrier island stand out.

If a walk on a pristine, deserted beach is your thing, then Bald Head is your place. Except for a few service vehicles, there are no cars on the island so transportation is by foot, bicycle and electric cart. You can rent bikes and carts on the island to reach shopping, restaurants and the beaches. All Bald Head beaches are public with access via paths from the road. You will pass several trails along the way that wind through the forest and marsh.

While you are exploring be sure to stop by Old Baldy, the original Cape Fear Lighthouse and the Keeper's House and one of the oldest standing lighthouses (built in 1817). You can climb the 108 steps and the ladder to the lantern room for a wonderful view of the entire area.

NAVIGATION: Bald Head Island is easily reached either from the ICW, which turns to the west at Southport or from the ocean. It is an excellent jumping-off or landing point to or from a voyage south. Bald Head Island's deep-dredged and well-marked channel lies southeast of flashing green "13A" on the Smith Island Range of the Cape Fear River (east of Jay Bird Shoals).

Bald Head Island

America's Waterway Guide Since 1947 — **Chapter 6**

Bald Head Island, NC

BALD HEAD ISLAND		Largest Vessel	VHF	Total Slips	Approach/Dockside Depth	Floating Docks	Gas/Diesel	Repairs/Haulout	Min/Max Amps	Pump-Out Station
1. Bald Head Island Marina WiFi 2.8 mi. S of MM 309.0	(910) 457-7380	115	16	175	8.0 / 6.0	F	GD		30 / 100	P

WiFi Wireless Internet Access
Visit www.waterwayguide.com for current rates, fuel prices, website addresses and other up-to-the-minute information. (Information in the table is provided by the facilities.)

Scan here for more details:

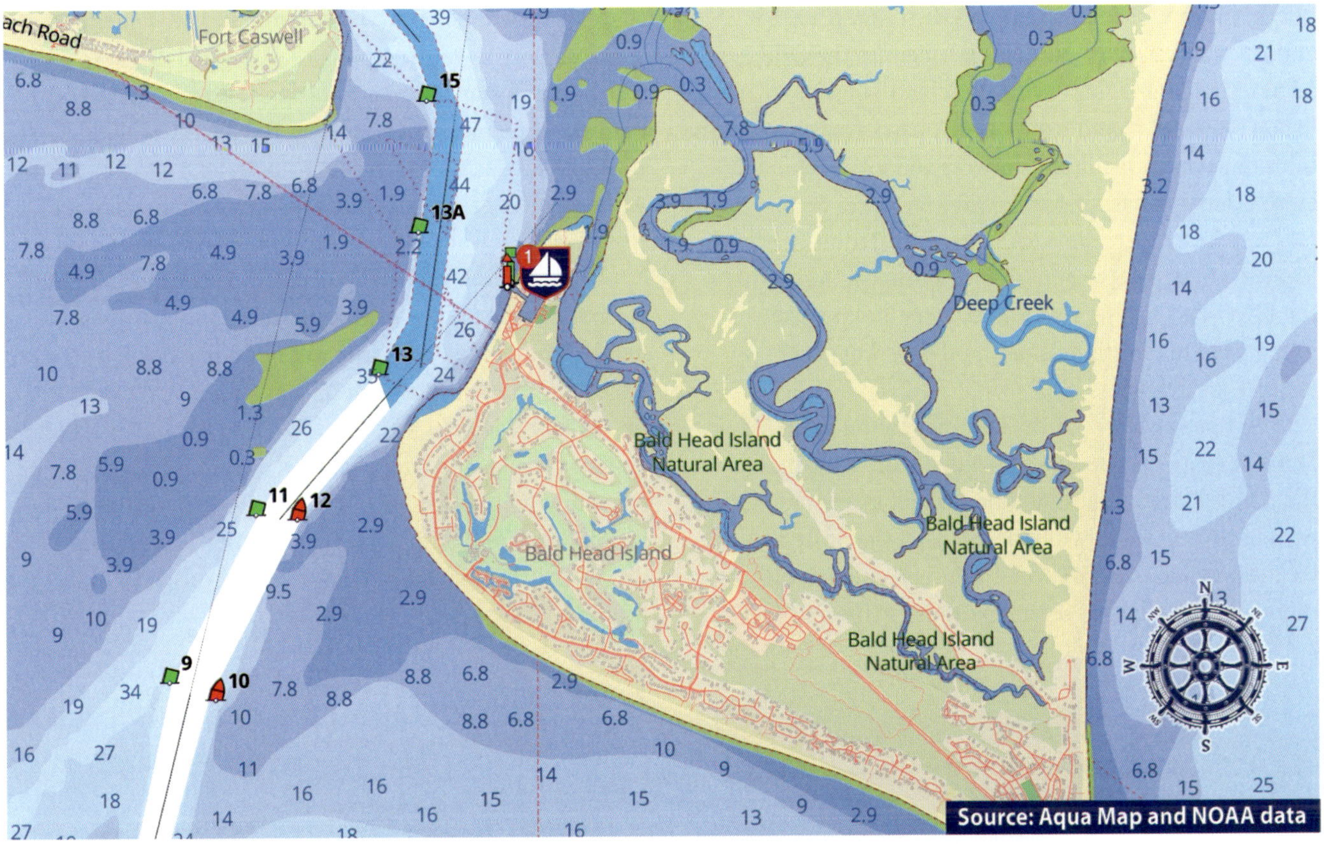

The ebb and flood currents range from 2 to 3 knots and run perpendicular to the island's entrance channel. The entrance channel is narrow and care must be exercised to maintain control of your vessel in the current. Do not try to enter if another boat is exiting the channel fairway. Call the dockmaster on VHF Channel 16 for guidance if needed.

Dockage: Bald Head Island Marina is located in a 10-acre protected harbor with neatly lined floating docks and surrounded by an adorable village. Along with dockside conveniences such as showers, laundry facilities, some groceries, boating supplies and casual dining, marina guests can enjoy the island's fine dining, outstanding golf and pristine beaches. The marina can accommodate vessels to 115 feet and 8-foot drafts. Call ahead for availability, docking instructions and assistance (monitoring VHF Channel 16). There is no room for anchoring in the enclosed basin.

Southport–ICW Mile 309

About 2 miles north of the Cape Fear River Inlet (to the Atlantic) the ICW leaves the river, takes a hard turn to the west, enters a dredged land cut and arrives in the peaceful little village of Southport.

Southport's numerous restaurants and much of its business district are within easy walking distance of the waterfront. The downtown combines all the charm of a laid-back coastal village with historic southern architecture and style.

> **NOTE:** A "drive on" (car) ferry terminal is 2 miles north of Southport and runs to the tip of Fort Fisher at the mouth of the Cape Fear River. The enjoyable 45-minute one-way trip is filled with unique, beautiful views and is a bargain at $7 per carload.

MID-ATLANTIC EDITION

Chapter 6: Beaufort to Southport, NC

NAVIGATION: Shoaling has been observed along Southport's waterfront and the nameless island just southwest of the village so stay in the channel. When entering the ICW channel from the Cape Fear River, there is no shortcut. The two rectangular condo buildings on the point at Southport make a prominent landmark.

Dockage: At Mile 307 the modern Deep Point Marina offers comfortable dockage along with easy ocean, ICW and river access. The marina is adjacent to the Bald Head Island Mainland Ferry Terminal, which houses a snack bar (open seasonally) and restrooms. A harbormaster building offering laundry facilities, showers and a convenience store is located harborside.

Deep Point also manages Indigo Plantation & Marina located immediately south of the Southport basin on the ICW. This facility caters to boaters looking for a longer stay (a month or more) and does not accept short-term transients.

The floating docks at the entrance to the basin at Southport are private and associated with the condos on the point. Dockage is sometimes available at a few of the private slips in the town basin. (Check the posted signs.) Past these docks and in front of Provision Company there are four slips for dining patrons (910-457-0654). If you eat there, you can stay overnight at the dock. There is no water or power and it may be noisy when the restaurant is full.

Nearby Fishy Fishy may also have dockage for diners but call ahead (910-457-1881). The Southport Town Dock is open to the public and is being used as a dingy dock, but no overnight docking is allowed.

A short distance into the southbound ICW land cut a channel opens to the right at flashing red marker "2A" into Morningstar Marinas Southport, one of the largest and most amenity-laden marinas in North Carolina. The full-service marina has over 200 in-water protected slips with deep water access, a well-appointed ship store and a fuel dock. They also have a 220 unit dry storage facility.

At Mile 311 (daybeacon green "9"), Safe Harbor South Harbour Village offers a spacious 500-foot facing dock parallel to the ICW that can accommodate boats up to 200 feet. They offer all fuels, pump-out stations, ice and oil on the face dock.

The on-site Rusty Hooks Dockside Grill has great food (try the signature fish tacos), a bar and live music, while Joseph's Italian Bistro offers fine dining with European decor. This facility is known for being cruiser- and pet-friendly. Reservations are recommended.

Morningstar Marinas Southport

Southport Area, NC

DEEP POINT		Largest Vessel	VHF	Total Slips	Approach/Dockside Depth	Floating Docks	Gas/Diesel	Repairs/Haulout	Min/Max Amps	Pump-Out Station
1. Deep Point Marina WiFi MM 307.0	(910) 269-2380	100	16	82	6.0 / 6.0	F	GD		30 / 100	P
SOUTHPORT										
2. Morningstar Marinas Southport WiFi MM 309.3	(910) 457-9900	200	16	200	8.0 / 6.0	F	GD		30 / 100	P
OAK ISLAND										
3. Safe Harbor South Harbour Village WiFi MM 311.4	(910) 454-7486	200	16	153	15.0 / 12.0	F	GD		30 / 100	P
4. St. James Marina WiFi MM 315.0	(910) 253-0463	120	16	155	5.5 / 7.0	F	GD		30 / 50	P

WiFi Wireless Internet Access
Visit www.waterwayguide.com for current rates, fuel prices, website addresses and other up-to-the-minute information.
(Information in the table is provided by the facilities.)

Scan here for more details:

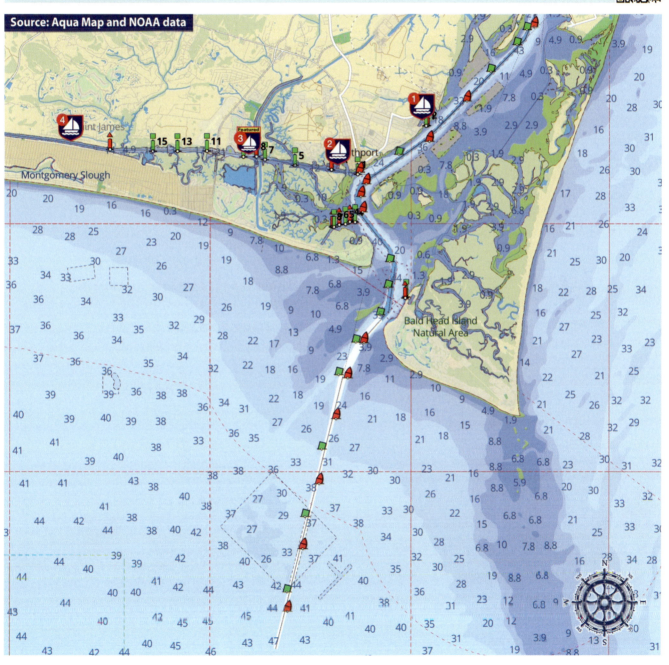

Source: Aqua Map and NOAA data

MID-ATLANTIC EDITION

Chapter 6: Beaufort to Southport, NC

Goin' Ashore: SOUTHPORT, NC

ATTRACTIONS

1. **Keziah Memorial Park**
   Lovely place for a walk and home to an ancient gnarled oak estimated to be more than 800 years old. Native Americans may have bent the young tree to mark the trail to their fishing grounds. Tree took root a second time, thus developing the unusual formation. You can't miss it at 113 W. Moore St. (910-457-7945).

2. **Fort Johnston - Southport Museum & Visitor's Center**
   Historic fort built in 1748 offering exhibits on Southport's history at 203 E. Bay St. (910-457-7927).

3. **North Carolina Maritime Museum**
   Housed in former officer quarters at Fort Johnston with collection covering shipwrecks, piracy, the Civil War, commercial fishing, hurricanes and a number of other natural and manmade events that have left a permanent mark on the North Carolina coast (204 E. Moore St., 910-457-0003).

4. **Old Brunswick County Jail Museum**
   Restored two-story brick jailhouse (circa 1904) featuring quarters with period artifacts at 318 E. Nash St. (910-457-7927).

5. **Old Smithville Burying Ground**
   Shaded by giant oak trees, peaceful and well-kept cemetery founded in 1792 (before the town). Occupants include ship captains, passengers from a steamship that sank in the 1800s and Civil War-era officers and soldiers. Located at 401 E. Moore St. and managed by the Southport Historical Society (910-457-7927).

6. **Old Yacht Basin**
   Where to go for fresh seafood and great views. Restauarants include Fishy-Fishy, Provision Company, Frying Pan and its popular bar, American Fish Company.

SERVICES

7. **Dosher Memorial Hospital**
   924 N. Howe St. (910-457-3800)

8. **Margaret and James Harper, Jr. Library**
   109 W. Moore St. (910-457-6237)

9. **Southport Post Office**
   206 E. Nash St. (910-457-4633)

MARINAS

10. **Morningstar Marinas Southport**
    606 W. West St. (910-457-9900)

America's Waterway Guide Since 1947 — Chapter 6

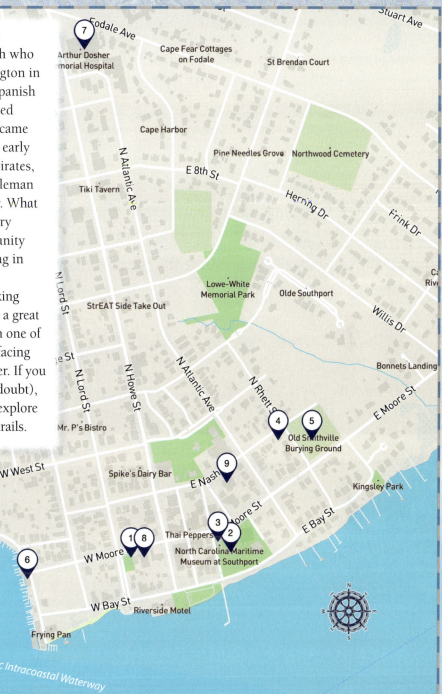

Southport was originally named Smithville after Benjamin Smith who served under Gen. George Washington in the Revolutionary War. The first Spanish explorers arrived in 1521 and settled up the Cape Fear River in what became known as Brunswick Town. In the early 1700 Southport was a harbor for pirates, including Stede Bonnet, the "Gentleman Pirate," who was a frequent visitor. What began as a small fishing and military town has blossomed into a community for retirees and commuters working in Wilmington.

Waterfront Park offers breathtaking views of the Cape Fear River and is a great spot for a leisurely walk or a rest on one of the many front porch-style swings facing the water. There is also a fishing pier. If you run out of things to do (which we doubt), take a ferry to Bald Head Island to explore its beaches, lighthouse and nature trails.

Chapter 6: Beaufort to Southport, NC

Oak Island Lighthouse

SAFE HARBOR SOUTH HARBOUR VILLAGE AWAITS

Two Waterside Restaurants
Bathhouses, Showers & Laundry
Pump Out Service
Complimentary Parking
Dog Park
Home Port Events
Multiple Fuel Locations on the Transient Dock

Scan to learn more

SAFE HARBOR
— SOUTH HARBOUR VILLAGE —

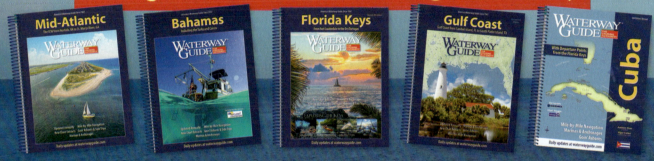

Chapter 6: Beaufort to Southport, NC

Anchorage: Across from Deep Point Marina at Mile 307, there is a remote cove behind the spoil islands that is out of the way of traffic and mostly quiet. Good holding in 8 to 10 feet MLW with no wakes or traffic. No shore access but, nonetheless, a good overnight stop.

The Southport Basin is shallow (3- to 7-foot MLW depths) with poor holding and is open to the south and ICW wakes, which is why we don't recommend this as anything other than an emergency anchorage. The entrance to Dutchman Creek at Mile 310.2 has shoaled to 5.5 feet, as has the anchorage on the west side of Pipeline Canal Basin. In short, this is a good area to plan on taking a slip.

If you must anchor, enter Dutchman Creek just past green daybeacon "5" on the east (ICW north) side of the creek for deeper water. The bottom is mud and sand, and the creek is narrow enough that two anchors is a good idea. Wake protection from all directions. Expect mild wind protection from the northeast but exposure to wind (marsh) in all other directions.

Pipeline Canal Basin is north of red daybeacon "8" at Mile 311. Be careful where you choose to drop the hook, as it shallows to the north. The muddy bottom holds well but will make a huge, stinky mess on your boat when the hook comes up. This anchorage does, however, offer excellent shore access at a nearby boat ramp.

Oak Island–ICW Mile 312

From Oak Island through Long Beach you will pass through several small towns and a series of beach developments. You will likely encounter numerous small fishing boats testing the waters for red fish and flounder. These are also some of the most beautiful sections of the ICW.

Oak Island Lighthouse offers sweeping views over Caswell Beach and Bald Head Island. Tours to the second level (12 steps up to a solid concrete floor) are offered during the summer months on Wednesdays and Saturdays. Reservations are not required but if you wish to take a tour to the top (up 131 steps to an outside balcony) we recommend making a reservation (and well in advance). All tours are free.

NAVIGATION: Oak Island (NC 133) Bridge (65-foot fixed vertical clearance) at Mile 311.8 is the first bridge encountered after Snows Cut. There is another high-level bridge–Middleton Street Bridge with 67-foot fixed vertical clearance–between Oak Island and the mainland at Mile 316.8.

From Mile 310 to Mile 396 below Myrtle Beach, the National Ocean Service (NOS) tables do not provide information on currents. In general the flood runs south in this area but expect current reversals as you pass inlets.

Dockage: Continuing west on the ICW, the well-managed St. James Marina at Mile 315 is a full-service marina with everything you need on a 15-acre site. They have 12 reserved transient slips for vessels to 120 feet and a dry storage facility. This is part of a large residential development and includes a small general store and a gift shop. This is a remote location; transportation is required for provisioning.

Lockwoods Folly, NC to McClellanville, SC

Chapter 7

Chapter 7: Lockwoods Folly, NC to McClellanville, SC

■ TO MYRTLE BEACH, SC

The distance from Southport, NC, to Little River Inlet, SC, is 32 miles and will take you about 4 hours in an 8-mph trawler. Time and tide is a concern because this stretch of the waterway contains two of the ICW problem areas: Lockwoods Folly and Shallotte Inlet.

You will want to pass through this area near high tide, giving you 4+ feet more depth and a lot of extra breathing room. Little River and Southport tides are similar so the logical departure time heading either north or south would be around 2 hours before local high tide to pass these two inlets around high tide.

Most boaters will not be doing this segment in a vacuum. If headed south, you will be moving behind Myrtle Beach in the ICW. If going north, you will be looking at going up the Cape Fear River. Tying two or more of these pieces together will require some thought.

Lockwoods Folly Inlet–ICW Mile 321

Approaching Lockwoods Folly Inlet, the shoreline shifts to low marshland extending back to scrub trees. Along the banks at Holden Beach just below the inlet an increasing number of houses have appeared on the ocean side of the ICW. This section carries heavy commercial and recreational boat traffic, particularly on weekends, and there are long stretches of No-Wake Zones.

If you make the passage in late June when North Carolina rivers are open for fishing, you will find a lot of boat traffic. Boats vary from outboard-powered skiffs and center consoles with families aboard to miniature shrimp boats. Although the traffic is chaotic and some skippers are uncooperative, one reward is that a fresh shrimp or fish meal is readily available at almost any tie-up.

ICW Bridges will not delay openings if boats are already waiting, so you must know your speed and calculate your transit carefully; slow boats may not be able to synchronize their passages with the openings.

NAVIGATION: Just past Mile 321 the ICW crosses the junction of Lockwoods Folly Inlet and Lockwoods Folly River. The proximity of the ICW to the ocean in this area makes conditions extremely changeable at both Lockwoods Folly Inlet crossing and Shallotte Inlet crossing a few miles farther south.

Strong ebb and flow currents alone continually move the sand, while storms off the ocean can reshape the bottom in hours. Be aware of crosscurrents and adjust your heading as required.

Lockwoods Folly Inlet, NC

HOLDEN BEACH		Largest Vessel	VHF	Total Slips	Approach/Dockside Depth	Floating Docks	Gas/Diesel	Repairs/Haulout	Min/Max Amps	Pump-Out Station
1. Zimmerman Marine - Holden Beach MM 322.5	(910) 842-5488	72	68	8	/			RH	30/50	
2. Holden Beach Marina MM 324.0	(910) 842-5447	45		10	7.0/5.0	F	GD	R	30/100	
3. Holden Beach Transient Dock MM 324.0	(910) 842-6488	60		3	/	F			20/50	P

WiFi Wireless Internet Access
Visit www.waterwayguide.com for current rates, fuel prices, website addresses and other up-to-the-minute information.
(Information in the table is provided by the facilities.)

Scan here for more details:

Source: Aqua Map and NOAA data

The channel past Lockwoods Folly Inlet usually has extra floating markers (which can be readily moved) that are not shown on the NOAA chart, plus other charted markers may be missing. As always, honor the marks, which are close to shore. Look for the ICW yellow triangles and squares so you do not confuse the inlet markers with those for the ICW. The best track can be seen on Waterway Explorer at www.waterwayguide.com.

At Mile 323.6 you will pass under the **Holden Beach (NC 130) Bridge** (65-foot fixed vertical clearance). This area has more boating traffic each year, especially during spring and summer. This is not a good place to anchor. Plan to take a slip.

Dockage: Holden Beach Marina just above Mile 323 is primarily a dry-stack marina but they do reserve a few of their 15 slips for transients. You can walk to a grocery store and several restaurants. The nearby Provision Company (910-842-7205) has good seafood, a casual atmosphere, dockage and live music on weekends.

The municipal Holden Beach Transient Dock is at Mile 324 with a 100-foot floating dock with power, water and pump-out service. The facility also has a nice laundry and anything you need within walking distance. Reservations can be made at the town office (910-842-6488).

Zimmerman Marine–Holden Beach operates hauling and marine services including fiberglass, mechanical, carpentry, rigging and systems installation and repair. Their original yard remains on Mobjack Bay (Mathews) with additional locations in Herrington Harbor, MD, Solomons, MD; Deltaville, VA; Oriental, NC; and Charleston, SC.

Chapter 7: Lockwoods Folly, NC to McClellanville, SC

Welcome to South Carolina!

The canals and dredged cuts of NC give way to the wide river mouths, large sounds and coastal inlets of SC. The natural waterways are deep to the banks of low, marshy grasslands that are backed by hummocks of trees, including stately moss-covered oaks. At low tide, the vast salt marshes will teem with bird life.

Beyond Charleston, there is a noticeable increase in tidal currents and heights. The tidal range runs about 8 feet and depths can change quickly. Shoaling is an issue in some areas, and strong tidal currents throughout the region can change depths overnight. This section of the ICW also has many bridges, including many fixed high-level (65-foot vertical clearance) bridges. All SC bridges monitor VHF Channel 09. Be aware of the South Carolina Department of Transportation (SC DOT) Hurricane Evacuation Rule (posted on most opening bridges): Draw and swing bridges will not open when wind reaches a sustained 25 knots or if mandatory evacuation is ordered. During periods of strong winds, these bridges may be closed. (Swing bridges are especially vulnerable to damage from high winds.) Boats with taller masts must run outside from Beaufort, NC, to Georgetown or Charleston, SC, both of which are safe, big ship inlets. Be sure to refer to the Waterway Explorer at www.waterwayguide.com for navigational alerts, tidal information and bridge restrictions and schedules.

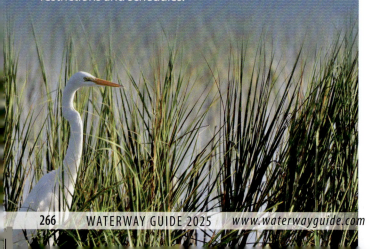

Shallotte Inlet–ICW Mile 330

At both Holden Beach and Ocean Isle Beach, long colonies of oceanfront houses (many on stilts) are on Florida-style dredged canals from the ICW to the ocean. Houses on the mainland side are more substantial, spaced farther apart and appear among the trees facing toward the ocean beach. You need to stay in the middle of the channel in this area due to rapid shoaling outside the channel.

> NOTE: The name Shallotte was derived from the original settlement name Charlotte and is pronounced "sha-LOTE" (with a long "o" sound).

NAVIGATION: The Shallotte River makes off northward at Mile 329.6 and leads to the rural town of Shallotte, NC. Call Coastal Machine and Welding on VHF Channel 16 for advice if you are considering venturing up the Shallotte River, which has a spring tidal range of 6 feet.

On the ICW at Shallotte Inlet, boaters can expect a sudden lateral push from the current coming through the inlet during a rising tide. You will experience a "pull" toward the ocean during an ebb tide. This pushing and pulling is more likely to put you aground than any shoaling along the ICW channel, so it would be wise to time your crossing at minimum tidal flow.

Shallotte Inlet maintains 9.5 feet MLW in the middle of the channel; do not hug any buoys. Keep in mind that one storm can completely change the inlet. Because of this, we do not advise use of Shallotte Inlet, even with local knowledge. This inlet is used primarily by local small fishing boats.

Anchorage: At red daybeacon "76" (Mile 229.5) near Shallotte Inlet there is a fairly large anchorage area with great holding and 10 feet MLW. Most of the shore is private docks but there is a restaurant that you could dinghy into for pets and/or food and drinks.

Little River Inlet–ICW Mile 342

NAVIGATION: The route from Shallotte Inlet is straightforward. Ocean Isle (NC 904) Bridge at Mile 333.7 is a fixed 65-foot span. Between the Mannon C. Gore (Sunset Beach) Bridge at Mile 337.9 and the Little River intersection with the ICW at Mile 341.9, stay in mid-channel to avoid the frequent shoals, which often crop up where various creeks cross to the ocean. There are no viable anchorage areas along this stretch.

About 1 mile above the junction of the ICW and the channel from the Little River Inlet, SC the route crosses

Little River Inlet, SC

OCEAN ISLE		Largest Vessel	VHF	Total Slips	Approach/Dockside Depth	Floating Docks	Gas/Diesel	Repairs/Haulout	Min/Max Amps	Pump-Out Station
1. Ocean Isle Marina & Yacht Club WiFi MM 335.5	(910) 579-6440	75	16	28	12.0 / 6.0	F	GD	RH	30 / 100	

WiFi Wireless Internet Access
Visit www.waterwayguide.com for current rates, fuel prices, website addresses and other up-to-the-minute information. (Information in the table is provided by the facilities.)

Scan here for more details:

Source: Aqua Map and NOAA data

the border from North Carolina into South Carolina (Mile 340.9). You can assume that you are in South Carolina when you make the turn below flashing red "116."

Just inside the South Carolina State Line the ICW crosses Little River, which offers relatively easy and well-marked access to the ocean through the well-maintained channel between jetties. Little River Inlet, SC is deep, wide and busy with a steady flow of tourist and fishing boats.

Little River Inlet has jetties and is relatively stable. This inlet is used regularly by casino boats and head boats docked at Little River. Casino boats are not required to have AIS transponders and many do not. There is a 5-foot shoal just off the east jetty that is awash at low tide. Note that the aids to navigation are frequently moved here to mark shifting shoals. Seek local knowledge before traversing the inlet.

Dockage: At Mile 335.5, Ocean Isle Marina & Yacht Club offers general boat maintenance, winterization, detailing services and more and has some reserved transient space to 75 feet.

Anchorage: This is a scenic anchorage next to a great beach at Bird Island in the inlet. Expect good holding and protection from north and northeast winds but there is a fairly swift tidal current so check the anchor. This is a great place to walk the four-legged crew members.

You can anchor in Calabash Creek on the mainland side of the junction between the ICW and Little River Inlet, SC at Mile 342. At extreme low tides the entrance bar carries around 5 feet. You will be subject to wakes from the ICW if you anchor toward the mouth of the creek. This is a pleasant spot otherwise with a golf course on the wooded northern shore.

Chapter 7: Lockwoods Folly, NC to McClellanville, SC

Give Calabash Creek red daybeacon "2A" (not the ICW red daybeacon "2," which features the distinctive ICW yellow triangle) a wide berth to avoid the shoal at the entrance. Then turn toward the row of charted dolphins and drop the hook near the north side of the center of the river. There is increasing shoaling on the opposite shore just upstream of the dolphins.

Do not anchor near the creek entrance as other vessels may arrive after you. Use two anchors in bad weather or if the anchorage is too crowded for normal swinging room. As always, show an anchor light. Shrimp boats and sightseeing vessels, whose wakes may disturb you, use the channel at night.

Little River–ICW Mile 346

The village of Little River is a good stopping point for boats coming from the north or south. About a one-day run from Wrightsville Beach to the north and just before the long stretch of the ICW behind Myrtle Beach, it is the northern gateway to popular vacation resorts, which line the ocean beach for more than 20 miles as you head south.

The mild climate has attracted permanent residents as well as vacationers. It also attracts anglers who come to patronize its charter fishing boats as well as golfers, who come to take on the 100-plus golf courses. This area is very busy with small boats, especially on weekends and holidays.

NAVIGATION: The high point between Little River Inlet and Winyah Bay below Georgetown is located near the **Socastee (SC 544) Hwy. Bridge** (Mile 371.2) behind Myrtle Beach. Water heading north falls 23 miles to the Little River Inlet. High tide here is 3 hours later than it is at the inlet and low tide is almost 4 hours later. This can be used for an advantage when moving through this stretch of the ICW.

If you are southbound from Little River you will have approximately 3 hours of travel in an 8 mph trawler to make it through the Rock Pile and to the summit. A departure from Little River 2 hours before local high tide will result in a beneficial following current all the way up the ICW to Socastee Bridge.

Leaving earlier would offer a greater advantage but transiting Shallotte Inlet at half tide puts you at Little River Inlet just about 2 hours before that local high tide. In this case we will take what we can get.

If you are heading north from Myrtle Beach, time your arrival at Little River Inlet about an hour after local low tide to take advantage of up to 2 mph of tidal lift. This will allow an arrival at Shallotte Inlet just before local half tide, with at least 2 feet of extra water under your keel to help you on your journey towards Lockwoods Folly and Southport.

Nixon Crossroads has two bridges: **Nixon Crossroads Bridge** at Mile 347.2 (fixed vertical clearance 65 feet) and the **Captain Archie Neil "Poo" McLauchlin (Little River) Swing Bridge** at Mile 347.3 with a closed vertical clearance of 7 feet. (The Little River Swing Bridge was renamed in 2018 after a lifelong

Little River Swing Bridge

Little River, SC

COQUINA HARBOR

COQUINA HARBOR		Largest Vessel	VHF	Total Slips	Approach/ Dockside Depth	Floating Docks	Gas/ Diesel	Repairs/ Haulout	Min/Max Amps	Pump-Out Station
1. Cricket Cove Marina WiFi MM 345.0	(843) 249-7169	60	16	73	10.0 / 7.0	F	GD		30 / 50	
2. Coquina Yacht Club WiFi MM 346.0	(843) 249-9333	102	16	87	8.0 / 8.0	F			30 / 50	P
3. Myrtle Beach Yacht Club WiFi MM 346.0	(843) 249-5376	110	16	153	8.0 / 10.0	F	GD		30 / 100	P
4. Lightkeepers Marina WiFi MM 346.0	(843) 249-8660	80	16	125	7.5 / 7.5	F			30 / 50	P

WiFi Wireless Internet Access
Visit www.waterwayguide.com for current rates, fuel prices, website addresses and other up-to-the-minute information. (Information in the table is provided by the facilities.)

Scan here for more details:

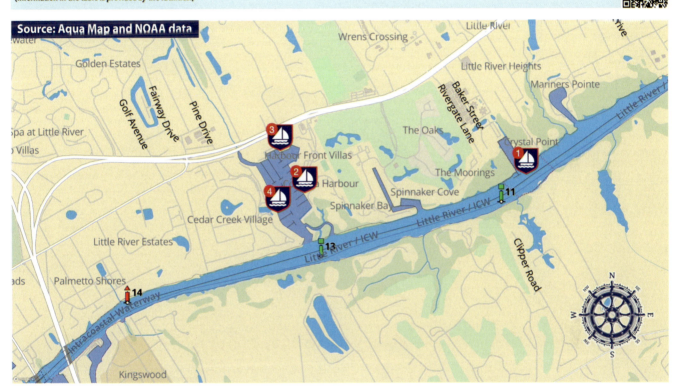

Source: Aqua Map and NOAA data

resident.) The bridge opens on request. The Captain Poo Swing Bridge is old and frequently in need of repair.

NOTE: The Nixon Crossroads Bridge and the Captain Archie Neil "Poo" McLauchlin (Little River) Swing Bridge denote the dividing line between fresh and saltwater. Southwest of the bridges where the water becomes fresh you need a freshwater fishing license to do any angling.

Coquina Harbor, a large deepwater basin on the west side of the ICW at Mile 346 (green daybeacon "13") is home to several marinas serving transients. A black and white lighthouse replica marks the harbor entrance. The entire harbor is surrounded by a 3-mile boardwalk.

Dockage: Cricket Cove Marina at Mile 345 has one of the largest indoor dry storage facilities in the Myrtle Beach area plus 73 wet slips (including transient slips). The popular Snooky's on the Water (843-249-5252) is on site.

Southbound boaters headed for Coquina Harbor need to proceed slightly south of the entrance and come back to the north and enter at an angle. Do not try to cut the corner on this well-marked channel; it is shallow outside the entrance markers. Deep-draft vessels should call ahead for entrance information.

Coquina Yacht Club has 12 transient slips to 102 feet with full amenities. Across the harbor is Lightkeepers Marina, a large but quiet marina adjacent to a condo development. They have limited transient space so it's a good idea to call ahead.

Transients to 46 feet are welcome at the well-regarded Myrtle Beach Yacht Club at Coquina Harbor. They have all the usual amenities plus a restaurant (the Officers Club), which you can visit as a guest of the marina manager.

MID-ATLANTIC EDITION

Chapter 7: Lockwoods Folly, NC to McClellanville, SC

North Myrtle Beach Area, SC

NORTH MYRTLE BEACH		Largest Vessel	VHF	Total Slips	Approach/ Dockside Depth	Floating Docks	Gas/ Diesel	Repairs/ Haulout	Min/Max Amps	Pump-Out Station
1. Cherry Grove Marina (formerly Anchor Marina) MM 347.0	(843) 427-7008	48	16	108	7.0 / 6.0	F		RH	30 / 50	
2. Harbourgate Marina WiFi MM 347.7	(843) 249-8888	100	16	100	8.0 / 6.0	F	GD	R	30 / 50	P
3. North Myrtle Beach RV Resort and Marina WiFi 348.1	(843) 390-4386	30	9	36	8.0 / 5.0	F	GD	H	30 / 50	P

WiFi Wireless Internet Access
Visit www.waterwayguide.com for current rates, fuel prices, website addresses and other up-to-the-minute information.
(Information in the table is provided by the facilities.)

Scan here for more details:

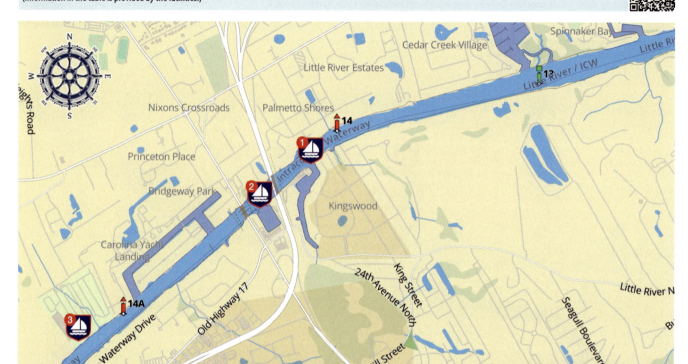

Source: Aqua Map and NOAA data

The convenient Cherry Grove Marina (formerly Anchor Marina) is located just before the Nixon Crossroads Bridge (Mile 347.2) on the south side of the ICW. This 100-slip facility maintains just 3 transient slips to 48 feet and offers a variety of professional boat services.

Harbourgate Marina directly on the ICW at Mile 347.7 (nestled between the bridges) is part of a condominium complex with numerous amenities. Call ahead; they have limited transient space on their floating docks. A large shopping plaza with groceries and a West Marine is within walking distance.

Two miles south of Coquina Harbor is North Myrtle Beach RV Resort and Marina with resort amenities. Private showers, laundry facilities, a pool and an on-site bar and grill are among the offerings. They are set up for smaller vessels (to 30 feet) but can accommodate larger vessels on the face dock. Call ahead.

To Myrtle Beach Area–ICW Mile 354

Barefoot Landing at Mile 354 (North Myrtle Beach) is a large complex featuring two theaters, plus over a dozen restaurants and 100 plus specialty shops. This open air "mall" has ponds, bridges, turtles, alligators and birds in addition to shopping and dining.

There has been almost continuous new shoreside development between Barefoot Landing at Mile 354 and about Mile 362 on both sides of the ICW. Golf is very popular here with over 100 courses in the greater Myrtle Beach area. Single-family homes, docks and huge condominium developments surrounding golf courses line much of the ICW.

Supermarkets, marine supplies and restaurants are within walking distance of most marinas and are too numerous to list here, which is why there is no

Myrtle Beach Area, SC

BAREFOOT LANDING		Largest Vessel	VHF	Total Slips	Approach/ Dockside Depth	Floating Docks	Gas/ Diesel	Repairs/ Haulout	Min/Max Amps	Pump-Out Station
1. Barefoot Marina (WiFi) MM 354.0	(843) 390-2011	150	16	142	8.0 / 12.0	F	GD		30 / 50	P

(WiFi) Wireless Internet Access Scan here for more details:
Visit www.waterwayguide.com for current rates, fuel prices, website addresses and other up-to-the-minute information.
(Information in the table is provided by the facilities.)

Goin' Ashore for Myrtle Beach. They do a better job than we can at Visit Myrtle Beach (www.visitmyrtlebeach.com).

NAVIGATION: Below Little River the ICW route enters a 26-mile-long high-banked land cut known locally as Pine Island Cut. There is a tall white sign ("Danger Rocks") that marks the start and the ending of this stretch of the waterway. New development and clearing along this once-heavily wooded area give the illusion that the channel is wider than it really is. Be extremely careful to remain in the center of the channel.

Check on VHF Channels 13 or 16 to see if any tug or barge traffic is passing through the area. Stay in the center of the channel and follow the markers. It is wise to make a "Sécurité" call on VHF Channels 13 or 16. Keep to mid-channel and watch for shoaling at bends and places where drainage ditches enter the waterway. When passing or being passed by another boat do not crowd too close to the edge of the channel. Keep an eye out for flotsam and snags. Numerous trees have toppled into the cut, and many woodpiles on the banks appear ready to follow. There is heavy development along much of this stretch.

CAUTION: The stretch between ICW Mile 349 to around Mile 352 is known as the "Rock Pile" due to the rock ledges along both sides of the channel. A number of charted daybeacons mark the most worrisome of the rock ledges, many of which are visible only at low tide. Not all of them are marked so keep a sharp watch.

Chapter 7: Lockwoods Folly, NC to McClellanville, SC

Robert Edge Parkway Bridge (also known as North Myrtle Beach Connector Bridge) with 65-foot fixed vertical clearance crosses the ICW at Mile 349.1.

The **Barefoot Landing Swing Bridge** (31-foot closed vertical clearance) crosses at Mile 353.3. The bridgetender at the swing bridge monitors VHF Channel 09, and the bridge opens on signal. Two dolphins are on the edges of the channel on the east side of the bridge between the bridge and the docks.

Just beyond Barefoot Landing you will pass under the **Conway Bypass (SC 22) Bridges** (65-foot fixed vertical clearance) at Mile 355.5. Shoaling has been observed near the drainage ditches between this bridge and the bridges at Mile 365.4. At Mile 356 cables for an overhead gondola giving access to a now defunct golf course across the ICW may look too low for comfort but the clearance is at least 67 feet as clearly charted.

At Mile 358.3 is **Grande Dunes Bridge** (65-foot fixed vertical clearance) spanning both sides of the ICW. Be careful not to confuse the small floating markers at the two entrances to the Marina at Grande Dunes just south of the bridge with ICW markers. Should you need it, Grand Strand Medical Center (843-692-1000) is located adjacent to the Grand Dunes development. Another fixed 65-foot high-rise bridge, **Grissom Parkway Bridge**, is at Mile 360.6.

The fixed 65-foot **U.S. 501 Bridge** crosses the ICW at Mile 365.5 along with a **SCL Railroad Bridge** (16-foot vertical clearance), which remains open. ICW veterans and commercial skippers refer to these two bridges as the "Combination Bridges."

At Mile 366 numerous cypress stumps and a lone tree encroach into the north side of the ICW from the extensive stone riprap meant to prevent soil erosion around one of the many condominium developments along this stretch. The 65-foot **Fantasy Harbor Bridge** at Mile 366.4 is the connector to access the defunct Freestyle Music Park.

Socastee Swing Bridge (which opens on request) at Mile 371.0 has an official closed vertical clearance of 11 feet, although its tide board shows less. It opens on signal. Use the southeast draw. The Socastee (pronounced "sock-a-stee") Swing Bridge is old and frequently in need of repair. Call the drawtender on VHF Channel 09 or by phone (843-302-8640) for up-to-date status.

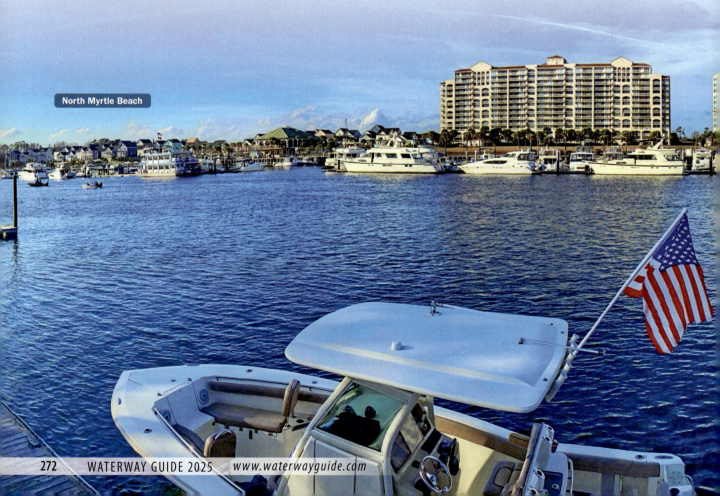

North Myrtle Beach

Chapter 7
America's Waterway Guide Since 1947

CAUTION: Benjamin E. Thrailkill, Jr. (SC 544) Bridge at Mile 371.3 frequently has less than the charted 65 feet of clearance due to high rainfall during storms, especially after a hurricane. A graph that shows bridge clearance versus water gauge height can be found online at Socastee Water Gauge Height. Sailboats with tall masts should check conditions carefully here.

The **Carolina Bays Parkway (SC 31) Bridge** crosses the ICW at Mile 372.4 with 65-foot closed vertical clearance.

Dockage: Free daytime dockage is available at The Dock at Barefoot Landing. This is a great place to stop for lunch or shopping but absolutely no overnight docking is allowed. There is some current, and you will be docking with the current on the beam.

Barefoot Marina is across the ICW from the shopping area. Access to all the expected amenities plus a resort-style pool are among the perks here as well as 1,100 feet of concrete floating docks available for transient dockage. The marina provides free transportation (by golf cart) to the Barefoot Landing shopping area (1 mile walk across bridge), or you can dinghy across the river and tie up for even easier access.

Grande Dunes Marina at Mile 357 offers a protected harbor for vessels up to 120 feet. The on-site restaurant, Anchor Café, is the only restaurant in Myrtle Beach on the ICW. The marina is also the trailhead for scenic walkways along the ICW. Several dining options are within walking distance as is a grocery store and other shopping.

The family-oriented Osprey Marina, located at red daybeacon "26" (Mile 373), has dry storage plus floating transient slips to 200 feet, pump-out service and a dockmaster's building with all the necessary amenities. The entrance to the protected basin is well marked and has 10-foot MLW depths.

NOTE: Once in a slip here, expect a welcome from dozens of turtles looking for a handout. This may be your first experience with "southern" turtles and yes, they do know how to beg. If you don't happen to have turtle food aboard, they are glad to accept hush puppies, crackers, pet food or anything else you throw their way.

MID-ATLANTIC EDITION

Chapter 7: Lockwoods Folly, NC to McClellanville, SC

Myrtle Beach Area, SC

GRANDE DUNES		Largest Vessel	VHF	Total Slips	Approach/ Dockside Depth	Floating Docks	Gas/ Diesel	Repairs/ Haulout	Min/Max Amps	Pump-Out Station
1. Grande Dunes Marina WiFi MM 357.0	(843) 315-7777	120	16	126	10.0 / 6.0	F	GD		30 / 50	P

WiFi Wireless Internet Access
Visit www.waterwayguide.com for current rates, fuel prices, website addresses and other up-to-the-minute information.
(Information in the table is provided by the facilities.)

Scan here for more details:

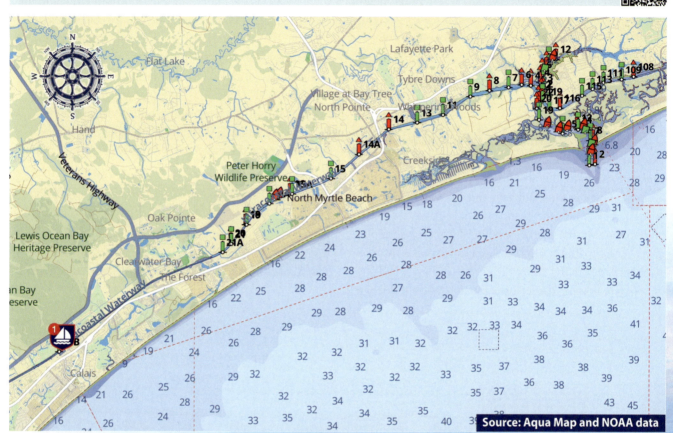

Source: Aqua Map and NOAA data

North Myrtle Beach Boardwalk

Myrtle Beach Area, SC

MYRTLE BEACH

		Largest Vessel	VHF	Total Slips	Approach/ Dockside Depth	Floating Docks	Gas/ Diesel	Repairs/ Haulout	Min/Max Amps	Pump-Out Station
1. Osprey Marina WiFi MM 373.0	(843) 215-5353	90	16	119	10.0 / 9.0	F	GD		30 / 50	P

WiFi Wireless Internet Access
Visit www.waterwayguide.com for current rates, fuel prices, website addresses and other up-to-the-minute information.
(Information in the table is provided by the facilities.)

Scan here for more details:

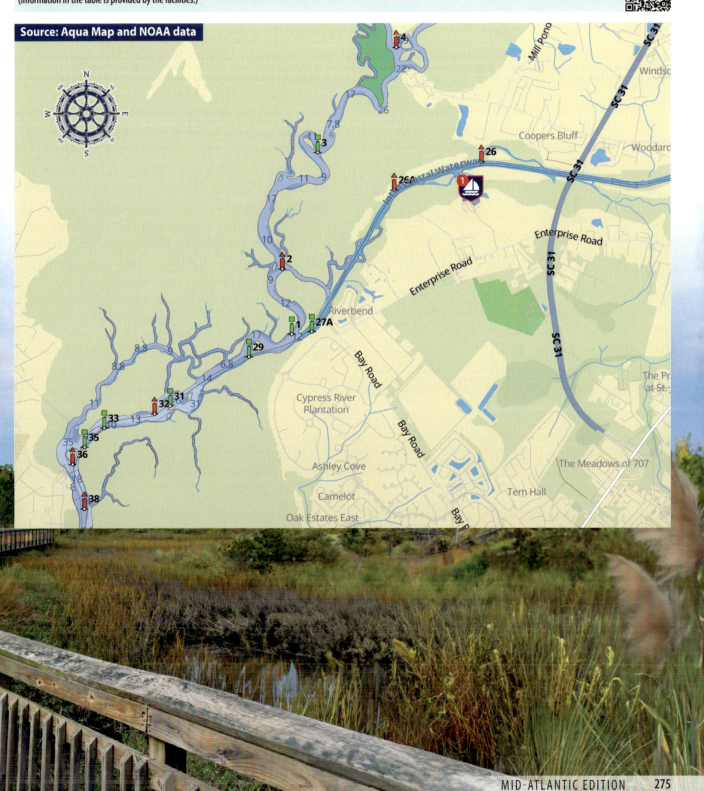

Source: Aqua Map and NOAA data

MID-ATLANTIC EDITION

Chapter 7: Lockwoods Folly, NC to McClellanville, SC

Anchorage: The upper Waccamaw River is laden with great anchorages. See details at Waterway Explorer.

This is one of the most rewarding areas to anchor south of the Chesapeake Bay, but bass-boat fishermen may sometimes come full-bore around the bends, so bear that in mind when picking your spot. Always use your anchor light. Also be aware the bugs can be troublesome in this area of the river. Screens are a must all the time.

■ TO MCCLELLANVILLE

When you talk to cruisers about their favorite rivers there seem to be several that are always mentioned for their beauty: the Hudson, Tennessee, St. Johns and Waccamaw seem to be on everyone's list. The ICW leaves the cut and joins the Waccamaw River at Enterprise Landing (Mile 375).

The river is deep to its wooded banks and is easily the most scenic part of the ICW. Moss-draped cypresses line its side streams and turtles sometimes sun themselves along the shore. Wildflowers of all descriptions grow in cypress stumps and the water looks like tea. Your boat's bow will get a brown mustache but that is easy to remove with lemon juice or a commercial cleaner. Ospreys abound and there are some eagles.

Peaceful anchorages are plentiful but be careful: You may be sharing the space with one of the local alligators!

Side Trip: Upriver to Conway–ICW Mile 375

Conway is a beautiful and interesting side trip 15 miles north of the ICW. You'll find some eclectic shops and good cafés in this quaint southern town.

NAVIGATION: At Enterprise Landing (Mile 375) the ICW enters the upriver waters of Waccamaw River. Although the ICW route continues downriver on the Waccamaw, the upriver 15-mile-long stretch to Conway carries 4.5-foot MLW depths. The channel is no longer marked but staying in the middle will get you safe passage.

Stay to the outside of the bends and be prepared to face a speeding bass boat or two as you round the curves. Set your depth sounder alarm and hold down your speed.

The **Church St. (US 501) Bridge** south of Conway has a 65-foot fixed vertical clearance. The bridge to the north (**Main St. Bridge**) has no clearance gauge but charts show a charted 35 feet of vertical clearance. The basin has 10 feet MLW but when entering, make sure to stay center as the sides shoal.

This section of the Waccamaw is highly trafficked by local boats. Tugs with tows frequently announce their presence in the narrow and winding upper Waccamaw River with a "Sécurité" call on VHF Channel 16 or occasionally on VHF Channel 13. Watch for flotsam along the entire length of the upper Waccamaw

Conway, SC

Waccamaw River, SC

BUCKSPORT

		Largest Vessel	VHF	Total Slips	Approach/ Dockside Depth	Floating Docks	Gas/ Diesel	Repairs/ Haulout	Min/Max Amps	Pump-Out Station
1. Bucksport Plantation Marina & RV Resort WiFi MM 36	(843) 397-5556	200	16	50	20.0 / 8.0	F	GD		30 / 50	P

WiFi Wireless Internet Access
Visit www.waterwayguide.com for current rates, fuel prices, website addresses and other up-to-the-minute information.
(Information in the table is provided by the facilities.)

Scan here for more details:

Source: Aqua Map and NOAA data

River. It can vary from harmless bundles of reeds to a whole tree or a water-soaked log (or deadhead) with only the top exposed.

Dockage: Two floating docks in Conway are marked as transient docks with electricity but no water. Contact the Conway City Marina office (located at Waccamaw Outfitters) for staying (843-488-3121). There are pair of longer docks a short walk away available for day docking only. The marina has a gas dock, pump-out service ($5) and two restrooms with showers behind the store/ marina office.

Anchorage: At Conway you can anchor upriver between the high-level US 501 Bypass Bridge and the Main St. Bridge (35-foot fixed vertical clearance) in 5 to 6 feet MLW with good holding in mud. Make sure you stay out of the channel. From here you can dinghy to shore and the town of Conway.

Enterprise Landing (Bucksport)–Mile 375

Enterprise Landing at Mile 375 was once the departure point for huge shipments of yellow pine and cypress. This was the domain of Capt. Henry Buck, who brought over 100 shipwrights from Bucksport, ME, to Bucksport, SC, where they built the 210-foot sailing ship Henrietta, which carried cargo worldwide for over 30 years. Bucksport lies on a sharp bend where the Waccamaw River begins to widen, making navigation easier.

NAVIGATION: There is a large, busy public boat ramp on the southeast side of the ICW at Enterprise Landing north of green daybeacon "27A" (around Mile 375) so watch for small-boat traffic. There is also a series of private docks here extending toward the ICW channel.

Chapter 7: Lockwoods Folly, NC to McClellanville, SC

The 36 miles between Enterprise Landing (Mile 375) and Estherville-Minim Canal (Mile 410.6) is the longest tidal segment of the ICW. Slower boats will carry a fair current all the way to Georgetown (Mile 403) when leaving Enterprise Landing about 1.5 hours after high tide.

Dockage: The friendly Bucksport Plantation Marina & RV Resort, located on the west side at the bend in the river at Mile 377, is easy to access with 700 feet of parallel docking. They can handle vessels to 100 feet (with reservations). The bathhouse is shared with the campers and there is an on-site tiki bar and camp store.

Anchorage: There is a good anchorage in mud at the oxbow just south of Enterprise Landing in Enterprise Creek (Mile 374.8) with at least 6 feet MLW and all-around protection. You can anchor on either side of the charted island that splits Enterprise Creek and the Waccamaw River. The south side (Waccamaw River - Enterprise Landing) has more swing room.

A better anchorage option is at Mile 375.5 in the deeper loop north of Enterprise Landing on the north side of the river across from flashing green daybeacon "29" (Waccamaw River Oxbow G29). The holding is fair in 13 feet MLW near the southern part of the oxbow. This spot will hold 3 or 4 boats and may be full on a weekend.

We recommend the use of an anchor trip line in case you snare a submerged stump or log and make sure your anchor is set. It is a short run up the river to the county launching ramp where you can dinghy your pet ashore.

Pawleys Island Area– ICW Mile 385 to Mile 396

Pawleys Island at Mile 388 on the ICW is known for its beaches, sand dunes and hammocks. The original Pawleys Island Hammocks has been in the business of producing rope hammocks since 1889 and that's still their mainstay, along with fabric hammocks and hammock-inspired swings. At the opposite end of this stretch is Butler Island (near Mile 396), a scenic natural area.

NAVIGATION: South of Mile 385 the Waccamaw River becomes wider and straighter, making navigation easier but it is important for slow boats to note that tidal currents here can have an impressive effect on your progress.

Coming north during a wet spring, boats should respect the ebb tide, which is accelerated by spring rain runoff. Conversely, there may be no advantage on flood tide when offset by this runoff.

The 4-foot tide starts at the inlet of Winyah Bay and moves up the Waccamaw River beyond Enterprise Landing, where the ICW moves off the river and into the canal behind Myrtle Beach. Timing your transit to the 2.5- to 3-hour offset in tides between the mouth of Winyah Bay and the Socastee Swing Bridge can be used to a boater's advantage.

As with other long tidal runs, there is also a significant offset between change of tide and change of current flow measured near the Estherville-Minim Canal Cutoff. Both ebb and flood continue about 90 minutes beyond low and high tide, respectively, and can reach maximum current speeds about 2.5 to 3 hours after published tide times.

For maximum advantage, when heading south an 8-mph trawler should leave Enterprise Landing to arrive at South Ferry Island 1 hour on either side of low tide.

If headed north towards Myrtle Beach, you will definitely want the flood tide behind you. The best time to leave South Ferry Island is between 2 and 4 hours after low tide. When headed south, you can expect to get as much as a 2-mph lift; if heading north on the flood tide, you will get slightly less.

Dockage: Just to the south of Bucksport is Wacca Wache Marina in an idyllic harbor at Wachesaw Landing. There is a current to contend with so it is worth it to look north of the fuel dock to see if there is a spot available on the face dock. Helpful dockhands will help you find transient berthing. Nice bathhouses and a good restaurant, Walter's on the Waterway, are among the amenities. Beautiful views and sunsets are included. Note that this is also a large boat and jet ski sales and rental destination and can be busy.

It is interesting to note that the address at Wachesaw Landing is actually Murrells Inlet, although the inlet is several miles away and not connected by water to the ICW. The village of Murrells Inlet is a popular fishing resort with many seafood restaurants and good shopping opportunities.

Safe Harbor Reserve Harbor at Mile 388 no longer accept transients.

Heritage Plantation Marina to the south at Mile 394 is directly on the ICW at Pawleys Island. This friendly marina is also part of an upscale gated community. They welcome transients to 150 feet.

Waccamaw River, SC

WACHESAW LANDING		Largest Vessel	VHF	Total Slips	Approach/Dockside Depth	Floating Docks	Gas/Diesel	Repairs/Haulout	Min/Max Amps	Pump-Out Station
1. Wacca Wache Marina WiFi MM 383.0	(843) 651-2994	150	16	100	25.0 / 8.0	F	GD	H	30 / 100	P

WiFi Wireless Internet Access
Visit www.waterwayguide.com for current rates, fuel prices, website addresses and other up-to-the-minute information.
(Information in the table is provided by the facilities.)

Scan here for more details: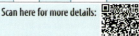

Anchorage: One of the prettiest, most secluded anchorages anywhere is at Prince Creek east of the ICW across from flashing red "44" at Mile 380.4. The north and south entrances both have approximately 15-foot MLW depths but neither end offers protection from ICW wash. The lower end is wide enough to warrant only one anchor but you may need two at the upper end or narrower parts. If you give the points of Prince Creek a wide berth, you can run the length of Longwood Island and rejoin the ICW south of Mulberry Landing at flashing green "53" (at Mile 381.7).

Just south of the northern entrance to Prince Creek (Mile 381.2), you may turn west off the ICW at flashing red "48" marking the entrance to Bull Creek. Give this marker a very wide berth. This has better holding and more swing room than other anchorages on the Waccamaw River. Anchor in at least 15 feet MLW with a mud bottom. Go up past the first bend to avoid the wake of ICW traffic and anchor where depths suit. Hunters frequent this area in season so prepare to awaken early to the sound of shooting in season.

A secluded anchorage is available at Mile 383.5 in Cow House Creek. This is somewhat exposed to the north and south but has excellent holding (7 to 12 feet MLW) and is very scenic. It is a great spot to watch the alligators and other wildlife, which is why we don't recommend swimming here!

Sandhole Creek at Mile 385.5 is a nice stop. Make sure to enter on the side closer to red day beacon "66" as the other side is shoal, as shown on the charts. Trees line this creek, offering decent wind protection.

Another good spot to drop the hook is at Mile 389 in Thoroughfare Creek, which carries 14-foot MLW depths. Turn up Thoroughfare Creek at flashing green daybeacon "73" and anchor in 10 to 13 feet MLW with a sandy bottom. Be aware that Thoroughfare Creek is heavily used by locals on the weekends and it may not be the same tranquil spot it is during the week.

Schooner Creek at Mile 393.1 has depths of at least 8 feet MLW with protection in all directions. Enter in mid-

Source: Aqua Map and NOAA data

Chapter 7 — Lockwoods Folly, NC to McClellanville, SC

Waccamaw River, SC

PAWLEYS ISLAND		Largest Vessel	VHF	Total Slips	Approach/Dockside Depth	Floating Docks	Gas/Diesel	Repairs/Haulout	Min/Max Amps	Pump-Out Station
1. Heritage Plantation Marina WiFi MM 394.0	(843) 237-3650	150	16	40	30.0 / 30.0	F			15 / 50	P

WiFi Wireless Internet Access
Visit www.waterwayguide.com for current rates, fuel prices, website addresses and other up-to-the-minute information.
(Information in the table is provided by the facilities.)

Scan here for more details:

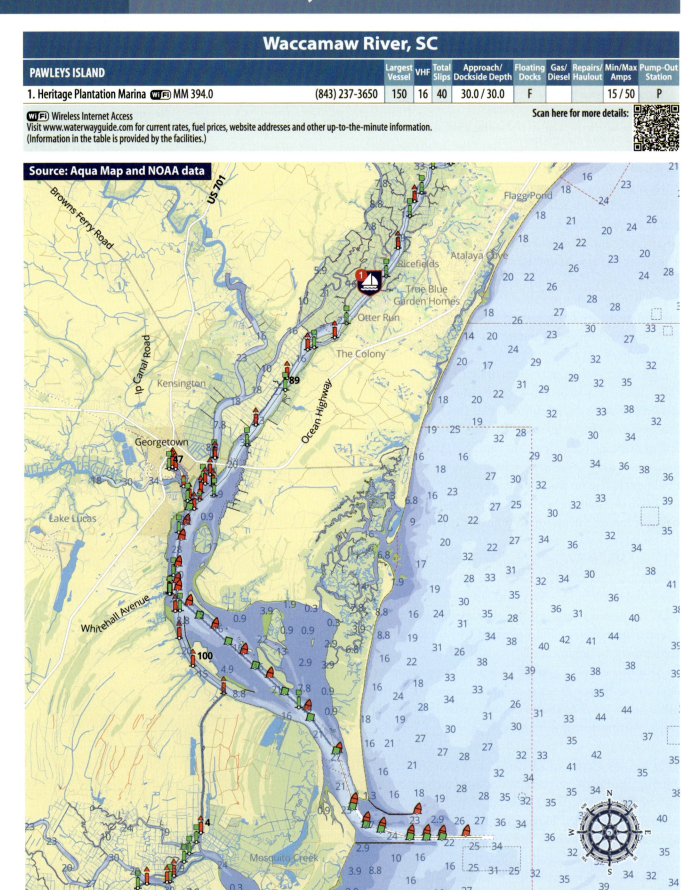

Source: Aqua Map and NOAA data

channel proceeding up to where the creek widens slightly just before the sharp bend to starboard.

At Mile 395 you can anchor in at least 9 feet MLW in Jerico Creek with good holding in mud. (The creek has 8-foot charted MLW depths at the entrance but deepens as you proceed.) Turn into Jericho Creek at Mile 394.9 before flashing green daybeacon "83."

Good protection from northwest winds can be found at Butler Island. Pass green can "1" to port and then proceed into the unnamed cove between Contentment Island and Butler Island. There is good holding in 15- to 30-feet MLW depths but use an anchor trip-line near the island. If you anchor on the channel side north of Butler Island, you will be jostled by wakes from fast-moving boats.

On the north end of Butler Island there is an underwater high voltage cable crossing. It is indicated on the chart as a cable area and there are signs ashore but they are difficult to read. Avoid this area when choosing your anchorage.

Georgetown Harbor–ICW Mile 403

The stretch of the Waccamaw River that includes Georgetown has become increasingly popular. There has been a proliferation of tour boats of many types–even amphibious craft–along the river and around the inlet at Winyah Bay. There are island tours, plantation tours and wilderness tours. Even vessels that create minimum wake should give these tour boats a slow pass.

NAVIGATION: The high-level **Ocean Highway (US 17) Bridge** (65-foot fixed vertical clearance) at Mile 401.1 is a short distance above Georgetown on the Waccamaw River. After passing under the bridge take the time to sort out the markers leading to the Georgetown Harbor entrance channel.

Four bodies of water converge below the big shoal extending south from Waccamaw Point: Waccamaw River, Winyah Bay, Great Pee Dee River and Georgetown's Sampit River. The buoys can be confusing. Near the junction of the four bodies of water is flashing (2+1) red "W." Read your chart carefully and do not cut behind this daybeacon, which sits in 5 feet MLW. Leave it to starboard when southbound.

The channel into Georgetown Harbor is wide and deep with at least 9 foot MLW depths. Once off the ICW and heading toward the harbor the channel for yachts and small commercial craft bears off to starboard just before flashing (2+1) red "S." The Sampit River turns abruptly to port and Factory Basin is straight ahead.

If your intention is to visit Georgetown take the channel to starboard. Exercise some care and do not cut too close to the starboard shore, which is infested with broken and submerged pilings. Once abeam of the first docking area, the harbor is relatively clear of obstacles.

The upper reaches of the small but attractive Sampit River are readily open to exploration. Beyond the twin-span 65-foot vertical clearance Rosen (US Hwy. 17) Bridge, the river is unmarked and uncharted.

The Great Pee Dee River channel is marked with red and green daybeacons leading upriver toward Georgetown Landing Marina, which is just before the Ocean Highway (US 17) Bridge (West) with 20-foot fixed vertical clearance. The Coast Guard station at Georgetown is next to this marina.

Dockage: The 171-slip Georgetown Landing Marina on the Great Pee Dee River is a good option when the Georgetown Harbor is full. Note that it is somewhat exposed, which can make the 680-foot transient face dock uncomfortable in a south wind. There can also be a strong current. They have a fully-stocked marine store plus full amenities.

Hazzard Marine in Georgetown Harbor is a full-service repair and refit facility that can accommodate vessels on 365 linear feet of transient dockage with full amenities. It is a one block walk to East Bay Park with an exercise path, tennis courts, playground and a dog park.

The well-regarded Harborwalk Marina–Georgetown is directly adjacent to Georgetown's business district with slips to 200 feet on their floating docks and all amenities. The marina is just a short walk from restaurants, museums and shopping. The knowledgeable and helpful staff can help you decide what to explore.

The marked entry channel to Belle Isle Yacht Club & Marina is just to the west of the ICW at Mile 406. Amenities in this gated community include two swimming pools, two tennis courts and a private oceanfront clubhouse at Pawleys Island (20 minutes away). The facility is surrounded by almost 640 acres of park-like gardens, woods and lakes, as well as a variety of wildlife.

Anchorage: There are several local boats anchored at Georgetown–South and at Georgetown–North but there is still room for transients to anchor. The bottom is deep mud, however, if you set your anchor well, it can be delightful with 10-foot MLW depths.

Chapter 7: Lockwoods Folly, NC to McClellanville, SC

GOIN' ASHORE
GEORGETOWN, SC

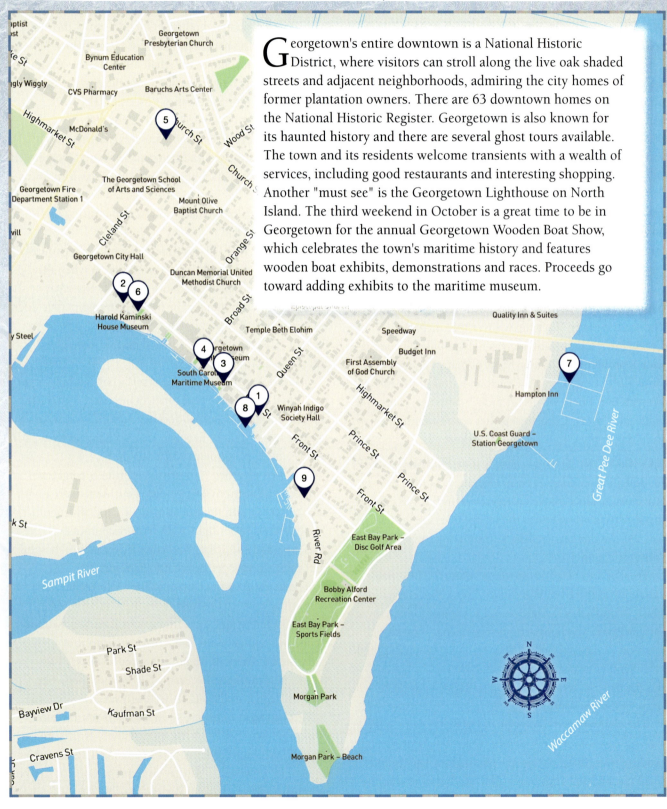

Georgetown's entire downtown is a National Historic District, where visitors can stroll along the live oak shaded streets and adjacent neighborhoods, admiring the city homes of former plantation owners. There are 63 downtown homes on the National Historic Register. Georgetown is also known for its haunted history and there are several ghost tours available. The town and its residents welcome transients with a wealth of services, including good restaurants and interesting shopping. Another "must see" is the Georgetown Lighthouse on North Island. The third weekend in October is a great time to be in Georgetown for the annual Georgetown Wooden Boat Show, which celebrates the town's maritime history and features wooden boat exhibits, demonstrations and races. Proceeds go toward adding exhibits to the maritime museum.

ATTRACTIONS

1. **Georgetown Chamber of Commerce**
   Located at 531 Front St. (843-546-8436). Trolley Tour leaves from 814 Front St. to tour revitalized downtown.

2. **Kaminski House Museum**
   Built in 1769 by a local merchant, now used as a teaching tool for the area's history. Admission by tour only. Museum shop on site at 1003 Front St. Call for hours and fees (843-546-7706).

3. **Rice Museum**
   Includes a 45-minute guided tour about the local rice culture, featuring the 1842 Clock Tower and the Kaminski Hardware Building. The third floor houses the skeleton of America's oldest known vessel, *Brown's Ferry*, an 18th-century all-purpose freighter. Housed in the Old Market built in 1842 at 633 Front St. (843-546-7423).

4. **South Carolina Maritime Museum**
   Small museum at 729 Front St. features photographs, documents, artifacts and interactive exhibits related to SC's maritime history. Exhibits include the prized Fresnel lens of the old North Island lighthouse, a photographic representation of the chronology of the Port of Georgetown and a model of the *Henrietta*, the largest wooden ship ever built in South Carolina. The ship was 201 feet long and the top of her mainmast was 147 feet above the deck. Free admission. Call for hours at 843-520-0111.

SERVICES

5. **Georgetown County Library**
   405 Cleland St. (843-545-3300)

6. **Harborwalk Veterinary Hospital**
   1001 Front St. (843-546-3355)

MARINAS

7. **Georgetown Landing Marina**
   432 Marina Dr. (843-546-1776)

8. **Harborwalk Marina**
   525 Front St. (843-546-4250)

9. **Hazzard Marine**
   200 Meeting St. (843-527-3625)

Chapter 7: Lockwoods Folly, NC to McClellanville, SC

Georgetown Area, SC

GEORGETOWN AREA		Largest Vessel	VHF	Total Slips	Approach/Dockside Depth	Floating Docks	Gas/Diesel	Repairs/Haulout	Min/Max Amps	Pump-Out Station
1. Georgetown Landing Marina WiFi MM 402.0	(843) 546-1776	200	16	171	19.0 / 17.0	F	GD		30 / 100	
2. Hazzard Marine WiFi 0.9 mi. N of MM 403.0	(843) 527-3625	200	16	37	10.0 / 9.0	F	GD	RH	30 / 50	P
3. Harborwalk Marina WiFi 1.1 mi. N of MM 403.0	(843) 546-4250	200	16	50	12.0 / 10.0	F	GD		30 / 100	P
4. Belle Isle Yacht Club & Marina MM 405.9	(843) 546-8491	40	16	80	3.6 / 6.0	F	G		30 / 50	

WiFi Wireless Internet Access
Visit www.waterwayguide.com for current rates, fuel prices, website addresses and other up-to-the-minute information. (Information in the table is provided by the facilities.)

Scan here for more details:

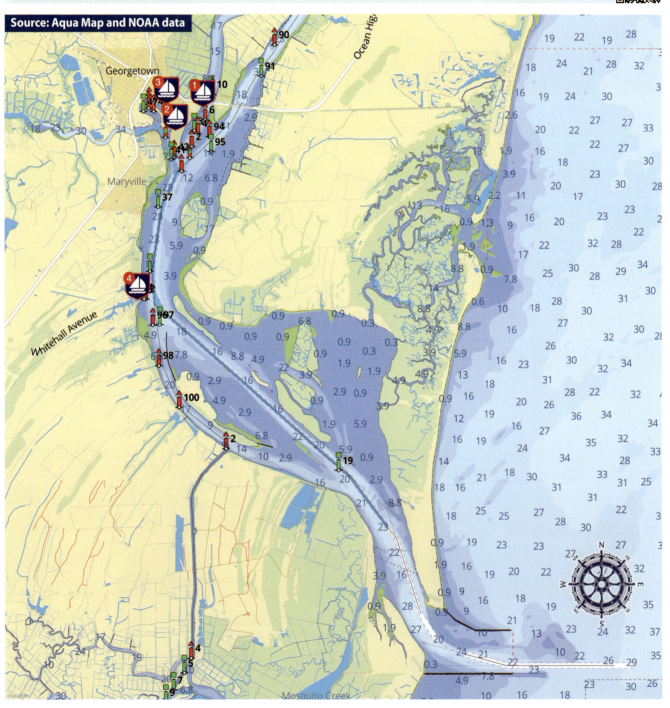

Source: Aqua Map and NOAA data

Shore access is easy thanks to the two public docks along the Harborwalk. The docks will accommodate anything from a dinghy to a 60-footer but both have signs indicating daytime use only, which is strictly enforced. One is at the south end of the walk behind the clock tower at Lafayette Park and the other is in the middle of the walk at Francis Marion Park (next to the South Carolina Maritime Museum).

Over the years, the "main channel" to the abandoned steel mill has shoaled to less than 2 feet MLW. If inbound for the Steelmill Channel anchorage nearest the mill, the safest approach is to take the channel through town. Keep the bifurcated "S" light to port and keep close to the docks all the way around.

Winyah Bay Entrance

For boats making the ocean run along the coast, Winyah Bay is the first large inlet south of the Cape Fear River and Southport, NC. The entrance to Winyah Bay is well marked and deep. It can present a challenge for underpowered vessels due to strong currents. It pays to watch the tide here and enter or leave with the current. Night entry is feasible due to well-marked ranges.

NAVIGATION:

CAUTION: If you bypass Georgetown to go down Winyah Bay, note that the aids to navigation at the junction of Georgetown's harbor channel and the ICW are colored and numbered as from seaward. Three miles below Georgetown at Mile 406 the ICW route leaves the Winyah Bay ship channel, bears off to the south and continues down the well-marked Western Channel to just past Mile 410. The ICW marking system resumes at the Western Channel.

It pays to watch the tide here and enter or leave with the current. Low-powered boats headed north should leave Georgetown 1 hour after slack tide before flood tide at Charleston to carry a fair current up the Waccamaw River. The Western Channel to the inlet, although unmarked beyond the ICW turn into the Estherville-Minim Creek Canal, is true to its charted depths.

If Winyah Bay Entrance is your goal, follow the main shipping channel beginning at Frazier Point. Georgetown Light, 85 feet above the water, shines from a white cylindrical tower on the north side of Winyah

Chapter 7: Lockwoods Folly, NC to McClellanville, SC

Bay entrance. Smoke from one or another of the stacks in Georgetown can often be seen from well offshore. The sea buoy is well out; recreational vessels can safely approach waypoint N 33° 11.570'/W 79° 07.040', which is just east of red buoy "4." From the waypoint, entry is straightforward on a heading of due west, turning to northwest at red buoy "8" and north-northwest after that.

Conditions can be particularly bad at the ends of the jetties when tide opposes wind. Also, much of the south jetty is visible only at low water. Northbound vessels need to be aware of the shoals to the south and west of the channel and not stray west of the waypoint. Anything under 20 feet MLW indicates you are too far west on your approach.

Anchorage: Currents in the Western Channel are strong–up to 3 knots on the ebb. Don't be tempted to anchor here. You can drop the hook behind the unnamed marshy island at the north end of the Estherville-Minim Canal in 10 feet MLW with good holding (Winyah Bay–Western Channel). There is a strong current but if you drag it would be in the current direction, not toward the shore. Expect traffic in the morning in season.

Estherville-Minim Canal to McClellanville– ICW Mile 410 to Mile 439

This area was one of the primary territories of Francis Marion (a.k.a. "The Swamp Fox") during the American Revolution. He earned a reputation for harassing the British troops and then disappearing into the swamp. Several attempts by the British to capture him failed.

If time permits, do visit the small community of McClellanville. There is a museum by the fire tower, a few shops and some restaurants. The town also boasts some amazing live oak trees draped with Spanish moss. Near the marina is the infamous Deerhead live oak, which is over 150 feet tall and 36 feet in circumference and estimated to be over 1,000 years old.

Be prepared for a rather eerie experience as the shrimpers come and go; you can only see the marsh grass and not the creeks they are in so they appear to be moving through the grass.

NAVIGATION: The ICW makes a sharp departure southward from the Western Channel at flashing red "2" into the Estherville-Minim Creek Canal. Split flashing red "2" and the shore for 17-foot MLW depths. Despite recent dredging, careful navigation is required. Just follow the

America's Waterway Guide Since 1947 — **Chapter 7**

McClellanville, SC

MCCLELLANVILLE		Largest Vessel	VHF	Total Slips	Approach/ Dockside Depth	Floating Docks	Gas/ Diesel	Repairs/ Haulout	Min/Max Amps	Pump-Out Station
1. Leland Oil Company WiFi 0.5 mi. N of MM 430.0	(843) 887-3641	75	16	8	10.0 / 10.0	F	GD		30 / 50	

WiFi Wireless Internet Access
Visit www.waterwayguide.com for current rates, fuel prices, website addresses and other up-to-the-minute information. (Information in the table is provided by the facilities.)

Scan here for more details:

Source: Aqua Map and NOAA data

markers but pass them by 50 to 60 feet off; do not hug them.

At Mile 411.5 Estherville-Minim Canal Bridge is open to vessel traffic except when a vehicle needs to cross (infrequent). Watch for flashing yellow lights on sign. In the open position the floating bridge rests against the east bank of the river. Continuing south on the ICW the channel turns to starboard just past Mile 415 and immediately crosses Minim Creek where it enters a long cut with shoal edges.

Be aware of strong currents at Mile 420 when crossing the South Santee River. It shallows to 8.2 feet MLW. Favor the green side of the channel and take care not to be swept into the shoal area at the southern end.

Shrimp boats have been observed using a surprisingly well-marked channel across from Jeremy Creek to access Five Fathom Creek (Mile 430). If you want to explore the Cape Romain area, it is an easy run to the ocean on this route.

Be careful to stay in the middle of the ICW channel as it shallows rapidly along the edges at Mile 431 from red daybeacon "35" to green daybeacon "65" but has shoaled. In general stay 50 feet off all marks, go slow and test the depths side to side. The bottom is soft mud. See details at Waterway Explorer.

With a strong east wind, the water can be a foot higher and with a west wind, a foot lower. A deviation of 30 feet can result in a change in depth of up to 2 feet.

From Mile 436 the ICW follows another land cut (Mathews Cut) for about 10 miles. On the mainland side Francis Marion National Forest Recreation Area offers picnic areas, campsites and a boat ramp but no facilities for transient boaters.

Chapter 7: Lockwoods Folly, NC to McClellanville, SC

Dockage: Jeremy Creek leading to McClellanville has been dredged to 10 feet MLW. Leland Oil Company in McClellanville provides easy in and out dockage with a 30-foot minimum. They also offer a $20 dock and dine option as well. They only have eight total slips so you may be encouraged to raft up, particularly during the annual shrimp festival each spring.

Anchorage: Although it has a good deal of tidal current, Minim Creek is the best anchorage for many miles to come. Either side of the creek has good holding but Minim Creek–West just below Mile 415 offers excellent protection with 8- to 20-foot MLW depths and all-around protection. You will have to dodge the crab pots and bugs will come visit at dusk but your reward will be a beautiful sunset and sunrise.

Minim Creek–East (across the ICW) has 8- to 11-foot MLW depths with excellent holding in mud and protection from all but north and southeast.

The anchorage on the west side of the South Santee River-West at Mile 420.1 (behind Brown Island) has 10- to 12-foot MLW depths, a sand and mud bottom and excellent holding. Crab pots usually line both sides of the river. Santee River–East has excellent holding with plenty of room for multiple boats.

There are many uncharted side creeks but these are of questionable depths for the tidal range. Five Fathom Creek–South at Mile 430 near McClellanville is pristine. Leave the ICW at green daybeacon "25" and proceed south about 0.50 mile on Town Creek. When you get to Five Fathom Creek turn to port (north) and go up Five Fathom 100 yards or more to anchor in 15 feet MLW. This gets you out of the main channel and is a wonderful anchorage. (Do have your bug screens ready.)

An option for shallow-draft vessels is Five Fathom Creek–North. Leave the ICW at green daybeacon "33" and head south into Five Fathom Creek. Hug the north shore to avoid the small charted island where creek meets ICW . Expect 4-foot MLW depths where the creek meets the ICW then 7 to 10 feet farther in.

Proceeding 2 miles south on Five Fathom Creek will afford another anchorage spot at its intersection with Bull River (Five Fathom Creek–Bull River). Depths vary so sound your way in. There are many "lost" crab pots and lines on the bottom in Five Fathom Creek. Use an anchor retrieving line and have a wire cutter ready as some lines are steel.

You can anchor east of the ICW at Mile 435.6 in Awendaw Creek opposite flashing red daybeacon "48." Go around the bend heading east and anchor in the 12-foot MLW spot shown on the charts. The bottom is sand and the anchorage is protected from waves but not wind. There is space for several boats. Your boat position will reverse in a good current.

There is shore access for pets at an oyster pile at the eastern end of the anchorage at any time other than high tide.

At Mile 439 there is good holding in sand in Graham Creek with protection from waves and slightly higher elevation on the west-southwest bank for reasonable wind protection. Approach the creek near red daybeacon "64" and proceed south down Graham Creek. Anchor midstream in 10-foot MLW depths or better up to the bend.

Francis Marion National Forest

Section 3: Charleston, SC to St. Marys, GA

Chapter 8: Charleston Area
Chapter 9: Stono River, SC to Ossabaw Sound, GA
Chapter 10: St. Catherines Sound to St. Marys, GA

MID-ATLANTIC EDITION

Chapter 8: Charleston Area

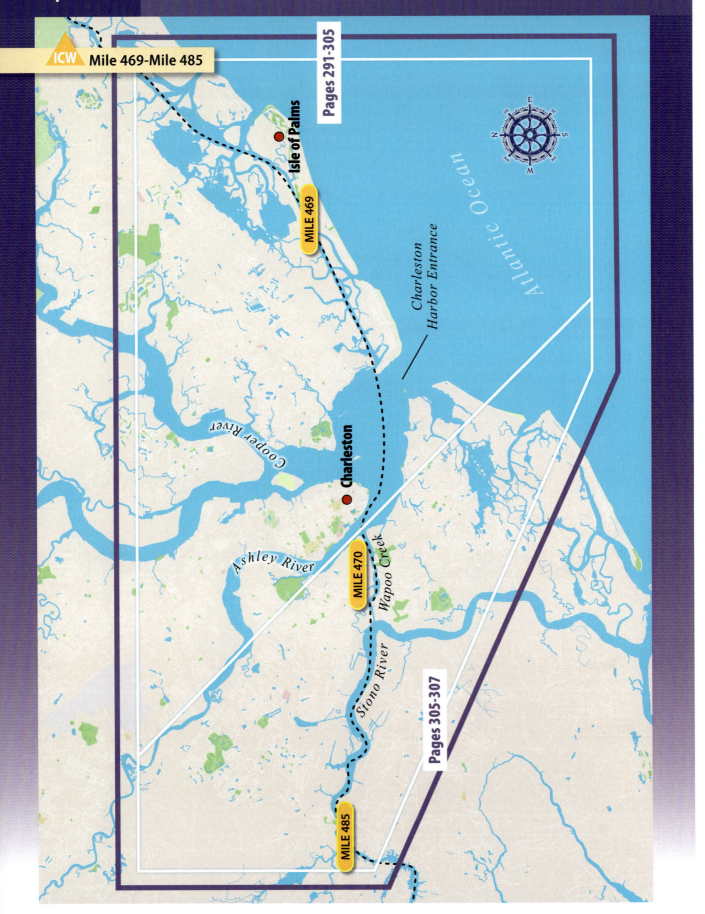

ISLE OF PALMS TO CHARLESTON, SC

The ICW north of Charleston offers wide scenic marsh views to the east and alternating marsh and forest on the west. Here the dredged ICW channel cuts through low marshy islets, across several small rivers and finally through a long land cut before reaching Charleston Harbor.

Numerous marsh streams and small rivers cross the ICW channel from all directions in this area. All of these can affect the tidal current flow and the side currents crossing the ICW channel. Slow boats need to pay more attention than fast ones but both should be aware that shoal areas can and do creep out near these crossings.

The charted depths are somewhat optimistic along this stretch so be more precise in keeping to the channel at low tide. Our advice is that keeping in the center of the channel is always the best. If the water gets too "skinny," then start slightly moving from side to side in an attempt to find good water.

NOTE: From Mile 415 to about Mile 450 the National Ocean Service does not provide tidal current information. Generally the flood tidal current runs north. From Mile 450 to Mile 460 the current reversals cancel each other out.

NO WAKE ZONE

This is not a No-Wake Zone but caution should be exercised through this congested area. Before this transit, tie down as if you were going to sea. It will be choppy and confused from the many boat and ship wakes, and you will likely get rocked on your way through by an inconsiderate boater or by residual wakes that you can't avoid.

To Isle of Palms—ICW Mile 469

At Mile 456.7 you pass through a land cut between Isle of Palms on the ocean side and Goat Island on the mainland side. The two islands are quite different. The Isle of Palms is well developed with golf courses, resort hotels and restaurants, while Goat Island was formerly inhabited by only a few hearty souls who commuted to their jobs by boat. Now, although the island remains relatively isolated, more and more weekend getaway cottages have appeared on Goat Island.

Chapter 8 — Charleston Area

Charleston Area, SC

		Largest Vessel	VHF	Total Slips	Approach/ Dockside Depth	Floating Docks	Gas/ Diesel	Repairs/ Haulout	Min/Max Amps	Pump-Out Station
ISLE OF PALMS										
1. Isle of Palms Marina WiFi MM 456.5	(843) 886-0209	220	16	55	12.0 / 12.0	F	GD		30 / 100	
SULLIVANS ISLAND										
2. Toler's Cove Marina WiFi MM 462.3	(843) 881-0325	110	16	162	8.0 / 8.0	F	GD		30 / 50	P

WiFi Wireless Internet Access
Visit www.waterwayguide.com for current rates, fuel prices, website addresses and other up-to-the-minute information. (Information in the table is provided by the facilities.)

Scan here for more details:

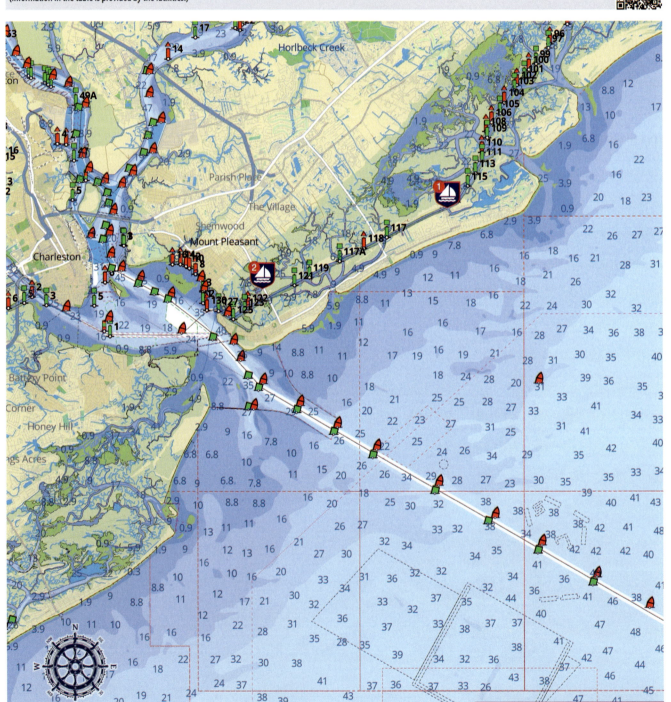

Source: Aqua Map and NOAA data

NAVIGATION: The ICW channel between Mile 439 and Mile 456 is among the straightest stretches along the entire ICW. Be sure to mind the markers. At Mile 444 watch your wake and exercise caution when passing Andersonville.

> **CAUTION:** There are areas of known shoaling and care should be taken when navigating these waters as depths change constantly. Make sure that you are using current information including local knowledge when transiting the area. Be prepared for additional ATONs and changed buoy locations to assist safe passage. See details at Waterway Explorer (www.waterwayguide.com).

At Mile 458.9 **Isle of Palms Connector Bridge** (65-foot fixed vertical clearance) crosses over the ICW to the Isle of Palms community. Based on stains on the tide boards there may only be 63 to 64 feet of clearance at high tide.

Ben Sawyer Memorial (SC 703) Bridge (31-foot vertical clearance) at Mile 462.2 opens on signal, except from 7:00 a.m. to 9:00 a.m. and 4:00 p.m. to 6:00 p.m. year-round Monday through Friday (except federal holidays) when the draw need not open. The bridge need only open on the hour from 9:00 a.m. to 7:00 p.m. on weekends and holidays. Use the western span.

Dockage: At Mile 456 near flashing red "116" is the municipal Isle of Palms Marina with transient slips on floating docks (30-foot minimum) and an easy access fuel dock. There are few provisions or amenities on the island but the well-stocked IOP Marina Outpost has everything you might need including a deli. This is a pleasant stop close to but out of the hustle and bustle of Charleston.

Just through the Ben Sawyer Memorial (SC 703) Bridge (31-foot vertical clearance) at Mile 462.5 on the mainland side is Toler's Cove Marina. This is part of a private condominium development and transients are welcome if space is available. They mostly cater to sportfishing boats. It is best to call ahead on VHF Channel 16 for slip availability.

Anchorage: You will find several lovely spots to drop the hook along the way to Isle of Palms. Price Creek at Mile 448 is a local favorite for weekend and holiday outings. Feel your way in near flashing red daybeacon "86" below the islet blocking the entrance (submerged at high tide) then proceed a short distance to a suitable spot in 7- to 8-foot MLW depths with a sandy bottom. To get it at low tide, go past the little island (if southbound) and approach from the south. (Four or less feet has been observed when approaching from the north at MLW.) Proceeding seaward, this winding creek widens into Price Inlet.

The farther up the channel you go from Price Creek, the deeper the water gets. You can anchor in about 10 feet MLW north of Bull Island at Capers and Bull. This offers good holding in the strong tidal current. It is an easy dinghy ride down Price Creek to the beaches on Bull Island (just past some uncharted mooring balls). Good beachcoming on the beach, but be aware of restrictions on dog access beyond the beach.

A tight little anchorage with enough room for four or five boats is available at ICW R90. Enter south of red daybeacon "90" and anchor in about 10 feet. Expect some tidal current. The mud bottom has good holding. No shore access.

Because of its proximity to Capers Island Heritage Preserve, Whiteside Creek at Mile 451.1 is a favorite overnight anchorage for skippers who are ready for an ocean swim or a hike along the beach. The creek can get extremely congested during the spring and fall. It is too deep for anchoring at the bend and shoals unpredictably upriver of the bend. Depths are generally shallower before the bend than shown on the charts.

Take the dinghy to the park dock at the western tip of Capers Island to visit Capers Island. A trail from the dock leads to an ocean beach after passing an impounded lake, which is home to numerous alligators. (No swimming!)

Capers Creek to the south is a wide-open anchorage for settled weather. Plenty of swing room and scenic views of the South Carolina lowlands and ocean inlet.

Dewees Creek (Mile 455) is wide and deep but the current flows swiftly and a commuter boat from the mainland serves the island residents. Bear these things in mind when dropping the hook.

On the opposite side of the ICW at Mile 455 is an anchorage between Dewey Island and Big Hill Marsh with deep (12 to 17 feet) water and protection from wind and wakes from all but the east. To reach the anchorage, you must navigate around the east side of the Big Hill Marsh by turning to port at green daybeacon "109" and following the deep-water channel around.

Chapter 8: Charleston Area

Dewees Island is privately owned so cruising boaters should not venture above the high-water line while walking on the beach.

At green daybeacon "109" you can enter Dewees Creek for several good anchorages. If you turn into the Unnamed Creek to the north off Dewees Creek, proceed 0.25 mile in and around the bend to the west for a nice anchoring spot in 20 to 30 feet MLW with good holding in mud.

There is lots of room for several boats with plenty of swing room where Long Creek meets Dewees Creek, just a short way off the ICW. Or you can proceed up Dewees Creek to Hamlin Sound (north of Eagle Island) and anchor in 15 to 25 feet MLW with a mud bottom.

At Mile 456, north of Isle of Palms Marina, Seven Reaches Creek offers 7-foot MLW depths with good holding in mud. To the south Hamlin Creek at Mile 458 offers a protected anchorage off the south side of the ICW near green daybeacon "117." Anchor before the 28-foot fixed vertical clearance Isle of Palms Connector Bridge in 7 to 10 feet MLW with good holding in sand. It is exposed to the northeast.

Inlet Creek at Mile 461 is a regular stop for cruisers heading north or south. It offers fair holding in at least 11 feet MLW and is exposed to the south. This is the last good anchorage before the large and busy Charleston Harbor, which you will want to enter in daylight if possible.

Charleston Harbor Entrance

It is difficult to enter the Charleston Harbor Entrance from the ocean and not take note of Fort Sumter on the northeastern tip of James Island. On April 12, 1861, Capt. Abner Doubleday fired the first Union shot of the Civil War defending Fort Sumter in Charleston Harbor. The fort fell to the Confederates 34 hours later and remained in their hands for the duration of the war. The Union placed it under siege for over 550 days and conducted 5 major bombardments, which effectively flattened the fort, but they never retook it.

Private boats should not attempt to tie up at the fort. According to the National Park Service, all ladders, cleats and lines are for the use of ferries and tour boats. You can either beach or anchor your boat on the western side of the fort.

NAVIGATION: During daylight the entrance markers and the forest of harbor buoys leading to Charleston Harbor are easy to sort out. If yours is a first-time passage, however, it is best to run rough compass courses without shortcutting any of the buoys. When leaving Charleston to head north, slow boats should leave a couple of hours before low-water slack tide for an easier run.

This is a heavily used ship channel and there is a great deal of commercial traffic here day and night. Smaller vessels are advised to stay to the edge of the channel until reaching the inlet jetties. When entering Charleston Harbor from the ICW–anytime after low-water slack tide

Arthur Ravenel Jr. Bridge

to about 2 hours before high-water slack for Charleston Harbor—the current will give slower boats a healthy boost up to the marinas on the Ashley River.

The sea buoy for Charleston Harbor Entrance, SC is 10 nm farther out than necessary for recreational craft. A waypoint at N 32° 42.860'/W 79° 47.550' between green buoy "15" and red buoy "16" saves considerable time, although southbound vessels need to be aware of the shoaling to the north and guide their course appropriately, coming in on a southwesterly heading.

Charleston (Cooper River)

On the east side of Charleston's peninsula the Cooper River enters from the north to meet the harbor at Shutes Folly Island, where historic Castle Pinckney stands. On the east side of the Cooper River at Hog Island is Patriots Point, where the aircraft carrier USS Yorktown, the submarine USS Clamagore and the destroyer USS Laffey DD-736 are permanently berthed. Check the museum schedule for available tours.

NAVIGATION: Those northbound for the Cooper River should continue using the Mount Pleasant Range. Follow this out of the channel, watching for flashing green "127" about 0.25 mile to the east marking the entrance to the northbound ICW.

Once in the harbor you can follow the well-marked channel to reach the facilities on the Cooper River at Patriots Point or Town Creek as well as those on the Ashley River. Be alert for commercial traffic when crossing the harbor and give these big vessels plenty of room.

Above Drum Island the Wando River feeds into the Cooper from the northeast. **Arthur Ravenel Jr. Bridge** over the Cooper River at Drum Island has a vertical clearance of 186 feet, and where the same highway crosses Town Creek on the west side of Drum Island the vertical bridge clearance is 65 feet.

Dockage/Moorings: Charleston Harbor Resort & Marina located on the eastern shore of the Cooper River at Patriots Point is a destination in itself but it is also a convenient place to dock for easy access to the adjoining Patriots Point Naval & Maritime Museum. Turn in at quick flashing red buoy "34" for the a slip on the floating docks or to take on gas and diesel at the 24-hour fuel dock near the entrance.

Amenities include a water taxi to Charleston and a free shuttle to a well-stocked gourmet grocery store nearby in Mount Pleasant. The on-site restaurant, The Charleston Harbor Fish House (843-284-7070), has a rooftop bar with a great view. This marina hosts the famous Charleston Race Week sailing regatta, which draws hundreds of boats.

Zimmerman Marine–Charleston is located at Charleston Harbor Resort & Marina and at Cooper River Boatyard offering boat repair services from rigging to mechanical and electrical. They have other yards in Deltaville, VA; Mobjack Bay, VA; Herrington Harbour, MD; Solomons, MD; Oriental, NC; and Holden Beach, NC.

Chapter 8: Charleston Area

Goin' Ashore
CHARLESTON, SC

ATTRACTIONS

1. Dock Street Theater
Reopened in 1937, first building in the U.S. designed specifically for theatrical performances at 135 Church St. (843-577-7183). Stunning interior.

2. Historic Charleston City Market
Four-block city market at 188 Market St. that is over 200 years old. Actually originated as market for food items, not slaves, as commonly thought. (The Slave Market is a few blocks away.) Best spot to see sweet grass basket weavers at work. Open daily at 9:30 a.m.

3. Old Exchange Building
Historic building that once housed a Revolutionary prison, known as the Provost Dungeon. Costumed docents lead tours daily every half hour between 9:30 a.m. and 5:00 p.m. (122 E. Bay St., 843-727-2165).

Charleston is a favorite destination for cruisers, offering superb protection in bad weather, and with its numerous marinas and boatyards, an excellent stopover point to attend to you and your boat's needs. Charleston's "Museum Mile" boasts six museums, five nationally historic homes, four scenic parks, numerous historic churches, the Old Market and City Hall. Frequent tours by the Historic Charleston Foundation and the Preservation Society offer a peek inside the old homes and their glorious gardens. Do take a carriage ride or one of the ghost tours if you have time. Even if it does not make your hair stand on end, you will have a new insight into the city's past. (Example: The cobblestone streets in the historic district were built from the rocks used as ship's ballast.) The 8-acre waterfront park runs 0.5 mile alongside the Cooper River at Vedue Range. Take a photo in front of the famous Pineapple fountain or snag a swing on the pavilion-covered pier.

The easiest way to move around downtown is aboard the city's free visitor-oriented system of shuttle buses: three routes that circulate around the most popularly-visited downtown areas, connecting with the central Visitors Center on Meeting Street.

America's Waterway Guide Since 1947 — Chapter 8

4. Rainbow Row
Series of 13 colorful historic houses located north of Tradd St. and south of Elliott St. on East Bay Street. Houses date back to the 18th century and are a popular photo spot.

5. South Carolina Aquarium
Liberty Square houses the aquarium where residents include an American alligator, playful river otters, bright green moray eels and horseshoe crabs. Numerous exhibits (both aquatic and wildlife), plus a 6,000-gallon stingray tank and two-story, 385,000-gallon Great Ocean tank, which houses a 220-pound loggerhead sea turtle and several tiger sharks. The best times to visit are weekdays before 11:00 a.m. or after 2:00 p.m. Call ahead for admission fees (843-577-3474).

6. The Charleston Museum
"America's first museum" founded in 1773 by the Charleston Library Society with changing exhibits and artifacts about South Carolina and also Confederate history. Located at 360 Meeting St. Call for hours and ticket prices (843-722-2996).

SERVICES

7. Access Urgent
233 Calhoun St. (843-853-8870)

8. All Creatures Veterinary Clinic
224 Calhoun St. (843-579-0030)

9. Charleston County Public Library
68 Calhoun St. (843-805-6930)

10. Charleston Post Office
83 Broad St. (843-727-1129)

11. Charleston Visitor Information
211 Meeting St. (843-573-4849)

MARINAS

12. Charleston Maritime Center
10 Wharfside St. (842-853-3625)

13. Charleston Yacht Club
17 Lockwood Dr. (843-722-4968)

14. Safe Harbor Bristol
145 Lockwood Dr. (843-723-6600)

15. Safe Harbor Charleston City
17 Lockwood Dr. (843 723 5098)

16. The Harborage at Ashley Marina
33 Lockwood Dr. (843-722-1996)

Chapter 8: Charleston Area

On the western shore of the Cooper River south of Drum Island is the municipal Charleston Maritime Center with some transient dockage adjacent to Liberty Square. The current at this marina can be challenging but it is convenient to most of the sightseeing attractions.

A free trolley that serves the downtown area stops in front of the South Carolina Aquarium (843) 577-3474), which is next to the marina. Charleston is a working commercial harbor and you can expect some surge from the passing ships when docked at the Maritime Center.

Seabreeze Marina is located just south of Arthur Ravenel Jr. Bridge. They offer deep-water transient slips on floating docks with first-class amenities, a ship store and on-site restaurant. A friendly and helpful staff round out the offerings.

Farther north at the entrance to Shipyard Creek is Cooper River Marina with 200 slips (35 reserved for transients) on floating docks. They can accommodate vessels to 42 feet (long term) or 150 feet (transients) and have a well-stocked store, climate-controlled showers and laundry facilities and pump-out service. This is a county-owned and -operated facility.

There is more dockage available on the Wando River. The South Dock of One River Landing at Daniel Island is available for day dockage (for a fee) and drop off and pick up for boaters using their moorings, which can accommodate vessels to 60 feet. (North Dock is reserved for Daniel Island Yacht Club members.).

Safe Harbor City Boatyard is located about 20 miles up the Wando River from Drum Island. The full-service boatyard offers complete yacht repair and service. While this facility may be a bit off the beaten path, they offer mobile service at any Charleston area marina, even emergency after-hours service.

Wando River Marina is located at the base of the Route 41 Bridge. Marina facilities include free pump-out service, restrooms, electricity and water at each slip, a ship store and a fuel dock with both non-ethanol gas and diesel. Call ahead for slip availability. Visitors arriving by boat to dine at the Wando River Grill can tie up for free at the designated docks.

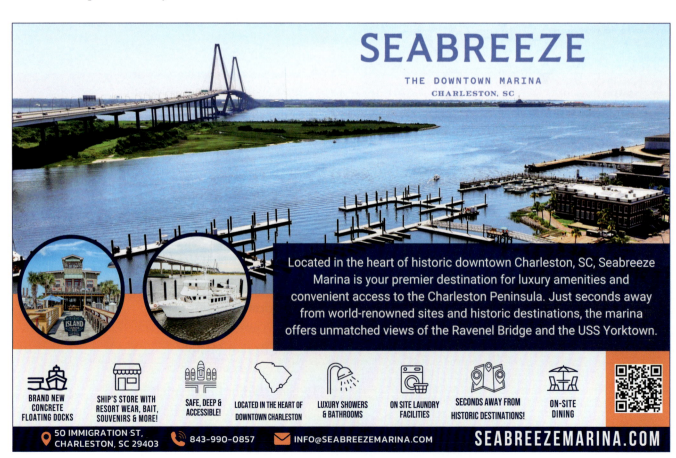

Charleston (Ashley River)

The Ashley River forms the west fork of the two rivers that flow along the peninsula of downtown Charleston. Note that the ICW leaves the Ashley River and enters Wappoo Creek across from and just past the Coast Guard Station in Charleston.

The shoreline along the city side of the Ashley River, marked by the row of colonial mansions, is known as The Battery. The name dates back to Charleston's earliest days when gun emplacements protected the city here.

On the west side of the Ashley River above the James Island Expressway Bridge (56-foot vertical clearance) and the US 17 (Ashley River) Bridges (18- and 14-foot closed vertical clearances, respectively) is Charles Towne Landing at Oldtown Creek. This is the site of the first permanent English settlement in South Carolina. This historic site recreates the colonists' daily lives and includes a full-scale replica of the trading vessel *Adventure* and is worth a visit if you are spending a few days in Charleston.

Additionally several beautiful plantation homes and gardens–including Middleton Place, Drayton Hall, Magnolia Plantation and Gardens and the Audubon Swamp Gardens–are upriver on the Ashley. Both Charles Towne Landing and the plantations are best visited by car. The historic downtown lends itself to the horse-drawn carriage tours but many of the areas attractions are outlying and will require transportation.

NAVIGATION: When heading into the Ashley River from the Charleston Harbor Inlet there are two clearly charted ranges–the South Channel and the Ashley River Approach–to assist you. This area is frequently dredged. Note that the current can be extremely swift, from 1 to 2 knots, with tides ranging 4 to 6 feet in this area.

There is plenty of water depth in the area, which is frequently dredged. Follow your chart's ICW magenta line to the Ashley River and allow for the stiff current (about 3 knots at flood). If the current is flowing contrary to a wind of any strength, prepare yourself for a rough crossing. Check the currents and winds carefully before entering any of the marinas and call for assistance if needed. Space during the traveling seasons can be at a premium, so reservations are highly recommended.

The marinas are located south of the James Island Expressway Bridge (56-foot vertical clearance) on the Ashley River. If you wish to cruise past the marinas and cannot clear the twin US 17 (Ashley River) Bridges with their respective 18- and 14-foot controlling vertical clearances, you will need to call ahead to request the bridges openings. The bridges open on signal daily, except from 4:00 p.m. to 9:00 a.m., when the draws will only open if at least 12-hour notice is given. The bridges are 0.10 of a mile apart. Beyond the turning basin the Ashley River's minimal depths prohibit all but small shallow-draft boats from proceeding. The Coast Guard base is to starboard about 1 mile up the river beyond The Battery.

Dockage: A convenient walkway under the James Island Expressway Bridge connects Safe Harbor Charleston City and The Harborage at Ashley Marina.

Safe Harbor Charleston City at Mile 469.5 welcomes transients of all sizes. They offer 3,000 feet of floating docks with high-speed diesel fueling stations, deep-draft slips with no height limitations and an impressive floating bathhouse with laundry. The Mega Dock (the main floating dock of the marina) is almost 0.25 mile long and, as the name suggests, you can expect to find megayachts tied there.

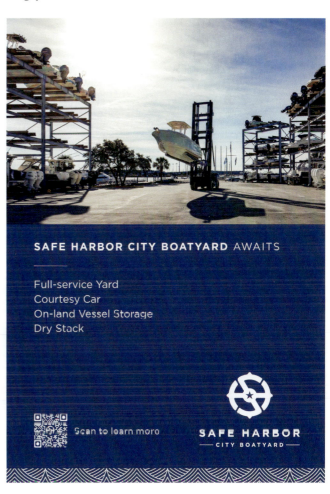

SAFE HARBOR CITY BOATYARD AWAITS

Full-service Yard
Courtesy Car
On-land Vessel Storage
Dry Stack

Scan to learn more

SAFE HARBOR
CITY BOATYARD

Chapter 8 — Charleston Area

Charleston, SC

		Largest Vessel	VHF	Total Slips	Approach/ Dockside Depth	Floating Docks	Gas/ Diesel	Repairs/ Haulout	Min/Max Amps	Pump-Out Station
PATRIOTS POINT										
1. Charleston Harbor Resort & Marina WiFi	(843) 284-7062	200	16	459	12.0 / 12.0	F	GD		30 / 100	P
2. Zimmerman Marine - Charleston	(843) 849-2458				/			R		
COOPER RIVER										
3. Charleston Maritime Center 0.5 mi N of MM 467.0	(843) 853-3625	180	16	30	30.0 / 20.0	F	GD		30 / 50	P
4. Seabreeze Marina WiFi	(843) 853-0932	420			/	F	GD		30 / 100	
5. Cooper River Marina WiFi	(843) 406-6966	150	16	200	45.0 / 25.0	F			30 / 100	P
WANDO RIVER										
6. One River Landing	(843) 471-1881		16		/	F				
7. Safe Harbor City Boatyard WiFi	(843) 884-3000	125	16		15.0 / 10.0	F		RH	15 / 50	
8. Wando River Marina	(843) 214-5990				/	F	GD		30 / 100	P

WiFi Wireless Internet Access
Visit www.waterwayguide.com for current rates, fuel prices, website addresses and other up-to-the-minute information. (Information in the table is provided by the facilities.)

Scan here for more details:

Source: Aqua Map and NOAA data

CHARLESTON'S ONLY RESORT STYLE MARINA
New 50% Larger Transient Docks (Easy Catamaran Docking)
Complimentary Shuttle to Downtown Charleston
Three Phase 480v Power • On Spot Wifi
24-Hour High Speed Fueling • Onsite Restaurants and Bars
Marina Boutique Shopping • 24-Hour Gym • Top Rated Spa

Mount Pleasant • South Carolina • 29464
843.284.7062 • Marina@CharlestonHarborResort.com
www.CharlestonHarborMarina.com

SAFE HARBOR CHARLESTON CITY AWAITS

Mega Dock
Winter Storage
Waterside Restaurant
Bathhouses, Showers & Laundry
Ship's Store

Scan to learn more

Charleston, SC Area

ASHLEY RIVER		Largest Vessel	VHF	Total Slips	Approach/ Dockside Depth	Floating Docks	Gas/ Diesel	Repairs/ Haulout	Min/Max Amps	Pump-Out Station
1. Safe Harbor Charleston City WiFi MM 469.5	(843) 723-5098	400	16	415	20.0 / 25.0	F	D		30 / 200+	P
2. Charleston Yacht Club-PRIVATE MM 469.5	(843) 722-4968				/ 8.0	F				
3. Ripley Light Yacht Club - PRIVATE WiFi MM 469.0	(843) 766-0908	100	16	83	5.0 / 6.0	F			30 / 50	P
4. The Harborage at Ashley Marina WiFi MM 469.5	(843) 722-1996	120	16	230	15.0 / 22.0	F	GD		30 / 100	P
5. Safe Harbor Bristol	(843) 723-6600	70	16	145	15.0 / 22.0	F			30 / 50	P
6. Dolphin Cove Marina WiFi	(843) 744-2562	65		95	35.0 / 8.0	F		RH	30	
7. Loggerhead Marina - RiversEdge Marina WiFi	(843) 554-8901	35	16	30	5.0 / 5.0	F	G	H	30 / 50	P

WiFi Wireless Internet Access
Visit www.waterwayguide.com for current rates, fuel prices, website addresses and other up-to-the-minute information.
(Information in the table is provided by the facilities.)

Scan here for more details:

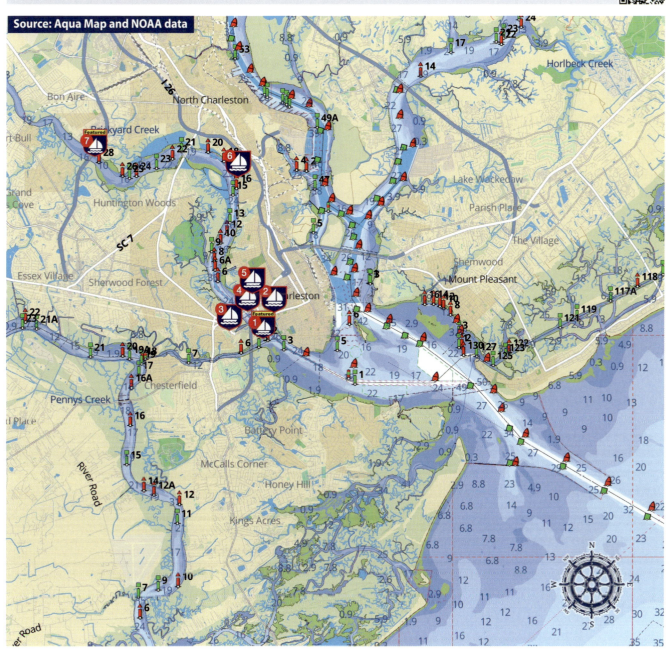

Source: Aqua Map and NOAA data

Chapter 8: Charleston Area

They also have a full-service convenience store, an internet café and a marina courtesy van that makes hourly trips to the downtown area and daily trips to West Marine. The marina is also home to the popular Variety Store Restaurant.

Charleston Yacht Club is private and does not accommodate transients but members of reciprocal clubs are welcome in their clubhouse.

The full-service The Harborage at Ashley Marina is north of the 56-foot fixed vertical clearance James Island Expressway Bridge and is capable of accommodating vessels up to 120 feet. The marina offers full amenities as well as a courtesy shuttle to take transients to and from many of downtown Charleston's most popular attractions. There are plenty of restaurants within walking distance and groceries within 2 miles. The marina is adjacent to two hotels, making it a great location for hosting visitors or crew changes.

The private Ripley Light Yacht Club across the river welcomes transients to 100 feet with all amenities.

Safe Harbor Bristol is located past the Ashley River Bridges and adjacent to the Citadel. It was designed and engineered for easy docking with 128 wet slips for boats less than 70 feet (14-foot maximum vessel height/air draft) and 63 drive-on docks for boats from 12 to 20 feet. They have a mobile pump-out station, cable and water at every slip and welcome transients.

Farther north on the Ashley River across from Duck Island is Dolphin Cove Marina, which offers some boat repairs and may have transient space (to 65 feet). This marina primarily caters to liveaboards and is one of the most economical in the area (but with less amenities). They also have a fully enclosed drystack.

Past the **SC 7 (Cosgrove Avenue) Bridge** (with a fixed vertical clearance of 50 feet) and before the **General William C. Westmoreland (I-526) Bridge** (with a fixed vertical clearance of 35 feet), you will find Loggerhead Marina–RiversEdge Marina. They offer indoor and outdoor dry storage for boats up to 35 feet and wet slips for boats up to 45 feet.

Anchorage: Boats swing differently in the current here so pay careful attention to how the boats around you are swinging (some on a single anchor, some on two; some on rode, some on chain) when you set the hook. There are three popular anchorages directly on the Ashley River.

There is a large designated anchorage at Charleston across from Safe Harbor Charleston City (near the Wappoo Creek entrance). It has good

Folly Beach

America's Waterway Guide Since 1947 — **Chapter 8**

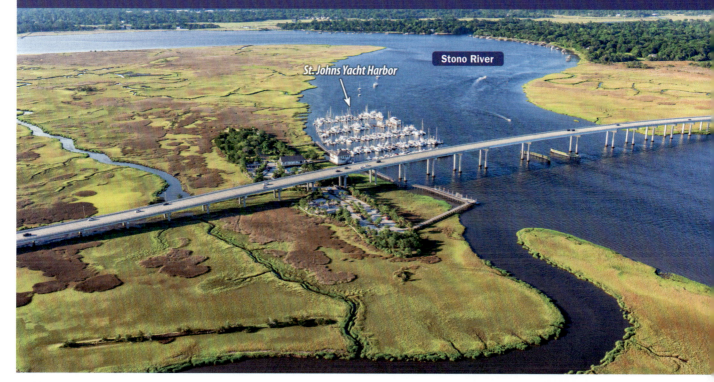

holding in mud (12 to 20 feet MLW) and is exposed to the northwest and southeast. You should also be aware that there are a lot of snags on the bottom.

Another anchorage is in the small area adjacent to the Coast Guard Station and before Safe Harbor Charleston City in 10 feet MLW with a mud bottom (Charleston–Coast Guard). It is exposed to the northwest through the southeast. There are a handful of long-term-anchored boats here taking up most of the useful space. Watch for crab pots.

Just north of the channel entrance to Ripley Light Yacht Club between the high rise and the bascule bridges is an anchorage (Charleston–North of Bridge) with 12 to 25 feet MLW with good holding in mud. Note that it is exposed to the northwest and southeast, is also home to a lot of local boats and is usually congested.

Anchored vessels may dock a dinghy at Safe Harbor Charleston City for a fee, at the nearby boat ramp or possibly at the private Charleston Yacht Club. With the strong current, do factor the current into your trip ashore.

> NOTE: Charleston Waterkeeper offers a mobile pump-out service in the lower Charleston Harbor. They will come to your slip or location at anchorage and pump out your holding tank for free. Pump-out service is performed once per week on weekends.

All requests for pump-out service must be received by 5:00 p.m. on Friday. Boat owners do not need to be present. Call 843-608-9287 to schedule.

■ WAPPOO CREEK & STONO RIVER

Wappoo Creek–ICW Mile 469 to Mile 472

From Mile 472 at Elliott Cut to Mile 535 at Beaufort, SC, the South Carolina Lowcountry scenery is lush and beautiful with water birds and marsh grass creating picture-postcard sights everywhere you look. Beaufort is a beautiful stopping place and the next community of any size past Charleston.

NAVIGATION: Continuing down the ICW on the Ashley River opposite the Safe Harbor Charleston City you enter Wappoo Creek, which then leads into narrow Elliott Cut. Running Elliott Cut at mid-tide is a memorable experience with as much as a 5-mph current. Immediately inside Wappoo Creek's northern entrance at Mile 469.7 is **James Island Expressway Bridge** (official fixed vertical clearance of 67 feet but there are no tide boards), followed by the **Wappoo Creek (SC171) Bridge** (33-foot closed vertical clearance) at Mile 470.7.

> **NO WAKE ZONE**
> This entire section through Elliott Cut is a patrolled No-Wake Zone. Almost every pier has a sign saying, "Slow, you are responsible for your wake." Go as slowly as you can, even though it may be difficult when the strong current is dead against you.

Chapter 8: Charleston Area

Stono River Area, SC

STONO RIVER		Largest Vessel	VHF	Total Slips	Approach/ Dockside Depth	Floating Docks	Gas/ Diesel	Repairs/ Haulout	Min/Max Amps	Pump-Out Station
1. St. Johns Yacht Harbor WiFi 1.0 mi. S of MM 472.5	(843) 557-1027	120	16	224	25.0 / 8.0	F	GD		30 / 50	P

WiFi Wireless Internet Access
Visit www.waterwayguide.com for current rates, fuel prices, website addresses and other up-to-the-minute information. (Information in the table is provided by the facilities.)

Scan here for more details:

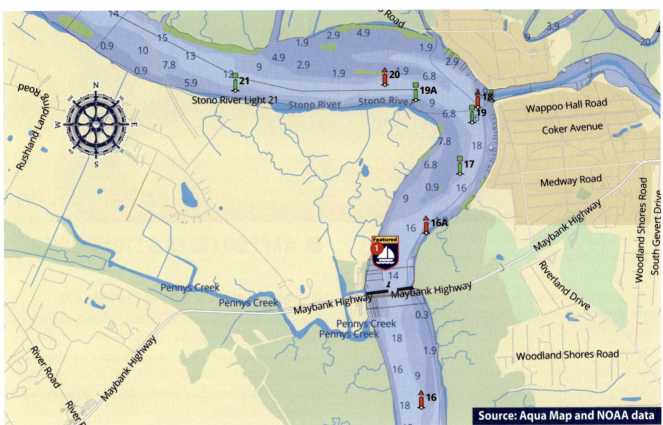

Source: Aqua Map and NOAA data

The draw will open on signal except from 6:00 a.m. to 9:29 a.m. and 3:31 p.m. to 7:00 p.m., Monday through Friday (except federal holidays), when the draw need not open. Between 9:30 a.m. and 3:30 p.m., Monday through Friday (except federal holidays), the draw need only open on the hour or the half-hour. A boat ramp is on the north side of the Wappoo Creek (SC171) Bridge.

⚠ *CAUTION:* Ebb tide begins at the entrance to Elliott Cut about 1 hour before it turns at the Charleston Entrance to Wappoo Creek. Flood tide occurs at about the same time on both ends of this 4-mile section of the ICW. Transiting the cut at the turn of the tide is strongly recommended for auxiliary-powered vessels and other craft with limited maneuverability.

Anchorage: The most protected overnight anchorage in the Charleston area at Mile 471 is just beyond the Wappoo Creek (SC171) Bridge (33-foot closed vertical clearance, restricted schedule) in 11 to 15 feet MLW behind the unnamed small island. The Wappoo Creek anchorage is narrow and not very large (with space for only a few small to mid-size cruising boats) and subject to strong current. It is a long dinghy ride to downtown but it is a quiet, secluded spot for those who get there early. It is in a residential area with private docks on the south side.

Stono River–ICW Mile 472 to Mile 485

From Elliott Cut, which leads from Charleston, SC, south to the Stono River, the ICW route continues along the Stono River for about 12 miles to the Beaufort, SC, area.

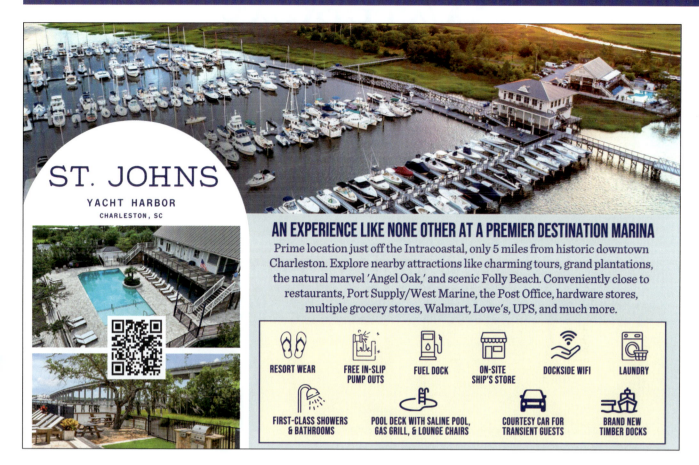

NAVIGATION: From Elliott Cut the ICW enters the Stono River just beyond Mile 472. Shoaling has been reported at the confluence of Elliott Cut and the Stono River near red daybeacon "18." The ICW channel up the Stono River begins with green daybeacon "19A." Make sure you are using the most up-to-date charts.

Downstream on the Stono River leads to the Folly and Kiawah Rivers, frequented by local recreational boaters. Folly and Kiawah Islands are home to several ocean resorts with beaches, shopping, restaurants and several golf courses.

A short distance beyond the **John F. Limehouse Hwy. Bridge** at Mile 479.3 (65-foot fixed vertical clearance), the Stono River narrows and the ICW channel follows a winding path past Johns Island. When heading north through the starboard side of the channel at the Limehouse Bridge be aware of small-boat traffic coming from the busy boat ramp north of the bridge.

Just beyond Mile 480 red daybeacon "40" marks a shoal off the creek to the north. This marker appears to be in the wrong place but it is not. Give it space as a shoal extends slightly farther into the channel from the creek. The current usually reverses at this point.

Dockage: A short side trip south from Elliott Cut down the Stono River brings you to St. Johns Yacht Harbor. They offer "yacht club amenities in a family-friendly environment." The facility has laundry facilities, a ship and sundries store, free in-slip pump-out services and a saltwater pool. They also offer a courtesy car. They are located just before the 65-foot fixed vertical clearance **Paul J. Gelegotis (Stono) Bridge**.

Anchorage: The best anchorage in this area is across the Stono from red daybeacon "16A" (at Mile 472.6 behind Buzzards Roost Point) in the 10-foot MLW charted area near St. Johns Yacht Harbor. There can be considerable current in the river; however, there is excellent holding here in clay.

Anchorage is also available at numerous locations up the Stono River including at Stono River R20 and Stono River R22 with good holding in mud in at least 7 feet MLW. There is minimum wake and wind protection.

At Mile 479.8 at Johns Island there is another somewhat protected spot on the north shore for more shoal-draft vessels with 4 to 6 feet MLW.

 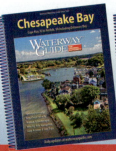   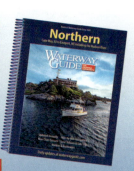

Plan with the experts

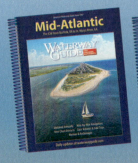    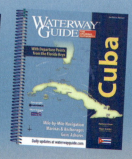

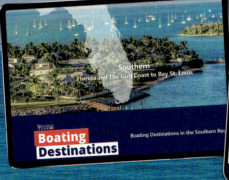 

Scan to subscribe now at www.waterwayguide.com

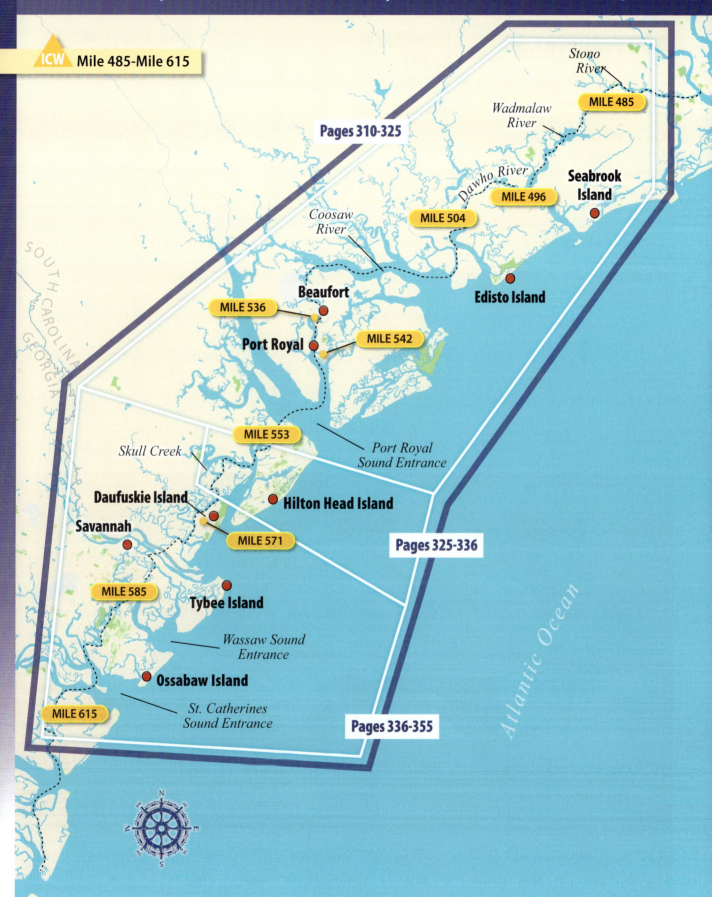

Chapter 9: Stono River, SC to Ossabaw Sound, GA

■ TO BEAUFORT, SC

CAUTION: Be aware when navigating these waters that depths change constantly. Make sure that you are using current information including local knowledge when transiting the area. Be prepared for additional ATONs and changed buoy locations to assist safe passage. Check www.waterwayguide.com for up-to-date information.

This stretch of lush and lovely South Carolina marsh is teeming with wildlife. The delicate colors of the grasses and the unique scents wafting off the marsh make cruising through these parts a unique experience. You are now in open country.

Wadmalaw to North Edisto River– ICW Mile 485 to Mile 496.6

NAVIGATION: The ICW leaves the Stono River at Mile 485 and enters a short land cut leading to the headwaters of the Wadmalaw River. The tides meet at Church Flats at Mile 485 (so named for the practice of going to church on the flood tide and coming home on the ebb.)

Near red daybeacon "78A" there are (charted) submerged rocks on both sides of the channel.

Several aids to navigation mark the shoals on the Wadmalaw River between flashing red daybeacon "82" and green daybeacon "101." Run the long stretch between quick-flashing red "92" and flashing red daybeacon "94" on a compass course and swing wide to the outside on curves.

If transiting at mid to high tide, check your position with respect to the current along the way to avoid the mud flats to the north and remain in deep water. Swing wide toward flashing red daybeacon "94" and avoid the shortcut to green daybeacon "95."

Red daybeacons "98" and "100" indicate a shoal area that is visible at low tide but can be difficult to spot at high tide. These two markers need to be given a wide berth.

Anchorage: There is an anchorage at Mile 487 at Church Creek - New Cut Landing, which is especially popular during the spring and fall. The holding here is good in about 15 feet MLW and the anchorage is fairly well protected.

To reach this anchorage turn off the ICW at green "77" and proceed east into Church Creek for less

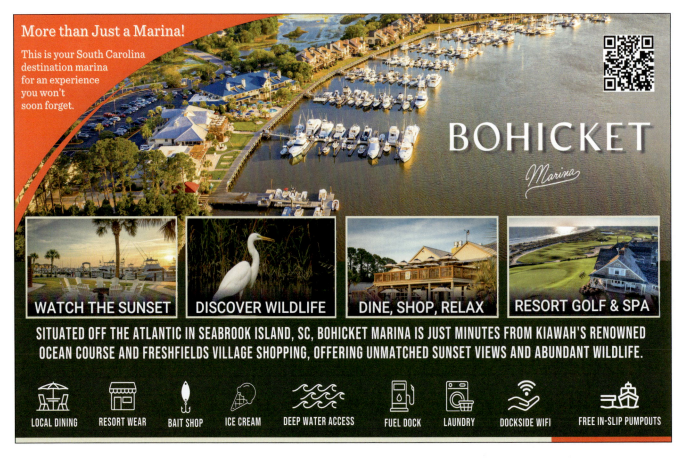

Edisto River, SC

BOHICKET CREEK		Largest Vessel	VHF	Total Slips	Approach/Dockside Depth	Floating Docks	Gas/Diesel	Repairs/Haulout	Min/Max Amps	Pump-Out Station
1. Bohicket Marina & Market ⓦⒾⒻⒾ 7.2 mi S of MM 497.0	(843) 768-1280	150	16	200	14.0 / 14.0	F	GD	R	30 / 100	P

ⓦⒾⒻⒾ Wireless Internet Access
Visit www.waterwayguide.com for current rates, fuel prices, website addresses and other up-to-the-minute information.
(Information in the table is provided by the facilities.)

Scan here for more details:

Source: Aqua Map and NOAA data

than 0.50 mile, taking care to stay an equal distance from the shores.

Low tide will reveal the hidden oyster beds on the north side and shallow mud flats on the south side. However, dropping anchor in the middle of the creek will give you plenty of swing room and depth to handle the tide change. This anchorage offers a lovely panoramic view of the sunset and sunrise.

A bit farther off the ICW you can find excellent shelter, all-around protection and no wakes at the Church Creek (alternate) anchorage. Many cruisers prefer this to the "original" location due to its remote location.

At Mile 495 leave the ICW and turn to starboard to enter Toogoodoo Creek. Use great caution when entering as there are large areas of mud banks on both sides at its entrance. You will find good holding in 10 to 15 foot MLW depths in packed mud. You will also be subjected to some wakes from passing fisherman but that settles down in the early evening.

If you continue on the ICW for another 0.50 mile, you will find Tom Point Creek with 8 to 20 feet MLW and good holding. Note that there is an uncharted shoal on the outside bend with less than 3 feet MLW. Stay in the center of the channel.

North Edisto River Inlet

NAVIGATION: At flashing red "108" (Mile 496.6) the Wadmalaw splits into the North Edisto and Dawho Rivers. The North Edisto heads off to the southeast and the Atlantic Ocean. About 6 miles south on the North Edisto River you can head up swift-running Bohicket Creek to the village of Rockville and Seabrook Island, both popular weekend destinations with Charleston-based boaters.

Chapter 9: Stono River, SC to Ossabaw Sound, GA

Edisto River

A side trip with access to the ocean can be made by continuing down the North Edisto River, which is well charted and easy to run, except for shoaling along both riverbanks.

North Edisto River Inlet is a straight shot with a charted shoal section (5 foot MLW) near flashing red "6." Up-to-date tide information is available online from NOAA Tides and Currents (www.tidesandcurrents.noaa.gov).

Dockage: The friendly Bohicket Marina & Market lies just north of the village of Rockville on Bohicket Creek off the North Edisto River. Maximum ebb and flood currents call for both advance planning and dockside help to assure a smooth docking and departure. The marina has 25 transient slips to 150 feet. Shopping and restaurants are available at the on-site Market.

Anchorage: Steamboat Creek to the south on the west side of the North Edisto River has an excellent anchorage in 17-plus feet MLW with a clay bottom but you might encounter some snags on the bottom. There is limited protection from the wind until you are well into the creek. There is also a boat ramp in this creek that has a small dock where you can land dinghies to exercise your pets.

There is a secluded anchorage and room for many boats farther west on Steamboat Creek Marker 497 (2 miles west off the ICW). The holding is good and there's a public dock nearby, should you need to get off the boat. You can explore the farther areas of the creek by dinghy.

Ocella Creek, just to the north of the North Edisto River Inlet is an anchorage option. Enter at high tide and stay in the middle of the river. This is quiet with plenty of space for when the boat swings.

Dawho River to South Edisto River– ICW Mile 496 to Mile 504

NAVIGATION: The ICW continues on the Dawho River at Mile 496.6, veering off to the southwest for 1 mile before turning to the northwest at flashing red "112."

The ICW enters a land cut at Mile 501 just before the McKinley Washington Jr. (SR 174) Bridge with a published fixed vertical clearance of 65 feet but closer to 63- to 64-foot according to the tide boards.

A portion of the old swing bridge is used as a fishing pier. Beyond the bridge the ICW passes through narrow North Creek and Watts Cut before emptying into the broad and swiftly flowing South Edisto River.

McKinley Washington Jr. (SR 174) Bridge is 35 miles from Lady's Island (Woods Memorial) Bridge (Mile 536.1), a little more than a 4-hour cruise in an 8-mph boat. No matter when you leave, you will face tides running in both directions for two-thirds of the trip. Taking advantage of a flood tide on the Coosaw heading south and the ebb tide heading north will make a difference of as much as 2 mph over the 12-mile-long river run.

Timing navigation for this stretch is more about water depth than speed. Watts Cut, Fenwick Cut and the Ashepoo Coosaw Cutoff all contain areas of serious shoaling that are better transited well away from low water.

The key tide station for this section is Brickyard Point (Mile 529.7) located on the ICW near the upstream end of the Coosaw River. Going in either direction, the best time is related to the turn of the tide to ebb at this station.

If southbound, aim to leave the McKinley Washington Jr. (SR 174) Bridge about 2 hours after Brickyard Point low tide, which is actually more into the rising tide locally. As the local tide range is 7 feet, this will provide at least a 2-foot margin above MLW at the start of the route and more depth for Fenwick Cut and Ashepoo Coosaw Cutoff. You will arrive at Brickyard Point close to high tide.

Heading north, enter the Coosaw River at high tide. This means a falling tide for your trip, but you should make it through Watts Cut about 2 hours before MLW. In a deep-draft vessel, consider leaving 1 hour earlier for extra water in that last section.

Anchorage: At Mile 501 you will notice a pair of sloughs coming into the Dawho River from the north. These little slivers of water actually connect behind marshland to form an oxbow. Do not be tempted to try to anchor in either slough as shoals become bare at low tide.

Just south of the McKinley Washington Jr. (SR 174) Bridge, it is possible to anchor in the approach to Fishing Creek. Be aware that the charted depth at its entrance is 4 feet MLW and that there are charted submerged piles outside the ICW channel here. If you decide to enter Fishing Creek, favor the red daybeacon "132" side when entering.

You will find at least 9-foot MLW depths inside and good holding, despite some current. There is some highway noise and it can be buggy; nevertheless, this is one of the best anchorages along this section of the ICW. As in all anchorages be sure to use your anchor light at night.

South Edisto River to Ashepoo Coosaw Cutoff– ICW Mile 504 to Mile 518

The main destination along the South Edisto River is Edisto Island overlooking the Atlantic Ocean. Edisto Island is home of the community of Edisto Beach and offers deep-sea fishing opportunities. The town has beautiful, well-preserved Colonial homes, a popular residential resort with golf course, an oceanfront state park and good stores and boutiques. You will find a slower pace that harks back to the 1950s; there are no high-rise motels or typical carnival type boardwalk activities here.

NAVIGATION: The South Edisto River is easy to follow. Remember, however, that you are in a strong tidal zone so do not cut too close to the markers or the bends in the channels. Starting at Mile 505 Range "A" and Range "C" mark the ICW course along the South Edisto River between Watts Cut and Fenwick Cut. These ranges keep boaters off the river's wide shoals and projecting points. Note that green daybeacon "161B," shown on some older charts, no longer exists.

At Mile 511 the ICW heads southwest along the Ashepoo River, while the South Edisto River meanders in a southeasterly direction toward the Atlantic Ocean. Despite dredging in 2023, shoals continually build at both the north and south entrances to Fenwick Cut and along its entire length. Exercise caution.

The ICW route continues to the southwest leading from the South Edisto River through Fenwick Cut and into a short section of the Ashepoo River. Once you have transited the Ashepoo River, the ICW enters the first part of the Ashepoo Coosaw Cutoff.

The Ashepoo Coosaw Cutoff soon jags in a northwesterly direction entering Rock Creek at Mile 515 before it continues as a narrow land cut toward the wide Coosaw River. This is another area of known shoaling so care should be taken when navigating these waters as depths change constantly. Depths to 4.5 feet MLW have been observed at the south end of the Ashepoo Coosaw Cutoff. Make sure that you are using current information including local knowledge when transiting the area. Be prepared for additional ATONs and changed buoy locations to assist safe passage.

> NOTE: Given the proximity of Port Royal Sound, Charleston and North Edisto Inlets, St. Helena Inlet should be skipped.

Dockage: The Marina at Edisto Beach is located behind Edisto Island on Big Bay Creek, 4.5 miles south from the ICW. This sportfishing-oriented facility has transient slips to 55 feet and a well-stocked ship store. Nature and fishing charters leave from here daily. Be sure to call the marina well in advance for slip availability.

There is a free dock at South Fenwick State Park on the Ashepee River with dockside depths of 4.5 feet MLW at a small 12-foot floating dock. This is a great place to walk the dog.

Chapter 9: Stono River, SC to Ossabaw Sound, GA

Edisto River, SC

EDISTO ISLAND		Largest Vessel	VHF	Total Slips	Approach/Dockside Depth	Floating Docks	Gas/Diesel	Repairs/Haulout	Min/Max Amps	Pump-Out Station
1. The Marina at Edisto Beach WiFi 4.5 mi. S of MM 511.0	(843) 631-5055	55	16	72	17.0 / 12.0	F	GD		30 / 50	
MOSQUITO CREEK										
2. B & B Seafood House Marina 1.8 mi. N of MM 513.5	(843) 844-2322	50	68	2	10.0 / 10.0	F	GD			

WiFi Wireless Internet Access
Visit www.waterwayguide.com for current rates, fuel prices, website addresses and other up-to-the-minute information. (Information in the table is provided by the facilities.)

Scan here for more details:

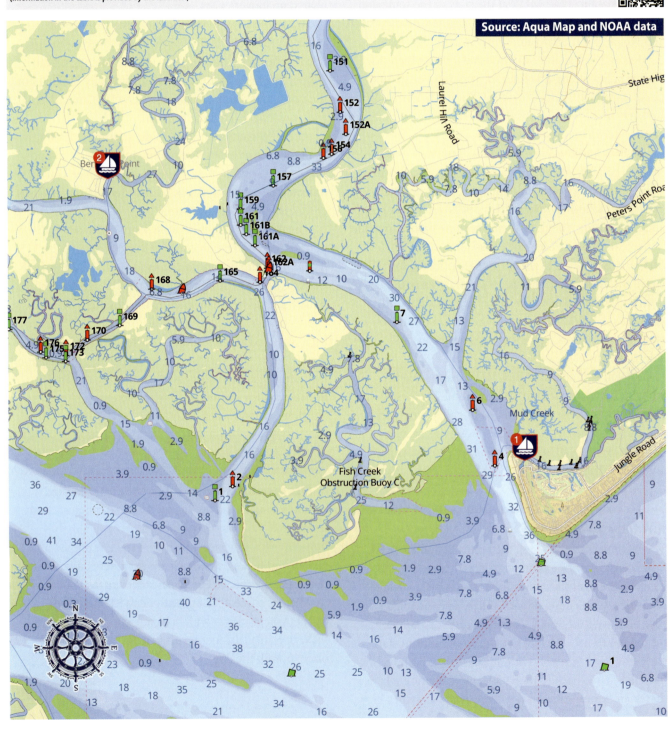

Source: Aqua Map and NOAA data

B & B Seafood House Marina is 1.8 miles off the Ashepoo River on Mosquito Creek. This is a seafood wholesale/retail outlet that can accommodate two vessels up to 50 feet but it is not a traditional marina. Do not try to tie up at docks until after 4:00 p.m. Call ahead to book. Power is available (30 amp) but you'll need a long cord to reach it. There are restrooms but no showers. The oysters and shrimp are fresh off the boat (in season) and very economical.

Anchorage: The South Edisto River provides a good fair-weather anchorage at Mile 504.2 (Sampson Island North). When southbound out of Watts Cut, bear off to starboard into the South Edisto River. Anchor in the middle about 1 mile from Watts Cut where the chart shows 10- and 11-foot MLW depths with a soft, mud bottom.

This is a wide open, relatively quiet spot with good holding, although we advise against anchoring here in any strong wind. There is considerable current (1 to 2 knots) just as with all the rivers in this area of the ICW, and conditions can become uncomfortable with opposing wind and current. Continuing around the next bend is an option. This is a good spot to wait if you are going north and want to time the tide through Dawho River.

Just past the lower end of the South Edisto River at Alligator Creek (Mile 509.4) and opposite green daybeacon "157" is an anchorage for settled weather with good protection from the northwest. Be cautious when entering this creek as it has been reported to have a shallow entrance. Once you are in sound your way toward the shore to avoid trap markers and anchor in 8 to 11 feet MLW, well off the channel. The current may reach 1.5 knots so vessels may lay to the current rather than the wind.

Continuing south toward the inlet, there is an anchorage up St. Pierre Creek south of the ICW (east side) with good holding in mud and 9- to 17-foot MLW depths.

Closer to the inlet at the South Edisto River Entrance you can anchor in soft mud in 10 feet MLW. Better holding can be found at Big Bay Creek where there is good protection and better depths than shown on the charts. This is a peaceful anchorage but it is open to wakes (usually small boats).

Most anchorages along the Ashepoo River are open but pleasant with good holding. There are two anchoring possibilities at Fenwick Island. The one north of the cut on the ICW is at Mile 511.6 and is fairly open with a strong current, making anchoring challenging. At Fenwick Island South, there is an anchorage with at least 11 feet MLW. This is a quiet and tranquil anchorage near South Fenwick State Park, which provides public access to a park but no other amenities.

Just past B & B Seafood House Marina is an anchorage on Mosquito Creek with at least 7 feet MLW with a mud bottom. This is 1.8 miles off the Ashepoo River.

The headwaters of Rock Creek at Mile 516 provide a narrow but well-protected anchorage with minimum 8-foot MLW depths to the second bend. Use the depth sounder to avoid the shoals on the inside of the turns in the creek; however, deep-drafted boats swinging on the current have also frequently grounded in this anchorage.

Coosaw River–ICW Mile 518 to Mile 529

While the Coosaw River is wide and unobstructed, it is always best to keep to the channel and run at least a rough compass course to help you spot the markers, which are spaced fairly far apart.

NAVIGATION: The Combahee River at Mile 518.5 and the Bull River at Mile 521.5 flow off the north side of the Coosaw River. Approximately 2 miles west of flashing red "186" Parrot Creek leads south off the Coosaw River to a marina at Morgan River and anchorages at Bass Creek and Lucy Point Creek. Depths exceed 10-foot MLW depths for the entire approach to Parrot Creek from the ICW.

Dockage: Dataw Island Marina is 3 miles south of ICW Mile 521 by following Parrot Creek and rounding the south side of Coosaw Island on the Morgan River. The marina is located inside a gated golf and tennis community also featuring pickleball, croquet and bocce (available to transient boaters with advance coordination). This marina offers transient dockage, dock and dine and dry stack storage. Morgan River Grill is a local favorite for fun fare in a casual atmosphere for lunch and dinner.

Anchorage: Many spots in this area are suitable for anchoring. At Mile 521 you can anchor inside Wimbee Creek off the Bull River just north of the ICW. Watch for the shoal below Summerhouse Point and leave the island to starboard. Holding is good here in 11 to 18 feet MLW, although the bottom also is hard with shells in some areas.

South of the ICW (Mile 521.5) there are anchoring possibilities east and south of Coosaw Island accessed by Parrot Creek. You can drop the hook in 7 to 12 feet MLW

Between Charleston & Savannah:

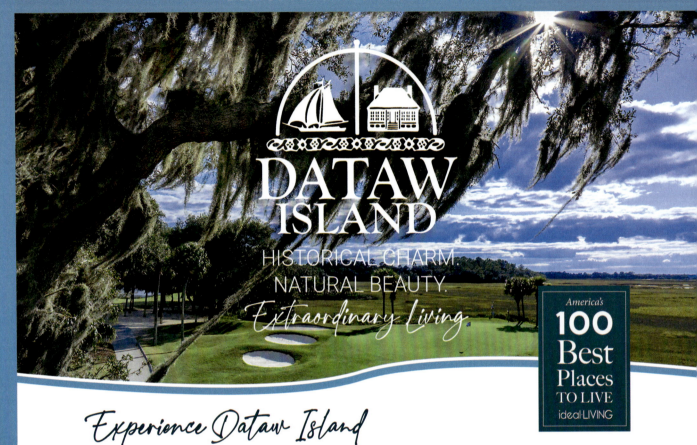

Experience Dataw Island

Dataw Island is an active lifestyle community located six miles east of the historic Lowcountry town of Beaufort, SC. Conveniently situated between Hilton Head, Savannah, and Charleston and close to the beach, shopping, history, and fine & performing arts, Dataw is away from it all but close to everything.

DATAW ISLAND MARINA: The Dataw Island Marina offers wet slips, dry stack, haul-outs, diesel & ethanol-free gasoline, complimentary laundry, showers, and wi-fi, a restaurant, bicycles, and more.

THINGS TO SEE & DO: With advance request, explore Dataw Island's two top-rated golf courses, Har-tru tennis courts, croquet lawns, bocce, pickleball, indoor & outdoor pools, fishing, crabbing, walking & cycling trails, dog runs ... Experience Dataw and experience extraordinary living!

Visit Dataw Island to see for yourself why the community has been called the *hidden gem* of South Carolina!

"Club of the Year"
(South Carolina Golf Association)

"Top Community to Follow Your Passion: Charitable Giving"
(Golf Home Network)

"Outstanding Tennis Facility"
(USTA)

"Best Kayaking"
"Best Island Community"
"Best Health & Wellness"
(ideal-LIVING)

"Best Community"
"Best Golf Course"
"Best Tennis Pro"
(Beaufort Gazette)

Learn more: | dataw.com | (843) 838-3838

Coosaw River, SC

DATAW ISLAND

		Largest Vessel	VHF	Total Slips	Approach/ Dockside Depth	Floating Docks	Gas/ Diesel	Repairs/ Haulout	Min/Max Amps	Pump-Out Station
1. Dataw Island Marina 3.0 mi. S of MM 521.0	(843) 838-8410	50	16	22	15.0/8.0	F	GD	RH	30/50	

WiFi Wireless Internet Access
Visit www.waterwayguide.com for current rates, fuel prices, website addresses and other up-to-the-minute information. (Information in the table is provided by the facilities.)

Scan here for more details:

Source: Aqua Map and NOAA data

off the grass banks of Morgan's Island. This is also known as Monkey Island, but you're unlikely to see the monkeys that love here, as it's quite far from the trees. It is very quiet and secluded. Bass Creek has 13 to 16 feet MLW and wave (but not wind) protection.

Back on the ICW at Mile 523, you can anchor north of Coosaw Island. Turn to the south at green daybeacon "189" and snug up to the shore for 15 feet MLW. Good protection from the south but open to wind from other directions.

Continuing south you can anchor past Dataw Island Marina at Lucy Point Creek. Even though there is an entrance to Lucy Point Creek directly off the ICW, the fixed 14-foot vertical clearance SC 802 Bridge at the mouth necessitates the "back door" approach.

Beaufort, SC–Mile 536

The ICW leaves the Coosaw River at Mile 529, where you will find a well-marked entrance range heading into Brickyard Creek. Military aircraft might buzz you as you travel south on Brickyard Creek. While the noise from the military aircraft in this area can disrupt a peaceful anchoring experience, the U.S. Marine Corps Air Station here–along with the nearby famous Parris Island Recruit Depot–is a major contributor to the local economy.

The City of Beaufort appears to starboard at about the point where Brickyard Creek becomes the Beaufort River. Beaufort's attractions include an entire downtown on the National Register of Historic Places, a multi-purpose park along the waterfront, an amphitheater, markets and a bandstand, all within sight of bed and breakfasts, attractive shops and meticulously restored historic houses.

Chapter 9: Stono River, SC to Ossabaw Sound, GA

Goin' Ashore: BEAUFORT, SC

ATTRACTIONS

1. Beaufort History Museum
Housed in Arsenal at 713 Craven St. (843-525-8500) built in 1798 to house the Beaufort Volunteer Artillery after fighting with the Continental Army during Revolutionary War. Features exhibits on the town's history and culture. Also serves as Visitor Center. Open daily except Sunday from 10:00 a.m. to 4:00 p.m.

2. Harry C. Chambers Waterfront Park
Riverfront park with landscaped green space, a playground and a performance stage. If all that is just too exhausting, grab one of the 20 bench swings and enjoy the water views, people watch or read a good book.

3. John Mark Verdier House Museum
Federal-style mansion built around 1790 and headquarters for Union forces during Civil War. Also hosted Marquis de Lafayette upon his return to the country after the Revolutionary War. Currently houses a museum and is open for tours at 801 Bay St. (843-379-6335).

4. Lowcountry Produce Market and Café
Cafe and market offering small plates and quick bites plus "grab & go" provisions at 302 Carteret St. (843-322-1900). Just a few blocks from the marina and popular with the boating crowd.

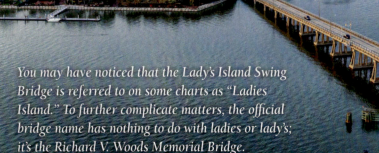

You may have noticed that the Lady's Island Swing Bridge is referred to on some charts as "Ladies Island." To further complicate matters, the official bridge name has nothing to do with ladies or lady's; it's the Richard V. Woods Memorial Bridge.

America's Waterway Guide Since 1947

Chapter 9

Beaufort is a thriving city surrounded by rivers and waterways with cool breezes and lush gardens under oak tree canopies that enchant the most seasoned visitor. Beaufort is known for its rich history and architecture, and several companies offer guided walking (or carriage) tours of the city's historic district. It is a gracious place that is true to its Southern heritage. Lazy summer days are spent casting a shrimp net, walking on an undeveloped island beach or kayaking down the river. People come for the Lowcountry seafood, tomato stands and the Sea Islands. If history is your thing and you have transportation, visit the Beaufort National Cemetery, established in 1863, and the final resting place for many Civil War soldiers and veterans from other wars. While out and about, the Pat Conroy Literary Center is dedicated to the life and work of beloved Southern author Pat Conroy, who called Beaufort home for many years.

5. Santa Elena History Center
Learn the story of Santa Elena, which was settled in 1566 on Parris Island. Encompasses religion, geopolitics, cultural clashes, war and struggles to survive. The area even served as the Spanish capital of Florida from 1569 to 1587.

6. St. Helena's Episcopal Church
Erected in 1724, the church at 507 Newcastle St. (843-522-1712) is surrounded by a wall built of bricks arriving from England as ship ballast. Church has ancient graveyard where tombstones served as operating tables for wounded soldiers during the Civil War.

SERVICES

7. Beaufort Post Office
501 Charles St. (843-525-9085)

8. Downtown Beaufort Library
311 Scott St. (843-255-6456)

9. Veterinary Wellness Care
1609 North St. (843-524-5972)

MARINAS

10. Safe Harbor Beaufort
1006 Bay St. (843-524-4422)

MID-ATLANTIC EDITION

Chapter 9 — Stono River, SC to Ossabaw Sound, GA

Beaufort Area, SC

		Largest Vessel	VHF	Total Slips	Approach/ Dockside Depth	Floating Docks	Gas/ Diesel	Repairs/ Haulout	Min/Max Amps	Pump-Out Station
LADYS ISLAND										
1. Lady's Island Marina WiFi 0.8 mi. S of MM 536.0	(843) 522-0430	210	16	75	7.0 / 14.0	F			30 / 50	P
BEAUFORT										
2. Safe Harbor Beaufort WiFi MM 536.2	(843) 524-4422	150	16	100	20.0 / 15.0	F	GD		30 / 50	P
PORT ROYAL										
3. Safe Harbor Port Royal Landing WiFi MM 539.0	(843) 525-6664	120	16	140	20.0 / 15.0	F	GD		30 / 50	P

WiFi Wireless Internet Access
Visit www.waterwayguide.com for current rates, fuel prices, website addresses and other up-to-the-minute information. (Information in the table is provided by the facilities.)

Scan here for more details:

Source: Aqua Map and NOAA data

The homes in Beaufort are typically West Indies-style in a T-shaped floor plan with a raised first floor, high ceilings and double porches. Over time Beaufort has spread gently southward along the western bank of the river toward Port Royal.

NOTE: Beaufort is pronounced "Bew'-fort" not "Boe'-fort" as when referring to Beaufort, NC. If you are new to cruising the ICW in the Carolinas, do take an extra moment to get the pronunciation of the two straight or you can just wait to be corrected by the locals.

NAVIGATION:

NO WAKE ZONE

A strictly enforced No-Wake Zone extends nearly all the way from the Lady's Island (Woods Memorial) Bridge to the fixed McTeer Memorial Twin Bridges (65-foot fixed vertical clearance) over the Beaufort River at Port Royal (Mile 539.6). Signs on both bridges warn that violators of the No-Wake Zone will pay a fine of $1,025 or spend 30 days in a South Carolina jail cell.

Stay to mid-channel where the ICW begins its 4-mile run along Brickyard Creek (the headwaters of the Beaufort River). There are flats along both sides of the channel, particularly where the Coosaw River enters Brickyard Creek. Slow boats should note that the current between Brickyard Creek and Beaufort changes at about flashing red daybeacon "224" (Mile 532.1). If you catch the end of the flood or the slack, you can usually ride the current to Beaufort.

Lady's Island (Woods Memorial) Bridge is at Mile 536.1 (closed vertical clearance of 30 feet). While there is ample maneuvering room both above and below the bridge, the strong side-current is tricky; adequate power and careful boat handling are required.

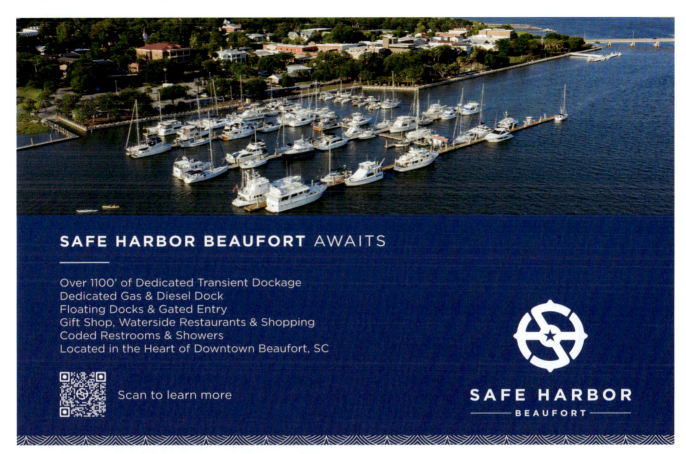

NOTE: You may have noticed that the Lady's Island (Woods Memorial) Bridge is referred to on some charts as "Ladies Island." To further complicate matters the official bridge name has nothing to do with ladies or lady's; it's the Richard V. Woods Memorial Bridge.

CAUTION: A temporary deviation is in place from March 25 through September 29, 2024, to test a proposed operating schedule during which the Lady's Island (Woods Memorial) Bridge opens on signal, except Monday through Friday, from 6:00 a.m. to 9:29 a.m. and 3:31 p.m. to 7:00 p.m., when the draw need not open to navigation. Also, between 9:30 a.m. to 3:30 p.m., the draw need open only on the hour. Between 9:30 a.m. to 3:30 p.m., the draw need open only on the hour and half-hour.

The bridge is slow and cumbersome to open and is frequently under repair. There may be lengthy delays so check ahead to see if there are any issues.

Dockage/Moorings: To port (south) just above Lady's Island (Woods Memorial) Bridge on Factory Creek is Lady's Island Marina. The marina has transient space at floating docks with all the usual amenities plus an on-site yoga studio, canvas shop, massage therapist and restaurant, Lady's Island Dockside (843-379-3288). Historic downtown Beaufort is one mile away, a scenic 15-minute walk (or take a courtesy bike from the marina) across the Lady's Island (Woods Memorial) Bridge.

At Mile 533 just north of green daybeacon "233" a marked channel leads into the well-regarded Marsh Harbor Boat Works on Ladys Island. Marsh Harbor is a small but efficient boat yard specializing in repair and painting. They generally do not take transients.

The Beaufort River and ICW lead to Safe Harbor Beaufort, which overlooks the Henry C. Chambers Waterfront Park. Restaurants, inns and charming shops open to the waterfront and the historic business district. The marina offers ample dockage and some marine services. Currents are very strong here with 7- to 9-foot tides so use considerable caution in docking. Call ahead to the marina for dockage availability and assistance. Floating docks on the T-head accommodate transient cruisers; even so, set ample fenders on approach.

A large portion of the anchorage area has been converted to a mooring field that is managed by Safe

Chapter 9: Stono River, SC to Ossabaw Sound, GA

Harbor Beaufort. There are 30 moorings. The fee includes the use of showers and the dinghy dock.

The original Beaufort Day Dock is west of the marina and has room for boats on the outside only (dinghies go inside). Smaller boats may also tie up to the 140-foot-long floating dock between the marina and the bridge at Waterfront Park.

Beaufort "East" Day Dock has a 3-hour limit enforced by the City to allow access for more boats during the day. No overnight docking and no docking between 1:00 a.m. and 6:00 a.m.

Anchorage: Just off the ICW to the north of red daybeacon "206" Jack Island Sound is an open area without much wind protection, but very little current and far enough off the ICW to prevent wakes. No shore access.

Brickyard Creek at Mile 530.1 has 5 to 9 feet MLW with a mud bottom and all-around protection. The deep-water channel is very narrow and residential docks extend far out from the shore so we recommend exercising caution when anchoring here.

While essentially just a pull-off of the ICW, the anchorage at Pleasant Point gets you a good distance from the channel. Enter the anchorage across from the boat ramp and move WNW into the pocket of about 10 to 15 feet MLW. (Note the east end of the charted islet is marked by green daybeacon "229A.") There is less water deeper into the pocket and also more crab pots. Holding is good in mud with shells. There is a lot of current so expect to turn with the tides. The boat ramp provides shore access for a quick dog walk.

A more protected anchorage is available in Factory Creek, which opens just north of and parallel to the Lady's Island (Woods Memorial) Bridge (at Mile 536). This anchorage is somewhat narrow for larger vessels. Enter as if heading to the Lady's Island Marina, favoring the red side of the channel as there is only 6 feet MLW near green daybeacon "1." Anchor in a minimum of 7-foot MLW depths past the marina.

Anchored boats can pay a fee to dock dinghies at Lady's Island Marina or can anchor closer to the public boat ramp before the marina and dinghy ashore there. The current is less intense here than on the ICW and you will not be rolled by nighttime traffic.

It is also possible to anchor west of Safe Harbor Beaufort at Beaufort–Downtown if you keep well clear of

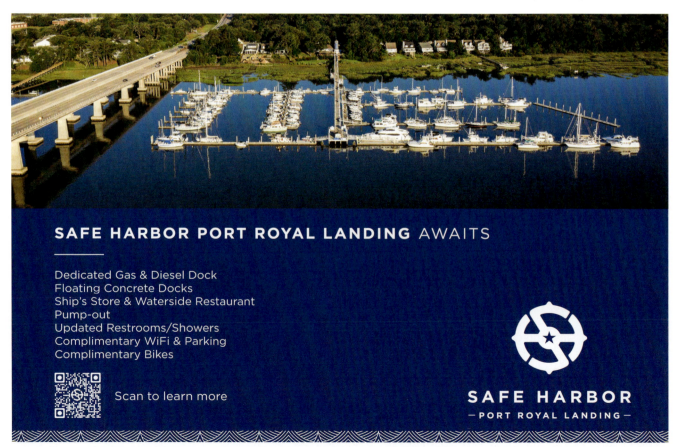

SAFE HARBOR PORT ROYAL LANDING AWAITS

- Dedicated Gas & Diesel Dock
- Floating Concrete Docks
- Ship's Store & Waterside Restaurant
- Pump-out
- Updated Restrooms/Showers
- Complimentary WiFi & Parking
- Complimentary Bikes

Scan to learn more

SAFE HARBOR — PORT ROYAL LANDING —

VISIT
BEAUFORT
PORT ROYAL ◆ SEA ISLANDS

Let the Lowcountry tides guide you.

Refuel in more ways than one in historic Beaufort, SC, from convenient marinas and stunning natural beauty to authentic culture and cuisine. Experience the transformative beauty of a place that has turned countless overnight anchorages into week-long retreats - and lifelong cruisers into locals.

FIND INSPIRATION FOR YOUR GETAWAY AT BEAUFORTSC.ORG.

DISCOVER
South Carolina

Chapter 9 — Stono River, SC to Ossabaw Sound, GA

ICW traffic and anticipate the effects of strong southerlies, substantial tidal-current swings and lots of boat traffic. The 30 moorings here are closely spaced (with more to come) making it difficult to anchor. It is best to anchor near the turn in the river. The depths are generally 10 to 20 feet MLW with a mud bottom with good holding.

The staff at Safe Harbor Beaufort asks that vessels anchor at least 200 feet away from their facility. This is part of a city ordinance of which even some locals are not aware. And, as always, use a light when anchored. You can dock your dinghy behind Beaufort Day Dock next to Safe Harbor Beaufort.

There is a large area behind the Unnamed Island shown on the charts dividing the Beaufort River. This offers good holding with room for many boats. Enter from the south near flashing red 242 (Mile 538.6) off Spanish Point. Proceed east, and then turn north between the marsh island to the west and the marshes to the east. Set your hook in 15 to 20 feet MLW over a sandy bottom. Do not try to re-enter the Beaufort River proper (to the north) due to severe shoaling.

Port Royal–ICW Mile 540

The Beaufort River runs broad and deep and its well-marked main channel is easy to follow past Port Royal and Parris Island (the Marine Corps Recruit Depot) to the Port Royal Sound Entrance. There is plenty of commercial fishing traffic in the channel and much to see ashore as the river arcs along between Parris Island and St. Helena Island.

NAVIGATION: Battery Creek joins the Beaufort River from the west. On Battery Creek's north shore is Port Royal, the deep water commercial shipping center for the Beaufort area. If headed up Battery Creek, keep red daybeacon "42" to starboard and follow the channel to Port Royal. Farther upstream is the fixed **US 21 Bridge** (45-foot vertical clearance). The creek carries 12-foot MLW depths or more for 4 miles upstream and is charted but no markers are present.

If northbound on the ICW, be sure to make the turn to the north on the Beaufort River between red nun "40" and quick flashing green "41," beyond which you will pick up the ICW markers again, rather than continuing straight westerly into Battery Creek and Port Royal. Both routes have bridges visible ahead and this mistake has been known to dismast sailboats.

CAUTION: From flashing green "41" (Mile 541.7) to flashing red "26" (Mile 547.8), the ICW joins the Port Royal ship channel and the familiar ICW marker system reverses: Keep red to port. Care should be taken to ignore red daybeacon "42" which takes you off the ICW and into Battery Creek.

The ICW returns near Parris Island Spit as you make the turn to cross Port Royal Sound towards Hilton Head Island. Stay clear of the Spit and the shoaling in that area. To do so, when leaving the Beaufort River channel for the 5-mile crossing of Port Royal Sound lay a course from ICW flashing red daybeacon "246" off Parris Island Spit to red nun buoy "2" and then to flashing green daybeacon "3" just past Dolphin Head. It can be bumpy if wind and tide oppose.

Port Royal Sound Entrance is wide, deep and very long. If you are headed south offshore, this is not the best option as a point of entry as you will backtrack some distance to re-enter the ocean. However, it is a great exit to use to make an overnight run south to St. Marys.

From the Port Royal Sound Lighted Buoy "P" head north and follow the range to flashing red buoy "14," then veer to the west to quick flashing green buoy "25," where you can head west as noted to the southbound ICW and Hilton Head Island, or north to Beaufort, SC. There are ranges northbound to quick flashing green buoy "37" on the Beaufort River.

When a cold front passes through the area expect breaking ocean swells throughout the Port Royal Entrance channel until rounding Bay Point. Under these conditions the going will be tedious but still negotiable for well-found vessels. More difficult is the combination of a stiff onshore breeze against an ebb tide (driven here by local tides of 9 feet); this is a situation best avoided.

Dockage: Three miles south of downtown Beaufort immediately north of the **McTeer Memorial Twin Bridges** (65-foot fixed vertical clearance) is Safe Harbor Port Royal Landing with full amenities, an easy-access floating face dock with gas and diesel fuel, a fully stocked Ship Store and a courtesy car. It is less than one-mile drive to a supermarket, liquor store, drug store, ATM and West Marine. Be sure to phone ahead for reservations or hail the marina on VHF Channel 16 before you approach to check for dockage availability and directions to a berth on its floating docks.

Anchorage: You can drop the hook at Mile 538.6 in the eastern fork of the Beaufort River - Port Royal Landing just before the McTeer Memorial Twin Bridges. This provides easy access via dinghy to Safe Harbor Port Royal Landing.

There is another anchorage at Port Royal on Battery Creek with 8 to 20 feet MLW and a sand bottom. It is protected from all directions except southeast. There have been reports of debris on the bottom so make sure your anchor is well set.

If you really want to get off the beaten path, explore the upper reaches of Cowen Creek off the ICW at Mile 544.5. You will find deep water throughout the creek. On Cowen Creek–Distant Island Creek tuck into the deep water slot behind the unnamed island between Distant Island and the marsh for complete solitude in at least 12 feet MLW.

■ HILTON HEAD ISLAND AREA, SC

NO WAKE ZONE

As you progress through this are you will notice many commercial and private docks along the way. Note the No-Wake Zones and proceed at slow speed in these areas. These signs are sometimes small and hard to spot. As on any waterway, be courteous and do not let your wake roll into the docks. Local marine patrols are frequently in this area and will stop boaters throwing a wake into the marinas.

A bustling but beautiful year-round resort, Hilton Head Island is probably the best known of South Carolina's Sea Islands. As one of the largest barrier islands on the Atlantic Coast, it is amply endowed by nature and history and offers something nearly year-round for everyone

Chapter 9: Stono River, SC to Ossabaw Sound, GA

Goin' Ashore: HILTON HEAD, SC

ATTRACTIONS

1. Aerial Adventure Hilton Head
If you feel adventurous, try the 50 in-the-tree challenges on 6 ability courses at this playground in the sky located next to Broad Creek Marina (33 Broad Creek Marina Way). Or see the world from heights of up to 75 feet in the salty air as eight interconnected ziplines take you from a tree platform to a suspended bridge to an aerial staircase ("don't look down") to a 75-foot tower tour. Harnesses and helmets provided. Call 843-682-6000 for fees and hours.

2. Coastal Discovery Museum
Learning center offering a wide range of activities including guided tours (walking and by boat or kayak) of 68 coastal acres of the Honey Horn property. Trails, gardens, horses and a butterfly enclosure are at 70 Honey Horn Dr. Open daily. Call ahead for exact hours (843-689-6767).

3. Harbour Town Lighthouse
The landmark red and white striped lighthouse rises 90 feet above Calibogue Sound. "Climb through time" allows you to learn about a different period in SC history on each of the 10 floors. Open daily from 10:00 a.m. to sundown.

4. Stoney Baynard Ruins
Ruins of a 1793 Civil War plantation home and slave quarters with rumored ghost sightings at Plantation Drive.

SERVICES

5. Hilton Head Post Office
10 Bow Circle (843-785-7002)

6. Sea Pines Circle Immediate Care
2 Greenwood Dr. (843-341-2700)

7. Heritage Animal Hospital
130 Arrow Rd. #101 (843-842-8331)

8. Hilton Head Island Visitor & Convention Bureau
1 Chamber of Commerce Dr. (843-785-3673)

MARINAS

9. Broad Creek Marina
18 Simmons Rd. (843-681-3625)

10. Harbour Town Yacht Basin
149 Lighthouse Rd. (843-363-8335)

11. Palmetto Bay Yacht Center
86 Helmsman Way (843-785-5000)

12. Shelter Cove Harbour & Marina
1 Shelter Cove Ln. (843-593-9116)

America's Waterway Guide Since 1947

Chapter 9

Most people know Hilton Head Island for its red and white striped lighthouse, a popular photo op, but this is also a great family getaway with walking and bicycle-friendly trails through well-preserved natural areas. The Island is known for its beautiful beaches, including Coligny Beach Park, which has beachfront shops, restaurants, and live entertainment. There are several large grocery stores for provisioning and more shopping at Shelter Cove Harbour at Palmetto Dunes, The Village at Wexford and along William Hilton Parkway (Hwy. 278). Hilton Head is also home to more than 30 golf courses, including some of the best in the country.

Nearby Pinckney Island National Wildlife Refuge is home to a variety of wildlife including alligators, turtles and birds and has several trails for hiking and biking. (Transportation required.)

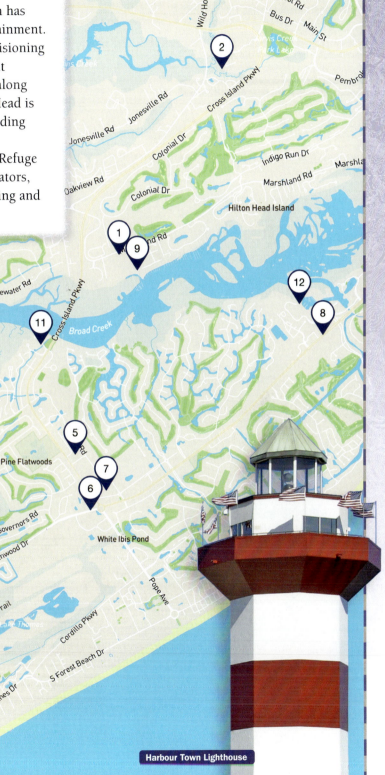

Harbour Town Lighthouse

MID-ATLANTIC EDITION

Chapter 9: Stono River, SC to Ossabaw Sound, GA

Hilton Head Area, SC

SKULL CREEK		Largest Vessel	VHF	Total Slips	Approach/ Dockside Depth	Floating Docks	Gas/ Diesel	Repairs/ Haulout	Min/Max Amps	Pump-Out Station
1. Safe Harbor Skull Creek WiFi MM 555.0	(843) 681-8436	200	16	179	12.0 / 10.0	F	GD		30 / 100	P
2. Hilton Head Harbor Marina WiFi MM 557.0	(843) 681-3256	100	16	101	30.0 / 20.0	F	GD		30 / 50	
3. Windmill Harbour Marina WiFi MM 558.3	(843) 681-9235	70	14	258	5.0 / 8.0		GD	R	30 / 50	P

WiFi Wireless Internet Access
Visit www.waterwayguide.com for current rates, fuel prices, website addresses and other up-to-the-minute information. (Information in the table is provided by the facilities.)

Scan here for more details: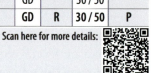

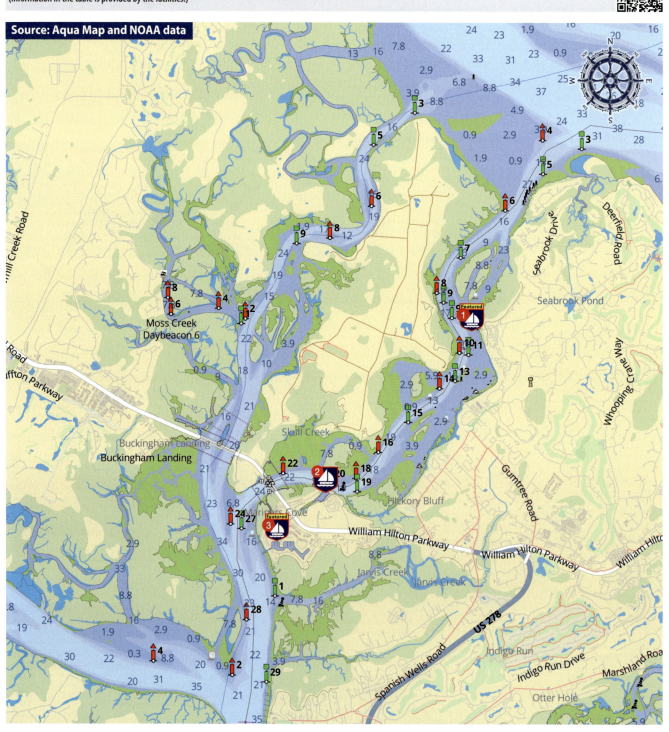

Source: Aqua Map and NOAA data

including a choice of excellent marina resorts. The ICW amenities offered on Hilton Head range from the ultra-luxurious to comfortable casual.

The numerous ferry boats plying the waters of Calibogue Sound between Hilton Head and Daufuskie Island can leave large wakes. The ferries usually slow down to "no-wake speed" when passing recreational boats. **Wilton J. Graves (U.S. 278) Hwy. Bridges** (65-foot fixed vertical clearance) at Mile 557.8 provide the only automobile access to and from Hilton Head Island.

Just opposite the spot where the ICW leaves Calibogue Sound for the Cooper River (Mile 565) is beautiful Broad Creek. To the north handsome houses, many with their own docks, line the creek at Shelter Cove. Oyster beds line the banks, crab pot markers dot the marsh flats and fishing drops are at the entrance to tidal streams along the way.

NAVIGATION: At Mile 553 you enter Skull Creek between Hilton Head Island and Pinckney Island (a wildlife refuge). Markers lead past oyster beds to Mile 555, where the first of Hilton Head Island's several marinas shows to port. Slack tide at the north end of Skull Creek is 2 hours after the south end. Watch for the shoal just in front of the marina to the north.

The proper entrance to Broad Creek and more dockage options is at green daybeacon "1." Give the marker a rather wide berth at low tide and enter between it and red daybeacon "2" on the opposite side. The shoal extends northeast of green daybeacon "1" so use caution.

Once you are inside, Broad Creek runs deep to its banks all the way to the marinas well upstream. Be aware that ferries to Daufuskie and other destinations use this creek.

CAUTION: The break between Brams Point and Buck Island at green daybeacon "29A" is too tricky for strangers. Do not attempt to use this secondary entrance to Broad Creek without local knowledge.

Dockage: The welcoming Safe Harbor Skull Creek at Mile 555 offers slips on modern concrete floating docks and can accommodate vessels to 200 feet. They have a complete lineup of modern amenities, and the area's sought-after beaches, resorts, golf courses and shopping are within reach.

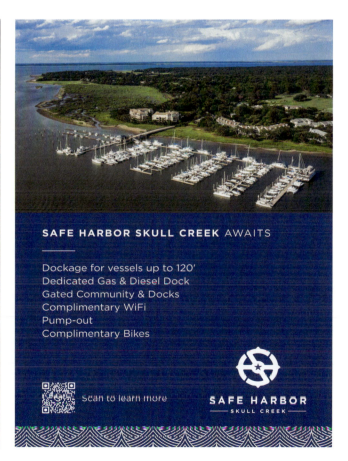

Chapter 9: Stono River, SC to Ossabaw Sound, GA

Hilton Head Area, SC

BROAD CREEK		Largest Vessel	VHF	Total Slips	Approach/ Dockside Depth	Floating Docks	Gas/ Diesel	Repairs/ Haulout	Min/Max Amps	Pump-Out Station
1. Harbour Town Yacht Basin WiFi MM 565.0	(843) 363-8335	140	16	100	8.5 / 8.0	F	GD		15 / 100	P
2. Palmetto Bay Marina WiFi 3.5 mi. E of MM 563.8	(843) 785-5000	200	16	65	20.0 / 20.0	F	GD	RH	30 / 100	P
3. Wexford Plantation-PRIVATE WiFi	(843) 686-8813	70	16	280	7.0 / 7.0	F			30 / 50	P
4. Broad Creek Marina WiFi 4.5 mi. E of MM 563.8	(843) 681-3625	100	16	55	23.0 / 16.0	F	GD	R		P
5. Shelter Cove Harbour & Marina WiFi	(844) 238-3237	160	16	178	/ 9.0	F	GD	R	20 / 100	P

WiFi Wireless Internet Access
Visit www.waterwayguide.com for current rates, fuel prices, website addresses and other up-to-the-minute information. (Information in the table is provided by the facilities.)

Scan here for more details:

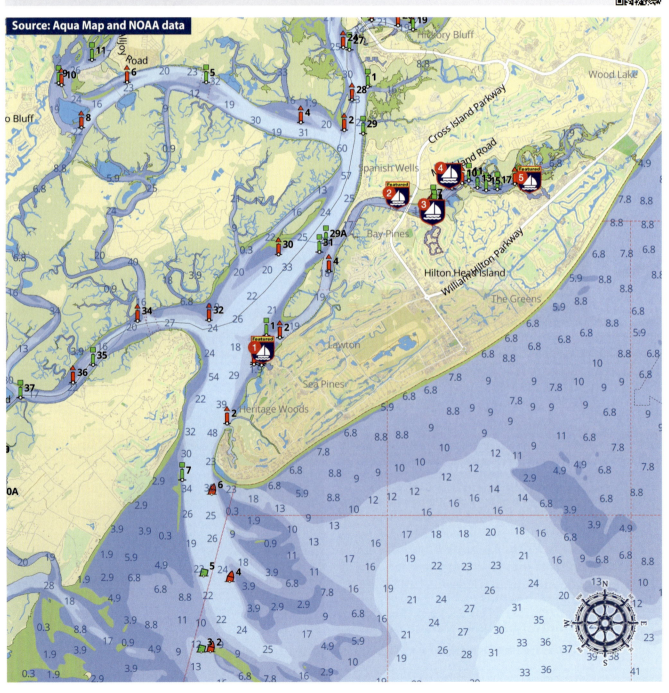

Source: Aqua Map and NOAA data

At Mile 557 Hilton Head Harbor Marina has an easily accessed fuel dock right on the ICW. The independently owned marina offers dockage in an enclosed basin and is also a luxury RV resort with resort amenities. They are also pet friendly. Car rentals and shuttle service are available upon request.

Note the direction and velocity of the current carefully as you approach the marina. When approaching from the north favor flashing green daybeacon "19" and give red daybeacon "20" just below the entrance channel a fair berth. A bar extends well up from the daybeacon.

In Calibogue Sound on the port side (to the east) before Jarvis Creek a pier marks the entrance to the lock leading into Windmill Harbour Marina, which lies in one of two secure, tide-free, lock-controlled harbors along the ICW. (The other is at the private Wexford Plantation, also on Hilton Head.) The harbormaster stands by on VHF Channel 14.

This harbor is home to the South Carolina Yacht Club and is surrounded by the well-maintained grounds of a gated residential community with a pool, restaurant and bar. Be aware that this is a sizable harbor (over 15 acres) and depending on where you are docked, it may be a hike to the bathhouse or to the club's dining room.

Perhaps one of the best-known features along this stretch of the ICW is the red and white striped 90-foot-tall lighthouse located east of Mile 564 and south of the entrance to Broad Creek. This marks Harbour Town Yacht Basin and the entrance to the original residential development on Hilton Head Island, Sea Pines. Enter between two jetties (the one to port is an observation pier) into Harbour Town's circular basin with its floating concrete docks. Villas, shops and multiple restaurants rim the circular basin. This is a full-service marina with many amenities plus beach access and a pool as well as fitness center access.

Palmetto Bay Marina is before the **Cross Island Parkway (U.S. 278) Bridge** (65-foot fixed vertical clearance) in Broad Creek. They offer over 7,190 linear feet of dockage, three restaurants and bars, fuel, laundry and showers, and complete yacht services.

On the starboard side of Broad Creek beyond the bridge is the private Wexford Plantation. They may have slips for members of reciprocal yacht clubs. Broad Creek Marina on the port side offers wet slips and dry storage plus both a mechanical shop and body shop. They also have a popular on-site restaurant.

Shelter Cove Harbour & Marina across from Palmetto Dunes Oceanfront Resort is an oasis for waterfront shopping, dining, water activities and tours and has spectacular water views. The marina offers resort amenities for vessels to 160 feet and a full-service marina store with boating gear, the latest coastal merchandise, snacks, convenience items, bait, tackle and more.

> NOTE: Broad Creek is a designated No-Discharge Zone. No onboard sewage—even that which has been treated—may be pumped overboard here. Y-valves and seacocks for overboard discharge must be wire-tied shut; simply closing them will not do. Fines will be levied if you are boarded and inspected, which can happen in this area.

Anchorage: It is possible to anchor outside the channel in Buck Island in at least 19 feet MLW. You may want to set two anchors because the area outside the channel is narrow and the current reverses strongly.

The holding in Broad Creek is excellent in thick mud. At the head of Broad Creek you can anchor behind Opposum Point. To reach this protected anchorage, leave the ICW and round green daybeacon "1" into Broad Creek. Follow Broad Creek for about 3 miles to just above Opossum Point. Anchor near the south shore below Palmetto Bay Marina. There is a public landing and boat ramp under the Cross Island Parkway (U.S. 278) Bridge.

You can anchor farther up the channel near green daybeacon "13" (Broad Creek G13) in at least 15 feet MLW or at green daybeacon "19" (Broad Creek G19), where holding is good in clay with 10-foot MLW depths in the middle of the creek. Access to Hilton Head is easy from either of these.

Side Trip: Bluffton, May River

The May River, which comes into the ICW at Mile 560, offers an interesting side trip north to the small town of Bluffton. The May River offers good anchorage almost anywhere past the bar at the mouth of its tributary stream, Bass Creek.

Anchorage: The May River has good holding in 15 feet MLW not too far north for easy access to the ICW. This is wide open with a lot of boat traffic on weekends. The anchorage at Bluffton offers better (all-around) protection in 10 to 20 feet MLW with a mud bottom. Shore access is available via Calhoun Street Public Dock with 3-hour tie-ups and no overnights. Some of the outside dock space is for 15 minutes for loading and unloading only.

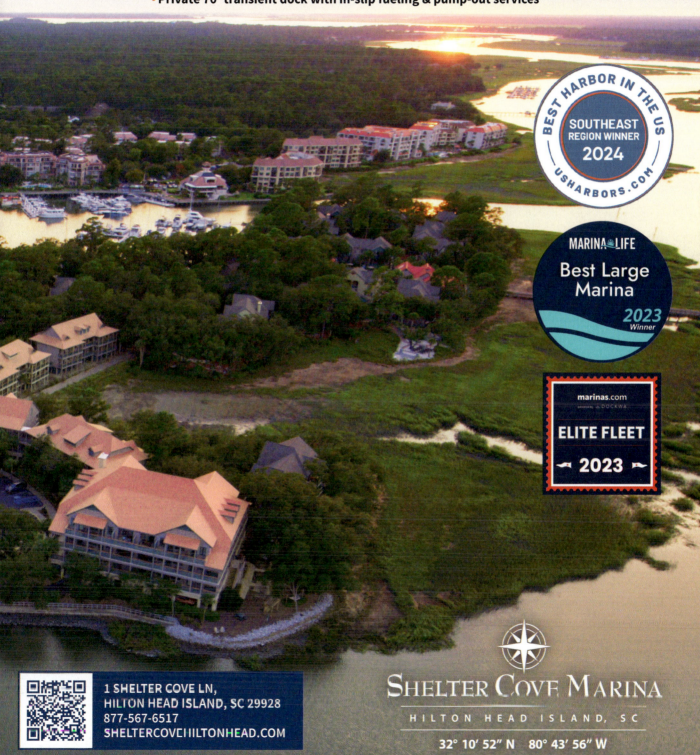

Located in the middle of Hilton Head Island, SC across from Palmetto Dunes Oceanfront Resort and just off the Intracoastal Waterway, Shelter Cove Harbour & Marina offers easy access to great shopping & restaurants plus bikes, watersports, golf, tennis & pickleball. The Ship's Store offers a large selection of apparel, accessories, convenience items & fishing tackle.

- **Floating docks / vessels up to 150'** • **Electrical: 30, 50, 100 amp** • **9' MLW, well marked channel**
- **Pump-out boat** • **Monitor channel 71/16** • **Restrooms, showers, laundry** • **Grocery store nearby**
- **Full service yacht maintenance** • **Wi-Fi internet access & cable available** • **Seasonal resort shuttle**
- **Private 70' transient dock with in-slip fueling & pump-out services**

1 SHELTER COVE LN,
HILTON HEAD ISLAND, SC 29928
877-567-6517
SHELTERCOVEHILTONHEAD.COM

Shelter Cove Marina
HILTON HEAD ISLAND, SC

32° 10' 52" N   80° 43' 56" W

COME ASHORE TO THE BEST OF HILTON HEAD ISLAND
Enjoy Harbour Town Yacht Basin and the unparalleled amenities of The Sea Pines Resort

Be surprised and captivated by The Sea Pines Resort and a luxury experience unmatched by any coastal resort destination. Experience miles of beautiful beaches, world-class dining, tennis and golf, including Harbour Town Golf Links, host to the PGA TOUR's RBC Heritage Presented by Boeing. For accommodations off the boat, stay at the stunning Inn & Club at Harbour Town, Hilton Head Island's only AAA Four-Diamond, Forbes Four-Star hotel, just steps from the Harbour Town Yacht Basin.

- LOA up to 150-foot vessels
- MLW 7 feet
- Daily/weekly/monthly dockage rates
- Electric: 30/50/100A, some 3-phase 100A
- VHF 16/68
- Fuel: High-speed gas and diesel; ValvTect fuels
- Complimentary pump-out
- Restrooms and showers
- Complimentary private washers and dryers
- Complimentary Wi-Fi internet

- Complimentary access to The Sea Pines Resort Fitness Center equipment
- Complimentary access to the Harbour Town Pool
- Beach access
- Access to the Harbour Town Clubhouse, Sea Pines Beach Club and Plantation Golf Club
- Resort Guest Amenity Card offering valuable benefits and room-charging privileges

    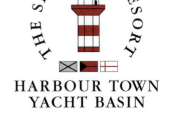

32° 08' 20" N / 80° 48' 40" W - St. Mile 564 | HILTON HEAD ISLAND, SC | **(843) 363-8335** | harbourtownyachtbasin.com

iNavX.com • WaterwayGuide.com

The Number One Handheld Chartplotter Just Got Better

 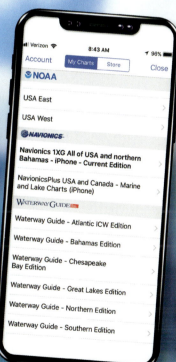 

iNavX

Navigate Confidently

Award Winning Technology and Data Delivery from iNavX and Waterway Guide

Chapter 9: Stono River, SC to Ossabaw Sound, GA

This is a sturdy floating dock in an idle speed zone. Depths on the inside of the dock are about 6 feet (MLW), while outside depth is closer to 20 feet MLW. There are power pedestals and water on the dock.

Calibogue Sound Entrance

NAVIGATION: Many boats use the Calibogue Sound Entrance, SC (pronounced "Cal-eh-BOE-gie") in fair weather and seas. It is a shortcut to reach the ICW from the ocean and is much shorter than the Savannah River approach. The markers, however, are widely spaced and sometimes difficult to locate.

It is approached from the Jones Island Range area of Tybee Roads. Note that if using this route to the Tybee Roads channel the northwestern end of the shoal marked by quick-flashing red buoy "2" and green buoy "3."

For South Hilton Head Island via Calibogue Sound, proceed as if entering the Savannah River but stay on Bloody Point Range after flashing red buoy "14," passing the lower range light and leaving green daybeacon "1" well to port.

Next, keep clear of the 5- to 6-foot deep shoal at the back Bloody Point Range, and then turn north toward quick flashing green buoy "3." Depths will briefly fall to 8 to 10 feet MLW from 14 feet, then rise again as you pass quick flashing green buoy "3."

At quick flashing green buoy "3," turn due north, and proceed to flashing green buoy "5," where you can then follow the remaining channel markers into Calibogue Sound.

■ TO OSSABAW ISLAND, GA

CAUTION: There are areas of known shoaling so care should be taken when navigating these waters as depths change constantly. Make sure that you are using current information including local knowledge when transiting the area. Be prepared for additional ATONs and changed buoy locations to assist safe passage. Be sure to check for depth updates and route suggestions at Waterway Explorer prior to traversing the area.

Daufuskie Island–ICW Mile 565

Heading south on the ICW, Daufuskie Island awaits at the confluence of Calibogue Sound and the Cooper River. (The ICW continues to run past Daufuskie Island as the channel goes south along the Cooper River, Ramshorn Creek and the New River.) With no bridge linking Daufuskie Island to the mainland the small native population (direct descendants of slaves brought from Africa) once lived an isolated life having little contact with the outside world. Nowadays, inspired by Hilton Head Island's development, Daufuskie Island continues to undergo extensive development of its own, with resorts and residential areas springing up each year. There is still, however, no vehicular access to the island.

NAVIGATION: The old lighthouse on Daufuskie Island at Haig Point serves as a landmark for spotting the lighted buoy at the entrance to the Cooper River. When passing Cooper River Landing on the Cooper River follow the dredged channel of narrow Ramshorn Creek into the New River, favoring the green side of the channel between flashing green daybeacon "39" and red flashing buoy "40" for 7.4 feet MLW. The tidal current reverses every 2 or 3 miles along this stretch and depths vary widely from year to year.

Slow down! Over the years, the wakes of passing vessels have damaged locally berthed craft at the floating dock and boat ramp at Daufuskie Landing.

Dockage: Near red daybeacon "36" on the Cooper River is Freeport Marina, which offers slips to 100 feet. This is a great place to get off the boat and rent a cottage (with a golf cart) and visit the nearby Old Daufuskie Crab Co. Restaurant (843-785-6652). Dockage at the marina is free during the day when you dine at the restaurant. This is a popular restaurant for boats in transit to stop for a quick lunch.

You can tie up for free at Daufuskie Landing at green daybeacon "39" during the day (no amenities). Be sure to stop in at the "not so general" General Store located just off the ferry docks for groceries and gifts or at the tiny and historic Silver Dew Winery, located in a building that dates all the way back to 1883. The building was originally constructed as a "wick house" for the nearby Bloody Point Lighthouse. Open daily for tours. (Call 843-342-8687 for details.)

Daufuskie Island, SC

COOPER RIVER

		Largest Vessel	VHF	Total Slips	Approach/Dockside Depth	Floating Docks	Gas/Diesel	Repairs/Haulout	Min/Max Amps	Pump-Out Station
1. Freeport Marina ⓦⓕ MM 568.0	(843) 785-8242	100		50	20.0 / 12.0	F	GD	H		

ⓦⓕ Wireless Internet Access
Visit www.waterwayguide.com for current rates, fuel prices, website addresses and other up-to-the-minute information.
(Information in the table is provided by the facilities.)

Scan here for more details:

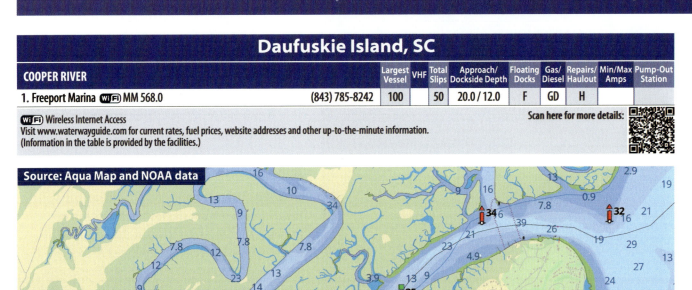

Source: Aqua Map and NOAA data

Anchorage: Across Calibogue Sound and the ICW at Mile 563 is well-protected Bryan Creek. When entering take care to clear the 2-foot MLW bar extending from the north. Once inside favor the west shore. Anchor in 8- to 11-foot MLW depths with a sandy bottom. This anchorage is pretty tight and can get buggy in warmer weather.

Bull Creek just past Mile 565 is a favorite anchorage and rafting site for local boats and ICW travelers alike. Just inside the entrance is good holding with sufficient depths but the currents are strong and there is no place to go ashore.

The best spot to anchor on Bull Creek is past the little creek to the west at Inner Bull Creek because shrimp boats use the lower part of the creek. This anchorage offers more seclusion and good holding. If you decide to anchor at Inner Bull Creek, navigate carefully at the sharp turn to the north. Deeper water is found farther from the eastern shore than shown on charts.

You can anchor in 8 to 15 feet MLW with excellent holding in mud on the northern branch of the Cooper River before green daybeacon "37" on the northwest side of Daufuskie Island. This anchorage is close to Freeport Marina and just outside the no wake buoys. Expect some boat traffic. Wind protection is provided by tall forests to the east.

Nearby Ramshorn Creek just north of the Cooper River offers good protection from wind and waves, depending on location. It is open to fetch from the southwest so proceed just short of the first bend for additional protection and a north wind break. Excellent swing room and room for numerous boats along this lengthy stretch.

Chapter 9: Stono River, SC to Ossabaw Sound, GA

Welcome to Georgia!

After passing through Fields Cut, you will encounter the Savannah River and the State of Georgia. Islands, estuaries, creeks and bars dominate the Georgia coast. If South Carolina is the Lowcountry then Georgia is the Backcountry, with miles of salt marsh, rushing tides, plentiful anchorages and mosquitoes (bring bug spray).

Georgia recently enacted legislation that restricts boaters choices for overnight anchoring. The Georgia Department of Natural Resources website includes an interactive map detailing the restricted areas under the section "Coastal Anchoring & Discharge."

"Anchoring Permits" are required in Georgia if you plan to anchor in one place for more than 14 days in a year. ("One place" is defined by a circle of 1 mile radius.) "Anchoring Restriction Areas" apply to overnight anchoring in these areas:

- Within 300 feet of a marina
- Within 150 feet of a marine structure (such as a private dock)
- Within 500 feet of an approved shellfish

You often hear about skippers choosing to run offshore to avoid Georgia but with good planning and prudent navigation, this isn't necessary. While you can easily jump outside at Tybee Roads or St. Simons Sound, you would miss the natural beauty of these pristine waters and endless sky.

South of flashing green "39" at Mile 570 the New River anchorage south of Page island has 8- to 20-feet MLW depths with excellent holding in mud. Enter from the south side of the river, watch your depth gauge and avoid the shallow water to the northwest.

Walls Cut/Fields Cut–ICW Mile 572

NAVIGATION: Leaving South Carolina you will pass through several shallow land cuts before reaching the Savannah River at the end of Fields Cut. This has typically been an area of concern due to constant shoaling. Depths are holding except where otherwise noted. The tidal range here is 8 to 9 feet so most boats will have no trouble at mid to high tide. Be sure to check for depth updates and route suggestions at Waterway Explorer prior to approaching the cuts.

Be advised that when approaching flashing red "50" at Mile 575.3 you will be entering the Savannah River. This river carries very heavy large shipping traffic that can create significant swells. Keep your radio on and lookout for these large ships. They are visible above the marsh grass. You might have to wait to cross the river and it is definitely advisable to do so.

NOTE: Heading south on the ICW you can pick up the beginning of the flood current and carry a fair (flood) current all the way through Walls Cut (Mile 572) and Fields Cuts to just south of Thunderbolt (Mile 585). (An ebb current gives the same advantage to northbound vessels.)

Anchorage: In calm weather cruisers will sometimes anchor south of the ICW and Walls Cut in the Wright River at Mile 572.2 (Turtle Island). There is 10 to 15 feet MLW here and a mud bottom. This is a convenient spot to stop north of the Georgia border with good holding and wave/wake protection. It is pretty anchorage but has little wind protection and no amenities.

Continue west across Field Cut on the Wright River for another anchoring option. Stay closer to the deeper waters on the southern side upon entry for 6 foot MLW then anchor in the center for more water. There is a little wind protection from the east provided by a small section of trees. This is a very peaceful location.

Chapter 9

America's Waterway Guide Since 1947

Savannah River

As you cross the Savannah River between Fields Cut and Elba Island Cut you leave South Carolina and enter Georgia. From here until the sheltered waters of Florida pay close attention to currents and depths as well as markers and ranges.

Study your charts before beginning this passage since the next 140 miles down the ICW are visually interesting and also physically demanding. You will use your GPS, compass, depth sounder and binoculars as you wind along serpentine rivers and cross open sounds that can be choppy and downright nasty when the wind kicks up.

The route winds past Georgia's barrier islands and then becomes an entirely different kind of ICW when you cross into Florida.

The channels are narrow here with wind-driven tides and sizable mud banks. It is best to travel on a high tide, especially through the challenging Hells Gate channel south of Savannah, the Sapelo River (ICW Mile 635) and Cumberland Dividings into Cumberland Sound.

The charts may not represent the most recent placement of navigation aids, which are frequently moved by the Army Corps of Engineers to mark the shifting channels. (As always, listen on VHF Channel 13 for dredging operations and give them a wide berth.) Refer to the Waterway Explorer for navigational alerts and updates.

It is especially important to stay in the channel, use the charted magenta ICW line as a guide (except where noted in the text), make use of the numerous navigational ranges and give markers–especially those at turns in natural rivers–a wide berth. Plan ahead in timing your arrival at the known trouble spots.

If it is low tide when you arrive, drop the hook for a while to wait for higher water; it doesn't take long for the tide to come up a foot or two. "Mid-tide and rising" is always preferable in these areas. Remember that strong winds and the lunar cycle affect tidal range. Conditions change so check the latest *Local Notice to Mariners* before you go.

> NOTE: The Bonaventure Cemetery, made famous in the book "Midnight in the Garden of Good and Evil," is visible from the ICW along the Wilmington River between quick-flashing red "30" and flashing green daybeacon "31" (past Mile 580) on the west side of the route.

St. Simons Lighthouse
St. Simons Island, GA
St. Simons Sound
Atlantic Ocean

Chapter 9: Stono River, SC to Ossabaw Sound, GA

Savannah River, GA

TYBEE ISLAND		Largest Vessel	VHF	Total Slips	Approach/ Dockside Depth	Floating Docks	Gas/ Diesel	Repairs/ Haulout	Min/Max Amps	Pump-Out Station
1. Tybee Island Marina WiFi	(912) 786-5554		16	54	18.0 / 16.0	F	GD	RH	30 / 50	P

WiFi Wireless Internet Access
Visit www.waterwayguide.com for current rates, fuel prices, website addresses and other up-to-the-minute information. (Information in the table is provided by the facilities.)

Scan here for more details:

Source: Aqua Map and NOAA data

You have to make a decision when you reach the Savannah River:

- Turn east to head to the Tybee Roads (Savannah River) Entrance and out to sea;
- Head west up the river to beautiful Savannah; or
- Continue on the ICW through the Elba Island Cut to the Wilmington River.

Option 1: To Tybee Roads (Savannah River) Entrance

Sixteen miles down the Savannah River from Savannah is the Tybee Roads (Savannah River) Entrance. This is an active inlet offering entry to Savannah via the ICW and Savannah River. Slower boats bound for the Savannah River on this route should enter Tybee Roads with a favorable current, if possible, as the effects of the current start many miles offshore in the Atlantic.

NAVIGATION: Entering the channel from the sea buoy (Savannah River Entrance Channel Lighted "T" at N 31° 57.700'/W 80° 43.100'), follow the Tybee range to quick flashing red bell buoy "8," turning north to follow the Bloody Point Range to flashing red "14." Turning to port here, follow the Jones Island Range to flashing red buoy "18," and then turn slightly southwest and continue in on Tybee Knoll Cut Range to flashing red buoy "24." Here, you will have Oyster Bed Island to your north and Cockspur Island to the south.

Pick up New Channel Range and follow the channel markers. Note the partially submerged breakwater that begins just past flashing red buoy "18," which is marked by a flashing white light, noted as "Fl 4s 16ft 5M" on your chart.

Coming from the north, mariners need to be aware of Gaskin Banks, an extensive shoal area extending nearly 8 nm out from Hilton Head. Also to be avoided is a

America's Waterway Guide Since 1947 — **Chapter 9**

Savannah River, GA

SAVANNAH AREA		Largest Vessel	VHF	Total Slips	Approach/ Dockside Depth	Floating Docks	Gas/ Diesel	Repairs/ Haulout	Min/Max Amps	Pump-Out Station
1. The Westin Savannah Harbor Golf Resort & Spa WiFi	(912) 201-2021	300		25	27.0 / 16.0	F			30 / 200+	
2. River Street Market Place Dock WiFi 8.0 mi. W of MM 576	(912) 629-2644	250			24.0 / 18.0	F			30 / 100	
3. John P. Rousakis Riverfront Plaza (East)	(912) 651-6477				/					

WiFi Wireless Internet Access
Visit www.waterwayguide.com for current rates, fuel prices, website addresses and other up-to-the-minute information.
(Information in the table is provided by the facilities.)

Scan here for more details:

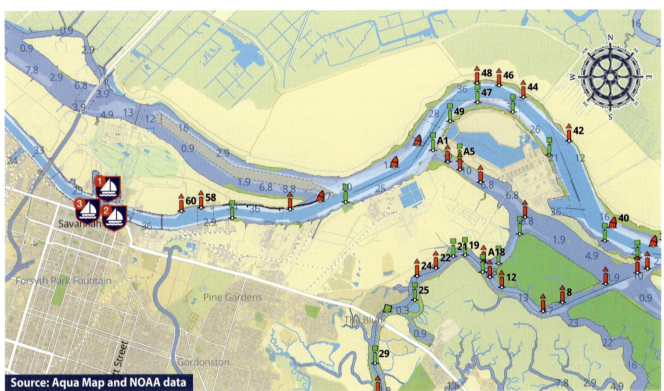

Source: Aqua Map and NOAA data

submerged breakwater north of and roughly parallel to flashing red buoy "12" and flashing red buoy "14."

Dockage: The entrance to the Savannah River near Tybee Island, Savannah's primary beach area, makes a good fuel stop for powerboaters going south on the outside run down the Atlantic. Tybee Island Marina offers wet slips and dry boat storage, fishing charters, a boat launch and a restaurant. The marina is on the south side of the Savannah River's mouth but the 35-foot fixed vertical clearance **SR 26/US 80 Bridge** over the marina's access channel restricts usage by sailboats.

Option 2: Upriver to Savannah

Described on Visit Savannah as "...a sweet Southern sanctuary where art, architecture and ghost tales collide under a shroud of Spanish moss," Savannah is a worthwhile diversion. Known for manicured (cobblestone) parks, horse-drawn carriages and antebellum architecture, a trip to Savannah is a trip back in time.

NAVIGATION: Savannah is about 8 miles north on the Savannah River from ICW Mile 576. Expect strong currents, a 9-foot tide and heavy commercial traffic on the way. Those with low-powered boats should check the tide tables and plan arrivals and departures accordingly.

Following the Savannah River another 170 miles will bring you to Augusta, home of the Professional Golf Association's annual Masters Championship.

When returning to the ICW you can do so via the south channel (below Elba Island), assuming you can navigate under the 35-foot fixed vertical clearance **Elba Island Road Bridge**.

MID-ATLANTIC EDITION

Chapter 9: Stono River, SC to Ossabaw Sound, GA

GOIN' ASHORE: SAVANNAH, GA

ATTRACTIONS

1. American Prohibition Museum
Artifacts and displays about the ban of alcohol from 1920-1933 at 209 W. St. Julian St. At night (Wednesday through Saturday) a retro speakeasy opens upstairs serving classsic cocktails and offering cocktail classes (912-220-1249).

2. City Market
In the heart of the Historic District four blocks of warehouses have been renovated to represent the 18th century marketplace. Features artists working in their lofts and exhibits of works for sale, as well as open-air cafés and shops offering crafts, accessories and gifts (219 W. Bryan St., 912-232-4903).

3. River Street Market Place
Housed in one-time cotton warehouses, there are more than 75 boutiques, galleries, artists' studios, restaurants and pubs on the river at 502 E. River Street (912-441-2664).

4. Ships of the Sea Maritime Museum
Founded in 1966 and featuring nine galleries of ship models, plus maritime paintings and artifacts from the 18th and 19th centuries. Collection is housed in elegant home built in 1819 for William Scarbrough, one of the principal owners of Steamship Savannah and president of the Savannah Steamship Company (41 Martin Luther King Jr. Blvd., 912-232-1511).

5. Telfair Museums
Includes three museums: Jepson Center, Telfair Academy and Owens-Thomas House and Slave Quarters. Telfair Academy is one of the south's first public museums and was built as a mansion in 1812. The 1938 bronze Bird Girl statue, made famous on the cover of John Berendt's novel "Midnight in the Garden of Good and Evil," is on display at 121 Barnarrd St. (912-790-8800).

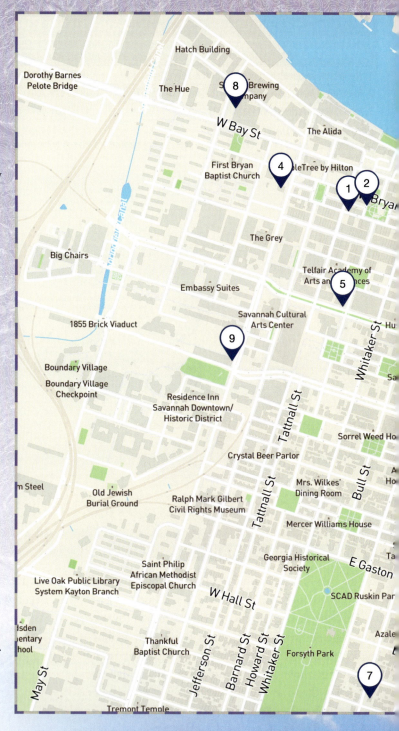

America's Waterway Guide Since 1947 — Chapter 9

Savannah sits serenely on a bluff 40 feet above the banks of the Savannah River, where General James Oglethorpe and 120 passengers landed in 1733 to found Britain's last American colony. General Oglethorpe laid out the city in a series of 24 squares, 22 of which remain as lovely parks surrounded by a mix of architectural styles, including Federal, Georgian, Victorian and Italianate. Walking and driving tours, carriage tours, audio tours and guided bus tours highlighting the historic homes built around Savannah's squares are all available. The free Express Shuttle runs daily and connects the Visitors Center, ferry and 18 stops in the historic district.

Another "must see" is Bonaventure Cemetery, one of the most famous in the country and home to stunning monuments, sculptures, and mausoleums. You can book a guided tour of the cemetery that includes transportation there (4 miles from downtown).

6. Waving Girl
This statue commemorates Florence Martus (1868-1943), unofficial greeter of all passing ships on the Savannah River at 2 E. Broad St. Legend has it she waved a handkerchief by day and a lantern by night and never missed a ship in her 44 years on watch.

SERVICES

7. ExperCARE Urgent Care
818 Abercorn St. (912-800-0110)

8. Savannah Post Office
2 N. Fahm St. (912-235-4666)

9. Savannah Visitor Center
1 W. River St. (912-651-6662)

MARINAS

10. River Street LLC
318 E. River St. (912-232-4252)

11. River Street Market Place Dock
502 E. River St. (912-629-2647)

12. The Westin Savannah Harbor Golf Resort & Spa
1 Resort St. (912-201-2000)

Chapter 9: Stono River, SC to Ossabaw Sound, GA

Dockage: The Westin Savannah Harbor Golf Resort & Spa on Hutchinson Island is directly across from River Street in Savannah with slips on floating docks. Their deep-water slips can accommodate vessels to 300 feet and they offer resort-style amenities. Be sure to call well in advance for reservations. Water ferry service is available to reach the other side of the harbor.

Across the channel River Street Market Place Dock offers concrete floating dockage with few amenities but direct access to downtown. The River Street Market features re-creations of the sheds that stood on River Street in the mid 1800s and houses an open-air market.

John P. Rousakis Riverfront Plaza (East), which was previously a free dock, is now charging an overnight fee that includes power and water. It is first-come, first-served (no reservations). Add extra fenders and expect wakes from the passing container ships, ferries and riverboat tours. See on-site signage for payment instructions. This location still allows free tie-up during the day (3-hour limit).

The Savannah River Dock across the channel is free but with no amenities (power, water, etc.), as is Eastern Wharf, a long concrete floating dock near a condo/apartment complex. If you are going to dock here, make sure your bow is facing west/upstream. Both can be rolly so put out good fenders and spring lines fore and aft.

Option 3: ICW to Thunderbolt—ICW Mile 576 to Mile 585

Thunderbolt is an important seafood-packing center with good marinas and restaurants. The shore is lined with shrimp boats, often rafted two abreast. Bus service is available with stops about close to Thunderbolt's marinas. (A taxi is better for the trip to Savannah.)

NAVIGATION: The ICW passage is not straight across the Savannah River but diagonal. When you cross the Savannah River, allow for the strong river current. Slow boats may have to correct course several times.

Watch for big ships, which will announce their presence on VHF Channels 13 and 16. They approach fast from both directions and port pilots have had many close encounters with pleasure boats in the river where the ships have no room to maneuver in the narrow, swiftly running channel.

Depths are well maintained here but since the tidal range is between 8 and 9 feet MLW be sure to stay in the channel. From Elba Island Cut the ICW heads briefly westward along St. Augustine Creek. It then enters the winding upper reaches of the Wilmington River, which is not nearly as intricate as it appears on the chart and then approaches the town of Thunderbolt. Multiple sets of ranges guide you through this area.

NO WAKE ZONE

Causton Bluff (Sam Varnedoe, SR 26) Bridge at Mile 579.9 has 65-foot vertical clearance. The old bascule bridge will remain in the open to navigation position until the spans are permanently removed from the waterway. Note that both sides of the bridge are No Wake Zones.

Note that the tidal current reverses between the **Causton Bluff (Sam Varnedoe, SR 26) Bridge** and the high-rise **State Of Georgia Memorial (U.S. 80) Bridge** (65-foot fixed vertical clearance) at Mile 582.5. (The bridge is known locally as the Thunderbolt Bridge.) At Thunderbolt and farther down the ICW at Isle of Hope (Mile 590), the current and direction of flow must be considered when docking. Marina personnel are

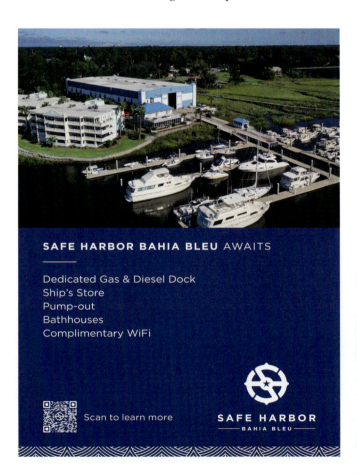

SAFE HARBOR BAHIA BLEU AWAITS

Dedicated Gas & Diesel Dock
Ship's Store
Pump-out
Bathhouses
Complimentary WiFi

Scan to learn more

SAFE HARBOR
BAHIA BLEU

Wilmington River, GA

THUNDERBOLT AREA		Largest Vessel	VHF	Total Slips	Approach/ Dockside Depth	Floating Docks	Gas/ Diesel	Repairs/ Haulout	Min/Max Amps	Pump-Out Station
1. Hinckley Yacht Services Savannah WiFi MM 582.4	(912) 629-2400	100	16	30	12.0 / 12.0	F		RH	30 / 50	P
2. Safe Harbor Bahia Bleu WiFi MM 582.6	(912) 354-2283	100	16	45	26.0 / 20.0	F	GD	RH	30 / 50	P
3. Thunderbolt Marine WiFi MM 583	(912) 356-3875	200	16	45	20.0 / 20.0	F	GD	RH	30 / 100	P
4. Savannah Yacht Club-PRIVATE	(912) 644-4100	45		60	20.0 / 20.0	F	GD		30	

WiFi Wireless Internet Access
Visit www.waterwayguide.com for current rates, fuel prices, website addresses and other up-to-the-minute information. (Information in the table is provided by the facilities.)

Scan here for more details:

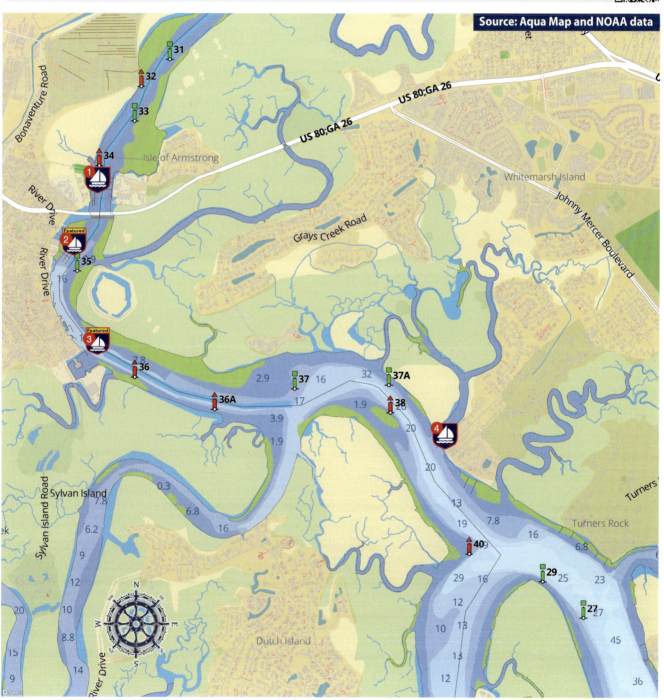

Source: Aqua Map and NOAA data

Chapter 9: Stono River, SC to Ossabaw Sound, GA

THUNDERBOLT MARINA
FULL SERVICE MARINA AND YACHT REPAIR
INTRACOASTAL MILE 583 - MARKER 35

THUNDERBOLT MARINE INC.
Marina Reservations
912-210-0363
VHF CHANNEL 16
dockmaster@thunderboltmarine.us

- Best Fuel Prices
- Fuel: Diesel & Gas
- Pump Out
- Ship's Store
- WiFi Available
- Minutes to Historic Savannah
- Restaurants within Walking Distance
- Catamaran Haulout to 28' Beam via Travelift
- Syncrolift Haulout for wider Beam

- Gated Security - Guard on duty 24/7
- Courtesy Car Available
- Spacious Laundry Room
- Clean Showers & Restrooms
- 14' at Low Tide
- Floating Concrete Docks
- No Height Restrictions from Wassaw Sound

Book Online: DOCKWA / SNAG A SLIP

Yacht Repair 912 352 4931

www.thunderboltmarine.us

Thunderbolt Marine
Safe Harbor Bahia Bleu
Wilmington River
Thunderbolt, GA

generally knowledgeable and when assigning berths, they try to put the less maneuverable, single-screw boats in slips that are easy to enter and leave in this area of high tides and swift currents.

If no attendant is around, it is best to put in at the fuel dock to size up the situation and then locate someone who can give directions or lend a hand. All marinas at Thunderbolt have floating docks.

When heading south from Thunderbolt take flashing green daybeacon "37" a little wide and then favor flashing green daybeacon "37A" avoiding the shoal near quick-flashing red "38."

Dockage: Hinckley Yacht Services Savannah, located to starboard just northwest of the State Of Georgia Memorial (U.S. 80) Bridge, is a premiere yacht care and service facility. They have just eight reserved transient slips so call ahead.

At Mile 582 Safe Harbor Bahia Bleu on the south side of the State Of Georgia Memorial (U.S. 80) Bridge is convenient to the ICW and to Thunderbolt's restaurants and shops. They can accommodate vessels up to 200 feet at their deep-water docks. They also have a well-stocked ship store and offer boat detailing and storage.

Thunderbolt Marine is at Mile 583 with transient dockage close to town and full-service repairs. Their lifts are capable of hauling the smallest to the largest of yachts. They also have spacious laundry facilities and pump-out facilities. Restaurants and a bus stop are within walking distance.

The private Savannah Yacht Club is about 2 miles past Thunderbolt to port. The yacht club has a reciprocity policy and requires 24-hour notice prior to arrival.

Savannah Marina on Turner Creek accommodates vessels of all sizes with first-class hospitality and full-service amenities. They are currently undergoing renovations, upgrades and expansion so call ahead for slip availability.

The former Hogans' Marina (now Sun Life Wilmington Island) is a dry storage facility and charter fishing base. They do not maintain transient slips but may have space for you. Do call ahead.

Farther south on the Wilmington River is Landings Harbor Marina with just a few reserved transient slips to 40 feet. The friendly marina crew will make you feel welcome.

Anchorage:

CAUTION: Georgia has enacted legislation that restricts boaters choices for overnight anchoring. Be sure to check the interactive map online at the Georgia Department of Natural Resources before dropping the hook. "Anchoring Permits" are required if you plan to anchor in one place for more than 14 days in a year. ("One place" is defined by a circle of 1 mile radius.) "Anchoring Restriction Areas" apply to overnight anchoring in these areas: within 300 feet of a marina, within 150 feet of a marine structure (such as a private dock) or within 500 feet of an approved shellfish area.

A mile or so below Thunderbolt the Wilmington River widens and the channel begins to straighten out. The popular Herb River anchorage is located at Mile 584.5. Most skippers anchor along the east bank before the first turn. The river bottom is a bit irregular and very deep at the bend but holding is better than in the lower stretch of the river where there is an oyster bank.

Local boat traffic is minimal and the tidal currents moderate. Depths are good at 13 to 15 feet MLW with a mud bottom but be sure to set the anchor well and, as always, show an anchor light. This anchorage is well protected.

It is possible to anchor before or after the fixed **Spence Grayson Bridge** (35-foot vertical clearance) on Turner Creek and dinghy into the boat ramp dock below the bridge to get ashore for access to shopping and restaurants. You can also anchor above the bridge if you can handle the clearance restriction.

Wassaw Sound Entrance

Wassaw Sound Entrance, the next Atlantic inlet south of Tybee Roads, provides quick access to the Savannah area from the Atlantic Ocean. A fair amount of local traffic regularly uses this inlet but we do not recommend it except with up-to-date local knowledge, excellent visibility, calm seas and at mid-tide. This is not an inlet for dark and stormy arrivals as it is poorly marked and surrounded by shoals nearly 5 nm out from the entrance.

This inlet is sometimes used by vessels bound for Thunderbolt Marine and unable to clear the 65-foot **State Of Georgia Memorial (U.S. 80) Bridge** over the Wilmington River at Mile 582.8.

Chapter 9: Stono River, SC to Ossabaw Sound, GA

Wilmington River, GA

		Largest Vessel	VHF	Total Slips	Approach/ Dockside Depth	Floating Docks	Gas/ Diesel	Repairs/ Haulout	Min/Max Amps	Pump-Out Station
TURNER CREEK										
1. Savannah Marina WiFi SE of MM 585.4	(912) 897-2896	120	16	55	7.0 / 10.0	F			30 / 50	P
WILMINGTON RIVER										
2. Landings Harbor Marina WiFi	(912) 598-1901	40	16	29	20.0 / 8.0	F	GD	RH	30 / 50	P
BULL RIVER										
3. Bull River Marina WiFi 4 mi. NE of MM 586	(912) 897-7300	110	16	70	25.0 / 18.0	F	GD	R	30 / 100	P

WiFi Wireless Internet Access
Visit www.waterwayguide.com for current rates, fuel prices, website addresses and other up-to-the-minute information. (Information in the table is provided by the facilities.)

Scan here for more details:

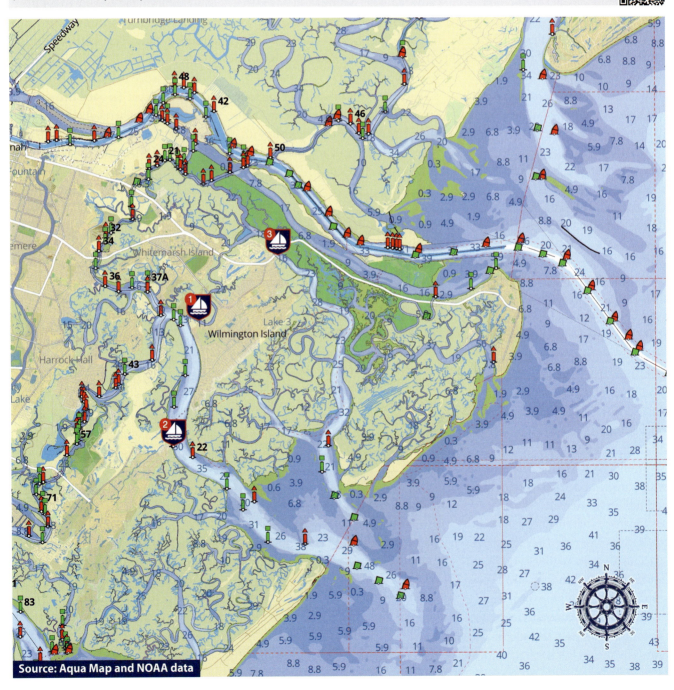

Source: Aqua Map and NOAA data

348 WATERWAY GUIDE 2025 www.waterwayguide.com

NAVIGATION: The entrance to Wassaw Sound changes continually so red buoys "4," "6" and "8" are not charted. Before beginning this inlet, mark a boundary line on your chart running due south from flashing red buoy "10." From flashing red buoy "2W," head west-northwest and curve to the north around the shoal to starboard until you reach the above noted line from flashing red buoy "10." Head due north to green can buoy "9" and turn northwest to follow the markers; depths will be 20 feet MLW or better.

Stay to the center of Wilmington River until you turn to the north after flashing red "22" and then stay to the east side of the river for deep water. Wassaw Sound and the Wilmington River carry about 25-foot MLW depths between flashing red buoy "10" in the Atlantic Ocean to flashing green daybeacon "29" at Skidaway River (Mile 585.6).

The 2 nm from the sea buoy to the first markers are tricky, with shoals on both sides, breakers and no markers. Just east of green can "9" and flashing red can "10" there is extensive shoaling. If you draw more than 5 feet, think twice before entering this inlet. This is not an inlet for dark and stormy arrivals, as it is poorly marked and surrounded by shoals nearly 5 nm out from the entrance.

Local boats anchor off a beautiful sandy beach at a spit on the northeast corner of Wassaw Island for day outings.

Dockage: Bull River Marina is accessible from Wassaw Sound with no bridges or other height restrictions but with a shallow bar (6- to 7-foot MLW spots charted) across its entrance channel. It is located 4 miles from ICW Mile 586 on the Bull River before the 20-foot fixed vertical clearance **US 80 (Bull River) Bridge**. The marina is home to boat rentals, fishing charters, excursions and the Daufuskie water taxi. They can accommodate vessels up to 110 feet.

Skidaway River & Narrows–ICW Mile 585

Isle of Hope at Mile 590 is a charming village of winding roads and old houses scattered among the tall pines and oaks located on the shore of the Skidaway River. It is 7 miles by water down the twisting ICW from Thunderbolt but only half that by road.

The town stands on a bend high above the river and is listed on the National Register of Historic Places. Signs politely request that you slow down as you pass and keep your wake to a minimum; better yet, tie up here to enjoy a walk among the antebellum homes.

About 1 mile from the Isle of Hope Marina is the Wormsloe Historic Site (912-353-3023) with a museum, ruins of a fortified house and a nature walk. Wild deer and pigs leave their tracks and sometimes appear on the grounds. The on-site Wormsloe Mansion is not open to the public because it is a private residence still occupied by the descendants of Noble Jones, one of the earliest Georgia settlers and the original owner of the property. You can visit the site on foot, bike or by tour bus from Savannah.

NAVIGATION: Turn southwest into the Skidaway River at Mile 585 for a meandering 5-mile cruise to Isle of Hope. Skidaway Narrows, immediately below Isle of Hope, is a twisting stretch of the ICW that weaves erratically back and forth around curves and bends. Take your time, cut your speed as necessary, watch your course and enjoy this winding creek with its fringes of salt marsh extending back to distant woods.

> NOTE: Skidaway Narrows is the preferred swimming hole of the local river otter population. Pay attention!

The pretty Vernon View at Mile 596 is a Savannah suburb overlooking the Burnside River portion of the ICW. This begins at Skidaway Narrows' southern end about 6 miles below Isle of Hope. Private docks line the shore (and are well charted) but there is no public marina. Remember that you are responsible for your wake here.

Slow boats should note that high slack water at Mile 592 (Skidaway Narrows) occurs 49 minutes before the Savannah River Entrance. This is good to keep in mind as arriving at Skidaway Narrows at slack water provides the most favorable currents from Mile 585 to Mile 603. Tidal currents reverse in the vicinity of the fixed 65-foot vertical clearance **Diamond Causeway (Skidaway) Bridge** at Mile 592.9.

The channel narrows from red daybeacon "46A" (Mile 590) to the bridge. Favor the eastern bank until red daybeacon "50." A boat ramp just below the bridge creates considerable small-boat traffic so keep alert. There is also a buoyed-off swimming area. Note the Slow Speed signs here.

On the Burnside River (Mile 596) favor the north side of the channel between red daybeacon "76" and flashing green daybeacon "79," which marks the turn

Chapter 9: Stono River, SC to Ossabaw Sound, GA

Wilmington River, GA

SKIDAWAY RIVER		Largest Vessel	VHF	Total Slips	Approach/ Dockside Depth	Floating Docks	Gas/ Diesel	Repairs/ Haulout	Min/Max Amps	Pump-Out Station
1. Isle of Hope Marina WiFi MM 590.0	(912) 354-8187	220	16	125	12.0 / 15.0	F	GD		30 / 100	P

WiFi Wireless Internet Access
Visit www.waterwayguide.com for current rates, fuel prices, website addresses and other up-to-the-minute information. (Information in the table is provided by the facilities.)

Scan here for more details:

Source: Aqua Map and NOAA data

into the Vernon River. A shoal is building out along the southeast side of the Burnside River so don't cut flashing green daybeacon "79" too closely and watch for shoaling to flashing green daybeacon "81."

Dockage: Located in one of the most beautiful settings on the entire ICW, the convenient Isle of Hope Marina provides large slips at concrete floating docks with full amenities including laundry facilities and a pool. The marina also offers a courtesy car and bicycles. There are food markets, a West Marine, Walmart and restaurants within courtesy car range.

Note that this is the last fuel stop on the ICW (southbound) for 90 miles. This is also the logical jumping-off point for the long run south and the first landing near Savannah when you are headed north with bus service to the city.

Anchorage: The first viable anchorage on this stretch is at Mile 585.9. There is good holding and room for several boats on the west side of Skidaway River, north and south of the "No Wake" sign. Depth is good to the marsh but expect 180-degree current swings and anchor accordingly.

Turtleneck Bend to the south (Mile 586.3) is a nice little anchorage in front of the UGA Marine Education Center and Aquarium. Anchor in 12 feet MLW with good protection from south wind. Make sure you are out of the channel and at least 150 feet from any dock.

Anchor just north of the Diamond Causeway (Skidaway) Bridge on the eastern shore just before slight bend at Mile 592.9 (Skidaway Narrows). This area shoals up quickly (depth of 15 feet MLW and tide of 7 feet) but is protected and offers small beaches for dog walking. Beware of your swing and don't anchor in the middle of the channel.

Isle of Hope Marina
Voted Savannah's Best!

- Complimentary high-speed WiFi
- 30-50-100 amp electrical service
- 4,000ft of floating concrete docks
- 600ft of deepwater face docks
- Gas, diesel, and pump-out facilities

- Complimentary loaner cars
- Marker 46A Clubhouse
- Ship's Store and laundry facilities
- 2,000 sq ft overwater pavilion
- Private restrooms and showers

ISLE OF HOPE
TPG MARINAS

LIFE STARTS ON THE WATER

50 Bluff Drive
Savannah, GA 31406
912.354.8187
ioh@tpgmarinas.com
iohmarina.com

Chapter 9: Stono River, SC to Ossabaw Sound, GA

Moon River, made famous by songwriter Johnny Mercer, is just short of Mile 595. Boaters have reported shoaling to around 4-foot MLW depths at the entrance although depths are still charted at 8 feet MLW with shoaling indicated. Anchor behind Marsh Island and remember that in periods of strong and prolonged westerly wind and during the new and full moon phases tides can be much lower than normal charted depths. Stay clear of flashing red daybeacon "74" and the shoaling before heading northwest up the river.

If you give the long shoal off Possum Point a wide berth, you can turn northward up the Vernon River well off the ICW to drop the hook south of the village of Montgomery. This is a pleasant anchorage in more than 14-foot MLW depths. Anchor before the charted 1-foot MLW bar, which extends out to the middle of the river. Currents can be strong here and you should allow for an 8-foot tidal range. Possum Point is another option in light winds.

You will probably share these anchorages with a shrimp boat or two during the season. They usually anchor on one long stretchy nylon rode and keep their arms down so give them plenty of space to swing.

To Ossabaw Island–ICW Mile 605

NAVIGATION: The Vernon River runs wide and deep until you reach Hell Gate, a land cut leading from the Vernon River to the Ogeechee River. If strong northeast winds kick up, you might see swells breaking up the long fetch of both the Vernon and Ogeechee Rivers.

The Ossabaw Inlet to the ocean at Mile 601 is used by small local craft but is not really suitable for use by cruising vessels other than in very calm weather and with a lot of local knowledge.

Hell Gate at Mile 601 is one of the most notorious sections of the ICW for shoaling. The channel is not as deep as shown on the charts and has shoaled in some places.

Do not hug green daybeacon "89." Pass by 80 feet off. Go slow and watch the depthsounder. Mid-tide and rising is the safest time to go through these questionable areas of the ICW and stay in the center of the channel.

There are strong side-sweeping currents at Hell Gate, especially on the ebb when entering from the north (Vernon River) so keep track of your progress by looking both ahead and astern.

Ossabaw Sound, GA

		Largest Vessel	VHF	Total Slips	Approach/ Dockside Depth	Floating Docks	Gas/ Diesel	Repairs/ Haulout	Min/Max Amps	Pump-Out Station
DELEGAL CREEK										
1. Delegal Creek Marina WiFi 1.0 mi. E of MM 601	(912) 224-3885	88	16	58	3.5 / 15.0	F	GD		30 / 50	P
LITTLE OGEECHEE RIVER										
2. Coffee Bluff Marina	(912) 231-3628	200		20	25.0 /	F	GD	H	30 / 50	P
OGEECHEE RIVER										
3. Ft. McAllister Marina WiFi 6.0 mi. W of MM 605.5	(912) 727-2632	85	16	60	15.0 / 20.0	F	GD	H	30 / 50	P

WiFi Wireless Internet Access
Visit www.waterwayguide.com for current rates, fuel prices, website addresses and other up-to-the-minute information. (Information in the table is provided by the facilities.)

Scan here for more details:

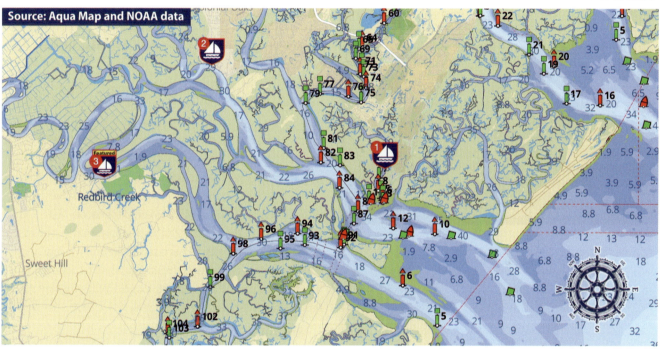
Source: Aqua Map and NOAA data

Leaving Hell Gate run beyond flashing green daybeacon "91" and round quick flashing red "92." Pay particular attention to the markers at the passage through Middle Marsh.

Carefully follow the markers, changing course as indicated to pass safely between Middle Marsh to the south (which is obscured at high tide) and the shoal north of red daybeacon "94" off Charles Creek's entrance.

Three miles north of Hells Gate, the ICW channel turns south off the Ogeechee River at Mile 605. The Ogeechee River is Georgia coast's second largest river and has a particularly strong ebb current.

From here, the Florida Passage flows into the Bear River, running the length of Ossabaw Island. One of Georgia's eight major Sea Islands, Ossabaw Island is pierced by a number of narrow but deep creeks fanning out from the Bear River.

Dockage: Delegal Creek makes off to the north at Mile 601 on the Vernon River just before Hell Gate. The marked channel leads to the well-regarded Delegal Creek Marina, a 60-slip marina in a beautiful setting. Marina guests can enjoy dining, tennis, pool and golf privileges offered by The Landings Club during their stay.

This is a well-known stopping point for transient boaters and the facility welcomes boats up to 150 feet. Call ahead on VHF Channels 16 or 68 to check depths and get directions for entering the marked channel prior to docking.

To the north on the Little Ogeechee River is Coffee Bluff Marina, which offers easy access and plenty of depth. If you score a slip, the sunset will be worth the effort.

Five miles up the Ogeechee River from flashing red daybeacon "98" (Florida Passage intersection) is Ft. McAllister Marina. This friendly marina has 15 acres of

Chapter 9: Stono River, SC to Ossabaw Sound, GA

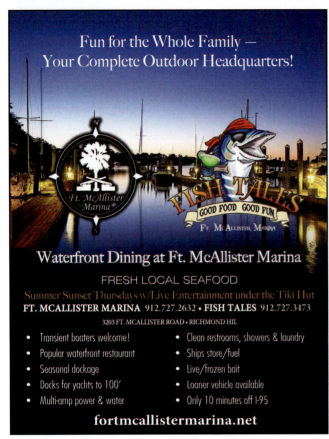

boat/RV storage (covered and open storage), offers repairs and has slips to 80 feet on floating docks. The on-site Fish Tales Restaurant (912-727-3473) is a lively waterfront eatery with a Caribbean flair at reasonable prices. They have live music most weekends.

To access Ft. McAllister Marina, continue north past the ICW turnoff at Mile 605 on the Ogeechee River. You will need to cross from the north to the south side of the river after passing charted Shad Island. The dockmaster can see vessels approaching and may contact you to offer guidance. If not, you should call the marina for directions on your approach.

This is one of those times when local knowledge is imperative. There are signs here that some find to be confusing, and it is easy to fetch up on the sandbar without proper directions. To further complicate matters, the channel in this rapidly flowing estuary is constantly shifting and even current charts may not be wholly accurate. Study charts carefully before heading upriver and refer to suggested tracks on Waterway Explorer (www.waterwayguide.com) before attempting passage.

At Mile 614 on the Bear River you can turn westward into Kilkenny Creek at ICW green daybeacon "107." The Texaco sign at the entrance is a good landmark. About 1.5 miles up from the marker is rural Kilkenny Marina, which welcomes transients to 100 feet. The marina reports that its entrance channel carries 10 feet MLW if you stay 30 feet north of the center of the creek.

Anchorage:

> NOTE: Parts of the St. Catherines Sound area (Bear and Medway River) are subject to anchoring restrictions. Be sure to check the interactive map online at Georgia Department of Natural Resources before anchoring.

Green Island Sound is a charted anchorage on the Vernon River and a great place to overnight in preparation for a transit of Hells Gate. Expect good holding and some protection from the east. Be sure not to anchor too close to the marker due to 180-degree swings.

There is a fine selection of anchorages in Redbird Creek north off the Florida Passage at Mile 606.8. Here you will find 6- to 18-foot MLW depths and good holding in mud. The current is very strong here so be sure to set your anchor well. Queen Bess Creek is directly across the Florida Passage with at least 4 feet MLW.

Ossabaw Sound, GA

KILKENNY CREEK		Largest Vessel	VHF	Total Slips	Approach/ Dockside Depth	Floating Docks	Gas/ Diesel	Repairs/ Haulout	Min/Max Amps	Pump-Out Station
1. Kilkenny Marina WiFi MM 614.0	(912) 727-2215	100	16	10	8.0 / 6.0	F	GD	H	30 / 50	

WiFi Wireless Internet Access
Visit www.waterwayguide.com for current rates, fuel prices, website addresses and other up-to-the-minute information.
(Information in the table is provided by the facilities.)

Scan here for more details:

At Mile 608.5 stay on the range until you are well past red daybeacon "102" then turn eastward up the Bear River to Cane Patch Creek or Buckhead Creek, then pick a spot with suitable depths and set the anchor well. Depths vary from 10 to 30 feet here and the current is exceptionally strong.

At Mile 612 you can turn north into Birthday Creek and anchor in 9- to 14-foot MLW depths with good holding in mud. Nearby Big Tom Creek at Mile 612.5 is a popular overnight anchorage. Anchor either near its entrance or around the first bend in 9-foot MLW depths.

Lincoln Creek, which branches off Kilkenny Creek south of the marina is open and exposed to all winds but offers great holding. Expect deep water (at least 10 feet MLW) from the ICW to the anchorage. There is plenty of swing room during tidal changes.

Kilkenny Creek provides a popular but peaceful spot to drop the hook with 15-foot MLW depths and a mud bottom. This anchorage borders the marsh, making insect screens and repellent essential.

For better protection, continue north past Kilkenny Marina to Kilkenny Creek North (2 miles north of the ICW). This anchorage offers 360-degree protection from waves and wind protection from the west.

Marker 107 Restaurant located just north of the marina provides shore access and a delicious meal with beautiful views of the creek.

There is considerable nighttime traffic from shrimp boats in Kilkenny Creek during the harvesting season so be sure your anchor light is working properly.

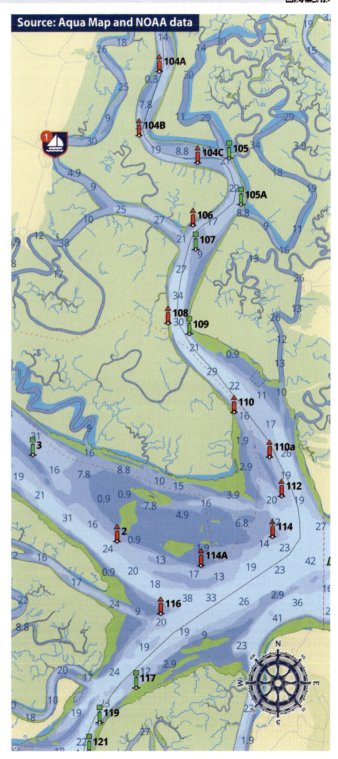

Source: Aqua Map and NOAA data

St. Catherines Sound to St. Marys, GA

Chapter 10

Chapter 10: St. Catherines Sound to St. Marys, GA

■ TO ALTAMAHA SOUND

> **CAUTION:** There are areas of known shoaling so care should be taken when navigating these waters as depths change constantly. Make sure that you are using current information including local knowledge when transiting the area. Be prepared for additional ATONs and changed buoy locations to assist safe passage. Be sure to check for depth updates and route suggestions at Waterway Explorer (www.waterwayguide.com) prior to traversing the area.

St. Catherines Sound–ICW Mile 618

NAVIGATION: St. Catherines Sound Entrance has a wide, uncomplicated entrance with good depths within. As with other smaller inlets in Georgia, channel markers are widely placed and it can be difficult to visually pick them out. Even though the offshore sea buoys are in their charted position and easy to locate with GPS, some of the smaller markers are frequently moved to locate better water.

Heading west from St. Catherines Sound Lighted Buoy "STC", turn in between green can "1" and flashing red "2" and head north to flashing green "5" in no less than 12 feet at MLW. (Or head straight from red and white "STC" to flashing green "5" where you may see 9-foot MLW depths.) The channel turns west toward green can "7."

For slow-moving northbound or southbound boats, the best time to arrive at St. Catherines Sound Entrance (Mile 618) is at low slack water, which occurs within 20 minutes of low tide at the Bear River Entrance NOAA station (#8673171). (See at www.tidesandcurrents.noaa.gov.) Tidal range is 7 to 8 feet.

Watch your course between Miles 615 and 617 and take care that wind and current do not set your vessel too far to the west.

To Sapelo River–Mile 635

NAVIGATION: A protected but seldom-used alternate to the ICW route along the exposed North Newport River is the charted Walburg Creek channel, which flows past the western shore of St. Catherines Island to join with the ICW route at Mile 623.

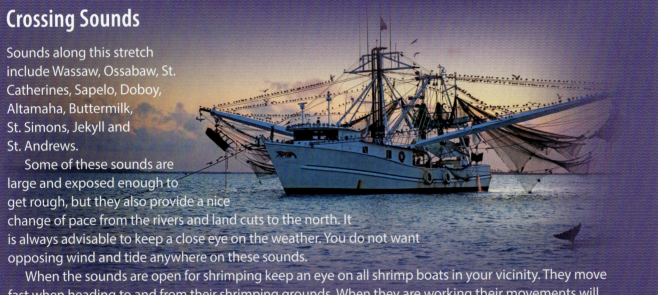

Crossing Sounds

Sounds along this stretch include Wassaw, Ossabaw, St. Catherines, Sapelo, Doboy, Altamaha, Buttermilk, St. Simons, Jekyll and St. Andrews.

Some of these sounds are large and exposed enough to get rough, but they also provide a nice change of pace from the rivers and land cuts to the north. It is always advisable to keep a close eye on the weather. You do not want opposing wind and tide anywhere on these sounds.

When the sounds are open for shrimping keep an eye on all shrimp boats in your vicinity. They move fast when heading to and from their shrimping grounds. When they are working their movements will be erratic and they will be occupied with their trailing nets so you will be the one to take evasive action.

Shrimpers often travel with their long "arms" extended so even if you are under sail, do not expect shrimp boats to alter course or raise their booms. They have been known to go under bridges with their "arms" partially or fully down, leaving no room for other boats. Stand well clear of them and keep your horn handy; five blasts is the danger signal.

America's Waterway Guide Since 1947 — Chapter 10

St. Catherines Sound, GA

MEDWAY RIVER		Largest Vessel	VHF	Total Slips	Approach/ Dockside Depth	Floating Docks	Gas/ Diesel	Repairs/ Haulout	Min/Max Amps	Pump-Out Station
1. Sunbury Crab Co. Restaurant & Marina WiFi MM 618.0	(912) 884-8640	125		28	/23.0	F	GD		30/100	

WiFi Wireless Internet Access
Visit www.waterwayguide.com for current rates, fuel prices, website addresses and other up-to-the-minute information.
(Information in the table is provided by the facilities.)

Scan here for more details:

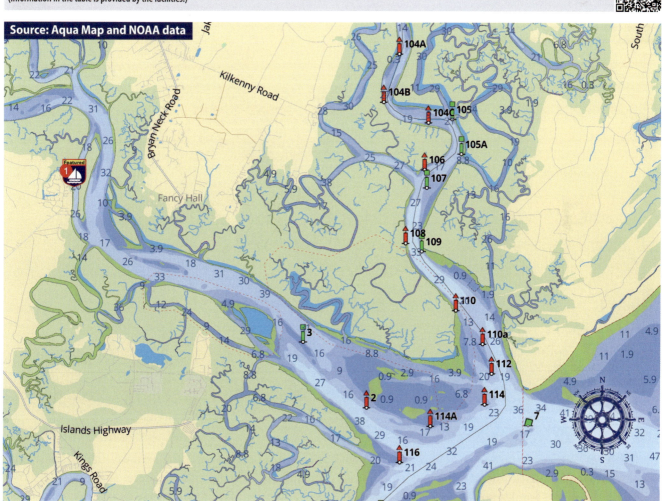

Source: Aqua Map and NOAA data

Green can buoy "7," which marks the end of the shoal at Middle Ground in St. Catherines Sound approaching Walburg Creek, needs to be honored if you intend to enter and anchor in Walburg Creek. Although the northern entrance to Walburg Creek (from St. Catherines Sound) is straightforward, the southern passage back into the North Newport River is tricky with depths of 4 to 5 feet MLW.

Beyond Mile 620 the ICW enters the mouth of the North Newport River and follows along that river to about Mile 623, where the North Newport River bears off to the west. The ICW channel continues south along Johnson Creek. Heading south along the ICW you will exit Johnson Creek for a short run along the South Newport River to its mouth.

MID-ATLANTIC EDITION

Chapter 10: St. Catherines Sound to St. Marys, GA

St. Catherines Sound, GA

THE HALFMOON

		Largest Vessel	VHF	Total Slips	Approach/ Dockside Depth	Floating Docks	Gas/ Diesel	Repairs/ Haulout	Min/Max Amps	Pump-Out Station
1. Halfmoon Marina WiFi 6.0 mi. W of MM 622.5	(912) 884-5819	100	16	10	15.0 / 60.0	F	GD		30 / 50	

WiFi Wireless Internet Access
Visit www.waterwayguide.com for current rates, fuel prices, website addresses and other up-to-the-minute information. (Information in the table is provided by the facilities.)

Scan here for more details:

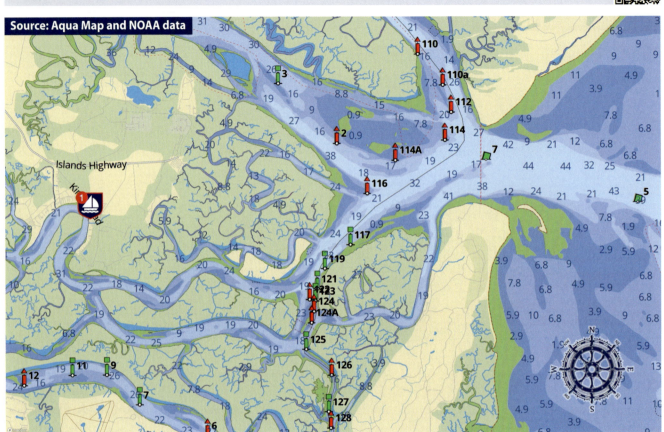

Source: Aqua Map and NOAA data

The ICW route heads up Sapelo Sound to the Sapelo River, running past Sapelo Island.

Dockage: About 6 miles northwest of St. Catherines Sound (from ICW Mile 618) on the Medway River is the popular Sunbury Crab Co. Restaurant & Marina. This is one of those fun, off-the-beaten-path places that is worth the few extra miles to go visit. The staff is friendly, they offer transient dockage to 125 feet and the restaurant offers large portions at reasonable prices in a relaxed, laid-back atmosphere. This place is funky, eclectic and fun.

To reach Sunbury pass between red flashing "114A" and "116" upriver and follow the chart. Cross to the west side of the river at Fancy Hall Creek (to starboard). There are no markers, just watch your depth sounder. As you approach Sunbury hug the western shore and enter the Sunbury channel between the unnamed island and the shore. Sunbury Crab Co. Restaurant & Marina will be the next to last docks on your left. (Look for signs.)

From flashing green daybeacons "119" and "121" (Mile 623.7) turn to the west and cruise 7 miles up the North Newport River to the small Halfmoon Marina, which offers space for transients at a competitive rate. You can also get there via the Timmons River a couple miles farther down the ICW.

Be advised that there are no markers on either side of these rivers in this area. Call the marina for directions and follow your chart plotter and depth sounder very carefully. The Halfmoon Marina is the last marina near the ICW southbound for the next 40 miles.

Anchorage: Walburg Creek can be accessed by traveling south from Mile 620 and provides splendid anchorages. There is a calm weather anchorage right off the ICW at Walburg Island Beach on the southwest corner of the island. The beach is not fully covered with water at high tide and is a nice place to let the dogs run. Note that the St. Catherines Island Foundation owns the island and limits visitation.

Enter the creek on the north side and drop anchor close to shore in at least 8-foot MLW depths. There is virtually no protection in any direction, so if winds exceed 5 or 10 knots, you'll be rocking. Expect some wake from passing boats.

For better protection, you can drop the hook in 15- to 20-foot MLW depths with good holding farther up Walburg Creek. Avoid anchoring in the bend of the creek off the southern tip of Walburg Island, where the water is deep and currents run swiftly. Shrimp boats often use this anchorage too so be sure that your anchor light is working properly.

On the North Newport River, pass green daybeacon "125" and proceed west for 500 yards or so. There is a muddy bottom here with about 9-foot MLW depths.

Cattle Pen Creek, south of Johnson Creek at Mile 625.5, provides a fine overnight anchorage for boats up to about 40 feet in length but may be too narrow for larger boats that need more swinging room. While the charted depths inside Cattle Pen Creek are good, expect entrance depths to be closer to 7 feet MLW rather than the 14 feet MLW shown on charts.

The marsh does not provide much protection from wind but the water is narrow enough that it does not get rough in the anchorage. It provides good holding in mud. The current can be strong but if you set your anchor well, there should not be a problem. As in all the marsh anchorages, this may be buggy.

Sapelo Sound Entrance

Sapelo Sound Entrance at Mile 632 is a favorite of area fishermen and shrimpers, not to mention legendary pirate Edward Teach (Blackbeard). You will pass just north of Blackbeard Island and Blackbeard Creek while transiting this inlet.

NAVIGATION: On Sapelo Sound, as well as other large sounds, give both lighted aids and daybeacons a wider berth than usual, especially around low tide. Keep track of your markers, running a compass course between distant ones. Many boats have erroneously run for an outlying sea buoy instead of a marker leading into a nearby tributary.

Mind the markers at the western end of Sapelo Sound where the ICW route enters the Sapelo River. At low tide approach the whole stretch with caution.

NOTE: Shrimp boats came and go at all hours and often have their outriggers down increasing their beam up to 120 feet, which consumes a large part of the channel.

Sapelo Sound

Chapter 10: St. Catherines Sound to St. Marys, GA

Current and trustworthy local knowledge required. From the sea buoy, proceed first to red nun buoy "2" and then head slightly south of west to green can buoy "3." Depths will drop from more than 20 feet down to 12 feet MLW along the way. If you see 10-foot MLW depths, you are in trouble and need to reverse course.

At green can buoy "5," you will see 20-plus-foot MLW depths return, and it is a simple matter of following the red buoys in until you meet up with the ICW past red nun buoy "10." (Note that some buoys may be off station or missing.)

Southbound cruisers hoping to avoid the Georgia ICW rarely use this inlet, preferring to jump offshore through the big ship channels at Charleston or Port Royal, SC, or Savannah, GA. This is not the best inlet in rougher weather due to extensive shoals to the north and south of the inlet.

Note that low slack water on Sapelo Sound Entrance occurs 30 minutes before it occurs at the Savannah River Entrance.

Anchorage: On the South Newport River you can anchor just out of the channel between green daybeacon "1" and red daybeacon "2" with good holding. There is very little light pollution, making this a good spot for star gazing.

Southbound out of Johnson Creek, the Wahoo River makes off the South Newport River portion of the ICW at Mile 630 and is a fine overnight anchorage. When entering the river be wary of the shoal that is located between the mouth of the Wahoo and the Newport River.

Proceed slightly past the mouth of the Wahoo River and turn back to avoid the shallow, well-marked shoal. Go northwest 1.2 miles and anchor by the stand of trees on the north shore. If you go as far as the 90-degree bend to the west be careful of the shoal on the north side as it is encroaching farther into the channel. The depth range throughout this area is 10 to 15 feet MLW in mud. This anchorage offers good wind protection from all sides and little traffic so no wakes. A primitive beach allows dog access but is very muddy. Watch for deer, snakes and wild boars on land.

To Doboy Sound–Mile 650

Continuing south the ICW route leaves the Sapelo River and enters the Front River. The Front River is narrow but deep in mid-channel. Many of the hammocks of land west of the channel show piles of ballast stone, which is all that remains of a once-prosperous riverside community.

The ICW route continues south along the Front River before heading into Creighton Narrows at Mile 642. Along the stretch through Creighton Narrows a succession of daybeacons and lights mark the channel; observe them carefully. When leaving Creighton Narrows and entering the Crescent River run straight past red daybeacon "156" until passing flashing green daybeacon "157" to avoid shallow depths to the west.

The marked channel leads you into Old Teakettle Creek, which widens as it reaches Doboy Sound at Mile 649. There is a constant shoal on Old Teakettle Creek between red daybeacons "158A" and "160."

Follow the outside of the bend passing red "160" by at least 170 off for 24 feet MLW.

Arriving at Doboy Sound at low slack water will speed up your run from Mile 644 to Mile 654. (Trying to hit low slack water at either Sapelo Sound or Buttermilk Sound is not quite as critical, as both of these sounds provide more open waters and easier currents to navigate.)

Doboy Sound Entrance with 7-foot controlling depths is not our first choice in bad weather. On the other hand, if you have to get in or out, it is uncomplicated and the breakwaters may give you some protection from south-setting waves once behind them. The preferred St. Simons Sound Entrance is 18 nm to the south.

To access the Doboy Sound Entrance, head slightly north of west from the sea buoy and continue in past the breakwaters to the north of red nun buoy "4." The channel shoals to 7 feet MLW approaching green can "3," then deepens again. Continue to red nun "8" on the northerly point of land in 20- to 40-foot depths.

Once in the sound, keep an eye out for shoaling. Breakwaters to the north and a long easterly shoal on the south side are the main hazards here. Aside from the sea buoy and flashing red "8," all of the aids to navigation in this inlet are unlighted, making it a difficult–if not dangerous– nighttime passage.

Anchorage:

NOTE: Parts of the Sapelo Sound area including the Mud River are subject to anchoring restrictions. Be sure to check the interactive map online at Georgia Department of Natural Resources before dropping the hook.

America's Waterway Guide Since 1947 **Chapter 10**

Some boats anchor to the west of where Creighton Narrows empties into the Crescent River at Mile 644. One of the main attractions is the sandy beach for pet relief by red daybeacon "156," which is dry during an 8-foot low tide.

You can also drop the hook farther upriver on the Crescent River (north) in 12- to 16-foot MLW depths. Nearby Cedar Creek is another option.

The most popular anchorage between Sapelo Sound and Doboy Sound is New Teakettle Creek at Mile 646.5. The charted depths are good (15 to 20 feet MLW) and the best protection lies around the first bend to starboard. Be careful to avoid the charted 2-foot MLW lump in New Teakettle Creek just past Mary Creek.

Another attractive anchorage is up the Duplin River at Mile 649. Go past the very busy ferry dock at Marsh Landing 1 mile or so to the high ground of Little Sapelo Island and anchor in 15 to 16 feet MLW. Note the overhead power cable upstream on the Duplin River with a 38-foot vertical clearance.

The holding here is very good and you will have plenty of swinging room as it is wide and deep to its banks. The current is swift but this is a good spot to spend the night. A lot of boats anchor here in order to stage for a favorable tide to transit the Little Mud River. Dinghy to the ferry dock and take a hike on the island. There are restrooms at the ferry dock.

To Altamaha Sound—ICW Mile 656
NAVIGATION:

CAUTION: Low slack water at Mile 655 occurs 38 minutes before it occurs at the Savannah River Entrance. At Mile 660, only 5 miles away, low slack water occurs 2 hours and 6 minutes before it does at Savannah. NOAA provides up-to-date tide tables online.

The ICW continues down Doboy Sound to quick-flashing red daybeacon "178" at the mouth of the North River (Mile 649.5). Follow the channel carefully here and in the dredged areas past the Darien, Rockdedundy and South Rivers. The range markers for this area that are shown on older charts have been removed. Mariners are advised to use extreme caution while transiting the area.

Darien River Waterfront Park & Docks along the Darien River

Chapter 10: St. Catherines Sound to St. Marys, GA

Darien Area, GA

DARIEN RIVER	Largest Vessel	VHF	Total Slips	Approach/Dockside Depth	Floating Docks	Gas/Diesel	Repairs/Haulout	Min/Max Amps	Pump-Out Station
1. Darien River Waterfront Park & Docks WiFi 7.0 mi. W of MM 655 (912) 437-3625	40		4	25.0 / 25.0	F			20 / 50	

WiFi Wireless Internet Access
Visit www.waterwayguide.com for current rates, fuel prices, website addresses and other up-to-the-minute information. (Information in the table is provided by the facilities.)

Scan here for more details:

The ICW follows a channel down Little Mud River (dredged only south of red daybeacon "194") to the Altamaha Sound and into Buttermilk Sound. Boaters consistently report shallower depths than the charts show in this area. Stay in the 75-foot dredged channel by following the track detailed at Waterway Explorer (www.waterwayguide.com).

It is best to plan this transit for a rising two-thirds tide. Crosscurrents can quickly push slow vessels out of the channel when exiting narrow stretches like the Little Mud River to enter open water like Altamaha Sound.

The Coast Guard has removed all markers from the Altamaha Sound entrance channel to and from the Atlantic Ocean (not part of the ICW) due to shoaling. Do not attempt to use this inlet to or from the ocean.

Watch for bare-land areas near the ICW channel in Altamaha Sound during extreme low tides, particularly in areas where the charts show less than 3 feet MLW.

Anchorage: If you know that the tide will be too low when you reach one of the well-known shallow areas like the Little Mud River, anchor for a while and let the tide rise before you enter.

There is an anchorage at the south end of Doboy Island (Mile 651.3) at Back River. The channel at the north entrance of the river is deeper than charted and expect to anchor in 8 to 11 feet MLW with good holding in sand. It provides protection from all except westerly winds. There is no shore access.

The Little Mud River at red daybeacon "182" is also a great anchorage. There is plenty of swing room and you can drop your anchor in 12 to 18 feet MLW with good holding. The current is moderate in this entire area. Local fishing boats will come by but that usually dies down around dinner time.

Side Trip: Darien River–ICW Mile 651.6

NAVIGATION: The Coast Guard has placed channel markers all the way to Darien, located 7 miles up the Darien River, which shrimp boats use heavily. Plan your passage for mid-tide and rising going off the ICW up the river. Some southbound cruisers have been tempted to return to the ICW from Darien via the slightly shorter route on the Rockdedundy River. We do not recommend this route. There are no markers of any kind on the Rockdedundy River and 3-foot MLW shoaling has been observed at the bends in the river as shown on the most recent NOAA chart.

Dockage: Cruising boats making the trip up the Darien River can find dockage at Darien River Waterfront Park & Docks. Be aware that there is an 8- to 9-foot tide and a ripping current. Dockage is limited and is strictly first-come, first-served and is not free but is very reasonable. There is a dockmaster available most times of the day. Reservations are recommended. Skipper's Fish Camp at Darien has dockage for diners (no shore power). This dock is available on a "first-come, first-served" basis. Call 912-437-3474.

■ THE GOLDEN ISLES

The "Golden Isles" area includes Little St. Simons Island, St. Simons Island, Sea Island, Brunswick and Jekyll Island. The largest of its sea islands, St. Simons Island is a draw for history buffs, golf and tennis players, nature lovers and, of course, boaters.

On the island's ocean side exclusive Sea Island is home to the fashionable 5-star Cloister Hotel and beautifully landscaped residences. Golf courses are plentiful on the islands and one near the Cloister hosts a yearly PGA tournament.

The downtown district in Brunswick (on the Brunswick River) features a growing mix of antique shops, specialty shops, art galleries, theaters and restaurants. With daily shrimping excursions heading in and out of Brunswick's harbor, there is plenty of fresh, local seafood to be had at Brunswick restaurants.

Finally, Jekyll Island is a staff favorite at Waterway Guide because of its historical significance and the natural beauty of the island. It is home to one of the Rockerfeller's favorite vacation homes, the Jekyll Island Club, which to this day has an air of wealth and sophistication.

To St. Simons Sound–ICW Mile 678

NAVIGATION: Heading south from Buttermilk Sound several sets of ranges guide you over the flats to the headwaters of the southward-flowing Mackay River. The South Althama River intercepts the ICW at Mile 662 (west side), while the Hampton River branches to the east at Mile 664. There are docking facilities up each of these rivers.

> NOTE: You may encounter high-speed, outboard-powered boats manned by uniformed personnel in the Althama River. You will find almost a dozen of these docked at Two Way Fish Camp, located 5 miles west of the ICW at Mile 662. They are operated by the nearby Federal Law Enforcement Training Center. This is where Customs and Border Patrol, marine patrols and other federal agents receive their boat training.

Flashing green "237" marks shallow water on the east bank. Keep red daybeacon "238" to starboard and continue along the Mackay River. The ICW turns to the west and continues down the Mackay River until it intersects with the lower end of the Frederica River and enters St. Simons Sound. Current charts show this correctly but some skippers still attempt to take the wrong route around the eastern side of Lanier Island only to be stopped by the 9-foot fixed vertical clearance bridge over the Frederica River.

The fixed **F.J. Torras Causeway Bridge** (65-foot vertical clearance) spans the Mackay River portion of the ICW at Mile 674.9. The current under this bridge is very strong. The 5-mile stretch from Mile 673 to Mile 678 is straightforward. The only problem area is the shoal south of Lanier Island. Leave flashing green "245A" and "247" well to port when passing. Flashing green daybeacon "249" has been moved and appears to be far to the east of the ICW channel. Leave this to port as well.

> *CAUTION:* There are areas of known shoaling so care should be taken when navigating these waters as depths change constantly. Make sure that you are using current information including local knowledge when transiting the area. Be prepared for additional ATONs and changed buoy locations to assist safe passage. Be sure to check for depth updates and route suggestions at Waterway Explorer prior to traversing the area.

Chapter 10: St. Catherines Sound to St. Marys, GA

Hampton River, GA

LITTLE ST. SIMON ISLAND AREA		Largest Vessel	VHF	Total Slips	Approach/ Dockside Depth	Floating Docks	Gas/ Diesel	Repairs/ Haulout	Min/Max Amps	Pump-Out Station
1. Two Way Fish Camp WiFi 5.0 mi. W of MM 664.0	(912) 265-0410	70	16	110	/ 15.0	F	GD	RH	30 / 50	
2. Hampton River Marina WiFi 3.5 mi. E of MM 664.0	(912) 638-1210	40	71	20	12.0 / 14.0	F	GD	R	30 / 50	
ST. SIMONS ISLAND										
3. Morningstar Marinas Golden Isles WiFi N of MM 677.0	(912) 434-4751	200	16	137	10.0 / 18.0	F	GD	R	30 / 100	P

WiFi Wireless Internet Access
Visit www.waterwayguide.com for current rates, fuel prices, website addresses and other up-to-the-minute information.
(Information in the table is provided by the facilities.)

Scan here for more details:

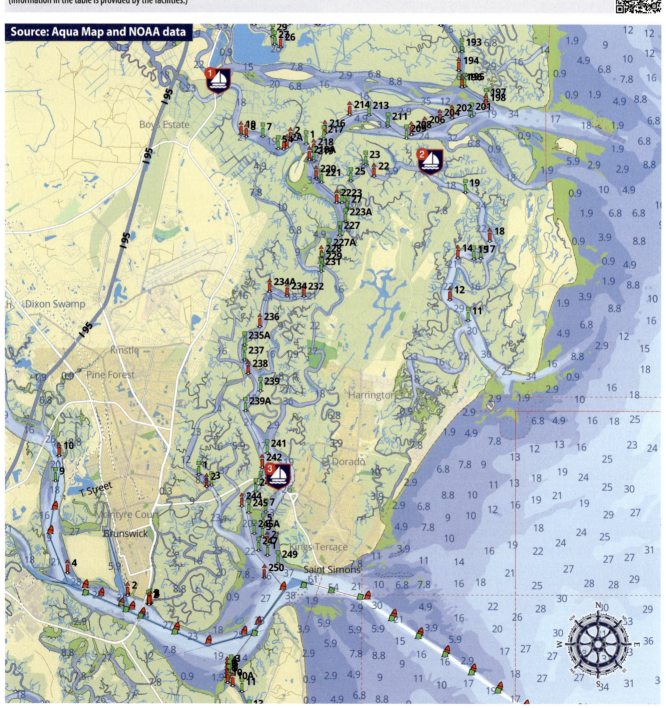

Dockage: Two Way Fish Camp, located 5 miles west of the ICW at Mile 662 on the South Althama River, usually has transient space in a natural setting with friendly people. Bait, tackle and sundries are available in the ship store. Mudcat Charlie's (912-261-0055) is on site offering good food at reasonable prices.

The current here can be fierce. If approaching the fuel dock during times of maximum current flow, stand by until the current slackens before you approach the dock. Contact the fuel dock for instructions.

About 3 miles up the marked channel of the Hampton River at Mile 664, you will find the Hampton River Marina set amidst the naturally beautiful marsh. The full-service marina welcomes transients if space is available (with slips to 40 feet). This 6-acre operation includes are wet slips, dry stack and trailer storage, boat maintenance, a ship store and bait. Call before making plans to stop here.

To reach Hampton River Marina follow the Hampton River abruptly back to port at Mile 664 between flashing green "223" and "223A." Note that shoaling extends into the channel from both riverbanks up to green daybeacon "27." Proceed slowly and watch the depth sounder. Daybeacons farther downstream mark some of the shoals so pass wide of the markers. At green daybeacon "21" the chart shows a slot of 4 foot MLW but there are reports of the water being substantially deeper.

Morningstar Marinas Golden Isles is 2 miles north of Mile 676 on the east side of Lanier Island. This facility is south of the low bridge (9-foot vertical clearance) across the Frederica River connecting Lanier Island with St. Simons Island so it must be approached from the south. When entering and exiting the marked channel to the marina, follow the chart carefully and do not confuse these channel markers with the ICW markers nearby. The markers may differ from what is shown on your NOAA chart.

A pool, laundry facilities and a fully-stocked ship store are among the ample amenities at Morningstar Marinas Golden Isles. On site are charter fishing, a dive shop, boat brokers and a restaurant. The marina provides immediate access to historic St. Simons Island located just over the bridge. The configuration of the docks eases current issues, although there is still a strong current running parallel to the docks so be sure you have fenders rigged before you come alongside.

Anchorage: At Altamaha Sound you can anchor behind Dolbow Island at Mile 659 where there is 13 to 20 feet MLW and fair holding in soft mud. This is a quiet anchorage close to the inlet and the ICW.

The South Altamaha River at Mile 662 is deep and well marked with a 7-foot MLW bar at the entrance near red daybeacon "218." Holding is good in 7 to 20 feet MLW with a mud bottom and is protected from all but the southeast. The anchorage is large but the current tears through it so we recommend using two anchors. A sandy beach and pine tree-covered bank is accessible by tender where the river enters the waterway.

At Mile 666.5 west off the main ICW route (Mackay River), Wallys Leg opens up to the west into a good anchorage but only in fair weather. Wind from the east can be annoying but if out of the west, it will blow your socks off!

Enter mid-stream opposite flashing green "231" and then favor the north shore; go in slowly and use the depth sounder. Anchor in 10- to 12-foot MLW depths off the clump of trees to the north. Holding is good but the current is strong so know the state of the tide and set your anchor well. This anchorage can get crowded in season but there is room for several boats.

Jove Creek at Mile 671 off the Mackay River is an anchoring option near red daybeacon "238." This offers wave protection but little wind protection. The bottom gets harder deeper into creek and around the first bend. Stay closer to the mouth for better holding.

The popular Hawkings Creek anchorage on the Frederica River offers good holding and deep water (17 to 20 feet MLW). There is shore access at the 2-hour free dock just north of the bridge. There is a beautiful park with live oaks and sandy paths. Clean restrooms and a filtered water machine are here as well.

Just slightly below Morningstar Marinas Golden Isles, south of the 9-foot fixed vertical clearance bridge, the Coast Guard has established a special anchorage area in 10 to 14 feet MLW (Lanier Island South). Yachts measuring 65 feet or less are not required to show anchor lights in the area but it is a good idea to do so anyway.

The bottom is hard in some places and it is difficult to get the anchor set. Pick a spot clear of the few (private) moorings and be mindful of the current. Wakes can be a problem at the outer end of the anchorage near green daybeacon "7."

Chapter 10: St. Catherines Sound to St. Marys, GA

St. Simons Sound Area, GA

		Largest Vessel	VHF	Total Slips	Approach/ Dockside Depth	Floating Docks	Gas/ Diesel	Repairs/ Haulout	Min/Max Amps	Pump-Out Station
BRUNSWICK										
1. Brunswick Landing Marina, Inc. WiFi NW of MM 680.0	(912) 262-9264	250	16	347	36.0 / 12.0	F	GD	RH	30 / 100	P
JEKYLL ISLAND										
2. Jekyll Harbor Marina WiFi MM 684.5	(912) 635-3137	120	16	49	12.0 / 10.0	F	GD		30 / 100	P

WiFi Wireless Internet Access
Visit www.waterwayguide.com for current rates, fuel prices, website addresses and other up-to-the-minute information. (Information in the table is provided by the facilities.)

Scan here for more details:

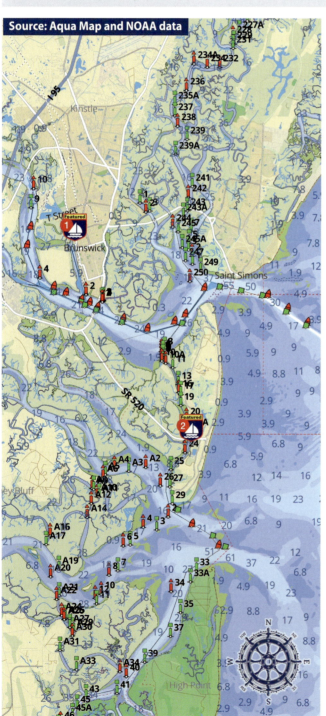

Source: Aqua Map and NOAA data

Morningstar Marinas Golden Isles provides dinghy dockage for a fee. The dinghy area is the slip directly behind the office on dock. Transportation will be needed for provisioning of any type.

Gascoine Bluff Park Free Dock is nearby with 45 feet of dockage space on the end of a fishing pier and a 2-hour, daytime use only restriction. This is a nice place to stretch your legs after day of cruising. You may even catch a ride to the grocery store (located almost 2 miles away).

Alternate Route: Frederica River (North)– ICW Mile 666

Fort Frederica National Monument preserves the archaeological remnants of a fort and town built by James Oglethorpe between 1736 and 1748 to protect the southern boundary of the British colony of Georgia from Spanish raids. About 630 British troops were stationed at the fort. A Visitor Center (with a bookstore and restrooms), a 23-minute informational movie and ranger programs make this worth a visit (912-638-3630).

NAVIGATION: At Mile 666 and flashing green "229" the Frederica River heads off the ICW to the east. This makes for a fun side trip as you wend your way north or south along the ICW. Slightly more scenic than the ICW in this area, the Frederica River flows past St. Simons Island, rejoins the ICW farther down the Mackay River at approximately Mile 674 and then continues under the 65-foot fixed F.J. Torras Causeway Bridge (Mile 674.5).

Take care if you are entering the Frederica River with the current. A bar protrudes from below flashing green daybeacon "229" and the current seems to split here. Keep well to the north side at the entrance and don't hesitate. Do not confuse flashing green "229" (flashing every 2.5 seconds) with flashing green daybeacon "231" (flashing every 4 seconds) at the entrance to Wallys Leg. Though winding and unmarked, this slightly longer side route runs deep to the shore except at the mouth of the lower

America's Waterway Guide Since 1917

Chapter 10

Lanier Island

ICW

Morningstar Marinas Golden Isles on the Frederica River

end at Manhead Sound where the water depth is 5 feet MLW midway between the two banks.

Anchorage: Many cruisers like to anchor in the Frederica River (North) off the Fort Frederica National Monument in 9 to 20 feet MLW. Visits ashore are possible at some states of the tide but be mindful that the tide can sometimes rise and fall 2 feet in an hour during the middle of the cycle. During a low tide dinghies can be left high and dry making re-entry into the water difficult, if not impossible.

Brunswick

Known as the "Gateway to the Golden Isles," the "Land of Five Flags" and the birthplace of the original Brunswick stew, Brunswick now boasts a revitalized commercial and residential historic district. (If you are visiting in November, don't miss the Brunswick Rockin' Stewbilee featuring live music, a cook-off competition and plenty of stew to sample.)

The British gave the town its name from Braunsweig, Germany, the ancestral home of King George III; however, five nations have claimed this area of Georgia as their own. First, explorer Hernando de Soto raised the Spanish flag in 1540; followed by Frenchman Jean Ribault in 1562; then the Spanish expelled the French in 1565 and ruled again until 1736, when the British flag flew until the Revolutionary War. The American flag was lowered during the Civil War, replaced by the stars and bars of the Confederate flag until 1865, when the United States flag was raised once again. All these flags can be found flying at the marina.

Brunswick has been a port city since the 1700s and in addition to the cargo and shrimp traffic, the J.A. Jones Company built 99 Liberty Ships in three years during World War II. The shipyard set an unbroken record in December 1944 by constructing seven ships in one month. See a scale model of a Liberty ship at the Mary Ross Waterfront Park at 209 Gloucester St. (912-267-2600).

NAVIGATION: St. Simons Sound Entrance is the straightforward entrance to Brunswick and an all-weather inlet; nevertheless, it can be rough when the wind and current are opposed. From the sea buoy, proceed northwesterly to quick flashing red buoy "16" on the range, then turn to port and pick up Plantation Creek Range. Be sure to start from the sea buoy due to shallows that extend quite far from shore. Channel shallows very rapidly outside of the markers, and ebb current is quite strong at the mouth of the inlet. This is a busy entrance; keep watch for big ships transiting the inlet.

Extra care should be taken and be sure to study the weather before venturing into St. Simons Sound. Heading north you can arrive at Mile 678 at low slack water and ride the flood current up the Mackay River.

MID ATLANTIC EDITION

Chapter 10: St. Catherines Sound to St. Marys, GA

Brunswick Landing Marina, Inc.

When heading up the Brunswick River in the vicinity of red flashing "20A" and "22" note that the charted sandbar to the north is a spoils island created with dredge material from a deepening of the entrance to St. Simons Sound. A rock bulkhead surrounds the island, which is highly visible in daylight; however, if you are traveling at night or in other conditions of poor visibility be sure to stay in the marked channel as the warning beacons around this island are not lit or currently charted.

This route leads in a westerly direction before turning north at flashing green "1" and heading to downtown Brunswick. Crossing the shipping channel is the Sidney Lanier Bridge, which carries SR 17. The suspension bridge has more than 185 feet of clearance, is visible for several miles and is one of the more scenic bridges on the ICW. The town of Brunswick is located just north of the bridge.

Dockage: In a hurricane hole off the Brunswick River, the 20-acre Brunswick Landing Marina, Inc. is in the center of Brunswick's Historic District. Head north at flashing green "1" then follow the Brunswick Harbor range markers to the marina just beyond the shrimp boat docks. This marina is protected from all directions and has little current making maneuvering easy. The marina's boatyard and lift are north of the transient facilities.

Anchorage: The anchorage at Blythe Island is near a cargo shipping dock and Blythe Park. This is a quiet spot with 14-foot MLW. There is a dock at Blythe Island Park that you tie a dinghy to for free. The park has a kids playground and picnic tables as well as open restrooms. You can anchor to the north in deeper water but less swing room and some traffic noise.

Jekyll Island–ICW Mile 679

With wide-open beaches, a treasure trove of historical sites and 24 miles of paths and trails, Jekyll Island is a "must see" coastal destination. Read more at Visit Jekyll Island (www.jekyllisland.com).

NAVIGATION: Heading south from St. Simons Island the ICW crosses St. Simons Sound and runs 3 miles up the Brunswick River to the mouth of Jekyll Creek (Mile 681), which flows between Jekyll Island and marshland. From there the ICW proper continues south down Jekyll Creek, which eventually flows into Jekyll Sound located farther south.

Jekyll Creek is dredged occasionally; however, this is a constantly changing area so be alert. The dredged channel is only 75 feet wide and has been moved farther east than the old channel.

> *CAUTION:* The tidal range for Jekyll Creek is 7 to 9 feet and is greatly affected by wind tides. An east wind of 15 knots or greater will add 1 foot to the depths, while a west wind will lessen the depths by 1 foot. The channel is also affected by the tugs that pass through. Conditions are going to be variable so plan to traverse the area near high tide or at least on a rising tide.

The charted Jekyll Island Range you will use to approach Jekyll Creek has unusual characteristics. The dayboard for green daybeacon "1," located on the front structure of this set of range markers, is difficult to see northbound and confusing to line up with when southbound. A range (labeled "Jekyll I Range" on the chart) leads past a single stone jetty on the red side between the red daybeacons at the entrance to the creek, which is submerged at high tide. Be aware that this jetty extends from the shore all the way out to flashing red "4." Because the current sets strongly to the side be sure to follow the range until past this jetty. Jekyll Island (SR 520) Bridge crosses the ICW at 684.6.

Dockage: Jekyll Harbor Marina is on the south side of the high-rise Jekyll Island (SR 520) Bridge. Transient slips are on the outside of the linear dock with easy tie-up but occasional wave action from passing boats. This is the last marina before St. Marys so be sure to fuel up and provision if necessary. Fuel will not be available again until Fernandina Beach at about Mile 716.

This service-oriented facility has slips for vessels to 120 feet and offers loaner bikes and golf carts. A grocery, package store, bank, Post Office and such are a 20-minute bike ride. The historic district is 10 minutes away.

Anchorage:

> NOTE: Parts of the Jekyll Sound area are subject to anchoring restrictions. Be sure to check the interactive map online at Georgia Department of Natural Resources before anchoring here.

Southwest of Jekyll Harbor Marina drop your anchor for at least 7 feet MLW north of red daybeacon "24" (Jekyll Island R24). Holding is excellent to the north or south of the daybeacon.

You can land the dinghy at the marina for a daily fee and have access to their many amenities. This is perfect for taking your dog to shore or just for getting out and stretching your legs.

Across from Jekyll Island there is a good anchorage in Umbrella Creek with 10 to 15 feet MLW, good holding in mud and no traffic. There is, however, no wind protection and lots of current.

■ TO ST. MARYS, GA

> *CAUTION:* There are areas of known shoaling so care should be taken when navigating these waters as depths change constantly. Make sure that you are using current information including local knowledge when transiting the area. Be prepared for additional ATONs and changed buoy locations to assist safe passage. Be sure to check for depth updates and route suggestions at Waterway Explorer prior to traversing the area.

Cumberland River

The ICW route at the mouth of St. Andrew Sound just north of Cumberland Island marks the closest spot to the ocean on the ICW south of Norfolk, VA. Look to the northwest and you will be looking back at the ocean side of Jekyll Island.

Cumberland Island, behind which the ICW winds for more than 20 miles, was once the center of controversy over development plans. It achieved its protected status as a National Seashore decades ago, ensuring that most

Chapter 10: St. Catherines Sound to St. Marys, GA

Goin' Ashore
JEKYLL ISLAND, GA

ATTRACTIONS

1. Faith Chapel
Charming circa 1904 church at 375 Riverview Dr. that features whimsical animal carvings, terra cotta gargoyles, and Tiffany and Armstrong stained glass windows. Open daily, 8:00 a.m. to 10:00 a.m. Tour offered daily from 10:00 a.m. to 4:00 p.m. (included with purchase of museum tour or tickets sold separately).

2. Georgia Sea Turtle Center
Educational center that serves as a hospital for ill and injured sea turtles with interactive exhibits and experiences. Open daily from 9:00 a.m. to 5:00 p.m. at 214 Stable Rd. Call ahead for admission fee (912-635-4444).

3. Goodyear Cottage
White stucco home (circa 1906) on Riverview Dr. now used as a Center for Creative Arts, housing both the Jekyll Island Art Association and the Jekyll Island Pottery Guild. Exhibits change monthly.

4. Indian Mound Cottage
William and Almira Rockefeller's spacious vacation home, named for the on-site Indian burial mound. Daily tours are offered of the house and a collection of historic artifacts on the hour from 10:00 a.m. to 4:00 p.m. Located on Riverview Drive.

5. Jekyll Island Club Resort
Established as a retreat for wealthy families in 1888. Castle-like resort includes five buildings at 371 Riverview Dr. (888-445-3179).

6. Jekyll Island Museum
Housed in a former stable with exhibits, a gift shop and tour opportunities at 100 Stable Rd. (912-635-4036). Open daily from 9:00 a.m. to 5:00 p.m.

7. Plantation Oak
Largest and oldest tree on the island at 375 Riverview Dr. Dates to the mid-17th century and is 7 feet 8 inches in diameter.

SERVICES

8. Jekyll Island Post Office
17 Pier Rd. (912-635-2625)

MARINAS

9. Jekyll Harbor Marina
1 Harbor Rd. (912-635-3137)

America's Waterway Guide Since 1947

Chapter 10

From early settlers to America's social elite to today's young explorers, the story of this Georgia barrier island has captured imaginations for generations. Strolling along the wide, cabbage palm and oak-lined streets is a pleasant way to check out the Colonial, antebellum and Victorian homes, several of which are now inns. The best way to explore Jekyll Island is by bicycle. More than 20 miles of well-marked paths lead to majestic forests, saltwater marshes, wide-open beaches, historic ruins and opulent cottages. Stop at Driftwood Beach, known for its driftwood trees and a popular spot for photographers.

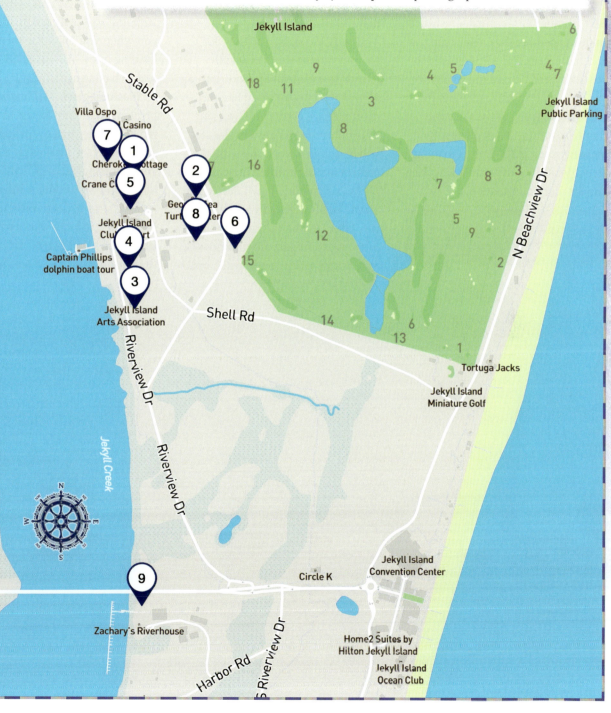

MID ATLANTIC EDITION 373

Chapter 10: St. Catherines Sound to St. Marys, GA

of the island will remain in its primitive state. No road or causeway from the mainland will ever be constructed. Public land acquisition continues today and the federal government owns approximately 85 percent of the island.

Most visitors arrive via ferry service from St. Marys, a 45-minute trip. However you arrive, you will find 50 miles of maritime forest trails, undeveloped beaches, wide marshes and more than 150 wild horses that have survived here in the wild since the Spanish originally set them free. Dungeness, ruins of the Carnegie family mansion, is a good spot for viewing some of the horses roaming freely. Visit the National Park Service site for more information.

NOTE: You will need insect repellent on Cumberland Island in the spring, summer and fall.

NAVIGATION: The ICW route becomes progressively more complicated as it approaches the Cumberland Dividings Channel and Cumberland Sound. This whole route is subject to shoaling (including St. Andrew Sound inlet), which is why many cruisers opt to jump outside at the preferred St. Simons Sound Entrance just a few miles to the north.

The ICW passage crosses St. Andrew Sound south of Jekyll Island. A stiff onshore wind running against the current can make the short passage across very wet and uncomfortable. As always, the seas will be calmest when the wind and current are in the same direction.

After transiting Jekyll Creek, give a wide berth to Jekyll Point. Green can "29A" marks the end of a shoal in the seaward part of St. Andrew Sound; this point continues to build out. You can see the remains of a sunken shrimp boat at low tide close inshore of flashing green "29."

Set your course for quick-flashing red "32," the more easterly of two red lighted buoys far out in the sound. If timed correctly, you will have a fair current on the ICW from about Mile 685 to a little past Mile 700. Otherwise, the current will be going with you in one direction and against you when you make the turn at red flashing buoy "32" (Mile 689) with seas behaving accordingly.

Flashing green "31" marks the breakers to the northwest of flashing red "32." This area of shallow water and breakers is marked by the two green floating aids ("31" and "31A") but is slowly building southward and the strip of deep water marked by flashing red "32" has narrowed. Inside the flashing red "30" and "32" the bottom not only shoals but also

Cumberland Sound

shelters the sunken remains of old wrecks. A shoal has built out approximately 150 feet east of red buoy "32."

Once you round flashing red buoy "32" you can safely head into the wide entrance of the Cumberland River and southward down the ICW. Heading south into the Cumberland River you will pass two markers at the northern tip of Little Cumberland Island: flashing green "33" on the northern tip and green daybeacon "33A" just beyond.

> NOTE: Even though there is a large house visible on the St. Andrew Sound shore of Little Cumberland Island, a sign on the island warn against any landings as this is a wildlife sanctuary.

An alternate route with 6 feet MLW can be taken when heavy seas are running at flashing red buoy "32." This entails turning southwest at green can "29A" and following the marked channel to green daybeacon "7." Turn east here into the deep (unmarked) channel and follow to flashing green "33" (and the ICW) at Cumberland Island.

Anchorage: There are many options for anchoring along this route. On the Cumberland River in the bight just east of flashing green "37" at Mile 693 you will find a fair-weather anchorage protected only from east and southeast winds. Avoid the shoal marked by flashing green daybeacon "37" and drop the hook in about 10 feet MLW.

This anchorage is away from the Cumberland River traffic but gets uncomfortable with wind from any direction except east. Pull in farther behind the unnamed island at flashing green "37" for more protection.

Holding is great with there is plenty of swing room at Floyd Creek off the Cumberland River (Mole 695.6). Expect at least 17 feet MLW. Nighttime commercial shrimp boat traffic makes this a less desirable anchorage.

Shelbine Creek at Mile 698 is a lovely anchorage in the middle of the marshes. Enter the creek at green daybeacon "43" and drop anchor in the first creek to the southwest. Pull in halfway to the charted sandbar in 12 feet at MLW.

To the south at Delaroche Creek (Mile 702) is another great spot. You will find at least 12 feet MLW east of the junction with the (unnamed) creek coming in from the south.

South of the Brickhill River you can anchor in the Crooked River west of the ICW with charted depths of 8 to 13 feet MLW at Mile 703.8. Here you will find soft mud so anchor accordingly.

Side Trip: Brickhill River

NAVIGATION: At Mile 703.5 the deep but unmarked Brickhill River joins the ICW route above Cumberland Sound at quick-flashing red "60A." Note that markers are frequently missing in this area and the entire area is subject to shoaling. Enter the Brickhill River slowly and watch the depth sounder. Favor the green side for the channel.

Anchorage: On the Brickhill River North, 1.5 miles northeast of ICW Mile 696, you can anchor in 9 to 20 feet MLW just north of the Plum Orchard Plantation dock on Cumberland Island. Much of Brickhill Creek is deep (25 to 30 feet MLW). If the anchorage is full, anchor just past the bend on the inner side with good holding over a large area.

You can anchor just north of the dock at Plum Orchard Plantation (Cumberland Island). If coming from the south, enter the Brickhill River slowly and watch the depth sounder.

Dinghy ashore and you will be rewarded with a walk among huge live oaks draped with Spanish moss and a view of the well-preserved mansion. Plum Orchard, one of the Carnegie family estates, was built in 1898. If you are fortunate, you may encounter a family of wild horses grazing on the lawn or alligators swimming in the anchorage. (No swimming!)

Alternate Route: Umbrella, Dover and Floyd Creeks–ICW Mile 686

NAVIGATION:

> *CAUTION:* There are areas of known shoaling so care should be taken when navigating these waters as depths change constantly. Make sure that you are using current information including local knowledge when transiting the area. Be prepared for additional ATONs and changed buoy locations to assist safe passage.

If you want to avoid St. Andrew Sound and the Cumberland River, a 15-mile-long alternate, foul-weather route avoids the direct crossing. This shallow route, via Umbrella, Dover and Floyd Creeks, is charted and reasonably easy to run. It will add approximately 5 miles to the ICW route and there are some very shallow spots. Shallow-draft vessels may attempt this route but only on a rising tide.

A set of markers leads across Jekyll Sound at Mile 686 and into the Little Satilla River, where you can enter Umbrella Creek via the land cut at flashing green "A5." Enter Umbrella Cut dead on its centerline instead of trying to line up with the two markers. During strong northeast winds, high water makes it more difficult to navigate by obscuring much of the marsh grass along the shores of Umbrella Creek.

Dover Cut, which connects Umbrella Creek with Dover Creek, is narrow and winding with 8-foot MLW charted depths. Continuing along this alternate route a straight land cut connects Dover Creek to the Satilla River, which is easily followed for 1.75 miles to the entrance of Floyd Creek, the next section of the alternate route.

One shoal area to watch for is at the junction of Floyd Creek and Floyd Basin from green daybeacon "A21" to just past green daybeacon "A31" with a charted controlling depth of 8.5 feet MLW. From here on it is smooth sailing out to red daybeacon "40" in the center of the Cumberland River and back on the ICW at Mile 696.

St. Marys River Entrance

NAVIGATION: The Cumberland Sound Range starts at Mile 705. Take time here to sort out the mosaic of lights, markers and ranges now serving the huge government installation on Kings Bay at Mile 708. This stretch is well marked and sufficiently deep but watch the depth sounder. Shoaling also exists near the range markers northwest of Drum Point Island.

The ICW fronts the Kings Bay Naval Submarine Base near Mile 708 and Navy security patrols carefully monitor traffic from both directions, especially when submarines are passing through Cumberland Sound and the St. Marys River Entrance. Kings Bay and the area west of the ICW channel here are strictly off limits to cruising skippers. No-Wake Zones have been established in this vicinity and are strictly enforced.

The active Kings Bay Naval Submarine Base continues to be the reason for the frequent dredging and renumbering of buoys, beginning where the ICW joins the

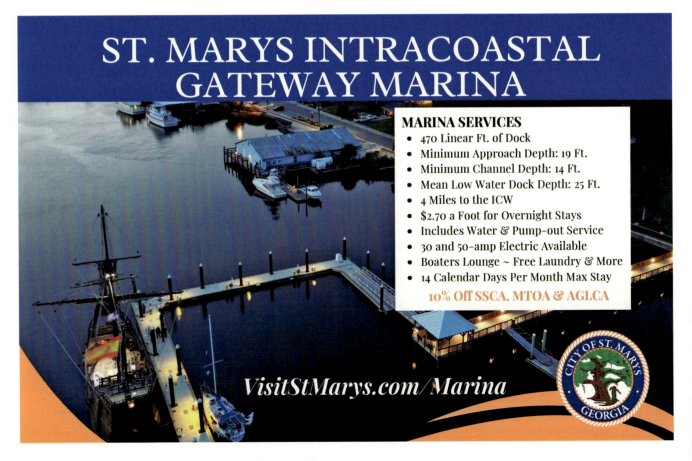

ST. MARYS INTRACOASTAL GATEWAY MARINA

MARINA SERVICES
- 470 Linear Ft. of Dock
- Minimum Approach Depth: 19 Ft.
- Minimum Channel Depth: 14 Ft.
- Mean Low Water Dock Depth: 25 Ft.
- 4 Miles to the ICW
- $2.70 a Foot for Overnight Stays
- Includes Water & Pump-out Service
- 30 and 50-amp Electric Available
- Boaters Lounge ~ Free Laundry & More
- 14 Calendar Days Per Month Max Stay

10% Off SSCA, MTOA & AGLCA

VisitStMarys.com/Marina

Chapter 10

Cumberland Sound, GA

ST. MARYS		Largest Vessel	VHF	Total Slips	Approach/Dockside Depth	Floating Docks	Gas/Diesel	Repairs/Haulout	Min/Max Amps	Pump-Out Station
1. St. Marys Intracoastal Gateway Marina	(912) 540-7230	130	16	12	14.0 / 25.0	F		R	30 / 50	P

WiFi Wireless Internet Access
Visit www.waterwayguide.com for current rates, fuel prices, website addresses and other up-to-the-minute information.
(Information in the table is provided by the facilities.)

Scan here for more details:

Source: Aqua Map and NOAA data

head of Cumberland Sound and continuing to the ocean inlet. Older charts may not show this change. Remember, the ICW daybeacons all have a yellow square or yellow triangle to designate them as ICW markers.

Patrol boats will ask you to move outside of the ICW channel if a submarine is in the vicinity and there is plenty of water off of the main channel. Patrol boats respond on VHF Channel 16. The submarines travel at high speeds in open water creating very large wakes.

St. Marys River Entrance at Mile 714 is a relatively easy entry and exit point conveniently located just off the ICW. The inlet is deep, wide and jettied. The entrance is well marked starting with lighted sea buoy "STM." From red daybeacon "10" proceed due west into Cumberland Sound. The current in this inlet is very strong and dictates appropriate boat handling to compensate.

Both the St. Johns Entrance Channel and the St. Simons Inlet involve long entry channels and strong currents to return to the ICW so be careful and try to plan exits and entries with a slack current or fair tide.

Slower boats are well advised to time their passages for slack water or a favorable tide. There are poorly marked jetties on both the north and south sides that are mostly SUBMERGED at high tide. Don't cut the corner and make sure you account for the single mark at the end of the jetty. Some shoal sections to the north of the channel inside the jetty.

> NOTE: When continuing southbound out of Cumberland Sound to the Florida line, the green markers will be left to starboard until you pick up quick-flashing green buoy "1" in the Amelia River near Mile 715.

St. Marys

St. Marys is a relaxing stop known for its Southern charm. Attractions include the downtown historic district, the St. Marys Submarine Museum and Crooked River State Park. St. Marys is a "cruiser friendly" location. There is even a "Cruisers Net" at 8:00 a.m. daily on VHF Channel 68. During the net you can get information about town activities and announcements along with help, if needed, and also make arrangements for transportation.

The ferry that takes visitors to Cumberland Island leaves from St. Marys. You can buy tickets at the Cumberland Island Visitor Center (912-882-4336). The ferry makes several trips a day from the waterfront and runs daily March through November. December through February finds a reduced schedule of Thursday through Monday.

MID-ATLANTIC EDITION

Chapter 10: St. Catherines Sound to St. Marys, GA

Goin' Ashore: ST. MARYS, GA

St. Marys is the southernmost point along Georgia's 110-mile coastline and is easily accessible from the ICW from the St. Marys/Cumberland Sound Entrance. St. Marys' small-town setting is idyllic & the opportunities to enjoy the laid-back vibe are endless. There's an array of historic sites, attractions, and events to ensure a great visit and the charming downtown area is lined with locally owned shops, historic homes, and restaurants serving up coastal-casual fare. There's no shortage of things to do, from a trip to Cumberland Island to attending a concert in the park, a memorable experience is up for grabs.

Come discover for yourself why *Southern Living Magazine* lists St. Marys among "Georgia's Best Coastal Towns."

Chapter 10 — America's Waterway Guide Since 1947

ATTRACTIONS

1. Cumberland Island National Seashore Museum
Houses artifacts from the island including the famed Carnegie lifestyle and the Timucuan Indians. War of 1812 Display Room demonstrates the events that occurred as one of the last battles of the war was fought at St. Marys' Point Peter area (129 Osborne St., 912-552-4336).

2. NPS Visitor Center
Hosts exhibits of island life and ecology with great views of the St. Marys River. Departure point for the ferry to Cumberland Island National Seashore. Ferry runs daily March to November with limited schedule December through February at 113 W. St. Marys St. (912-882-4336).

3. Farm to Family
Specializes in produce, small batch and specialty foods, cheeses, meats and Georgia wild caught shrimp. Located within walking distance of the marina at 605 Osborne St. (912-540-0825).

4. St. Marys Submarine Museum
Home to submarine service memorabilia, models, WWII patrol reports and a working periscope. Part of the Georgia WWII Heritage Trail (102 W. St. Marys St., 912-882-2782).

5. St. Marys Welcome Center
Located at 400 Osborne St. with curated self-guided brochure options, maps and expert advice for what to do during your stay (912-882-4000).

MARINAS

6. St. Marys Intracoastal Gateway Marina
200 E. Bryant St. (912-540-7230)

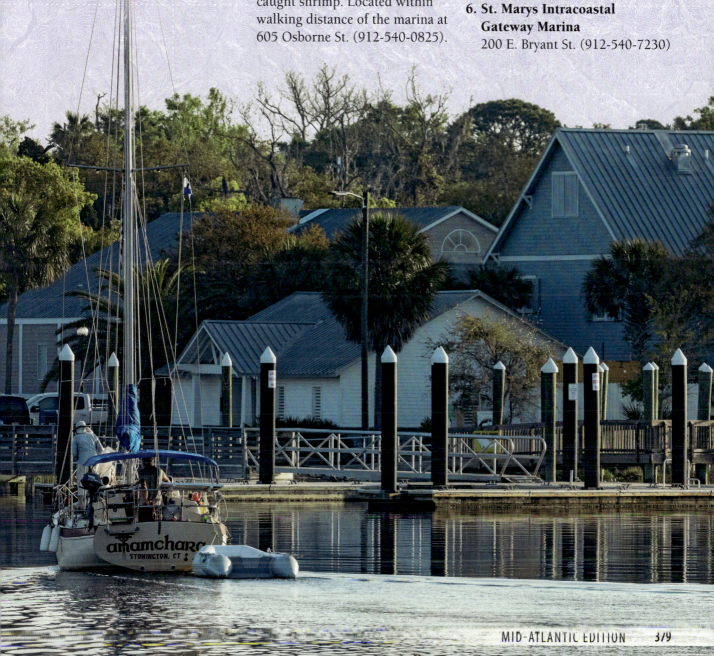

MID-ATLANTIC EDITION

Chapter 10: St. Catherines Sound to St. Marys, GA

NAVIGATION: The charted and well-marked St. Marys River enters Cumberland Sound from the west. Favor the center of the river and pass flashing green "3" wide to starboard. Follow the markers to avoid extensive shoaling of the west bank from red daybeacon "6" to flashing red "10."

Dockage: St. Marys Intracoastal Gateway Marina welcomes vessels to 100 feet with electric, water and slip-side pump-out service included in the daily rate. Other amenities include a boaters lounge, free (24-hour) laundry and loaner bikes. A staff member will shuffle you via golf cart (if available) should you need to go farther afield.

For maintenance or repairs, St. Marys Boat Services on the North River is a terrific DIY yard but they do not typically offer transient slips. Turn off the St. Marys River at green daybeacon "3" to access this facility.

St. Marys Day Dock has been completely rebuilt after being closed for several years due to hurricane damage. The east floating docks are ADA accessible and can be used for loading and unloading equipment and the west floating docks will accommodate a few 35-foot vessels for a 6-hour period. Overnight dockage is not allowed. The docks accommodate a wet and dry kayak launch protected from the current.

Anchorage: There is a substantial anchorage area in front of St. Marys with 8- to 13-foot MLW depths. Tidal currents run swiftly here so keep that in mind when dropping anchor and be sure to set your anchor well.

Navigate with the Cruising Authority

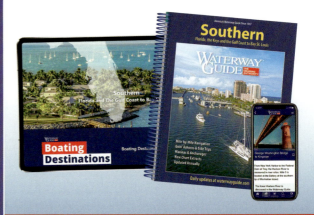

Subscribe today for the full package
(Guidebook of your choice, mobile app & online subscription)

Scan to shop now at www.waterwayguide.com

Marina/Sponsor Index

Sponsors are listed in **BOLD** and are highlighted in yellow in marina tables.

A

Albemarle Plantation Marina, 138, 139

Alligator River Marina, 161, 162

America's Great Loop Cruisers' Associate (AGLCA), 7

Anchorage Inn & Marina, 206, 208, 209

Annapolis Boat Shows, 11

Atlantic Yacht Basin, Inc., 122, 123, 124

B

B & B Seafood House Marina, 314, 315

Bald Head Island Marina, 255

Barefoot Marina, 271, 273

Bath Harbor Marina, 174, 175

Bayliss Boatworks, 154, 155

Beaufort Docks Marina, 219, 221, 222, 223, 224, Back Cover

Beaufort Yacht Basin, 219, 221, 222

Belhaven Marina, 164, 166, 168, 171

Belhaven Town Dock at Wynne's Gut, 166, 168, 171, 172

Belle Isle Yacht Club & Marina, 281, 284

Bishop's Marina and RV Park, 214, 215

Blackwell Point Marina, 190, 192

Bock Marine, 214, 215, 216

Bohicket Marina & Market, 310, 311, 312

Bridge Tender Marina, 241, 242, 245

Bridgeton Harbor Marina, 196, 197

Broad Creek Marina, 176

Broad Creek Marina, 326, 330, 331

Brunswick Landing Marina, Inc., 368, 370

Bucksport Plantation Marina & RV Resort, 277, 278

Bull River Marina, 348, 349

C

Cape Fear Marina, 249, 250

Carolina Beach Marina and Mooring Field, 247, 248

Carolina Beach State Park, 246, 247, 248

Carolina Beach Yacht Club & Marina, 247, 248

Casper's Marina, 233, 234, 236

Charleston Harbor Resort & Marina, 295, 300, 301

Charleston Maritime Center, 297, 298, 300

Charleston Yacht Club-PRIVATE, 297, 303, 304, 305

Cherry Grove Marina (formerly Anchor Marina), 270

Church St. Town Dock, 233, 234, 236

Clancy's Marina, 187, 190, 192

Coffee Bluff Marina, 353

Coinjock Marina & Restaurant, 126, 127

Columbia Marina, 145, 146

Columbia Municipal Dock, 145, 146

Cooper River Marina, 298, 300

Coquina Yacht Club, 269

Cricket Cove Marina, 269

Customs House Marina, 99, 100, 103, 105

D

Darien River Waterfront Park & Docks, 363, 364, 365

Dataw Island Marina, 315 316, 317

Deep Point Marina, 256, 257, 262

Delegal Creek Marina, 353

Dockside Yacht Club-PRIVATE, 228, 230

Dolphin Cove Marina, 303, 304

Dowry Creek Marina, 162, 168, 169, 171, 172

Duck Creek Marina & Boatyard, 196, 197

Dudley's Marina, 233, 234, 236

E

Edenton Harbor, 141-143

Edenton Marina, 141, 143

Ensign Harbor Marina, 188, 189

MID-ATLANTIC EDITION 381

Marina/Sponsor Index

Sponsors are listed in **BOLD** and are highlighted in yellow in marina tables.

F

Federal Point Yacht Club Marina, 247, 248

Franklin County, FL, 26-27

Freeport Marina, 336, 337

Ft. McAllister Marina, 353, 354

G

Gallants Channel, 217-219, 221, 222

Galley Stores Marina, 194, 197, 198

Georgetown Landing Marina, 281, 283, 284

Grand Banks, Inside Back Cover and Inside Back Flap

Grand Manor Marina NC, 160, 166, 168, 170, 171, Inside Front Cover

Grande Dunes Marina, 273, 274

Great Bridge Battlefield & Waterways Museum, 121, 122

Greater Beaufort-Port Royal CVB, 24-25, 323

H

Halfmoon Marina, 360

Hampton Marine & Dry Storage, 100, 102, 103

Hampton River Marina, 366, 367

Hampton, VA, 20-21

Hampton Yacht Club-PRIVATE, 100, 103, 105

Harborwalk Marina, 281, 283, 284

Harbour Town Yacht Basin, 325, 326, 330, 33, 334

Harbour Village Marina Inc., 239, 240

Harbourgate Marina, 270

Hatteras Boatyard, 202

Hatteras Harbor Marina, 203, 204

Hatteras Landing Marina, 203, 204

Hazzard Marine, 281, 283, 284

Heritage Plantation Marina, 278, 280

Hertford Bay City Dock, 138, 139

Hilton Head Harbor Marina, 328, 331

Hinckley Yacht Services Savannah, 345, 347

Holden Beach Marina, 265

Holden Beach Transient Dock, 265

Homer Smith Docks and Marina, 217, 219, 221, 222

Hurricane Boatyard, 183

I

Inland Waterway Provision Company, 191

Inlet Watch Yacht Club - PRIVATE, 247, 248

Isle of Hope Marina, 349, 350, 351, 352

Isle of Palms Marina, 291, 292, 293, 294

J

Jekyll Harbor Marina, 368, 371, 372

John P. Rousakis Riverfront Plaza (East), 341, 344

K

Kilkenny Marina, 354, 355

L

Lady's Island Marina, 320, 321, 322

Lamb's Marina, 132, 133

Landings Harbor Marina, 347, 348

Leland Oil Company, 287, 288

Lightkeepers Marina, 269

Loggerhead Marina - Boathouse Marina, 222, 223

Loggerhead Marina - RiversEdge Marina, 303, 304

M

Mackeys Marina, 144, 145

Manteo Waterfront Marina, 147, 149, 150, 151, 152

Marine Craft, 188, 189

Marshes Light Marina, 149, 152, 154

Masonboro Yacht Club and Marina, 243, 246

McCotters Marina & Boatyard, 176, 179

Mona Black Marina, 247, 248

Morehead City Transient Docks, 227, 228, 230

Morehead City Yacht Basin, 225, 227, 228, 229, 230

Morehead Gulf Docks, 227, 228, 229, 230

Morningstar Marinas Golden Isles, 366, 367-369

Morningstar Marinas Southport, 256, 257, 258

Moss Landing Marina, 177, 179, 181

Myrtle Beach Yacht Club, 269

N

New Bern Grand Marina Yacht Club, 193, 194, 196, 197, 198

Norfolk Yacht and Country Club-PRIVATE, 107

North Myrtle Beach RV Resort and Marina, 270

Northwest Creek Marina, 193, 197, 198

O

Ocean Isle Marina & Yacht Club, 267

Ocean Yacht Marina, 110, 112, 113, 115

Oden's Dock, 203, 204

Old Point Comfort Marina, 102

Onancock, VA, 16-17

One River Landing, 298, 300

Oregon Inlet Fishing Center, 156, 157

Oriental Harbor Marina, 187, 190, 192

Oriental Marina & Inn, 184, 187, 190, 192

Osprey Marina, 273, 275

P

Palmetto Bay Marina, 330, 331

Pecan Grove Marina-PRIVATE, 190, 192

Pirate's Cove Marina, 152, 154

Plymouth Landing Marina, 144

Port City Marina, 249, 250, 253

Portside Marina, 227, 228, 230

Portsmouth Boating Center, 110, 113

Portsmouth, VA, 111

Potter's Marine, 173, 174

R

R. E. Mayo Seafood Marine Supply, 182, 183

Rebel Marina, 104, 105

Ripley Light Yacht Club - PRIVATE, 303, 304, 305

River Dunes Marina at Grace Harbor, 185, 188, 189

River Forest Boatyard/Shipyard, 165, 166, 171, 168

River Street Market Place Dock, 341, 343, 344

S

Safe Harbor Bahia Bleu, 344, 345, 347

Safe Harbor Beaufort, 319, 320, 321, 322, 324

Safe Harbor Bluewater, 100, 102, 103

Safe Harbor Bristol, 297, 303, 304

Safe Harbor Charleston City, 297, 299, 302, 303, 304, 305

Safe Harbor City Boatyard, 298, 299, 300

Safe Harbor Jarrett Bay, 214, 215, 216, 220

Safe Harbor Outer Banks, 151, 154, 155

Safe Harbor Port Royal Landing, 320, 322, 324, 325

Safe Harbor Skull Creek, 328, 329

Safe Harbor South Harbour Village, 256, 257, 260

Sailcraft Service, 187, 190

Salt Ponds Marina, 98, 99

Sanitary Fish Market & Restaurant, 228, 230

Savannah Marina, 347, 348

Savannah Yacht Club-PRIVATE, 345, 347

Sawmill Point Marina, 249, 250

Sea Gate Marina, 214, 215

Seabreeze Marina, 298, 300

Seapath Yacht Club & Transient Dock, 241, 242, 245

Seven Seas Cruising Association (SSCA), 11

Marina/Sponsor Index

Sponsors are listed in **BOLD** and are highlighted in yellow in marina tables.

Shallowbag Bay Marina, 149, 152-154

Shelter Cove Harbour & Marina, 326, 330-333

Silver Lake Marina (Ocracoke NPS Docks), 205, 208

Southall Landings Marina, 98, 99

St. James Marina, 257, 262

St. Johns Yacht Harbor, 305, 306, 307

St. Marys Intracoastal Gateway Marina, 376, 377, 379, 380

Sunbury Crab Co. Restaurant & Marina, 359, 360

Swan Point Marina, 239

T

Teach's Lair Marina Inc., 203, 204

The Docks at Downtown Hampton, 99, 100, 103, 105

The Harborage at Ashley Marina, 297, 299, 303, 304

The Marina at Edisto Beach, 313, 314

The Multihull Company, 6, Inside Front Flap

The Westin Savannah Harbor Golf Resort & Spa, 341, 343, 344

Thunderbolt Marine, 86, 345-347

Tidewater Yacht Marina, 110, 112, 113, 115

TJ's Marina & Boatyard, 166, 171, 168

Toler's Cove Marina, 292, 293

Top Rack Marina, 121, 122

Town Creek Marina, 217-219, 221, 222, 223

Two Way Fish Camp, 365, 366, 367

Tybee Island Marina, 340, 341

U

Urbanna, VA, 18-19

V

Village Marina Hatteras, 203, 204

W

Wacca Wache Marina, 278, 279

Wando River Marina, 298, 300

Washington, NC, 22-23

Washington Waterfront Docks, 177, 179, 181

Washington Yacht & Country Club-PRIVATE, 176, 179

Waterside Marina, 109, 110, 111, 113

Wayfarers Cove Marina & Boatyard, 193, 196

Westmoreland County, VA, 14-15

Wexford Plantation-PRIVATE, 330, 331

Whittaker Creek Yacht Harbor, 187, 189, 190

Whittaker Pointe Marina, 189, 190

Willoughby Harbor Marina, 104, 105

Wilmington Marine Center, 249, 250

Windmill Harbour Marina, 328, 329, 331

Wrightsville Beach Marina, 241, 242, 244, 245

Z

Zimmerman Marine, Outside Front Flap

Zimmerman Marine - Charleston, 295, 300

Zimmerman Marine - Holden Beach, 265

Zimmerman Marine - Oriental, 189, 190

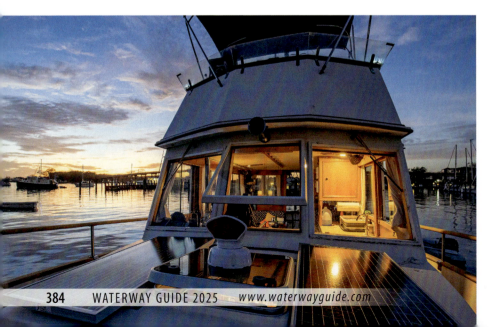

Subject Index

Most relevant pages are listed in **BOLD**

A

Adams Creek, 193, 214-217, 229

Albemarle Sound, 125-126, 136-137, **138-146**, 147, 157, **160-161**, 173, 200-201

Alligator River, 145-146, 160, **161-163**

Alligator River-Pungo River Canal, 163, 165, 171

Altamaha Sound, 358, 363-364, 367

Ashepoo Coosaw Cutoff, 312-313

Ashley River, 295, **299-305**

B

Bald Head Island, 254-256, 259, 262

Bath Creek, 174-176

Beaufort, NC, 116, 201, 215, **217-225**, 266, 320

Beaufort, SC, 305, 306, 310, **317-324**

Beaufort Inlet, 68-69, 210-213, 215, 221, **225**, 227

Belhaven, 160, 163, **164-173**

Bluffton, 331, 336

Bogue Sound, 213, 227, 231-232

Brickhill River, 375

Broad Creek, 163, 176, 179

Brunswick, 250, 258-259, 365, **369-370**, 371

Bucksport, 277-278

C

Calibogue Sound Entrance, 336

Cape Fear River, 201, 231, 246, **248-250**, 251, 253-256, 259, 264, 285

Cape Fear River Entrance, 72-73, 254

Cape Lookout, 125, 200, **209-210**, 219, 225

Charleston, 189, 213, 230, 265, 266, 285, 291, 293-294, **295-305**, 306, 313, 362

Charleston Harbor Entrance, 78-79, 294-295

Chowan River, 138-141, 144

Coinjock, 125-128, 160, 162

Columbia, 145-146, 160

Conway, 272, 276-277

Cooper River, 295, 296, **298**

Coosaw River, 313, 315-317, 320

Croatan Sound, 147, 149, 157-158

Cumberland River, 371, 374-376

Currituck Sound, 125

D

Darien River, 363, 365

Daufuskie Island, 329, 336-338

Dawho River, 312-313, 315

Dismal Swamp Canal Route, 128-133, 160

Doboy Sound, 89, 362-363

Dover Creek, 375-376

E

Edenton, 138, 140-143, 144

Elizabeth City, 130, 132-136, 160

Elizabeth River, 97, 106-107, 111, 113-114, **116-117**, 128, 132

Enterprise Landing, 276-278

Estherville-Minim Canal, 278, 286-288

F

Fields Cut, 338-339

Floyd Creek, 375-376

Frederica River, 365, 367-369

G

Georgetown, 213, 266, 268, 278, **281-285**, 286

Great Bridge, 117, 120-123, 129-130

H

Hampton, 97-98, **99-105**, 106-107

Hampton Roads, 66-67, **97-99**, 105-106

Hatteras Island, 201-204

Hertford, 138-139

Hilton Head Island, 324, **325-334**, 336

Subject Index

Most relevant pages are listed in **BOLD**

I

Isle of Palms, 291-294

J

Jekyll Island, 365, 371-375

L

Little River, 264, 266-267, **268-270**

Little River Inlet, 74-75, 264, 266-268

Lockwoods Folly Inlet, 264-265

M

Manteo, 147, **148-153**, 154-155

Masonboro Inlet, 70-71, 225, 241, 243

McClellanville, 276, 286-288

Morehead City, 116, 200, 213, 215-217, 221, **225-230**, 231-232, 254

Myrtle Beach, 262-264, 268-269, **270-276**, 278

N

Neuse River, 157-158, 179, 182-183, **184-192**, 193, 196, 198, 201, 215-216

New Bern, 186, **192-198**

New River Inlet, 125, 236-237

New Topsail Inlet, 231, 238, 240

Norfolk, 105, **106-111**, 113, 116-117, 121, 130, 160

Norfolk Harbor, 106-107

North Creek, 173-174

North Edisto River Inlet, 80, 311-312

North Landing River, 120-124

O

Oak Island, 260, 262

Ocracoke Island, 172, 200, **204-209**

Oregon Inlet, 147, **155-157**, 158, 201

Oriental, **184-192**, 193-194, 265, 295

Ossabaw Island, 336, 352-353

Outer Banks, 102, 125, 138, 146-149, 155, 188, **200-210**

P

Pamlico River, 171-172, **173-179**, 180, 200

Pamlico Sound, 157-160, 167, 172-173, 184, 188, 192, **200**, 201-202, 206

Pasquotank River, 132-133, 136, 138, 160

Pawleys Island, 278-281

Perquimans River, 138-139

Plymouth, 144-145

Port Royal, 313, 320, 324-325, 362

Port Royal Sound Entrance, 82-83, 324

Portsmouth, 96-97, 106, 107, **110-115**, 116-117

Pungo River, 160, **165-173**, 179, 182, 200

R

Roanoke River, 143-145, 158

Roanoke Sound, **147-157**, 158

S

Salt Ponds, 99

Sapelo River, 339, 358-362

Sapelo Sound Entrance, 88, 361-362

Savannah, 336, 338-340, **341-344**, 347, 349, 350, 362-363

Savannah River, 336, 338, **339-341**, 343, 344, 349, 362-363

Savannah River Entrance, 340, 349, 362-363

Scuppernong River, 145-146

Shallotte Inlet, 264, 266, 268

Skidaway River, 349-352

Snows Cut, 240, 246-248, 251, 262

South Creek, 173

South Edisto River, 312-315

Southport, 189, 210, 251, 254, **255-260**, 262-264, 268, 285

St. Catherines Sound, 354, 358-361

St. Catherines Sound Entrance, 87, 358

St. Marys, 324, 371, 374, 376, **377-380**

St. Marys River Entrance, 92-93, 376-377

St. Simons Sound, 338-339, 362, **365-368**, 369-371, 374

St. Simons Sound Entrance, 90-91, 362, 369, 374

Stono River, 305-307, 310

Swansboro, 213, 231, **232-236**

T

Thunderbolt, 338, 344-347, 349

Topsail Beach, 238-239

Turner Cut, 130-132

Tybee Roads Entrance, 84-85, 336, 338, 340, 347

U

Umbrella Creek, 371, 375-376

V

Vernon River, 350, 352-354

Virginia Cut Route, **120-128**, 160, 162

W

Wadmalaw, 310-311

Walls Cut, 338

Wappoo Creek, 299, 304-306

Washington, 173, 176, **179-181**

Wassaw Sound Entrance, 86, 347, 349

Willoughby Bay, 105-106

Wilmington, 240, 244, **248-250**, 251-253, 259

Winyah Bay Entrance, 76-77, 268, 278, 281, **285-286**

Wrightsville Beach, 225, **240-245**, 246, 248, 268

Y

Yeopim River, 138-140

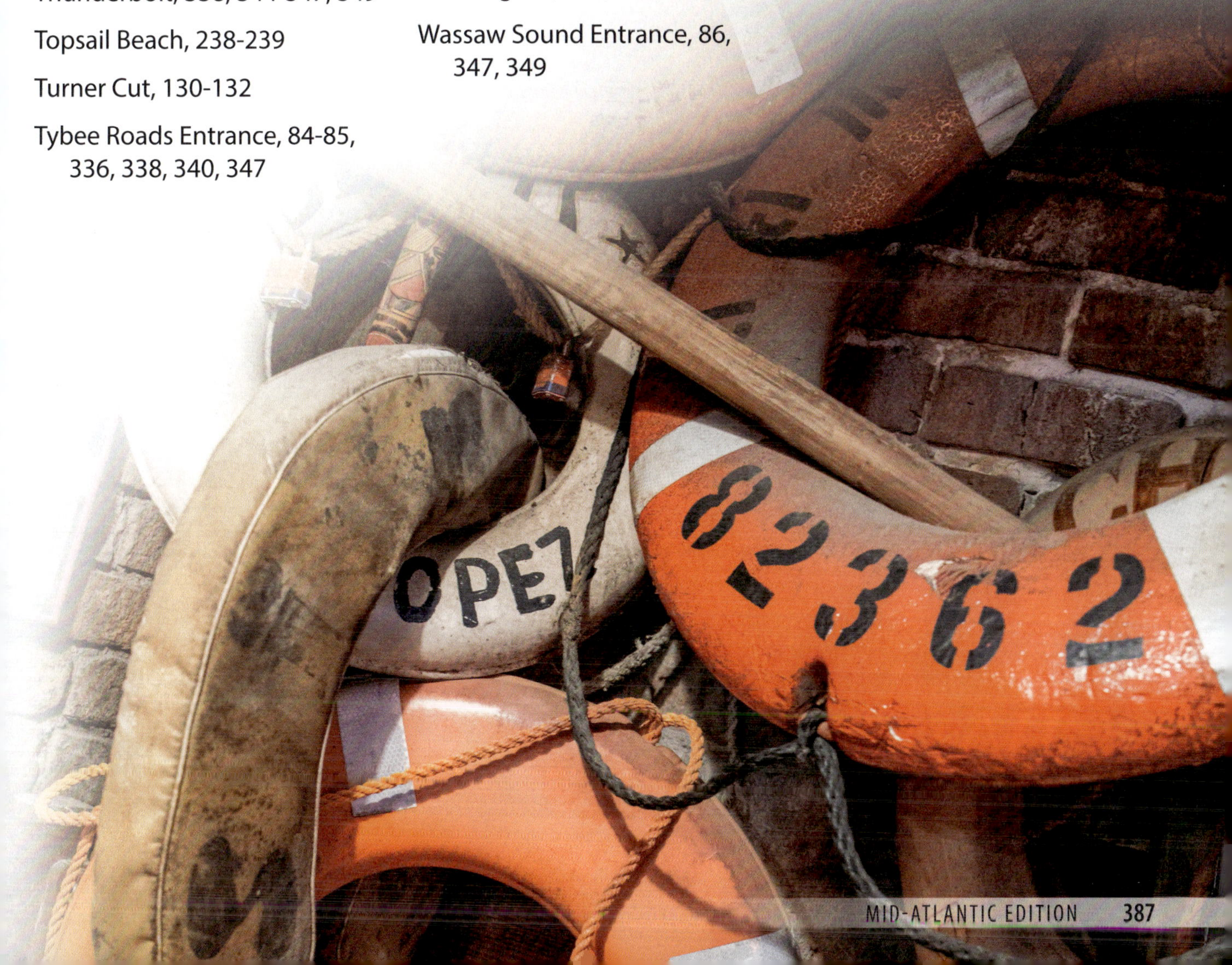

Goin' Ashore & Inlets Index

Goin' Ashore Index

- Beaufort, NC, 218
- Beaufort, SC, 318
- Belhaven, NC, 166
- Charleston, SC, 296
- Edenton, NC, 142
- Elizabeth City, NC, 134
- Georgetown, SC, 282
- Hampton, VA, 100
- Hilton Head, SC, 326
- Jekyll Island, GA, 372
- Manteo, NC, 148
- Morehead City, NC, 226
- New Bern, NC, 194
- Norfolk, VA, 108
- Ocracoke Island, NC, 206
- Oriental, NC, 186
- Portsmouth, VA, 114
- Savannah, GA, 342
- Southport, NC, 258
- St. Marys, GA, 378
- Swansboro, NC, 234
- Washington, NC, 180
- Wilmington, NC, 252
- Wrightsville Beach, NC, 244

Mid-Atlantic Inlets Index

- Beaufort Inlet, NC, 68
- Cape Fear River Entrance, NC, 72
- Charleston Harbor Entrance, SC, 78
- Doboy Sound Entrance, GA, 89
- Hampton Roads (Norfolk), VA, 66
- Little River Inlet, SC, 74
- Masonboro Inlet, NC, 70
- North Edisto River Inlet, SC, 80
- Port Royal Sound Entrance, SC, 82
- Sapelo Sound Entrance, GA, 88
- St. Catherines Sound Entrance, GA, 87
- St. Simons Sound Entrance, GA, 90
- St. Marys River Entrance, GA, 92
- Tybee Roads (Savannah River) Entrance, GA, 84
- Wassaw Sound Entrance, GA, 86
- Winyah Bay Entrance, SC, 76